The Fashion Industry and Its Careers:
An Introduction

Third Edition

The Fashion Industry and Its Careers: An Introduction

Third Edition

Michele M. Granger, EdD, ITAA
Missouri State University

Fairchild Books
An Imprint of Bloomsbury Publishing Inc.

B L O O M S B U R Y
LONDON · NEW DELHI · NEW YORK · SYDNEY

Fairchild Books
An imprint of Bloomsbury Publishing Inc

1385 Broadway
New York
NY 10018
USA

50 Bedford Square
London
WC1B 3DP
UK

www.bloomsbury.com

FAIRCHILD BOOKS, BLOOMSBURY and the Diana logo are trademarks of Bloomsbury Publishing Plc

1st edition published 2007
2nd edition published 2012
This edition published 2015

Library of Congress Cataloging-in-Publication Data
Granger, Michele (Michele M.)
    [Fashion]
    The fashion industry and its careers : an introduction / Michele M.
Granger. -- 3rd edition.
        pages cm
    Revised editon of: Fashion : the industry and its careers / Michele M.
Granger. 2012
        ISBN 978-1-62892-341-4 (paperback)
1. Fashion--Vocational guidance. 2. Fashion--Study and teaching. 3.
Clothing trade--Vocational guidance. 4. Clothing trade--Study and teaching.
I. Title.
    TT507.G68 2015
    746.9'2023--dc23

                                                    2014041188

Typeset by Lachina
Cover Design by Anna Perotti
Cover Image © Abbe Fenimore for Studio Ten 25 Interiors/Melanie Johnson Photography
Printed and bound in the United States of America

To Michael. My Love Always, Mimi

contents

extended contents

Unit 2   Careers in Fashion Design, Product Development, and Fashion Promotion   *119*

Chapter 6 Designing Apparel and Accessories for the Manufacturer   *121*

Unit 3   Careers in Fashion Retailing *191*

Chapter 9 Marketing for the Retailer *193*

Chapter 15 Visual Merchandising, Retail Design, and Interior Design *339*

Chapter 16 Beauty, Spa, and Wellness *367*

Appendix A Career Tracks and Salaries Chart *387*

Appendix B Résumé Tips, Interview Guidelines, Employer Research, and Résumé Samples *397*

Glossary *415*

Credits *437*

Index *441*

preface

The Fashion Industry and Its Careers: An Introduction, 3rd edition, provides an overview, or survey, of the global fashion industry with a focus on the career paths available within each level of the industry. It is written for the reader who is exploring career options, whether as a career change or as an entry-level position. It is designed to support the introductory college or university course in fashion design, fashion merchandising, product development, textiles, apparel, interior design, and career exploration. The third edition is fully updated with recent developments in technology, world economics and globalization, and effects on industry sectors and career opportunities. Through current, applied industry information and personal assessments throughout, students gain a critical understanding of what careers match their aptitudes, skill sets, and interests—and how to begin heading down a path toward a successful career in the fashion industry.

The book is based on the following four broad assumptions of postsecondary education and the fashion industry:

1. *People immerse themselves in studies they find personally and professionally relevant.* By examining the different levels or sectors of the fashion industry and exploring the career options that exist at each level, students have the opportunity to see themselves on career paths and, subsequently, define career goals to enhance and individualize their educational experiences.

2. *Fashion is a lifestyle that permeates many industry segments, from apparel and accessories to home fashions to beauty and wellness.* It includes all products and services that are influenced by changing trends in form, materials, theme, and color.

3. *The careers within the sectors of the fashion industry provide an ideal way to define and explain the industry and illustrate its various levels, from raw materials to ancillary services.* Exploring the industry by highlighting the careers in each industry segment provides a framework that allows students to see how the various levels work together.

4. *Effective career preparation requires across-the-board understanding of the following concepts:*
   - The apparel and textile industry operates in a global and high-tech market, making an understanding of cultural diversity, the world economy, and technological advances essential.
   - Activities of product development, manufacturing, and retailing are interrelated, from fiber and textiles to design and production to sourcing and merchandising.
   - Successful companies recognize that product decisions are consumer-driven.

Organization of the Text

The Fashion Industry and Its Careers: An Introduction, 3rd edition, is organized into four units, or parts, beginning with the creators and providers of raw materials and the manufacturers of products, followed by the manufacturers' designers who develop the concepts that will be produced, to the retailers who create and/or sell the products to the consumer, and ending with the auxiliary industries that support the work done by the product creators and product retailers. This edition has been reorganized to better align with the sectors of the fashion industry, moving from three to four units, with new units dedicated to Fashion Design and Fashion Retailing. The text is organized in the following sequence: Unit 1, Careers in Forecasting, Textiles, Manufacturing, and Resource Management; Unit 2, Careers in Fashion Design, Product Development, and Fashion Promotion; Unit 3, Careers in Fashion Retailing; and Unit 4, Careers in the Ancillary Businesses: Digital Media, Styling, Education, and Retail Design.

Unit 1: Careers in Forecasting, Textiles, Manufacturing, and Resource Management

The primary level of the fashion industry begins with the people responsible for the inspiration and conception of the fashion product's parts and raw materials (e.g., the forecasters, designers, and sourcing personnel). Unit 1 starts at the beginning of fashion product development and production. It provides an overview of the firms that supply the information, components, production, and design of fashion products that manufacturers produce. In addition, the back office departments of manufacturing firms are examined, to include sales, accounting, finance, and human resources. Chapter 1, Trend Forecasting, presents the trend forecasters who research, interpret, inspire, and predict shifts in fashion preferences and influence both the raw materials and the actual outcomes of fashion production. Chapter 2, Textile Design and Development, examines the textile product developers and designers who use colors, textures, patterns, and finishes to create the foundation on which fashion products are built. In Chapter 3, Sourcing, the personnel who locate the components and manufacturers of products are explored in greater depth. Chapter 4, Production, presents production in which employees work together to manufacture the final product. Finally, the offices that collaborate to support the fashion line (sales, finance and accounting, and human resources) have been consolidated into Chapter 5, Resource Management. Although positions in these support departments require some fashion industry knowledge, most employers require in-depth studies in other fields.

Unit 2: Careers in Fashion Design, Product Development, and Fashion Promotion

Unit 2 is composed of three chapters, Chapters 6 through 8, which explore the design sector of the fashion industry in greater depth. In Chapter 6, Designing Apparel and Accessories for the Manufacturer, careers related to designing apparel and accessories for the manufacturer are discussed, to include the fashion designer, assistant fashion designer, technical designer, specification technician, and pattern maker. Some retailers purchase finished fashion merchandise from manufacturers or wholesalers; others develop and manufacture products specifically for their clientele; many large retailers do both. Several large retail operations own a product development division that functions as a design and production source exclusively for them. In Chapter 7, Product Development by the Manufacturer and Retailer, the career tracks for director of product development, merchandiser, sourcing staff, product development designer, product manager, colorist, textile technical designer, product development pattern maker, and quality control manager are presented. Whether the fashion product is created and manufactured by the retailer or purchased from a manufacturer or wholesaler, it must be marketed to appeal to the consumer. In Chapter 8, Promotion for the Designer and Manufacturer, these marketing activities are explored through the career tracks of fashion stylist, public relations and social media directors, advertising research and promotion positions, and fashion event producer.

Unit 3: Careers in Fashion Retailing

The third level of the fashion industry represents the retailers of fashion products, from apparel to home furnishings, and those involved with creating a desire in the consumer for the retailer's fashion goods. Unit 3 has been revised to focus on marketing, merchandising, and management for the brick-and-mortar and/or e-commerce fashion retailer. As shown in Chapter 9, Marketing for the Retailer, the marketing, or promotion, division of a retail operation does just that through such professionals as the marketing director; product, brand, digital, and Web site marketing managers; art director; and copywriter. Chapter 10, Merchandising for the Retailer, explores the merchandising division of the retail operation—the buying and marketing of products. General merchandising managers, divisional merchandising managers, buyers/fashion merchandisers, assistant buyers, planners, distribution managers/allocators, and merchandising trainees work on the selection, pricing, and placement of merchandise on retail sales floors. In Chapter 11, Management for the Retailer, essential management careers in the retail sector are examined, to include those in stores—regional, store unit, associate, assistant, and department managers—as well as customer service managers. This chapter culminates in presenting the retail operation owners—all-in-one entrepreneurs who own and operate their retail businesses. Whether product or service—or brick-and-mortar, brick-and-click, or solely e-retailing—these entrepreneurs are rapidly contributing innovation and jobs to the fashion industry.

Unit 4: Careers in the Ancillary Businesses: Digital Media, Styling, Education, and Retail Design

Unit 4 presents a range of ancillary businesses that promote, educate, and provide support to the producers, retailers, and consumers of fashion goods. Whether working as freelancers or within a company, these ancillary business professionals frequently offer services, rather than tangible products. In a new Chapter 12, Digital Media and Visual Communication, the ever-growing careers in digital media are explored from the digital media director to graphic designer, to web designer and developer, and fashion journalist to blogger. In Chapter 13, Fashion Styling, Photography, and Costume Design, career options are discussed from the perspectives of company-employed and freelance positions. Fashion scholarship is now presented in its own chapter, Chapter 14, Fashion Curatorship and Scholarship, and includes coverage of museum and historical costume study, as well as teaching opportunities in high school and postsecondary education. Opportunities in the fashion or costume division of a museum discussed in this chapter include museum director, museum curator, assistant curator, collections manager, museum archivist, and museum conservator. The star of the fashion scholarship segment of the industry is the fashion educator, who instructs and/or conducts research in historical costume or many other facets of the fashion industry, from production to design and product development, to merchandising and entrepreneurship.

Chapter 15, Visual Merchandising, Retail Design, and Interior Design, now encompasses careers related to retail design, including architecture, interior design, and visual merchandising. Visual merchandising has become an important component of not only manufacturers' showrooms and retailers' sales floors, but it is also integral to online sales, social media, branding, and promotion. Fashion producers, designers, Web site and store retailers, and stylists all hire visual merchandisers to create a setting or an environment that will attract consumers and visually sell the merchandise. The primary career tracks discussed in Chapter 15 include architect, interior designer, visual merchandising professional, store planning director, mall manager, and assistant mall manager. An evolving sector is the beauty, spa, and wellness industry. Cosmetics, skin care, and hair care are growing areas of the beauty fashion industry. Chapter 16, Beauty, Spa, and Wellness, examines the careers of the beauty merchandising and marketing professionals. The careers of a makeup artist and hairstylist are also examined in Chapter 16 and can take place in a theater; on a film set or photo shoot; or in an individual's home, a salon, or a spa. Finally, the careers of the aesthetician and director of a spa are explored, as growth is expected to continue in spa and aesthetics companies. These ancillary businesses are evolving into full-service facilities that include services for makeup, hair, skin, and body. As we have watched health services integrate medicine and natural homeopathic remedies, we will continue to see fashion and beauty services integrated with health and fitness in the future, resulting in new career paths for those interested in beauty, health, and longevity.

Appendix A provides a chart of annual salary means by position and geographic location, as well as a listing of Web sites to research salaries. New online resources presented at the end of each chapter also provide current information on careers and industry trends. Appendix B features an assortment of résumé examples from several careers as suggestions for writing a résumé, researching employers, and interviewing. A glossary of key terms is also included at the end of the text.

Each chapter of *The Fashion Industry and Its Careers: An Introduction*, 3rd edition, provides current visuals, online resources, discussion questions, and key terms—the terminology used in the industry. These text features are developed to help clarify concepts, stimulate class discussion, and encourage critical thinking with applications and illustrations. Relevant education, work experience, personal characteristics, and career challenges are examined for each career track.

New to This Edition

- *Case Studies in Career Exploration* showcase profiles of companies, interviews with individuals, industry scenarios, and insider tips.
- *The Job Search* boxes feature sample advertisements for actual positions in fields discussed within each chapter.
- *Social Media Strikes* boxes interspersed throughout the text explore how social media trends are integrated into the various levels of the industry and describe the impact of Facebook, Twitter, Pinterest, Instagram, LinkedIn, and more. As new social media forces will continue to impact our lives and the fashion industry world, understanding the why and the how of social media today will help us anticipate the future.
- *New Profiles* are presented at the conclusion of chapters—from young executives and entrepreneurs, such as freelance trend forecaster and fashion entrepreneur Erin Burke (Chapter 11), Marivi Avalos Monarrez, Chief Marketing Officer and Managing Director for Asia at Fashionbi (Chapter 9), and Mandy Raines-Cordia, Women's Contemporary Apparel Buyer for Zappos.com (Chapter 10), to legends and true teachers, like David Wolfe, Creative Director of The Doneger Group (Chapter 1), fashion journalist Robin Givhan (Chapter 12), and fashion educator Dr. Catherine Amoroso Leslie at Kent State University (Chapter 14). The fashion industry and its careers are filled with remarkable, creative, intelligent, and hard-working people; in this book, about 25 of these people share their stories with you—the future faces of the fashion industry.
- *In-depth job titles and descriptions* for a wider range of careers now including Marketing Director (Chapter 9), Product Marketing Manager (Chapter 9), Brand Marketing Manager (Chapter 9), Digital Marketing Manager (Chapter 9), Web Site Marketing Personnel (Chapter 9), Creative Art Director (Chapter 9), Copywriter (Chapter 9), Customer Service and Customer Relationship Management (CRM) Staff (Chapter 9), Digital Media

Artist (Chapter 12), Graphic Designer (Chapter 12), Fashion Journalist (Chapter 12), and Fashion Blogger (Chapter 12).

- *A new Chapter 12* has been developed to familiarize readers with the growing career sector of digital media and visual communication. This chapter examines digital media, graphic design, Web site design, journalism, and blogging as career options. The chapter includes new boxed features such as "Top Digital Media Companies" and "Tips for Starting a Fashion Blog," plus a profile of fashion journalist Robin Givhan and an interview with fashion blogger Kristian Laliberte, former Senior Editor of Refinery 29.
- *Organizational changes* to the unit structure of this third edition align the content with current industry practice and emphasize career areas with the greatest growth potential.
- *A fully updated photo program* contains more than 75 new photographs and a *16-page color insert* of all-new full-color images.

Instructor's Resources

This edition includes an Instructor's Guide, Test Bank, and chapter PowerPoint presentations. The Instructor's Guide includes syllabi, class discussion topics, and exercises/assignments, and guest speaker suggestions. The Test Bank includes a separate answer key and a mixture of true/false, multiple-choice, and open-ended questions.

Resources can be accessed via www.BloomsburyFashionCentral.com.

Editor's Note

The prior edition of the textbook was titled *Fashion: The Industry and Its Careers*, 2nd Edition (9781609012250). This new edition has been retitled to better reflect the intended scope of the book as an overview of the fashion industry.

---

acknowledgments

- To my mother, a beautiful and brilliant role model who loved books, her career, and her fabulous wardrobe, but praised none of these—only her family. This one is for you, Sassy.
- To Annie and Armando. Thank you for being the best of parents to Michael and for taking such good care of each other.
- To my father, brother, sister, and my nieces and nephews. Thank you for your unconditional love.
- To my students—past, present, and future. You inspire me. Your enthusiasm energizes me, and your career success stories are a great source of pride. Special acknowledgment to former student Lauren Reiter, who shared her digital media and blogging expertise in Chapter 12, and current student Jared Bajkowski, who, using with his innate curiosity and charisma, conducted the incredible interviews in Chapter 1 while in New York interning for Cotton Inc. Thank you to graduate student Jacklyn Phillips for her excellent clerical and research assistance, as well as her great sense of style.
- To Olga Kontzias, emeritus executive editor of Fairchild Books. Paris, fashion, museums, family, great reads, and films—these passions we share. Thank you for starting me on this writing path and for being *mon amie*.
- To Amanda Breccia, Amy Butler, Edie Weinberg, Rona Tuccillo, Charlotte Frost, and all of Fairchild Books—Great gratitude for your direction and assistance throughout the writing process.
- To Abbe Fenimore, thank you for sharing the beautiful cover image, your interview, and the photographs of your work. We love your style.
- To the interviewees: Nancy Asay, Marivi Avalos, Malie Bingham, Chelsea Bommel, Erin Burke, Vince Camuto, Juan Carlos Gaona, Tom Julian, Joe Karban, Hannah Kimmerle, Kristian Laliberte, Dr. Catherine Leslie, Jeremy McCarthy, Melissa McGraw, Mandy Raines-Cordia, Nicole Narain, Jamie Ross, Stephanie Weiss, and David Wolfe. Thank you for graciously sharing your stories to help today's fashion students—the future of our industry.
- To the interviewers: Gernamno Felix, Tony Lisanti, Gail McInnes, Melissa McGraw, Pulkit Rastogi, and Amanda Irel Sajecki. Thank you for sharing your contacts and expertise.
- To the reviewers: Your thorough and helpful recommendations made this textbook much better than it ever could be as a solo project. The reviewers are: Thurlene Anderson, FIDM; Katherine Appleford, Kingston University London; Shawn Carter, FIT; Dana Connell, Columbia College Chicago; Crystal D. Green, Art Institute of Charlotte; Pandora Neiland, IADT Seattle; and Pam Stoessell, Marymount University.

UNIT 1

Careers in Forecasting, Textiles, Manufacturing, and Resource Management

Unit 1 starts at the beginning of fashion product conception and production. It explores the firms and people supplying the information, components, production, and support needed to manufacture fashion products to bring them to the retailers. In addition, the departments of manufacturing firms that support the people and profitability of fashion lines are examined, to include sales, human resources, finance, and accounting. Chapter 1, Trend Forecasting, presents the trend forecasters who research, interpret, inspire, and predict shifts in fashion preferences. Trend forecasters have tremendous influence on both the raw materials and the actual fashions. Chapter 2, Textile Design and Development, looks at the textile designers and developers who use color, texture, pattern, and finishes to create the foundation on which fashion products are built. In Chapter 3, Sourcing, the careers of sourcing personnel, who locate the components of products, are explored. Sourcing involves locating the materials that become part of the fashion merchandise. Sourcing personnel may also find factories, particularly overseas, to produce the merchandise. Chapter 4, Production, examines the careers of employees who work together to manufacture the final product. Finally, the offices that collaborate to support the fashion line (sales, human resources, finance, and accounting) have been consolidated into Chapter 5, Resource Management. Standing behind the production of the actual fashion line, these departments support the financial success of the fashion line and the growth of the company's employees. Although positions in these support departments require some fashion industry knowledge, most employers require in-depth studies in other fields.

When people who are interested in building a career in the fashion industry initially consider career tracks in the field, they often do not think about the primary level of the industry where fashion products begin. It is another world with a full range of job opportunities. The prospective fashion executive with a penchant for design can explore the world of textiles. Those with an interest in putting products together have immense opportunities in manufacturing. Others who have the skills and drive to sell fashion products are not limited to doing so in retailing; selling fashion lines to retail buyers provides both a new perspective and an array of new potential employers. For those who enjoy working with people or money, human resources and finance/accounting positions are available within every major fashion manufacturing company. It's a world the fashion consumer often does not think about, but it's one that you will next explore to broaden your career options and build your understanding of the fashion industry.

chapter 1

Trend Forecasting

Whenever you open a *Vogue* magazine, click on to HauteLook.com, and tune into *Project Runway*, you are introduced to the latest trends in fashion. From where do these concepts come? Who decided what the latest themes, colors, silhouettes, styling details, or fabrics would be? How far in advance of seeing these fashions on the runway (Figure 1.1), online, or in the fashion publication pages were these trends determined? What will next season's, or next year's, fashion trends be? No person or company uses a crystal ball to foresee the future of fashion. The people responsible for making these predictions, the rare and powerful, are referred to as **trend forecasters**, also *fashion forecasters* or *creative directors*.

Customers are often unaware of the amount of lead time that fashion products require. **Lead time** refers to the number of days, weeks, months, or years needed for the intricate planning, purchasing, and production steps to be implemented before fashion products actually land on the sales floors or Web sites of the retail operations. Lead time includes the time fashion forecasters need to analyze and project colors, design themes, silhouettes, fabrics, patterns or prints, and styling details—often years in advance of the actual manufacturing of the products. Without that proverbial crystal ball, fashion forecasters must combine their knowledge of fashion design, marketing, current world trends, and history with consumer research and business information. When trend forecasters identify and market their visions of the fashion future effectively, designers, retailers, and manufacturers in the textiles, apparel, accessories, and home environment sectors who subscribe to the forecasters' ideas have an edge, and their lines will be on point for their specific target markets. They will have lower purchasing risks and greater opportunities to increase their customer following and, ultimately, their sales volume.

The position of trend forecaster is one of the most influential career options in the fashion industry. Most fashion consumers and many prospective fashion industry executives wonder where the latest and greatest fashion trends originate. Trend forecasters continually monitor consumers and the industry through traveling, reading, networking, listening, and, most

■ Figure 1.1
The introduction of a designer's seasonal collection, as shown here on models backstage at Valentino's Spring 2013 Haute Couture runway show in Paris, is an important time for fashion forecasters, because these industry leaders have a great influence on future fashion trends.

important, observing. Trend forecasters attend trade shows, where they analyze the wholesale end of the business by looking at new products and fresh designs from established and new designers. They gather information from the media on population, design, manufacturing, and retail trends to determine what the new looks, silhouettes, colors, and fabrics will be for upcoming seasons. This career is illustrated in Box 1.1, an interview with creative director, Jamie Ross.

Many large corporations in all sectors—from agriculture to medicine—have research and development (R&D) departments. In the fashion sector, trend forecasters form the "R" component of the R&D departments in fashion businesses. They lead the research activities of the fashion industry and may also be involved in developmental functions. As researchers, trend forecasters (a) provide new knowledge to designers, buyers, and product developers; (b) assist in the development of new products; and (c) look for ways to update old products or to extend the life of popular products through modifications that rejuvenate them.

Forecasters search for consumer and business facts, as well as creative occurrences, and then analyze the findings to identify common threads that will become trends. Their goal is to isolate the major trends that will positively affect the amount and types of fashion products consumers will buy. Once the trends are classified, trend forecasters use words and images to communicate these to designers, buyers, product developers, and manufacturers in fashion. Images of the trend's mood and key terms, fabrications and colors, and styling details are composed on a "board," referred to as a **trend board**. In the past, these boards were created by hand; today, they are more likely created and disseminated to design and merchandising personnel digitally.

Technology is also impacting the way trend forecasters conduct research and development, market product concepts, and listen to the consumer. Box 1.2 provides more detail about the ever-changing world of trend forecasters by exploring the world of renowned trend forecaster, Li Edelkoort, and how her TrendTablet site and social media options reach out to creative people around the world.

Few career opportunities in fashion relate to all levels of the industry. Trend forecasting is one of the few. Population trends and interests, availability of raw materials, manufacturing capabilities, retail changes, merchandising and management developments, and entrepreneurial endeavors influence trend forecasting. This chapter introduces the world of trend forecasters, from those in color and textile forecasting to those in theme, style, and detail forecasting.

The Job of a Trend Forecaster

Types of Forecasters

In general, there are four primary types of trend forecasting firms: fiber and textiles, color, consumer population, and broad spectrum. First, there is the forecaster who works for a **fiber house**, or *fabric or textile house*, a company that represents a fiber source or a fabric. Examples include Cotton Incorporated or the Mohair Council of America. Second, there is the forecaster who specializes in color trends and is employed by a firm such as The Color Association.

CASE STUDIES IN CAREER EXPLORATION

Box 1.1 Chatting up Creative Director of The Doneger Group, Jamie Ross

Interviewed by Jared Bajkowski

Could you give us a little introduction?

I'm a Creative Director at The Doneger Group. There are four of us with very different functions, but my position probably overlaps the most with all the others. My focus is the youth market, which includes kids up to tweens and juniors. I also cover accessories, intimate apparel, and beauty (which is my other specialty).

What does an average day look like? What is the time frame for your work?

There's really no typical day, especially when we have markets. Then, I could be doing 10 to 20 presentations with clients. Other days, I could be analyzing runway shows, doing consultancy project meetings, or meeting with clients on more forecasting-driven stuff. Our publications are released 18 to 24 months in advance. With the Internet, we can constantly post updates. We can say, "This trend has reached saturation, you should pull back on it," or "This is a color we saw turn up that we weren't anticipating, and you should get into it." We can definitely update and react more often.

At what point did you realize that this was something you wanted to do?

Similar to many students, I didn't even know this career existed. I knew I had an interest in fashion, but prior to that, I had interests in art, history, and writing, so those were probably my strengths. When I first got into FIT [Fashion Institute of Technology], I thought I wanted to be a buyer or a stylist. After taking some buying courses, I realized that math was probably not my strength. By exploring and getting out into the industry, I was lucky enough to do two internships at the same time. One of them was with Vogue-Butterick and the other was with JC Penney. The Vogue-Butterick was really *The*

Box 1.1 Jamie Ross, Creative Director at The Doneger Group.

Devil Wears Prada type of fashion office with the fashion director coming in with the little dog in her bag every day. JC Penney was very down-to-earth and let me actually work with the fashion director on children's, men's, and women's wear.

JC Penney hired me and I moved to Plano, Texas, into a position they created in which I covered all the areas. When it moved its fashion office back and forth from New York to Plano a couple of times,

(continued on next page)

Box 1.1 *(continued)*

I moved and, in between, worked at J. Crew in the fashion office. At the JC Penney fashion office in New York, I had an opportunity to see David Wolfe speak and Doneger was at the top of my list. Abbey [Doneger] came over to look at some video equipment, and that's when he asked me if I wanted to come over and talk. I was very fortunate that I was in the right place at the right time, and there was an opening for a Creative Director. I've been here for 14 years.

What kind of skills does somebody in your position need?

It's important to be very analytical, and have strong editing and writing skills. You need to have a good eye, which you really can't teach somebody. Either you have it or you don't. We're all required to speak a lot. We give all sizes of presentations. Initially, that was something I had a problem with, and I probably still do. Normally, I'm a very shy person. I had a professor at FIT who said, "From your test scores you're probably the brightest person in the class, but if you don't learn how to speak up, you're never going to make it in this industry." From that point on, I just pushed myself.

At what point in your career did you really get to hone those skills?

I would say here [at Doneger]. At JC Penney, I was making presentations to the buyers and product development people, but it was not until here that I could be thrown into an audience of 200 people—or working with two people. In China last summer, I had an audience of 800. You have to have a certain comfort level with working all of those types of audiences.

What traits are really important for trend forecasters?

Flexibility. The people we've hired who go the furthest and stay the longest can be thrown into any kind of situation and rise to the occasion— you know, real team players. I think those are the people who get the most out of the experience. It just really helps to have a down-to-earth

personality and always be willing to pitch in on anything. We could get a phone call from a client and have to turn around a project in a couple of days. We're a small team, so everyone has to be super flexible—and *nimble*.

How do you get inspired?

Literally, being like a sponge. I'm that weirdo on the subway looking at everybody, from the person who's not interested in fashion to the fashionista. I'm really interested in everybody. When I have time to travel and to open myself up to everything around me, that's when I get most inspired.

What motivates you?

I never have a typical day. Every day is so different and so creative. I really have a great outlet for all of the things I love to do. To be able to write and do it creatively and feel like I'm helping my company, and to go out on the streets and photograph—I have no complaints.

How do you think trend forecasting has changed over the years?

When I first started, we used to cut and paste trend images down on sheets. It was crazy. We had a slide library of the collections and put them in carousels and did literal slide shows of the collections. If David [Wolfe] said, "Everybody in San Tropez is wearing lilac this summer. Everybody has to go buy lilac for next summer," it would happen. It doesn't work that way anymore. Once the Internet came along, our jobs changed tremendously, not just because of online free resources and competition, but also because clients can't wait a year to react to something. Our processes are *completely* different.

When did you realize that things were changing?

Once we subscribed to First View and then Style.com popped up, we were getting all these images. This drastically changed the way we did things as a department. I remember going to every fashion show and every party afterward— we would just be doing all-day-long shows. Then,

Box 1.1 *(continued)*

suddenly, we were sitting at our desks, analyzing. Now, I really pick and choose which one of the shows I'm going to, because I see less when I'm at the shows and I see more when I'm sitting at my desk. It's definitely changed the way that we look and analyze, and for everybody else, too. Most of our clients can instantaneously access the materials. The way that we provide value is that the clients don't have time to look through that many images and come up with an informed opinion.

Do you think there's any kind of drawback to predicting what is going to happen?

We always tell clients that we're making our best educated guess based on what we know now, and where we see things going. We're fortunate because of the way the office functions. Part of our office is merchandising, so they often hear back from stores firsthand what's happening in terms of sales results and what the customer is reacting to in terms of colors and hot items. They keep us grounded because, being creative people, we can make things very esoteric or kind of out-there. They bring us down to earth because they can say from experience that the customer is never going for that, or it's unrealistic. They keep us grounded and we push them.

Have you had any experiences where you were totally wrong or you left out something big from a report?

There are times when a client will say we missed something. Early in my career, when I first went to Barcelona, I thought there was a red pant trend. It wasn't until I went to Barcelona a couple of times that I realized that they just like red pants (laughs). We make our best educated guess, and sometimes we say things that don't make our clients happy. Take flared jeans, for example. When I first talked about flared jeans (at least three years ago), a lot of the clients said, "That's never gonna happen; we just got them into skinny jeans. It took them a long time to accept the skinny jean. They just found the right fit." Then they started seeing the sales and went—(throws hands up). I ultimately have to be the person to push it.

What kinds of applications are there for forecasting beyond fashion?

When I first started, I never anticipated we'd work with a lot of financial companies who have clients with investments in some of the designers and retailers that we're looking at. They ask, "Do you think it's a strong season for them?" They want to be able to tell their clients who have stock in the brand whether or not it's a strong season for that company.

Could you walk us through a case study of a past trend on which you worked?

There are several trends that we keep renaming and recycling. We're going to make a bigger deal out of the whole aspect of comfort going forward. I think it is related to the whole athletic sport idea. I can't tell you how many clients were asking, "Can we have a resource like Birkenstock?" When we first started talking about that, everybody said, "Nobody's going to want to wear Birkenstocks." It's so funny that the impact of the ugly shoe went upward. It was one of the few trends that I've seen that started with the feet and then worked its way up. Now, apparel is sort of matching, as is the whole attitude and the lifestyle. It's a big umbrella trend in every area—the idea of comfort.

Any advice for anybody who is aspiring to become a forecaster?

There are so few trend companies left, but I don't like to discourage anybody. I think that the best step is to pursue something in product development. I'm working with a retailer now that has as much access to the fashion services and the shows and all of the research tools that I do, but has an even bigger budget. It would be useful to do something for a retailer in its product development department. It's also important to have retail background to understand the psychology and lingo.

Courtesy of Henry Doneger Associates, Inc.

Box 1.2 TrendTablet

As a trend forecaster, Lidewij Edelkoort identifies the links among art, fashion, design, and consumer culture that will be prevalent in the future. She provides her design and lifestyle analyses for some of the world's leading brands through trend reports, seminars, and her magazines, *View on Colour*, *InView*, and *Bloom.* Over the years, Edelkoort's work has evolved into education and philanthropy. From 1999 to 2008, she was Chairwoman of the Design Academy Eindhoven. In 1993, she co-founded Heartwear, a nonprofit craft foundation that supports the sustainable production of art crafts in developing countries. In 2008, the French Ministry of Culture honored her as a Chevalier des Arts et des Lettres, and the Dutch Royal Family named her a Knight.

Edelkoort continues to move forward, now linking the worlds of technology, communication, and fashion. TrendTablet is the name of Li Edelkoort's online trend community. It is a curating trend tool, a social media platform designed to (a) share Li's concepts, (b) invite new design talents, and (c) interact with creatives worldwide. It is a place where you can see Edelkoort's most recent projects, learn where and when you can attend live presentations, and take part in a lively community of fellow designers, trend hunters, and innovators. One of the primary reasons for TrendTablet is to explain how trends grow, evolve, and flow, helping us to better perceive and understand how they interact with our daily life. You can become a fan of TrendTablet on Facebook to receive access to additional content, including behind-the-scenes images from Edelkoort's photographers, film outtakes from her directors, and more, or follow TrendTablet on Twitter for daily exclusives.

Source:
www.trendtablet.com and www.trendunion.com

Box 1.2 Li Edelkoort of Trend Union.

This forecaster provides information on color preferences and palettes for a wide variety of clients, from automobile manufacturers to flooring producers to apparel designers. Next, there is the forecaster who projects population trends and explores the social, economic, geographic, and technological changes in the world, as well as shifts in the population. The population trend forecaster tracks a population's age shifts; residential and geographic preferences; changes in family sizes and structures; entertainment preferences; spending patterns; influences by celebrities, films, and art; as well as other people-related topics, such as values and beliefs. Finally, there is the forecaster who is employed by a **broad-spectrum firm**, a company that provides forecasting services for a wide range of target markets and product categories or industries. The clients of broad-spectrum firms represent a variety of product categories, as illustrated by the following list of Li Edelkoort's clientele: the paper industry, automobile manufacturers, the food and drink industry, beauty products, and high-tech firms from telecommunications to electronic devices.

Companies like Trend Union, The Doneger Group, and Promostyl provide information on all of the trend areas for many target markets and product categories, including color, fabrications, silhouettes, fashion influences, design themes, and population trends. In essence, they offer a one-stop trend forecasting and strategy planning service, as illustrated in Box 1.3, an interview with Strategist and Men's Fashion Director, Tom Julian.

Sources of Information

Where do forecasters go for information? It depends on the market sector in which they specialize (e.g., color, demographics, apparel, or home) or consumer segment they are investigating (e.g., contemporary women, preteens, or men). There is, however, a range of information sources that most trend forecasters find to be valuable. Following is a list of popular trend forecasting resources:

- *Market research firms.* These companies provide specific information on consumer market segments for a fee. Population changes that can be quantified are referred to as **demographic data**, such as age, education, residence, family size, occupation, income, and expenditures. Additionally, more general government data on demographics is available on similar subjects at no cost through resources such as the U.S. Census Bureau (www.census.gov).

- *The couture collections.* Dior, Chanel, Celine, Gucci, Armani, Prada, Issey Miyake—the list of prominent and influential designers is a long one. The introductions of their seasonal collections are important times for trend forecasters, because these industry leaders have a great influence on future ready-to-wear and home trends.

- *New designers.* Trend forecasters often view the collections of up-and-coming designers with as much enthusiasm and interest as those of the established couturiers (Figure 1.2). Trend forecasters are often seeking new places for design talent, such as prestigious fashion schools around the world, or in countries providing government support and new opportunities for fashion entrepreneurial businesses, such as India, Canada, and Hong Kong.

- *Other fashion services.* Apparel and accessories forecasters may subscribe to other services, such as color forecasting services. Some subscribe to competitors' services to stay on top of what the competition is doing. The primary tangible product of a trend forecasting firm is referred to as a **trend book**, or *look book*, which features the recommendations and predictions of the company for the upcoming seasons.

■ **Figure 1.2**
Trend forecasters often view the collections of innovative designers, such as Gareth Pugh, with as much enthusiasm and interest as those of time-honored couturiers.

CASE STUDIES IN CAREER EXPLORATION

Box 1.3 Interview with Strategist and Men's Fashion Director of The Doneger Group, Tom Julian

Interviewed by Jared Bajkowski

Could you give us a brief introduction?

As Strategic Director of New Business, I help The Doneger Group as a company to realize new projects and new assignments that will take us into branding and marketing worlds. The second role I have is Men's Fashion Director. As a retail and merchandising organization, we have found that menswear is a growing and opportunistic category, so it makes some natural sense to use my skills and background in menswear to leverage it and market it to the menswear community.

Does strategy apply to everything you approach?

I think strategy is at the root of so many organizations and marketplace opportunities—and especially in our world of fashion today. Being strategic allows a business to bloom and grow. I think any successful organization today is more balanced between strategy and creativity, which means left-brain to right-brain, and I really try to balance that out. I think that's important.

What kind of recurring actions fill your time here?

Well, I think there's always recurring seasons, retail concepts, and marketplace shifts. At one time, you only worried about seasons four times a year and how they affected the consumer or the store. I think today we operate on 365 days a year. It is: *You're living for today, you're worried about tomorrow, you're looking to next year, but you understand what last year was about as well.* Right now, we are still talking about this season and researching the same season a year from now, but as a company we are past that and beyond. And we have to deal with every day.

What kind of skills does an aspiring trend, branding, or strategic executive need to develop?

Box 1.3 Tom Julian, Corporate Strategist and Men's Fashion Director.

I think you have to be a generalist, not a specialist. You have to be left-brain and right-brain. You have to be very cognizant that, even if you are in the merchandising world, you have to interface with the marketing and retail worlds. It all connects, and, therefore, you have to find out what the connectors are and what your role is in each and every part of it. I have always found that the most successful efforts and programs are those where corporate and marketing come to the table, interface with product, and then deliver the right thing in the right way. I will say the most important skillset for every executive at every level is a digital knowledge bank and project experience, and a consumer connection to it.

What inspires you?

I'm still inspired by the worlds that are in front of me every day, no matter what city I'm in. Culture, consumer, and experience. I've always prided myself on saying, "Give me 24 hours in a city and I will know the downtown area, the suburban area, the hot alternative destination area, the collegiate area, and the typical shopping area. Once I see that I will have a very good perspective on what is going

Box 1.3 *(continued)*

on. Even if I go on a vacation, I can see it from that level. It's just how I'm wired.

What's so important about what you're doing?

Every time I get involved with something, I say the bottom line of the business is so important. No matter how great a program, if it doesn't move the needle, it's not considered successful in corporate measurement style. One of my biggest challenges day in and day out in advertising and marketing was making sure that I was relevant and that the projects delivered. You have to show the results. You have to merchandise it; you have to sell it. I always say, "Show me. Don't tell me." Show the results in order to get the embrace.

Do you think the public is becoming more aware of marketing?

The consumer is very aware of everything today, and the consumer has a role and a voice. You can't ignore it. Ten years ago, the consumer would take anything that came out of fashion. Now, the consumer wants to see something that they've contributed to. It's true participation, and that is an ingredient that changes everything.

What have been the toughest challenges you've had to face in your career?

I've learned that you may not get the reward that is due you. You may have to look for other ways to get achievements. The entrepreneurial, start-up thing was not available to my generation because we were so traditionally schooled. Being a Pittsburgher brought up in a hard-working middle class, I wanted to work and work with passion. I wanted to believe in what I worked in and for. The hardest thing for me was to leave my emotion at the door. At the end of the day, it's either about the client or the product. Yes, you can be excited, but that can't be the only

driver. As a young person, you have to realize that sometimes your passion has to stop for the reality of what the business is or what the opportunity can be. That's hard when you're truly impassioned by it.

Is there any last advice to anybody with an aspiring fashion mind?

I keep hearing from industry executives that, in this virtual world, everything is transparent. Marketing executives will say about job candidates, "I want to see what they're doing and how they're doing it." If I see they are a part of a student group that's impacting the world, I know that is real and relevant. If they are online and they're making a difference with their message on Facebook, Instagram, or Tumblr, that's a very credible way for me to gauge them. If I see that they're self-promoters, and all they're doing is their pics of them and their friends in the coolest way, I'm not getting that they're hard-working individuals. Consider that whatever you put out there has to represent you and your brand, and it has to reinforce what you are going to contribute to the organization, because it is very accessible to anyone. I had a communications company say, "We will only hire a young person who has 5,000 Facebook followers, runs his or her own blog, and is tweeting 20 times per day. Why? Because they're approaching social media as part of their own, and that can help my business as well." What I see in young people today that is so dynamic is that they've got a great base of education; they're more worldly or have some type of international experience; and they've all had great internship experiences. That's pretty great. If you don't have that equation today, you need to figure out how you're going to get it, because you're kind of behind the eight ball without it.

Courtesy of Henry Doneger Associates, Inc.

- *Trade shows.* International fiber and fabric markets, such as Interstoff in Germany and Expofil in Paris (Figure 1.3), are primary information sources for forecasters who are researching color and textile trends. There are apparel and accessories trade shows at the markets in New York City, Dallas, Los Angeles, Las Vegas, and Chicago, to name a few. High Point, North Carolina, offers markets in home textiles and furnishings.

■ Figure 1.3
Expofil in Paris is among the world's premiere international fabric trade shows.

- *Communication with peers.* Networking is a key activity for trend forecasters. Updates from designers, buyers, and manufacturers can provide significant information on what is selling and what is not. Communication with representatives of key suppliers can assist the forecaster in identifying trends. Membership in professional organizations, such as the Fashion Group International, Inc. and the American Society of Interior Designers (ASID), also provides trend forecasters with the opportunity to network with others in the know in the fashion industry.

- *E-sources.* Web sites, blogs, online music programs, chat rooms, news sites, e-catalogs, and social networks are valuable resources that are easily accessible to trend forecasters. Also, forecasters may subscribe to specific online trend forecasting resources. Some of these sites are provided at the end of this chapter.

- *Design sources.* Reference books, historical costume collections and texts, vintage clothing shops, antique dealers, museums, bookstores, and libraries are excellent resources for forecasters who are exploring the influence of past eras on fashion, as in Figure 1.4. Videos and photographs of recent designer collections, fashion shows, trade show exhibitions, and fashion or art books are some examples of design resources that trend forecasters use for information on current designer and trend information.

- *Publications.* Trade journals and international consumer magazines are common, obvious sources for trend information. It is less apparent, however, that many apparel and accessories forecasters subscribe to home furnishings and home accessories magazines to identify color, fabric, and theme trends in the home. New colors in automobiles are often gleaned from successful hues in home furnishings and apparel. Auto, health, and celebrity magazines are also part of the trend forecaster's reading materials. Trend forecasters often read it all.

- *The arts.* Music concerts, visual art presentations, museum exhibits, dance performances, and theater plays can influence or interrelate with fashion trends. For example, a photography or apparel exhibit that travels internationally can influence fashion trends, as in Figures 1.5 and 1.6. Costume designer Patricia Field, as featured in Box 1.4, clearly influenced fashion through her work in *Sex and the City* and *The Devil Wears Prada*.

- *Entertainment headliners.* Celebrities greatly influence fashion trends. People in music and the news, on talk shows, on the red carpet, in videos, and on the big screen have the ability to set trends. For example, celebrity gowns are copied and made available to consumers in weeks (Figure 1.7). Forecasters often watch up-and-coming celebrities and project which newcomers have the star quality and visibility that will

■ **Figure 1.4**
Vintage clothing and antiques are excellent resources for forecasters who are exploring the influence of past eras on today's fashion.

■ **Figure 1.6**
The 2013 Esprit Dior exhibition at the Museum of Contemporary Art in Shanghai presented nine themes, grouping collections together from 1947 to the present day, and displayed eight of China's emerging artists as an homage to the designer of Avenue Montaigne.

■ **Figure 1.5**
"Fashion is not something that exists in dresses only. Fashion is in the sky, in the street, fashion has to do with ideas, the way we live, what is happening."
—Coco Chanel

CASE STUDIES IN CAREER EXPLORATION

Box 1.4 Fashion Designer, Stylist, Costumer, and Retailer Patricia Field

You may recognize Patricia Field, native New Yorker, as a fashion legend, with her name fitting into the category of designing women who do it their way and succeed, like Betsey Johnson and Vivienne Westwood. She is known for taking fashion risks, such as adding enormous flowers to garments, mixing high- and low-end fashions, combining day and evening looks, and creating a rainbow palette. She is also a groundbreaking fashion stylist and an Academy Award nominee and Emmy Award–winning costume designer for film and television: Think *Sex and the City* (SATC) and *The Devil Wears Prada*. Although you may know her as a trendsetter, designer, costumer, and stylist, did you know that she is also a retail entrepreneur?

Field's boutique in New York City has been a fashion landmark for nearly 50 years. Patricia began her career with the opening of her Greenwich Village boutique in 1966. In the late 1970s, she started her own line of clothing and accessories for club kids, ravers, and other wild personalities. Now, she helps launch the careers of many innovative young designers and stylists through her store. This downtown institution has been an internationally known favorite of celebrities and the fashion forward. If you can't get to Greenwich right away, you can visit her store Web site at www.patriciafield.com to shop vintage apparel, $9 jelly flats, a wig bar, and her Neoprene ICON bag in a rainbow of colors.

What has made Patricia Field so successful? A ton of hard work and gallons of talent combined with a bit of being in the right place at the right time. Whereas a lesser stylist working on *SATC* wouldn't have made as much of an impact, there's no denying that being able to capture millions of eyeballs every week was a huge coup and a boost to her career. The best thing about her, however, is her refusal to rest on her laurels. Patricia is continually pushing boundaries and trying new things. Of her success in the world of film and

Box 1.4 The wardrobe designer for a television series or film can impact fashion trends. Costume designer Patricia Field clearly influenced fashion through her work in *Sex and the City* and *The Devil Wears Prada*.

television, she says, "I never took it for granted and I sustained my business throughout. There is a certain truth about retail. If you listen to the customers, they will tell you."

Source:

www.patriciafield.com

make them future stars. Forecasters observe what they wear, who their favorite designers are, how they style their hair, and where they hang out with friends. Because forecasters have to anticipate the actual trends before they happen, identifying the people who will influence future trends is a critical part of the forecaster's job.

- *Fabrics.* Cotton Incorporated is a company that represents the cotton industry and provides trend information to designers and retailers. Fabric companies, such as Burlington Industries Group and Cone Mills Corporation, also develop trend information, which is often available on their Web sites.

- *Travel.* Vacation hot spots are often filled with people who influence fashion trends. Additionally, certain fashion trends develop in specific geographic locations. China and its fun fur fashions, Belgium with its deconstruction techniques in apparel, and Japan and its young and creative street fashions are all examples of the travel destinations where fashion trends have developed (Figure 1.8).

- *Consumer tracking.* **Consumer tracking information** refers to data that relates to customer spending, such as how much money is spent on clothing, entertainment, or food. It can also relate to how a customer makes a purchase—cash, Bitcoin, credit card, debit card, or (rarely) check. Purchases can be correlated with credit card data to examine who is actually buying what.

■ **Figure 1.7**
Anne Hathaway attends the 83rd Annual Academy Awards wearing a vintage Valentino haute couture gown with Tiffany & Co. jewels.

■ **Figure 1.8**
Designer Dries van Noten and his dog, Harry, on the rooftop of his Antwerp, Belgium headquarters. With its vacation appeal and fashion focus, Antwerp is an example of a travel destination where fashion trends develop.

- *Lifestyle trends.* **Lifestyle trends** refer to a population segment's values, interests, attitudes, dreams, and goals. Think about the following lifestyle trends: an increasing interest in health and fitness, the baby boomers' desire to entertain at home, and couples deciding to have fewer children and to start their families at a later age than previous generations. Next, ask yourself how these lifestyle trends influence fashion. Workout wear sales have increased. Patio furniture, cookware, and tabletop accessories have received a renewed interest in the home furnishings and accessories industries. The number of pieces sold in children's wear has decreased, but sales in this merchandise classification have increased as a result of higher unit prices. Two working parents who have launched their careers and waited to have children often have the finances and desire to provide their children with more. Lifestyle shifts influence what the customer wants to buy (Figure 1.9). **Psychographics** take this idea a step further: these include people's lifestyles and behaviors—where they like to vacation, the kinds of interests they have, the values they hold, and how they behave. Forecasters endeavor to become aware of these changes before they occur and identify the products that will meet consumer needs before customers know what they need.

- *Places where people gather.* Airports, concert stadiums, shopping malls, dance clubs, and Times Square on New Year's Eve are some of the locations where groups of people can be observed. Trend forecasters examine where these people are going, what they are wearing, and from whom and what they are buying.

- *Street scenes.* "I watch people anywhere and everywhere," one successful trend forecaster explains. "You never know where a trend will start." Worth Global Style Network (WGSN), a key forecasting resource discussed later in this chapter, recruits people from

■ Figure 1.9
Working parents, who have launched their careers and waited to have children, often have the finances and desire to provide their children with more. Celebrities have a tremendous impact on consumer preferences. Jennifer Lopez, working mother and celebrity, exemplifies both of these lifestyle trends.

■ Figure 1.10
A Japanese girl shows her own fashion style on the streets of Tokyo's Harajuku youth fashion district during Tokyo Fashion Week.

Figure 1.11
When a particular sport or activity, such as fly fishing, gains consumer interest, its active sportswear is often imitated or modified for streetwear.

colleges and other locations worldwide to submit trend information from their various communities. Every street in every city of the world, from WGSN's perspective, has the potential for fashion leadership (Figure 1.10).

- *Sports.* When a particular sport or activity gains consumer interest, its active sportswear is often imitated or modified for street wear. High-top boxing boots, surfer shorts, and yoga pants illustrate the influence of sports trends on ready-to-wear. As Figure 1.11 depicts, fly fishing is one of the sports currently impacting active and streetwear fashions.

The Career Path

Securing a position in trend forecasting does not happen quickly. Typically, many years of industry experience are required. Some successful forecasters have previously worked as designers or buyers before moving into the trend forecasting career field. A few of the fortunate begin with internships or assistantship positions in forecasting firms to gain direct experience, exposure, and contacts in the forecasting world.

Qualifications

Successful trend forecasters often meet or exceed the following qualifications:

- *Education.* At the very least, a bachelor's degree in one of a wide range of disciplines is required. These disciplines most frequently include business administration (e.g., marketing or consumer behavior), visual arts, fashion design, or fashion merchandising.

- *Experience.* Forecasters often begin in entry-level positions in the areas of retail, product development, design, merchandising, or fashion coordination. Some successful forecasters have held positions in several sectors of the industry, such as design, product development, and retailing.

- *Personal characteristics.* There are a few specific and unique qualities that trend forecasters display. Among them is an excellent understanding of people and human behavior, global population and industry shifts, and fashion trends. Successful trend forecasters have effective visual, written, and oral communication and presentation skills. They are often curious and creative people with superior networking abilities. Most important, they have an exceptional capability to analyze, synthesize, and organize observations into categories that are clearly communicated to clients. Think about viewing 15 couture collection presentations in a five-day period and then identifying the consistent trends among them. Trend forecasters have the ability to find the common threads and, later, classify and describe these trends for designers, manufacturers, and retailers who use the trend services.

The Trend Forecaster's Typical Career Path

Although the majority of college graduates prefer to start at the top, it is an essential advantage for a trend forecaster to understand all levels of the industry from a holistic perspective. Even the most entry-level retail sales positions provide valuable experience for future forecasters. As a sales associate, one is directly exposed to the customers' preferences and dislikes. Effective sales associates endeavor to understand who the customers are and identify their buying habits. As future trend forecasters progress to higher positions within the industry (e.g., product development or merchandising), it is important that they always keep in mind who the customers are and how they are changing. The work experience trend forecasters have acquired through the years is used on a daily basis when assisting designers, manufacturers, or merchandisers with future designs and purchases for upcoming seasons.

The Job Market for Trend Forecasters

The fashion industry has a limited number of trend forecasting positions in the areas of color, textile design, apparel and accessories design, and home furnishings. Because trend forecasting positions are limited, successful trend forecasters are well compensated for their knowledge and skills. Sometimes, a commission will be paid to trend forecasters based on how well their companies perform with their assistance.

Career Challenges

The pros of a trend forecasting career have been discussed, but what about the challenges? Because there are a limited number of successful forecasting firms, there are only a few jobs for a few good men and women. The job of a trend forecaster requires a tremendous amount of intelligence, skill, and exposure and, perhaps, a sixth sense. Forecasters must be aware of all of the external influences that may affect consumer behavior. The ability to observe, organize, and prioritize these outside influences is a rare skill. Trend forecasters who consistently identify the right trends develop strong reputations. Many wannabes who provide the wrong information for a season or two are no longer hired by clients, who depend on accurate fashion direction to make a profit. It can be stressful for trend forecasters to identify significant fashion influences seasonally or annually. Additionally, trend forecasters must be able to market their companies, their ideas, and themselves. The forecaster's knowledge, intuition, and experience truly form the ultimate product.

Examples of Trend Forecasting Companies

There are several successful trend forecasting companies around the world, with new firms constantly entering the mix. Some focus on a certain target market, such as teens or contemporary men, whereas others emphasize a specific fashion variable, such as color or fabric. Some offer a wide breadth of personal service, whereas others provide online reports. Whatever your fashion interest, there is a trend forecasting company to fill the bill.

Doneger Creative Services

Doneger Creative Services (www.donegercreativeservices.com), based in New York City, is the trend and color forecasting and analysis division of The Doneger Group. Doneger Creative Services offers a broad range of products and services, such as printed publications, online subscriptions, and live presentations. This division addresses the forecasting needs of retailers, manufacturers, and other style-related businesses. Doneger's creative directors and trend analysts cover the apparel, accessories, and lifestyle markets in the women's, men's, and youth merchandise classifications. Box 1.5 features an interview with associate trend analyst, Hannah Kimmerle.

Fashion Snoops

Fashion Snoops (www.fashionsnoops.com) is an online forecasting and fashion trend analysis service that covers the young men's, denim, junior women's, children's, and infant and toddler markets. Fashion Snoops was created about a decade ago by a team of designers and merchandisers who have extensive industry experience. The company's goal in bringing professionals together from various sectors of the fashion and licensing industries was to bring practical experience to creative teams. Fashion Snoops has a creative services division that provides consulting and outsourced services in the areas of research, design, merchandising, styling, and graphic art. The company serves hundreds of leading fashion firms in the United States, Canada, Europe, Australia, Asia, and South America.

Worth Global Style Network (WGSN)

Founders Julian and Marc Worth launched WGSN (www.wgsn.com), based in London, in 1998. It is one of the most successful online forecasting services to emerge. WGSN offers research, trend analysis, and news to the fashion, design, and style industries. Members of the 100-person staff travel extensively around the world. The WGSN team includes experienced writers, photographers, researchers, analysts, and trendspotters. **Trendspotters** are people located at universities and other locations worldwide who provide information to WGSN on the latest trends in each locale. The company tracks not only the latest fashion trends but also hot retail stores, new designers, emerging brands, and business innovations. WGSN maintains offices in London, New York City, Hong Kong, Seoul, Los Angeles, Melbourne, and Tokyo. Its client list is long and impressive and includes such designers and retailers as Giorgio Armani, Target, Mango, and Abercrombie & Fitch.

CASE STUDIES IN CAREER EXPLORATION

Box 1.5 Interview with Associate Trend Analyst of The Doneger Group, Hannah Kimmerle

Interviewed by Jared Bajkowski

Could you introduce us to yourself?

I'm an associate trend analyst with The Doneger Group. Coming from Iowa to New York to study fashion design, I interned in design and then began freelancing and interning in trend analysis. After graduation, I was hired by The Doneger Group, and I've been here for a couple of years.

What does an average day look like?

It depends on what season we're in and if there are any special client requests that we've gotten for that week. In the beginning of the season, we research color for the upcoming season, any relevant themes that we're feeling, and any overall movements as far as culture goes. What we start seeing on the runways and at trade shows—we bring all of that to the table, along with any relevant news. From there, we delve further into the runway looks and color. Then, clients come in and they want super-specific information, such as active graphics for women's spring/summer wear or kids' outerwear for fall/winter 2015. Whatever these requests are, we then do the research.

What does your research process look like?

I utilize social media as best I can, just because everyone's on it. I follow companies of interest on Twitter and Instagram. I also follow street style online, and take advantage of living in New York City. If there's an art gallery opening, getting out and about to people watch is important, as is attending fashion weeks and trade shows. Fashion and nonfashion events where people gather are the goal.

What kinds of things are you pulling from that aren't related to fashion?

I definitely grab mood shots (images) to give an overall feeling for a story—anything that would inspire me as a designer. With all of our products, we want to inspire our clients whether they're

Box 1.5 Hannah Kimmerle, Associate Trend Analyst.

designing, doing product development, or buying. Because we do a lot with color, we pull swatches to create collages to tell the overall story for the season.

What kind of special requests from clients have you encountered?

Requests for anything from toddler cold weather accessories to anything for activewear. Activewear is a definite hobby of mine. I get assigned those projects because we believe a person draws from his or her outside interests. If you have an interest in a product or activity a client wants to learn more about, you become a member of the team.

What other things do you enjoy researching?

My specializations in school were women's wear, sportswear, and activewear, For active clients, I

Box 1.5 *(continued)*

like anything new in terms of technology and draw inspiration from the most forward brands in the market. I love running and go to health expos, sign up for races, etc. When I go to those events, I see what people are into there—what they are wearing, talking about, listening to, etc.

Any shifts you're stuck on?

The shift of merging true activewear with true ready-to-wear. In ready-to-wear, you're seeing all of those high-tech fabrics such as mesh, and all those things that have that true sporting function. In activewear, you're seeing prints and patterns, matte and shine, which are things we've only seen in daytime fashion. Now, they're crossing over.

Can you tell us how you got into forecasting?

While a design student, I eventually wanted to move into something else after doing a couple of design internships. I wasn't really sure that I would like what I was doing every single day. My internship advisor helped me realize that I could keep my design major, but move into different avenues. From there, I sent my resume everywhere and was hired to freelance, doing illustrations and technical flats—later, interning there. From the very first day, I realized that I wasn't running errands and I wasn't bored and waiting for the clock to signal the end of the day. I practiced writing a lot—I wrote a lot of the reports that the company did. Later, I chose to go to a different company and meet new people. I joined The Doneger Group as an intern and then joined the team when I graduated.

What kind of skills do you think somebody who wants to get into trend needs?

It's important to develop your editorial eye, and it's important to consider the images that you pull in terms of their benefit to the client. You need to have a true reason behind each and every image that you put into a report. Definitely, practice writing; if you're not in a class, do it on your own. There's a weird mix of right-brain/left-brain. You need to be creative, but you also have to be analytical and work well in a corporate setting.

What kinds of traits are really sought after by trend companies?

Creativity is huge. Since our team is so small, we want our members to bring different, unique things to the table, because we can avoid the same issues being brought in for discussion. Attention to detail is big, too, because your work is being published.

What motivates you or inspires you about the career?

I love that fashion is changing all the time. I love how it affects everyone whether they know it or not. I would be doing this whether I got paid or not. It's just second nature, and this career has let me apply that.

Any advice for someone who wants to follow in your footsteps?

Definitely intern as much as possible. All of my interviews I got through people I met when I interned. It's a very close-knit community. If you're not at a trend agency, you can be at a retailer working in its trend division. Work on your own portfolio as much as you can. Sometimes, school projects restrain your creativity. You can put your true ideas into your own work. Do things on your own outside of school projects.

Courtesy of Henry Doneger Associates, Inc.

SnapFashun

To meet the needs of designers and manufacturers, members of SnapFashun (www.snapfashun .com) have access to its entire online archive of vector sketches and flats, based on 30 years of retail, street, and runway reporting from the fashion capitals of the world. The fashion library is updated with new details and silhouettes up to 14 times per year. SnapFashun is a source for Los Angeles and European retail reporting, merchandising trends, and original design ideas. The firm monitors up-to-the-minute looks at top-selling items in trendsetting cities.

Paris Trend Forecasters

Several trend forecasting services and trade shows are based in Paris, France. Carlin International is a forecasting and marketing firm dedicated to fashion trend information. The company's Web site, www.carlin-groupe.com, is available in English and French. Peclers Paris is a fashion trend forecasting service that specializes in textile design, fashion, beauty, consumer goods, and retailing. Première Vision is the world's leading trade show in fabric forecasting, promoting fabric trends for designers and manufacturers in the fashion industry. Première Vision teams with the company Première Vision S.A., a subsidiary of the French ___ ___ on for the Promotion of Textile Yarns, to produce the Expofil trade ___ ___ ld leader in yarn and fiber sectors, Expofil provides the te___ ___ colors, and materials.

Promostyl

Promostyl's mission is to pinpoint fashion, des ___ adapt to changing trends. The company bases its ___ lifestyles, believing that society makes fashion. ___ visual presentations, consults with companies, a ___ subsidiaries and agents. Three main offices are loc___

Color Forecasters

The Color Association of the United States is a ___ Web site, www.colorassociation.com, it is the oldes___ 1915, the Color Association has been issuing col___ committee panel of 8 to 12 industry professiona___ player in the color forecasting business is Doneger ___ color forecasting division is devoted to the apparel, ___

Cool Hunting

Cool Hunting seeks out trends in the form of "all ___ that there are no new ideas, just great executions. ___ he is always looking for both creative inspiration ar___ things. In 2003, he decided to start a catalog of wha___ Hunting. Today, Cool Hunting has a global team o___ innovations in design, technology, art, and culture, ___ at www.coolhunting.com. Cool Hunting is synonyr___ and videos highlight creativity and innovation in de___ travel. With a global team of editors and contributo___ publication, consisting of daily updates and weekly ___ designer's personal reference, Cool Hunting now has ___ creative people, who find its content on coolhuntin___ Vimeo, Instagram, Twitter, and Facebook.

Trend Union

Trend Union, created by Lidewij Edelkoort, speciali___ developing trend books for the fashion and textile i___ Paris and New York, Edelkoort is assisted by a highly ___ graphic artists, designers, artists, and consultants. ___

come a collection of biannual trend forecasting
, and lifestyles for seasons to come. These books
in advance of the major trends in the fields of
ear, Edelkoort creates a 20-minute audiovisual
y the significant future trends featured in the
e clients of Trend Union, with sessions in other

dustry. Accurate forecasting can make or break a
ust be aware of trend predictions to ensure their
t. Trend forecasters may be employed by broad-
anies specializing in color trends, or businesses
nformation by examining market research firms,
ws, art, design, e-sources, travel trends, lifestyle
hion forecasting is one of the few careers that
; therefore, it is essential for trend forecasters to
industry, from creative product development to
in this field without a number of years of prior
ter, you may anticipate a challenging career that
online and off, observe, absorb, organize, and

psychographics
trend board
trend book
trend forecaster
trendspotters

www.pantone.com
www.reddit.com
www.polyvore.com
www.trendhunter.com
www.trendwatching.com
www.wgsn.com

Discussion Questions

1. How conscious are you of current trends? Identify current color, design, art, textile, entertainment, and sociocultural trends for this season and the next.

2. Spot trends within the current season and trace their sources. Did these trends originate from the streets, art exhibitions, new technology, couture collections, or some other source?

3. Analyze current fashion publications and Web sites and compare the trends with fashion six months ago. Describe three themes cited as next year's top fashion trends.

4. What are some examples of companies outside of the fashion industry that rely on trend forecasting? Why are trends important to these businesses?

**, just for
re?**

or at The
g time.
n 1994,
r about
th to the
any; I was
been living
ad just
My world had
gner fashion.
the Milan
nds with
t. Ralph
to America
was shifting,
e epicenter
er of what
tood that the
sing and the
out.

consultant to
e they "ruled
been great. It
enth Avenue,
the founder,
he moment,
unters—and
ught, "Well,
eger, it would
area of
snob to really
cinated by it.
mething new
to start an
on. He was
dn't be buying
could be

Profile Figure 1 David Wolfe, Creative Director at The Doneger Group.

generating it here and selling it to the world at-large. That's how I ended up at Doneger.

It's an absolute dream situation for me because I'm treated like a star, which is very nice, and I do whatever I darn well please at this point 'cause I'm old. I mean, I'm 73. I have no intention of ever retiring, because I love what I do. About five years ago, I said to Abbey, "You know, I have to tell you that I can't do this anymore the way it's being done.

(continued on next page)

(continued)

Five years from now, it's going to be so invalid. And I do not want to be a dinosaur." He said, "What do you want to do?" I replied, "Well, what I'd really like to do is explain and teach people what's going on in the industry." He said, "Well, then that's what you should do."

I travel wherever I want to, and think about whatever I want to, and essentially do presentations around the world explaining what's going on. Every presentation, I remind people that fashion is a reflection of the society that wears it. If you want to know what's happening in fashion or what's going to happen in fashion, you have to know what's going on in the world so that you can figure out what's going to go on in people's heads. That's what's going to result in how they present themselves. I just could not be happier with my job.

What's an average day for you?

I'm always inputting information. I read a lot, shop, travel. My main responsibility is to produce PowerPoint presentations twice a year that are my introduction to a season before anybody starts on it. Right now, I've finished up Fall '15 and am about to start Spring '16. My presentations are about 60 percent fashion and 40 percent whatever I think is going on in the world that impresses me.

I spend a lot of time inputting and have three Web sites that I really count on—gizmag.com, springwise.com, and coolhunting.com. I gather a lot of information, and I'm very good at taking things that have nothing to do with fashion and seeing how they impact people's behavior, which will therefore impact what they want to wear and their feelings about color and things like that.

Do you ever spend a lot of time just imagining future landscapes?

Oh, yes. It's like a science fiction movie, I guess (laughs)—with a focus on the wardrobe. I am very good at not seeing that which is old and unimportant. I have selective vision. I'm the most ruthless editor imaginable. For a season,

we get probably 60,000 images from the various international fashion weeks. In three days, I can edit them down to the 600 that I work with for a season.

What is that editing process that you use for paring down to what's really important? Is that a skill you've had to develop?

I think most of it is gut, to be honest with you. When I'm first starting with a rough edit, I try to keep my mind blank, and have no preconceived notion of what I'm looking for. Simply, anything that strikes me as interesting, I take. Then, when I've amassed all of that, I look for the common denominators: Was there a color I kept choosing over and over again? Was there a silhouette I reacted to all the time? Really, because I'm a couple heartbeats ahead of the world, and always have been, I grow tired of things when they're still good. That's something that I've had to learn to do. At the beginning of my career, I was much too fast. I was trying to get people to do things according to my timing, rather than the timing that would make money for them.

One reason I love being at Doneger, and the reason I think Doneger is so unique in terms of color and trend forecasting, is that we have this whole huge retail consultancy that actually has day-by-day information about what's selling, and where it's selling, and how much it's selling for. Anybody else who's working in the industry doesn't have this real information, and it's really just about timing. If you do the right color a season ahead, it's not going to sell. And can you come back and do it again? Doneger helps me to fine-tune my thinking. I interact with a lot of the senior merchandising people and listen to them when they talk to me. We have a really interesting client base with most of the important retailers in the world. Our Tobe division has a dream client base. We've got this whole spectrum of information that I can use that no other forecaster gets. It keeps it really exciting and realistic. And I've always understood that the object is to make money, and lots of fashion people don't get that.

predict
ions that
alerted our
because
there is no
ion. When
de what
ey going to
one or two
do it in-depth
nybody who
iem? Or are they
e things and do it in

n observer or an
in. caster?

I used to be ᴅ   , but it's almost impossible
to be an influenc   . You can influence a
segment, but I woulᴅ   ver direct people the way I
would have 20 years ago. Most of our meetings now
are finding out from the clients who their markets

are, what they did well with last season, what failed
for them—all to fine-tune their timing.

**Can you give me any last advice for any aspiring
trend forecasters—or really any fashion mind?**

The most important thing for anybody who wants
to be in the field is to have a broad interest and
curiosity about the world at large. I think the worst
thing that can happen is that you specialize your
interest in fashion, because it's too narrow. You'll
never know what is going to happen next if there's
a big fence around your interest. You have to know
how to communicate your ideas. You have to not
just have a great idea, but you have to be able to
express it and sell it to people who can fund it or cut
the pattern or whatever. To create a perfect trend
forecaster, it would be somebody who has a big
general interest in culture at large, communication,
and everything in the world.

Courtesy of Henry Doneger Associates, Inc.

chapter 2

Textile Design and Development

Take a look at one of your favorite prints. It can be a blouse, a shirt, or that great pair of patterned shorts. Think about the colors, the texture, the weave or knit, and the art of the print. There are designers and design houses who have made their places in fashion history with their textile designs. Can you name a few? Louis Vuitton, Missoni, Gucci, and Emilio Pucci may come to mind. Somebody has to be the creative force behind these textile designs, and that somebody is a textile designer.

A **textile designer** creates original designs for the fabrics used in all sorts of industries. This person understands how to combine visual arts with technical and usage concerns. **Textile design** is the process of creating patterns, motifs, or surface interest for knitted, woven, or printed fabrics. Pattern and print designs are evaluated in terms of how they can be combined with printing, knitting, weaving, embossing, and embroidery processes. Textile designers often specialize in one type of textile or another (e.g., knits or wovens), and they collaborate with textile colorists. A **textile colorist** works with a design to determine **colorways**, the specific color selections for a particular pattern or print; these are sometimes referred to as a *color palette*. Figure 2.1 provides an example of a colorway for a woven print.

These two creative positions are examples of the numerous career paths in the textile industry, which is a high-touch, high-tech industry. In the high-tech sector of the textile industry, there are several other career options, including textile engineering and textile production. A **textile engineer** works with designers to determine how designs can be applied to a fabric. A **textile technician** works with the issues that are directly related to the production of **piece goods**, such as finishing. Newly constructed knit or woven fabric must pass through various finishing processes to make it suitable for its intended purpose. **Finishing** enhances the appearance of fabric and also adds to its suitability for everyday wear or rugged use. Finishes can be solely mechanical, solely chemical, or a combination of the two. Finishes

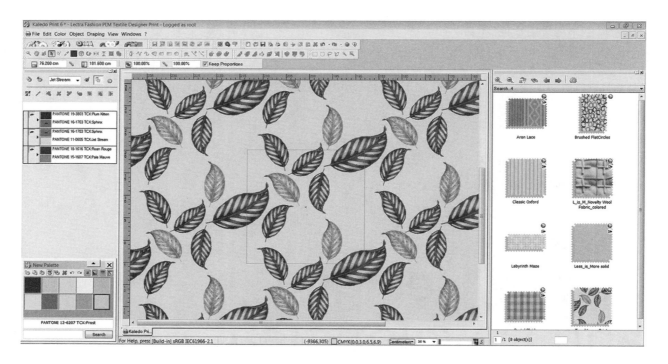

Figure 2.1
An example of a colorway for a woven print presented on Kaledo by Lectra.

that simply prepare the fabric for further use, such as scouring and bleaching in blue jeans, are known as **general finishes**. **Functional finishes**, such as durable press treatments, impart special characteristics to the cloth, such as waterproofing or flocking.

Job opportunities in actual textile production have dramatically declined in recent years because of inexpensive labor costs overseas. About 650 textile plants closed between 1997 and 2009, draining thousands of jobs and depressing communities.[1] It is true that textile manufacturing in the United States declined significantly in the 1990s and 2000s as cheaper labor pulled jobs overseas. In addition, automation and increased productivity of textile mills also cost jobs. More than 200,000 textile manufacturing jobs have been lost to automation in the last decade. However, things are changing overseas as well. Increasing wages in China and other countries, combined with higher transportation costs and tariffs, have prompted foreign and domestic companies to consider American manufacturing sites. The tide may eventually turn.

For now, a great number of U.S. fashion companies outsource much of their production work to companies in foreign countries. **Outsourcing** refers to having an aspect of a company's work performed by nonemployees in another company and, perhaps, in another country. Most outsourced jobs in the textile industry are low-paying production positions in countries with lower labor costs than those in the United States, such as those in the Pacific Rim, as well as South and Central America. The majority of American textile companies design domestically, but they outsource goods for production to take advantage of the free-trade agreements with low-wage countries. Despite the dramatic decline in U.S. jobs in the textile manufacturing industry, there is some light in that some job losses have been offset by creative and scientific tracks in design and product development.

In this chapter, the creative and scientific career opportunities in textile design and textile technology are examined. Whether one has a creative personality and an eye for pattern and color or a scientific mind that is interested in engineering and production, a job path in the textiles field can provide a fulfilling career.

Fashion Director

A **fashion director** for a textile company is responsible for determining the trends, colors, themes, and textures for piece goods, or fabrics, that the firm will feature for a specific season. Fashion directors are primarily interested in identifying the most important fashion trends for their companies and communicating these trends to textile designers, production managers, and customers. Fashion directors often work with trend forecasting firms to determine trend possibilities in color, form, theme, and fabric needs for each season.

Qualifications

The following is a list of qualifications for a career as a fashion director for a major textile firm:

- *Education.* A bachelor's degree in textiles, fashion design, fashion merchandising, visual arts, or a related field is a minimum requirement for employment as a fashion director.

- *Experience.* The majority of fashion directors moved up the ladder from within the ranks. Many of them were textile designers, product developers, buyers, or assistant fashion directors before obtaining key positions as fashion directors.

- *Personal characteristics.* The fashion director often has similar characteristics to the trend forecaster: curiosity, strong communication skills, a strong visual sensibility, leadership abilities, a good understanding of who the customers actually are, and the ability to work with a variety of constituencies—from designers to production managers to technical assistants.

Career Challenges

The challenges of the fashion director's career relate to two primary areas: securing the job and keeping it. Fashion directors are expected to have a strong foundation of work experience in the industry. It takes time, skill, and effort to be promoted through a variety of positions, for example, from technical textile designer to product developer to buyer. The best and the brightest climb quickly up the career ladder. Once in the position of fashion director, there is a great deal of pressure to be right—to be accurate about the color, pattern, style, and theme trends. If, for example, a fashion director determines that olive green is the color for a season, and it bombs at the retail level, then the company may lose a great deal of money from a high investment in olive green fabrics. As a result of this error, this fashion director may be searching for a new job. Additionally, the fashion director must collaborate successfully with a wide variety of people—designers, production personnel, and clients. It takes a person with a solid educational foundation in textiles, a well-balanced personality, and excellent communication skills to work effectively with so many different people.

Textile Designer

Textile designers create the images, patterns, colors, textures, weaves, and knits of the fabrics we wear and use, from our clothing and interiors to our automobiles and awnings (Figure 2.2). They can be classified as **surface designers**—knitters, weavers, or embroiderers for industries ranging from apparel to upholstery. To assist in textile design, there are **print services**, companies that sell art that becomes print designs to mills, wholesalers, product developers, and retailers. Many textile designers utilize **computer-aided design (CAD)**, which

■ Figure 2.2
Italian textile designer
Donatella Ratti with
fabric swatches of her
work.

■ Figure 2.3
A model on the runway
wearing a digitally
printed textile design by
Basso and Brooke.

is the process of developing garments, prints, and patterns on a computer screen. This process has greatly influenced the field of textile design, as it provides faster, more varied, and more personalized design options in textiles than were possible in past years.

Technological advances in CAD software and digital printing, several of which will be presented later in this chapter, offer unlimited creative opportunities to designers. For instance, a customer can now have a photograph of her pet pug transferred to canvas, which will then be used to create a handbag. An image of a Parisian street scene can be scanned and printed on fabric that will later become bedroom curtains. Once the print or pattern is developed, a strike-off is produced by the textile manufacturer. A **strike-off** is a test sample of printed fabric made to show and verify color and pattern before entering into production on larger quantities. Figure 2.3 shows a digitally printed textile design, and Box 2.1 provides information on the development of digital textile design and some of its designers.

A textile designer using CAD likely knows how to paint and draw well, but works specifically on the computer to create designs. A textile designer can take several different specialized career paths, including working with wovens, knits, or prints. For example, a textile designer may choose to focus on fibers and processes that are commonly used for knit goods such as sweaters, as illustrated in Figure 2.4. Another textile designer may decide to specialize in creating textile prints for woven fabrics by painting, or using CAD to create a **croquis** (Figure 2.5), a rendering or miniature visual of a textile pattern or print for a garment or an accessory, such as a scarf or handbag. The **assistant textile designer** supports the textile designer in accomplishing all of these tasks. What is the most important personal trait needed to be a successful textile designer? The key characteristic is to possess a mind that is simultaneously creative, business-oriented, and technically savvy.

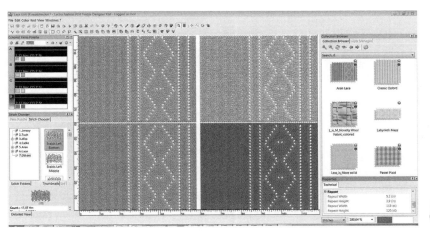

Textile Stylist

A **textile stylist** is the creative person who modifies existing textile goods, altering patterns or prints that have been successful on the retail floor to turn them into fresh, new products. The textile stylist may resize the image or develop new colorways for the modified textile print or pattern, and may collaborate with a textile colorist to accomplish this task.

Textile Colorist

A **textile colorist** chooses the color combinations that will be used in creating each textile design. Colorists frequently travel to fashion markets and belong to color forecasting organizations to stay on top of current and future color trends. There is a wide range of industries in which textile designers, stylists, and colorists are employed; they include the following:

- Knitted and woven textiles, used to make clothes and soft-good products, as well as upholstered products, such as home furnishings and automotive seats

- Rugs and carpets

- Prints for wallpapers, paper goods, flooring, or tiles

The responsibilities of textile designers, stylists, and colorists are as follows:

- Interacting with customers (e.g., apparel manufacturers or designers) to understand their needs and interpret their ideas accurately

- Collaborating with marketing, buying, and technical staff members, as well as design colleagues

- Understanding how textiles will be used, what properties textiles will need to function optimally, and how the addition of color dyes or surface treatments will affect these properties

■ Figure 2.4
A knit design and its colorways are presented on Kaledo by Lectra.

■ Figure 2.5
Croquis of a sweater design developed using CAD software.

CASE STUDIES IN CAREER EXPLORATION

Box 2.1 The Fabric as the Designer's Canvas

Lights, cameras, fabrics . . . Digitally manipulated prints have become big news on the runways. Martin Margiela, Peter Pilotto, and Mary Katrantzou belong to a new generation of designers who are literally creating not only the designs but also the printed fabrics they envision. "My training is as a textile designer and in traditional screen printing, but because of the nature of what I was doing with trompe l'oeil, digital collages give greater plasticity," explains Mary Katrantzou, a Central Saint Martins graduate, speaking of digital design's benefits. "With a screen print, 10 or 15 color separations need great expertise. With digital, there is no limitation. You can print a photographical version of anything," she adds.

Previously an instructor at the Royal College of Art and now a fabric consultant for Louis Vuitton in Paris, Susannah Handley compares the difference between traditional and digitally printed textiles as being similar to that of painting and photography. She tells the *International Herald Tribune*: "Directly

from computer to cloth is how many patterns are realized these days—it is a more clinical, faster method with the advantage that an instant result can be achieved."

The inkjet printing technology used in digital printing was first patented in 1968. In the 1990s, inkjet printers became widely available for paper-printing applications. You likely have one on your desk right now. The technology has continued to develop, and there are now specialized wide-format printers that can process a variety of substrates, everything from paper to canvas to vinyl and fabric. Although digital textile printing has been around for decades, it has only recently taken its place in the fashion industry. Digital textile printing provides the ability to print designs on fabric, directly from a PC or Mac. Inkjet printing is done on fabric in the same manner as it is completed on paper, and just as easily. This versatile technology is being used in many apparel and nonapparel markets. Digitally printed textiles can be used for a vast range of applications,

Box 2.1 Digital printing technologies continue to offer faster production and may grow to become the technology that provides the majority of the world's printed textiles.

Box 2.1 *(continued)*

including apparel, handbags, footwear, umbrellas, flags and banners, exhibition signage, furniture, curtains, drapes, bedding, towels, wall coverings, and carpets or other floor coverings.

For some companies and some products, digital textile printing can significantly reduce the costs associated with screen printing on textiles. Presently, the textile industry produces the majority of its printed textile fabric by screen printing, also referred to as analog textile printing. However, as we move through the digital age, developments in the digital printing of paper are increasingly being adapted for the textile market. Inkjet textile printing is growing, while growth in analog textile printing remains stagnant. As digital print technologies continue to offer faster production and larger cost-effective print runs, digital printing may grow to become the technology that provides the majority of the world's printed textiles. Currently, digital printing on textiles has several advantages over traditional textile printing methods, as follows:

• Lower production costs for short runs

• High productivity because of shorter lead times

• Fast turnaround

The only special requirement is that the fabrics used must be pretreated to hold the ink better and reproduce a wider range of high-quality hues. There are various types of treatments according to the fabrics and the inks being used.

Unlimited creative opportunities are often at the top of the designer's list when it comes to digital textile printing. Think about printing photographs on fabrics, using art as inspiration, creating a color palette that is unique to your design collection, and customizing products to meet an individual customer's desires. Digital printing on fabrics has also opened new opportunities for designers, manufacturers, merchandisers, and salespersons. For example, it is now possible to print a small piece of fabric, or enough for a garment, to create a sample of a new design.

Sources:

www.vogue.co.uk/news/daily/100413-the-digital-print-revolution

www.fashion-incubator.com/archive/introduction-to-digital-fabric-printing/

Ujiie, H. *Digital Printing of Textiles*. Centre of Excellence in Digital Ink Jet Printing, Philadelphia University, Woodhead Publishing Series in Textiles No. 53.

• Conducting research for ideas and inspiration, from antique embroidery to modern architecture to children's storybooks

• Experimenting with texture and pattern as it relates to color

• Producing design or color ideas, sketches, and samples and presenting them to customers

• Producing designs or color options for designs using CAD software

• Checking and approving samples of completed items

• Working to meet deadlines

• Working within budgets

• Keeping up to date with new fashions and population trends—current and projected

- Staying on top of new design and production processes

- Attending trade and fashion shows

Textile designers, stylists, and colorists need to consider such factors as how the designs will be produced, how the finished articles will be used, the quality of the materials used, and the budgets. They work standard hours, but they need to be flexible to meet deadlines. They are based in studios or offices. Prospective employers require a strong and relevant portfolio of work for review. Employers include large manufacturing companies and small, exclusive design houses. Some textile designers, stylists, and colorists are self-employed.

Qualifications

Requirements for employment in textile design, stylist, or colorist positions include the following:

- *Education.* A bachelor's degree in textiles, visual arts, computer-aided design, graphic design, fashion design, or a related discipline is a minimum requirement.

- *Experience.* Entry-level design positions provide the ideal starting place for college graduates. Additional experience in technical design (i.e., CAD) and color will assist the candidate in moving up the career ladder. Lectra's Kaledo Suite for textile design is becoming increasingly important in textile design, and experience in this program will give the job candidate an edge.

- *Personal characteristics.* Flexible computer skills; a strong visual sense for color, texture, and pattern; a creative personality; knowledge of how textiles are produced; effective business skills; an awareness of fashion trends; a practical understanding of skills such as sewing, knitting, weaving, and embroidery; and knowledge of the target consumer help make the textile designer, stylist, and colorist successful.

Career Challenges

The challenges for textile designers, stylists, and colorists are similar. They must interpret the trends designated by the fashion director. Sometimes, converting the words of the fashion director into the fabrics the director envisioned can be difficult. Textile designers, stylists, and colorists also must be aware of the technical requirements of fabric development, such as the printing requirements, durability, and application of finishes. Most important, they are often under pressure to meet quick deadlines and work within budget constraints.

Textile Technician

A **textile technician** either supervises the production facilities of a company or oversees the production as it is done by a **contractor**, a firm that is hired to manufacture the product line, either domestically or abroad. If a textile company owns its manufacturing facility, then the textile technician is responsible for the smooth running of the equipment used in textile production to maximize production. If a textile company contracts its production out to another company, then the textile technician works with the contractor to accomplish these goals. The primary responsibilities of the textile technician are as follows:

- Overseeing the regular routine maintenance of equipment, or the efficient production of the contractor

- Checking performance levels of equipment and/or contractors for optimal production

- Carrying out regular checks on production, spotting any difficulties, and dealing with them before they become problematic

In a large textile factory, a technician may specialize in one type of production technique, such as knitting or weaving; however, in a smaller company, the responsibilities of the technician may be more wide ranging. Technicians work approximately 40 hours per week, sometimes on shifts.

Qualifications

Requirements for employment as a textile technician include the following:

- *Education.* A bachelor's degree in textile technology, textile production, computer science, textile engineering, industrial technology, or a related field is required.

- *Experience.* Some textile technicians begin in entry-level technical design positions. They may move up into management of a team of technical designers that covers specific merchandise classifications, such as menswear or children's wear. Some technicians move into management or into specialized areas, such as quality control and research.

- *Personal characteristics.* High levels of technical knowledge and computer skills are extremely important personal qualifications in this career path. Strong practical and problem-solving skills are also essential. A thorough understanding of textile applications and usage assists the textile technician in making decisions about product development.

The career challenges for a textile engineer and textile technician are similar and are presented after the following discussion of the textile engineer's position.

Textile Engineer

Manufacturers are merging textiles with technology to create new products for the market. For instance, instead of being just wrinkle-resistant, fabrics have become truly wrinkle-free through a process patented by TAL Corporation of Hong Kong. The process involves baking a special coating onto the fabric, as well as innovative use of adhesives along the seams to prevent puckering. Other fabrics are coated with Teflon to resist stains. Materials have been developed to change color with body temperature changes, which is particularly appealing for hospital use. Figure 2.6 shows an additional example of innovative fiber technology. The career path that directly relates to these new products is that of textile engineer. A **textile engineer** works with designers to determine how designs can be applied to a fabric while considering practical variables, such as durability, washability, and colorfastness. A person in this position will have a background in textile science that often includes chemistry and manufacturing, in addition to textile analysis.

■ **Figure 2.6**
An enlarged image
of a crochet-look
bioimplantable surgical
patch.

Qualifications

Requirements for employment as a textile engineer include the following:

- *Education.* A bachelor's degree in textiles, textile technology, textile production, computer science, textile engineering, industrial technology, or a related discipline is a minimum requirement.

- *Experience.* Many textile engineers working for companies that own and operate their own manufacturing facilities move up from the production line to this position. Textile engineers working with firms that contract out production may have a greater job emphasis on information technology in their positions. Some textile engineers begin in apprentice positions as assistant textile engineers.

- *Personal characteristics.* A textile engineer has a broad knowledge of how textiles are produced. In addition, this position requires an understanding of technical considerations as they relate to textile applications, an awareness of consumer wants and needs, and a comprehension of textile science.

Career Challenges

Textile technicians and engineers face the challenge of understanding and anticipating the continually changing technologies in textile design and production. Deadlines are a constant potential source of stress. Communicating and problem solving with a variety of co-workers in different divisions, such as design and production, require a proactive approach, patience, and flexibility by textile technicians and engineers. The ability to identify a problem and solve it quickly is on ongoing task in these positions.

In addition to design, color, and technical positions in the textile industry, there are ancillary career paths. The resource room director or reference librarian and the account executive are two career paths that relate to the textile industry, yet require different sets of skills and backgrounds from those of the creative and scientific positions.

Resource Room Director/Reference Librarian

Many large companies maintain a **resource room**, or *reference library*, of textile samples, source books and magazines, Internet resources, print and pattern images, and, possibly, actual garments constructed from the company's fabrics or those of competitors. As portrayed in Figure 2.7, these items are used by fashion directors, designers, technicians, and sales representatives for design inspiration and reference. The **resource room director** oversees the procurement, organization, and removal or replacement of these materials. Some companies, such as large apparel manufacturers, fashion publishers, and fiber/fabric houses, maintain reference libraries. The **reference librarian** is responsible for managing the inventory of books and resources and procuring new ones.

■ **Figure 2.7**
Bunny Williams' design resource room. Resource rooms, also called reference libraries, hold items that are used by fashion directors and designers for inspiration and reference.

Qualifications

Requirements for employment as a resource room director or reference librarian include the following:

- *Education.* A bachelor's degree in textiles, fashion merchandising, fashion design, or a related discipline is a minimum requirement.

- *Experience.* For recent graduates with work experience in fashion retailing and textiles, strong academic performances, and impressive references, these can be entry-level positions. Some resource room directors or reference librarians later move into the design divisions of firms. Exposure to the references of a particular firm helps build the potential designer's background.

- *Personal characteristics.* Strong organizational skills, effective time management, first-rate communication skills, and attention to detail are personal qualities that fit the position of resource room director or reference librarian.

Career Challenges

Managing a resource room or reference library can be a daunting task. There is a constant flow of new acquisitions that need to be inventoried, labeled, and stored, often in minimal space. There must be a high level of organization for the resource room director or reference librarian to be able to pull samples quickly for the fashion director or designer who needs them immediately.

Account Executive

An **account executive**, also referred to as *sales* or *manufacturer's representative*, sells to and manages the accounts, or clients, of textile manufacturers. The account executive is responsible for the sales of textiles and usually is assigned to a specific territory, such as the southern or midwestern United States. As illustrated in the classified advertisement of Figure 2.8, account executives can be paid in several ways: a salary, commission, quota, or a combination of these. This is a great career for someone who prefers working independently and enjoys business, budgets, and sales, as well as the textile, fashion, and home furnishing markets.

Qualifications

Qualifications include the following:

- *Education.* A bachelor's degree in fashion merchandising, general business administration, or marketing is preferred.

- *Experience.* Retail or wholesale sales experience is most often required; however, an internship or employment as an assistant to an account executive is an excellent way to open the door to this career path.

- *Personal characteristics.* A strong understanding of accounting, effective sales skills, good communication abilities, and excellent follow-up skills are important attributes of successful account executives.

WANTED: TEXTILE SALES REPRESENTATIVE

JOB SNAPSHOT:
Location: New York, NY
Base Pay: $90,000 to $100,000 per year, plus benefits
Employee Type: Full-time
Industry: Fashion - Apparel – Textile Manufacturing
Manages Others: No
Job Type: Sales and business development
Education: 4-year degree
Experience: At least 5 years
Travel: Up to 50 percent

DESCRIPTION:
A global textile manufacturer seeks sales manager of textiles. Territory is international.

SUMMARY:
This position will be responsible for developing apparel textiles to the apparel industry sector worldwide.

RESPONSIBILITIES:
Receives orders from clients, coordinates with factories based on the orders received, imports finished products, and sells them to clients.
- Develops, implements, and revises sales strategy and tactics for customers.
- Develops and implements both short term and long range plans to expand sales.
- Maintains contact with customers in person, by the telephone, and in writing, to promote the sale and use of the company products in the territory.
- Develops, implements, and revises sales strategy and tactics for customers.

REQUIREMENTS AND PREFERENCES:
- Bachelor's degree in textile or business related field preferred.
- 5 years minimum of sales experience in the textile industry.
- Sales experience in casual wear, sportswear and women's suits preferred.
- Strong communication skills.
- Good computer skills in MS office.
- Chinese language skills are helpful, but not necessary.

NOTE: Please send your resume in MS Word format with your salary requirements.

Classified advertisement for a textile company representative. As illustrated in this classified advertisement, sales executives are responsible for the sales of a company's textiles and the solicitation and maintenance of accounts.

Career Challenges

Account executives are challenged to continually beat last season's or last year's figures. For some people, it is difficult to work independently and motivate yourself, despite rejections during sales calls and a fluctuating economy. Monitoring income and expenses, including many costs related to generating sales, is a juggling act for many account representatives who must ask themselves, "Will I make enough commission to earn a living and offset the costs of this travel to trade markets or to clients' offices?" Maintaining a positive outlook and a high energy level are requirements for the successful account executive.

Examples of Companies Employing Textile Designers and Product Developers

Several large companies employ textile personnel, from designers to resource room managers. Many of these firms are located in New York City and Los Angeles; some have satellite offices in Dallas, San Diego, and Atlanta, as well as cities abroad. Next, eight of the top textile firms are examined, encompassing fur as a type of textile.

Cotton Incorporated

■ **Figure 2.9**
Cotton Incorporated conducts research and promotion for cotton and cotton products, with the primary goals of increased demand and profitability.

Cotton Incorporated is a not-for-profit corporation established pursuant to the Cotton Research and Promotion Act of 1966. It provides fabric, color, and trend information for textile manufacturers, soft goods, and soft-good products for manufacturers, designers, and retailers. Funded by U.S. growers of upland cotton and importers of cotton and cotton textile products, Cotton Incorporated conducts research and promotion for cotton and cotton products with the primary goal of increasing the demand for and profitability of U.S. cotton and cotton products; its logo is illustrated in Figure 2.9.

The company offers technical services, such as fiber processing, fabric development, dyeing and finishing, and cotton quality management assistance. Information services provide data on cotton supply and demand, fiber quality, and consumer research trends. To keep cotton on the runway, Cotton Incorporated's fashion trend analysis team provides color and trend forecasts for cotton apparel and home products, highlighting the company's trend research and supplier information. Cotton Incorporated World Headquarters is located in North Carolina. Offices are located worldwide, including New York, Mexico City, Osaka, and Shanghai. The company's Web site, www.cottoninc.com, provides corporate information, research reports, and employment opportunity postings.

Australian Wool Services Limited (The Woolmark Company)

■ **Figure 2.10**
If you check the label of any quality wool or blended wool item you own, you are likely to find the famous Woolmark symbol, as shown here.

With more than 60 years of expertise in the wool industry and textile innovation, Australian Wool Services Limited is the world's leading wool fiber textile organization. The company provides unique global endorsement through ownership and licensing of the Woolmark, Woolmark Blend, and Wool Blend brands. The Woolmark Company, a subsidiary of Australian Wool Services, specializes in the commercialization of wool technologies and innovations, technical consulting, business information, and commercial testing of wool fabrics. If you check the label of any quality wool or blended wool item you own, you are likely to find one of the famous Woolmark symbols, as illustrated in Figure 2.10.

These brands and their corresponding brandmarks are protected by strict and extensive control checks to ensure product quality. Australian Wool Services Limited operates globally, working with textile processors, designers, and retailers in both the apparel and interior textile markets.

Fur Council of Canada

The Fur Council of Canada is a national, nonprofit organization incorporated in 1964, representing people working in every sector of the Canadian fur trade. This includes fur producers, auction houses, processors, designers, craftspeople, and retail furriers. The goals of the Fur Council programs include the following:

FUR COUNCIL OF CANADA

• Encouraging linkages between designers and other sectors of the fashion industry

• Sponsorship of competitions for both professional designers and students in Canadian fashion colleges

• Promotion of the work of innovative Canadian fur designers through advertising in top national and international fashion publications

• Providing accurate information about the Canadian fur trade to consumers, educators, and the public to counter criticisms that the industry's practices are cruel to animals. For example, in Canada, trappers must pass a mandatory course in which they learn how to use new humane trapping methods and how to apply the principles of sustainable use established by wildlife officials and biologists.

The Fur Council of Canada can be further investigated on its Web site at www.furcouncil .com; its logo is featured in Figure 2.11.

North American Fur and Fashion Exposition

In addition to headquartering the Fur Council, Canada also is the site of a major international fur market. The North American Fur and Fashion Exposition in Montreal (NAFFEM) is the largest fur and outerwear fashion fair of its type in North America and one of the most important fur fashion marketing events in the world. For more than 20 years, NAFFEM has attracted thousands of professional buyers from the world's finest specialty boutiques and department stores with its wide array of luxury furs, boutique furs, shearlings, leathers, cashmere, and accessories. During the annual trade show, more than 200 exhibitors represent designer labels and upscale women's and men's outerwear in fur and precious fabrics. The lines range from formal looks to casual wear, sportswear, and streetwear. More than half of the buyers viewing the lines of these exhibitors come from across the United States and abroad. Another area of the trade show features unique international accessory collections, including handbags, gloves, scarves, hats, wraps, and jewelry. NAFFEM is organized and managed by the Fur Council of Canada, as examined above.

Mohair Council

The Mohair Council is an organization exclusively dedicated to mohair, the fleece of the Angora goat. Established in 1966, the Mohair Council concentrates on marketing, education, and research as it relates to the mohair industry. The Mohair Council was created for mohair producers and is still financially sustained primarily by producers. It is a nonprofit organization

funded by interest and dividend dollars from the now-defunct Wool Act, a current voluntary producer mohair assessment program, and funds from the U.S. Department of Agriculture.

The council headquarters is located in San Angelo, Texas, on the edge of Edwards Plateau in the southwest part of the state. This rugged ranching region is prime goat country and has long been home to many of the finest Angora goat breeding flocks in the world. Ninety percent of the U.S. Angora goat population grazes within a 150-mile radius of the Mohair Council's national headquarters, making Texas the primary mohair region of the United States. The United States has developed into one of the three largest mohair-producing nations in the world, with an annual production in excess of 2.4 million pounds. The other principal mohair sources are South Africa and Turkey.

The main function of the Mohair Council is to promote American mohair and to find viable worldwide markets for this unique commodity. To market its product, the Mohair Council has a team of 11 professionals who travel the world in search of profitable foreign markets for American mohair. These individuals meet one-on-one with prospective buyers, discover their needs, and then work to put the mohair buyer and supplier together.

Another objective of the Mohair Council is to educate designers, manufacturers, retailers, and consumers about mohair and mohair products (logo illustrated in Figure 2.12). For example, did you know that, as a decorating fabric, mohair is valued for its flame resistance and high sound absorbency? It is ideal for public places such as theaters, hotel lobbies, and offices, as well as homes. In addition, mohair draperies are effective insulators, keeping heat in during cold weather and serving as a barrier against hot outdoor temperatures in the summer. The Mohair Council's Web site is www.mohairusa.com.

Cone Mills

Cone Mills, LLC, is one of America's leading textile manufacturers. Cone Mills is a privately held company owned by W. L. Ross and Company as part of the International Textile Group. It is headquartered in Greensboro, North Carolina, with five manufacturing facilities located in North Carolina and Mexico. The company operates regional sales offices in Greensboro, New York, Dallas, Los Angeles, and San Francisco. Established in 1891, Cone Mills aims to be the largest producer of denim fabrics in the world. It has been selling denim and casual sportswear fabrics internationally for more than 45 years, serves markets in more than 35 countries, and is the largest U.S. exporter of denim and apparel fabrics. Cone Industries has a strong interest in and commitment to safeguarding the environment. The company provides internship opportunities in textile production and environmental protection. Further information about the company and its job opportunities can be found at its Web site, www.conedenim.com.

Springs Global

Founded in 1887, Springs Global supplies leading retailers with coordinated home furnishings. The company headquarters is located in Fort Mill, South Carolina. Springs Global also produces and markets bed and bath products for institutional and hospitality customers, home sewing fabrics, as well as baby bedding and apparel products. This range of products is truly mind-boggling. Springs' bedding products include sheets and pillowcases, comforters and comforter accessories, bedspreads, blankets, bed skirts, quilts, duvet covers, pillow shams, decorative and bed pillows, and mattress pads. Its bath products include towels, bath and accent rugs, shower curtains, and ceramic and other bath accessories. Its window products include window hardware and decorative rods, blinds, shades, and soft window treatments such as drapes, valances, and balloon shades.

Through licensing agreements, Springs Global has extended its product lines to include kitchen and table accessories, flannel and knit sheets, blankets and throws, and lampshades. With such a vast array of product classifications, it is no surprise that Springs Global has approximately 30 manufacturing facilities in the United States, Canada, and Mexico and employs about 15,000 people. Five generations of the Springs family have led this private company. The company's Web site address is www.springs.com.

DuPont

When it was founded in 1802, E. I. du Ponte de Nemours was primarily an explosives company. Today, it is a company that has shown explosive growth. DuPont offers a wide range of innovative products and services for numerous markets, including agriculture, food and beverage, electronics, chemicals, packaging and printing, safety and protection, home and construction, transportation, and apparel. DuPont operates in more than 90 countries and is a Fortune 500 company.

DuPont's mission includes research and development as high priorities. The company has more than 40 research, development, and customer service labs in the United States and more than 35 labs in 11 other countries. The productive results of DuPont's research are illustrated by its products. DuPont's brands include Teflon coatings, Corian solid surfaces, Kevlar high-strength material, and Tyvek housing protective material. DuPont's innovative fabrics run the gamut of uses from hospital and medical care applications to firefighters' gear and sportswear. The company can be located online at www.DuPont.com.

Summary

As fashion companies in the United States now, more than ever, outsource much of their production work to companies in foreign countries, domestic job opportunities in textile production have dramatically declined. The majority of American companies design domestically but outsource goods internationally to take advantage of the free-trade agreements with low-wage countries. Although there is a loss in U.S. production jobs in the textile industry, there is an increase in the creative and scientific track, such as design, product development, and textile technology. Some of the key career tracks in the creative sector of textiles include fashion director, textile designer, textile stylist, and textile colorist. In the scientific and manufacturing areas of textiles, career options include textile engineer and textile technician. Additionally, there are ancillary career paths in textiles in a variety of areas, such as reference libraries and sales. The director of a resource room or reference library for a fiber association, such as Cotton Incorporated, maintains the fabric samples, garments, books, and trade journals that company employees use for inspiration and reference. The account executive is the sales representative for a fabric producer, selling piece goods to clients, such as the designers and manufacturers of apparel, accessories, or home furnishings. Whether you are interested in sales, technology, or design, there are career opportunities in the **primary level** of the fashion industry, the sector that includes fiber, fabrics, and manufacturing.

Endnote

1. Mercer, M., "Textile industry comes back to life, especially in South," *USA Today*, February 5, 2014.

Key Terms

account executive
assistant textile designer
colorways
computer-aided design (CAD)
contractor
croquis
fashion director
finishing
functional finish
general finish
outsourcing
piece goods
primary level

print service
reference librarian
resource room
resource room director
strike-off
surface designer
textile colorist
textile design
textile designer
textile engineer
textile stylist
textile technician

Online Resources

www.artdesignfashion.com/textile
www.cowtan.com
www.marimekko.com
www.pierrefrey.com

www.printsourcenewyork.com
www.texprint.org.uk
www.textilesource.com

Discussion Questions

1. In light of the trend toward outsourcing in textile production, what new career options do you believe will develop in the fiber and fabric sector of the fashion industry? What types of knowledge, training, and skills will best equip a job candidate to succeed in this industry over the next decade?
2. What are the differences between the textile designer, stylist, and colorist? The similarities?
3. Using the Internet, locate and describe two new technology programs, one that assists with textile design tasks and another that facilitates textile production.

Profile: Lectra and its Impact on Textile Design and Development

With more than 40 years' experience in fashion and apparel, Lectra's mission is to provide a complete spectrum of design, development, and production solutions to confront 21st-century challenges. From first creative spark to final product, Lectra addresses an end-to-end process, supporting the day-to-day operations of companies in more than 100 countries. From fast fashion to luxury to ready-to-wear, Lectra's 23,000 customers in markets as diverse as casual, sports, outdoor, denim, and lingerie represent every development and sourcing model imaginable.

Lectra Fashion PLM

Lectra Fashion PLM connects planning, design, development, and sourcing teams to help companies master the entire collection lifecycle from design to development to production. Specifically designed for the fashion and apparel

industry, this collaborative environment combines collection creation and management, textile and fashion design, product specifications, and design-to-cost for real-time decision making.

Lectra's Fashion and Textile Design Solution

Lectra's collaborative design solution keeps fashion and textile design teams focused on creative activities, allowing them to do digitally what they could never do by hand. With sketching and boarding tools, knit, print and woven textile design, and color development, Lectra's design solution provides tools for fashion companies to create new designs and trends.

Designers can easily share their creative work with other teams right from the beginning of the collection process, ensuring design quality and production feasibility. Better collaboration between

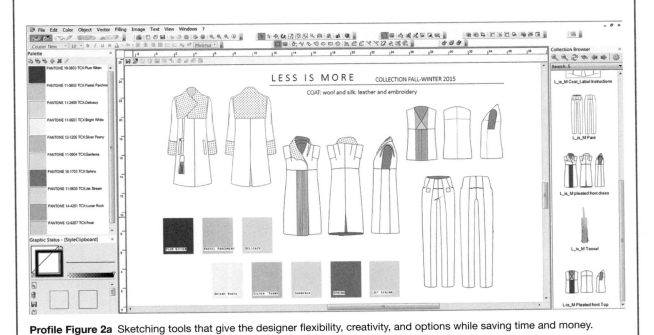

Profile Figure 2a Sketching tools that give the designer flexibility, creativity, and options while saving time and money.

(continued on next page)

(continued)

designers and product development teams reduces the number of errors and supports early decision making to significantly accelerate the design process.

Sketching tools help designers stay on top of trends and reduce the time it takes to get products from the drawing board to development and sampling. Fashion-specific tools cut down the time needed to create new styles and carry over bestsellers. Range plans and quick sketches jump-start fast visual concept development by turning creative trends into product ideas quickly. Detailed specification and production instructions reduce the need for clarifications when communicating product ideas to teams and suppliers.

Collaborative Textile Design Modules

Lectra's textile designer modules help textile designers create original concepts or adapt existing ideas from a textile archive by supplying industry-specific tools for woven, knitted, and print design production. Creating these visuals helps deliver clear specifications and design proposals with essential color, pattern, repeat, and scale information.

- *Lectra's collaborative print solution* turns creative ideas into production-ready, cost-effective prints. Print-specific tools help designers change repeat ideas, overlap, and dimensions; respect color limitations; group colors for tonal prints; and recolor from a seasonal palette to create unlimited colorways.

- *Lectra's collaborative weave solution* contains visual libraries of industry-standard weaves for an easy start, as well as the tools to customize and build on existing patterns. A yarn creation tool encourages designers to explore the effects of fibers, twist, and diameter on weave and knit patterns.

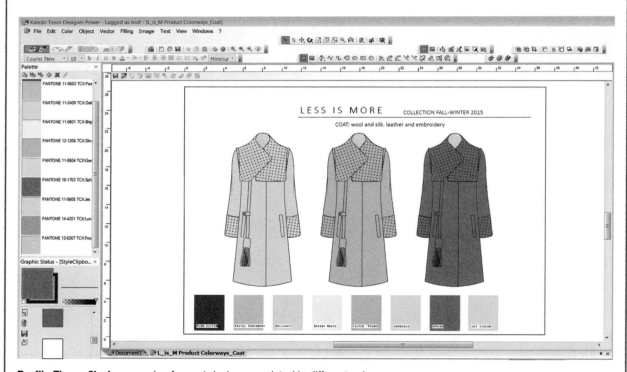

Profile Figure 2b An example of a coat design completed in different colorways.

(continued)

Profile Figure 2c Coat details are illustrated on the Lectra screen.

- *Lectra's collaborative knit solution* is driven by a unique three-dimensional stitch simulator that generates realistic knit fabric simulations. Designers can preview and check complex combinations of multicolor yarns and structured knits to get designs right the first time. An extensive library of knit structures coupled with this unique three-dimensional stitch simulator reduces the designer's time and the need for costly samples.

From palette creation to the preparation of print specifications, Lectra supports designers in the key steps of the print design process: (1) combine artistic tools and scanned images to create new print designs; (2) reduce and recolor flat and tonal prints; (3) create and vary print repeats; and (4) prepare print specifications with callouts, color information, text, and images for accurate communication with design, product development, and production teams.

chapter 3

Sourcing

If you have ever taken a clothing construction class, you have a headstart into the world of sourcing. You likely worked with interfacing, elastic, zippers, and buttons. As a result, you probably have an idea of how many components go into a garment, including some we do not even see. There is a person in the fashion industry whose job is to buy the materials that make up your favorite winter coat, your great leather belt, or your comfortable reading chair. Yet another person locates the manufacturing facility that produces the coat, belt, or chair. Both of these people are involved in the work of sourcing. **Sourcing** primarily refers to one of two activities: (1) the task of locating the suppliers of components needed to make a product, or (2) the job of securing manufacturers to produce end products and then collaborating with the manufacturer, contractor, or vendor while the products are being created. A **vendor**, or *supplier*, is any firm, such as a manufacturer or a distributor, from whom a company purchases products or production processes. Sourcing includes the following activities:

- Determining the amount of product needed

- Negotiating the best possible price and discounts

- Problem solving throughout the procurement and production activities

- Following up on actual shipments to make certain that due dates are met

- Assuring quality control is maintained

- Scheduling deliveries

Whether locating the components of a product or securing a manufacturer to produce it, sourcing takes a product from its conception stage to the sales floor or Web site.

Let's say a designer of an apparel line comes up with several amazing **collections**, or groupings of related styles. According to the designer's sketches, to actually turn the illustrations into apparel, the company will need several tapestry fabrics for jackets, silk chiffons for blouses, and colored denim for bottoms. Additionally, there will be the need for faux fur for the detachable collars, buttons for the jackets and tops, lining fabrics, interfacing, belting, and zippers—the list goes on and on. In some companies, the designer and an assistant locate the places from which to purchase these items. In larger companies, buyers source fabrics and related products for the items in the designer's line. In many midsized to large companies, the sourcing manager takes the designer's vision and helps turn it into reality.

Sourcing the Product

How do design companies locate the fabrics and other product parts necessary for producing their lines? Some career options focus on sourcing fabrics and other product components. Fashion production planners, piece goods buyers, and findings buyers are three examples of these career paths. Sourcing can encompass buying goods domestically and abroad. If products are purchased from an overseas vendor and shipped to the United States, then they are referred to as **imports**. In contrast, products that are bought by an overseas company from a vendor in the United States and sent out of the country are referred to as **exports**. Imports and exports are examined in further detail throughout this chapter.

Fashion Production Planner

Fashion production planners have the significant responsibility of material planning, anticipating all of the parts needed to make the final product. The primary tasks of fashion production planners are as follows:

- Reviewing forecasts of sales generated by the manufacturers' representatives and/or by analyzing past sales performance of line items

- Planning fabric production based on current orders and projected reorders

- Scheduling and monitoring works in progress

- Working with material manufacturers to determine the availability of goods

- Collaborating with key departments, such as design and product development, to anticipate future needs

- Meeting strict deadlines to keep shipments on time

Qualifications

A career as a fashion production planner requires the following qualifications:

- *Education.* A bachelor's degree in fashion merchandising, fashion design, business administration, marketing, international marketing, project management, or a related field is a requirement.

- *Experience.* Skills in a similar role within the fashion manufacturing sector of the industry are a hiring plus. Knowledge of offshore raw materials planning and purchasing as it relates to sales forecasts is essential. Experience in a large and varied manufacturing fashion company would be highly regarded. An internship with a manufacturer during college is an added bonus to postgraduate employment.

- *Personal characteristics.* The ability to communicate clearly is essential. Fabrics and findings are often sourced overseas; therefore, a multilingual background may be extremely valuable. A few of the languages that are currently important in the sourcing field are Mandarin, Taiwanese, and Spanish.

Piece Goods Buyer

The **piece goods buyer** works for a company that uses textiles in the production of its final products. This can be an apparel company, a home furnishings firm, an automotive manufacturer, or an accessories producer. The responsibilities of a piece goods buyer include the following:

- Shopping for textile supplies at trade markets and through textile manufacturers' representatives (Figure 3.1)

- Planning the amount of fabric, referred to as **yardage**, to purchase from various sources or determining from which vendors the piece goods will be purchased and communicating with these vendors

- Coordinating with production managers who advise on the delivery status of purchase orders; a **purchase order (PO)** is a contract for merchandise between buyers, as representatives of their firms, and vendors

- Communicating with accounts payable on payments and financing, to include proof of payments, wire transfers, and letters of credit; a **letter of credit** is a document issued by a bank authorizing the bearer to draw a specific amount of money from the issuing bank, its branches, or associated banks and agencies. It allows importers to offer secure terms to exporters.

- Working with warehouse managers on inventory management, such as availability and accessibility of fabrics

■ **Figure 3.1**
A piece goods buyer for
an apparel manufacturer
shops for textiles at
trade markets and
textile manufacturers'
showrooms.

- Monitoring quality control by inspecting shipments and dealing with **chargebacks**, credits for damaged merchandise and returns on defective goods

An **assistant piece goods buyer** often works with the piece goods buyer to accomplish this long list of responsibilities and as training for the position of piece goods buyer in the future.

Qualifications

A career as a piece goods buyer requires the following qualifications:

- *Education.* A bachelor's degree in fashion merchandising, fashion design, textiles, or a related field is a minimum requirement.

- *Experience.* Many piece goods buyers are promoted from the position of assistant piece goods buyer; others move into piece goods buying from the textile design track or the merchandising career path.

- *Personal characteristics.* A piece goods buyer has excellent quantitative skills, which are needed for calculating cost of goods, delivery expenses, and yardage amounts. This person must be able to work effectively under pressure, have excellent follow-up and communication skills, and be a successful negotiator.

Findings and/or Trimmings Buyer

The **findings buyer** is responsible for ordering findings and trimmings. **Findings** include such product components as zippers, thread, linings, and interfacings. Findings are functional and may not be visible when viewing the final product. **Trimmings**, however, are decorative components designed to be seen as part of the final product. Trimmings include buttons, appliqués, and beltings. The **trimmings buyer** is responsible for ordering these product components.

Locating findings and trimmings is an important job in which timing is critical. Think about the production line, quality control, and the end product. If the findings buyer orders skirt zippers that are too short, either the zippers will be installed and the customers will not be able to get into the skirts or production on the skirts will be halted until the correct zippers are received. If a button shipment is late, the trimmings buyer is held accountable, as the entire production has to be held until it arrives. Figure 3.2 shows a photo of Tender Buttons, a well-known boutique in New York City.

■ **Figure 3.2**
On a tree-lined street in Manhattan is a tiny brick townhouse, Tender Buttons, one of a few shops in America devoted entirely to the sale of buttons.

Qualifications

The education, experience, and personal characteristics required for findings and/or trimmings buyers are as follows.

- *Education*. A bachelor's degree in fashion design, fashion merchandising, product development, or a related discipline is a minimum requirement.

- *Experience*. Most findings and trimmings buyers work as assistants to the buyers before moving into this position, or they have worked in retail fashion merchandising. Internship experience and/or employment in either the manufacturing or design sector of the fashion industry are beneficial to securing these positions.

- *Personal characteristics*. High attention to detail is a critical asset to findings and trimmings buyers. Understanding product construction, sewing techniques, and product quality are essential skills. The abilities to locate vendors and negotiate with them are critical, as is following up on deliveries.

Career Challenges

Planners and buyers of raw materials, piece goods, and findings and trimmings share similar job struggles. It can continually be a source of stress to follow up on shipments needed to meet deadlines. Negotiating with vendors for priority shipping and competitive pricing can be a challenge. Written and oral communication skills may be tested when the buyer is putting together a deal with an overseas supplier. Currency exchanges, shipping costs, language barriers, and cultural differences can contribute to communication breakdowns. Attention to detail and written agreements are critical to minimizing these challenges. Finally, the buyer in sourcing is faced with constantly recalculating costs of goods. Shipping prices can change overnight. Handling fees may be added. Taxes may change. The dollar may fluctuate in currency exchange. Reviewing costs is a task that must be reexamined from the time an order is placed until the products reach the receiving dock. Fortunately, most buyers in sourcing enjoy the quantitative work that demands a high level of attention to detail.

Sourcing Manager

In addition to the positions responsible for sourcing materials needed to create the end product, some midsized to large companies have a position entitled sourcing manager, in which an individual is responsible for sourcing production. The **sourcing manager** communicates with the company manufacturing the product, referred to as the **contractor**. Sourcing managers work with overseas or domestic producers, discuss product specifications with them, and negotiate contracts. Next, the sourcing manager monitors the controls put into place to make certain that production is executed correctly by the outside vendor. After production begins, the sourcing manager oversees quality control and delivery schedules. Throughout the process, there are, more often than not, problems to be resolved.

Qualifications

Sourcing managers should possess the following qualifications:

- *Education.* A bachelor's degree in fashion merchandising, fashion design, product development, business administration, or a related field is a requirement.

- *Experience.* Strong knowledge of product construction is necessary for sourcing production, fabric, and findings. Also, a general technical knowledge of fabric applications, construction, and care is required. This position requires prior work experience. Two to three years as a retail buyer, a wholesale merchandiser, or a production manager provide a good background.

- *Personal characteristics.* Flexibility is often cited as the number-one quality for the successful sourcing manager. Keen observation skills and strong communication abilities are also important attributes. A large network of contacts in product components and manufacturing can make the sourcing manager's job easier. This network often results from professional relationships built during prior work experiences.

Career Challenges

The sourcing manager has to see far enough down the road to anticipate changes and potential problems and then be flexible enough to keep the work on track. Top sourcing managers are proactive, rather than reactive. Stamina is also a critical characteristic, as the job demands long hours that require tremendous focus and effort. Frequent travel may be required. Particularly for overseas travel, sensitivity to cultural differences is an asset. The abilities to learn from experience, negotiate effectively, and maintain a cool head reduce the stress level a sourcing manager can face. Box 3.1 is a sample of an online classified advertisement for a sourcing manager.

THE JOB SEARCH

Box 3.1 Sourcing and Logistics Manager

An international leader and innovator in the fiber, fabric, and fashion industry, we are currently seeking to fill the following position: Sourcing and Logistics Manager.

- Five-plus years of experience sourcing in China

- Background in source selection, vendor quality, and logistics

- Must come from a manufacturing background

- All candidates must be able to provide work-related references

Salary: $70,000–$85,000+bonus; excellent employee benefits

Location: Denver, Colorado

Merchandiser for a Manufacturer

The position of **merchandiser**, or *merchandise planner*, on the wholesaler's or manufacturer's side of the industry is very important to all departments, as this person works as the liaison among the design, production, and sales teams—from the showroom to the factory (Figure 3.3). One of the primary responsibilities of the merchandiser is to develop a merchandise line plan by month and by piece count or by **stock-keeping unit (SKU)**, a type of identification data for a single product. Some of the other duties of the merchandiser for a manufacturer include the following:

- Determining top sellers, referred to as **volume drivers**, and essential programs, retail pricing, and fabric recommendations for the collections based on past retail selling history

- Shopping the market and competition and, later, presenting a merchandising strategy to the design team

- Communicating changes in strategy, assortment planning, and allocation to technical, visual, and licensing teams

- Updating and maintaining the purchasing sheets on a weekly basis

■ **Figure 3.3**
One of the key duties performed by the merchandiser is shopping the market, reviewing the lines of current suppliers, and looking for new vendors.

- Providing input on budgets, sales, gross margin, and receipt flow

- Recommending line changes at department weekly meetings, based on actual sales trends as opposed to the sales plan for each style

- Identifying product opportunities for future seasons by translating trends

- Analyzing the current season's opportunities from retail sales

- Working with the sales teams to make sure their specific products needs are being addressed

Box 3.2 features a classified advertisement for a manufacturer's merchandiser, or merchandise planner.

Qualifications

Merchandise planners should possess the following qualifications:

- *Education.* A bachelor's degree in fashion merchandising, fashion design, product development, business administration, or a related field is a requirement.

- *Experience.* Strong knowledge of product components and product construction is necessary, as is general knowledge of production capabilities and technology. This position often requires prior work experience as a buyer or assistant merchandise planner. Applicants with work experience in both manufacturing and retailing have an edge over other candidates, as they have the ability to view the product from the manufacturer's and retail buyer's perspectives.

- *Personal characteristics.* Attention to detail, the ability to work accurately with numbers, and a futuring perspective are personal qualities that successful merchandise planners often have.

Career Challenges

Merchandisers (merchandise planners) must continually look ahead, preparing today for tomorrow's sales. They are constantly juggling several seasons at one time. It is a daunting task to be able to predict sales trends and to adjust production for the current season from slow-selling products into top-selling ones. Strong work relationships and effective communication skills help offset these challenges.

Import Production Coordinator

An **import production coordinator** is the apparel or home furnishings company's liaison with the manufacturer or contractor. The import production coordinator is involved in all aspects of the production process, works closely with the design team, and is the link between overseas factories (e.g., in China, Japan, Taiwan, India, and South America, to name a few locations) and the company's design and buying teams. The import production coordinator works on establishing the best possible **first cost**, or wholesale price, in the country of origin. The **country of origin** refers to the nation in which the goods were located and purchased.

Box 3.2 Merchandiser (Merchandise Planner)

An international brand and a leader in the design, marketing, and distribution of premium lifestyle products for more than 40 years in four categories: apparel, home, accessories, and fragrances. Seeking a merchandise planner at corporate headquarters.

Purpose and Scope:

The merchandise planner is responsible for partnering with the merchandising team to create annual and seasonal merchandise plans, forecasting the business based on changes in strategy and business climate, and managing inventory to support forecasts for our newest online business. In addition, this individual will have the opportunity to work on special projects to support the strategic and operating initiatives critical to success of the Web site and our continued growth and profitability.

Responsibilities:

- Forecast sales, margin, and inventory turn by month, at a department/class level, and communicate business performance during the monthly forecast

- Partner with merchant team to analyze current sales trends and on order at a brand level and adjust the forecast accordingly

- Create department and category level quarterly hindsight reports to drive strategic assortment decisions for future quarters and in-season management

- Plan and project receipt flow for basic items to support sales forecasts

- Prepare weekly sales recaps to aid in business analysis

- Track current selling to the plan and provide analysis around promotional events, as needed

Job Requirements:

- Expertise in retail math; strong analytical skills

- Ability to make confident and independent recommendations and accountability for managing and achieving business goals

- Decision-making capability clearly driven by conceptualizing future opportunities and developing strategic business initiatives

- Creative, assertive, and solution-oriented approach when faced with difficult business performance and/or challenging directives from senior management

- Ability to influence, present, and defend a business argument both one-on-one and in a group setting

- Superb presentation and communication skills, both spoken and written

- Ability to prioritize and direct multiple activities

- High level of organizational skills and attention to detail

An equal opportunity employer, offering dynamic career opportunities with growth potential and a generous company discount.

The main goal of import production coordinators is to ensure on-time delivery and quality of production. In addition, production coordinators negotiate price and track the supply chain from sample production to bulk delivery. A more detailed listing of the main responsibilities of an import production coordinator is as follows:

- Scheduling sample and line production in collaboration with design team

- Coordinating sample production and communicating any changes to the factory

- Establishing and maintaining strong relationships with offshore suppliers

- Anticipating the length of time it will take goods to be shipped and received from factories abroad

- Knowing import and export laws and how to complete the necessary documents to ship and receive goods and understanding how to work with customs

- Completing final sign-off on samples to begin production

- Managing critical time to ensure on-time deliveries

- Updating in-house computer systems on styling information

- Monitoring the production process and updating management on any changes or needs to create quality products

- Having an eye for detail and quality

- Identifying and resolving issues quickly and with cost efficiency

- Having the accounting knowledge needed to determine **landed costs**, the actual price of goods after taxes, tariffs, handling, and shipping fees are added to the cost of goods

Assistant importers work for the import production coordinator and follow up on orders with overseas suppliers. They also communicate with freight companies and customs agents, process documents, and check pricing agreements. They may also be responsible for arranging payments to overseas suppliers and serving as a liaison with internal customers to ensure goods arrive as expected.

Qualifications
The required qualifications for the import production coordinator are as follows:

- *Education.* A bachelor's degree in fashion design, fashion merchandising, product development, business administration, or a related field is essential.

- *Experience.* To secure this position, a prospective employee will need several years in previous import production experience within the apparel or home furnishings industry.

The position of import production coordinator often requires fluency in a foreign language (e.g., Japanese, Spanish, or Mandarin, to name a few). Intermediate to advanced Microsoft Office skills (e.g., Microsoft Word and Excel) are expected. Work experience may be obtained in the position of intern and/or assistant importer. This position often requires extensive travel. A proven background in importing, shipping, and client relationships is helpful.

- *Personal characteristics.* To be successful, import production coordinators need keen attention to detail, self-motivation, and the ability to work on a team. Excellent written, visual, and oral communication skills are required. They must be highly organized and able to work in a fast-paced environment. This person must have strong analytical skills and materials-planning knowledge to review product forecasts and plan raw materials to manufacture domestically and internationally. Effective negotiating and time-management abilities are key attributes, as problems often need to be resolved quickly and with consensus.

Career Challenges

The sourcing manager, import production coordinator, and assistant importer are faced with the primary challenge of effective communication to ensure on-time deliveries, the best prices, and top-quality products. They are often juggling many balls, working with the numerous vendors, production managers, and designers simultaneously. Although global travel may be an exciting adventure in the beginning of these careers, it can become a burden to pack a suitcase, jump on a plane to put out a production "fire," and return to the office, ready to work the next day. It takes a great deal of flexibility, stamina, and organizational skills to rise above the potential stress of a worldwide business operation.

Sourcing Career Options in the Global Community

The world has become one huge global market. Because many countries no longer produce all of the goods and services that they need and/or want, they have come to rely on one another to obtain what they cannot or choose not to produce. As this movement has evolved, the world's nations have become more economically interdependent. **Globalization**, the process of interlinking nations of the world with one another, is a growing trend in the fashion industry. **Global sourcing** refers to the process of locating, purchasing, and importing or exporting goods and services (Figure 3.4). When a retail buyer for a United States store, for example, buys saris from India and has them shipped to the United States, his or her company imports them. The country that provides and ships out the goods—in this case, India—exports them. Professionals in the sourcing field must understand international trade guidelines for importing and exporting, as well as remain abreast of any updates to those guidelines.

Buyer for a Store-Owned Foreign Buying Office

There are two types of retail organizations that operate **store-owned foreign buying offices**: retailers that are large enough to use and pay for this ancillary operation, and stores with very special images, such as exclusive boutiques and designer emporiums. Buyers who work in store-owned foreign buying offices support and advise other buyers of their respective stores. (In Chapter 10, the career track of the retail buyer is examined.) The buyers for a company- or store-owned buying office survey the market looking for new trends. They recommend

■ **Figure 3.4**
Global sourcing refers to the process of locating, purchasing, and importing or exporting goods and services from around the world. Here, a model showcases designer Anuradhaa Bisani's work during International Fashion Week in Chennai, India.

vendors and styles, develop catalogs and mailing pieces, and follow up on deliveries. Because they are employed by the retail store, they are, in essence, an extension of it. Buyers in many foreign buying offices are authorized to make purchases from vendors for the company, just as the domestic store buyers are when they shop the local markets. In some situations, the store buyers place purchase orders on the lots procured by the buyers of the foreign buying office. In other companies, the buyers of the foreign buying office place the orders. For example, a foreign buying office in Paris may be responsible for placing orders for the Chanel boutique in Amsterdam, as shown in Figure 3.5.

Companies with foreign buying offices generally locate these offices in major fashion capitals, such as Paris, London, Rome, Hong Kong, and Tokyo. Saks Fifth Avenue and Neiman Marcus are two examples of major retail operations that maintain store-owned foreign buying offices. Some large mass-merchandise chains also own foreign buying offices; Walmart and JCPenney are two examples.

Small to midsized stores cannot afford to own and operate their own foreign buying offices. Instead, they may choose to subscribe to the services of independently owned resident buying offices with foreign buying divisions. Independent buying offices do not represent retail store competitors in the same city or local area. They have **market representatives**, or specialized buyers of individual merchandise classifications (for example, junior sportswear, children's wear, or menswear), who work closely with their client stores, keeping them up to date on new product offerings in the marketplace, recommending new vendors, and assisting them in locating new goods. A great amount of the market representative's time is spent following up on the client's purchase orders to make sure they are shipped on time and as ordered. In Chapter 10, the qualifications and career challenges for a buyer are examined.

Licensing and Sourcing

Global sourcing has created a new fashion career path in licensing. Think of European designer names such as Dior, Chanel, Versace, and Gucci; American designers such as Donna Karan, Calvin Klein, and Ralph Lauren; American characters such as Mickey Mouse, Spider-Man, and Barbie; or manufacturers such as Harley-Davidson, Nike, and Hershey's. All of these companies offer product lines that are not central to their primary product lines. For example, in addition to a Fat Boy motorcycle, you can purchase Harley-Davidson belts, apparel, and sunglasses. Another example of international appeal for character product lines can be found at EuroDisney SCA in Paris, which features a range of Disney character products. The Disney boutique on the Champs Elysées is a prime retail location for the French and tourists alike.

Many well-known celebrities, fashion designers, and companies offer alternative product lines by working with manufacturers to produce goods under their names. For example, Fossil Inc. produces a line of watches for Donna Karan International Inc. The timepiece line fits the Donna Karan image, coordinates with her DKNY clothing and accessories, and features her name; however, Donna Karan International Inc. does not own the watch company. Fossil Inc., owner of the line, is the timepiece company that manufactures this product classification for and pays a fee and/or royalties to Donna Karan International Inc. The company also licenses its name to the likes of Estée Lauder (beauty products), Liz Claiborne (activewear), PVH (men's shirts), Oxford Industries (children's clothes), and Luxottica (eyewear).

This arrangement is referred to as a **license**, an agreement in which a manufacturer, the **licensee**, is given exclusive rights to produce and market goods that carry the registered name and brandmark of a designer (e.g., Ralph Lauren), celebrity (e.g., Jessica Simpson), character (e.g., Lego), or product line (e.g., Porsche). The owner of the name or brandmark is called the **licensor**. The licensor receives a percentage of wholesale sales or some other compensation for the arrangement.

Figure 3.6 provides an example of footwear licensed under the Jessica Simpson Collection. Camuto Group, Inc., based in Greenwich, Connecticut, coordinates the design, development, and distribution of women's fashion footwear as women's lifestyle brands on a global scale. The company is the master licensee for the Jessica Simpson Collection. Camuto Group, Inc. also develops and manages several exclusive brands for Tory Burch, BCBGeneration, BCBG Max Azria, Lucky Brand, and Sanctuary.

Today, many companies combine sourcing merchandise from overseas with importing and licensing. Additionally, many of these firms have finished products delivered from overseas manufacturers to retail operations abroad rather than solely importing the merchandise to the United States. It is truly a global market for many licensed products, one that can establish

and strengthen brand identity. As international distribution continues to develop, particularly in Asia, manufacturers in the United States need specialists with knowledge of sourcing, importing, exporting, and licensing regulations. These specialists are referred to as licensing directors.

Licensing Director

Licensing directors are responsible for overseeing the look, quality, labeling, delivery, and distribution of their companies' product lines. Sourcing is an integral part of this job. They work with the foreign and domestic manufacturers of various product lines, the licensees, to make certain that the products are branded correctly. The style, placement, size, and color of the brandmark and labels must be consistent across all product lines. Additionally, licensing directors make sure product lines meet quality expectations and fit within the design concepts of their company's primary line, whether it be Donna Karan Collection dresses or Kate Spade handbags. For example, in Jessica Simpson's lines, the apparel, handbag, and footwear will coordinate with similar colors and patterns, as illustrated in Figures 3.7a and b. The results that the manufacturers and designer desire are multiple sales to the consumers and a greater visual presence on retail floors.

Qualifications

The job requirements for licensing directors are as follows.

- *Education*. A bachelor's degree in fashion design or merchandising, business administration, marketing, international marketing, business law, or a similar field is a minimum requirement.

- *Experience.* Many licensing directors begin on the showroom floor of a manufacturer or as account representatives. Prior to this, retail sales experience during college provides a solid foundation in working with various product lines and customers. The position of licensing director is one that a candidate is promoted into after showing knowledge and skills in the business.

- *Personal characteristics.* The licensing director must manage many tasks at one time. The abilities to manage time, stay calm under pressure, and prioritize tasks are significant. Strong negotiation skills are a plus. Comprehension of product construction, quality, and design is a necessity. An understanding of import and export laws, branding regulations, and different cultures is critical to this career path.

Career Challenges

One of the greatest challenges in a licensing career is the need to clearly understand and stay up to date in a wide range of areas. The licensing professional must have a thorough knowledge of design and product development, branding specifications, import and export legislation and regulations, and manufacturing processes—all for a variety of products, such as sunglasses, gloves, sportswear, and footwear. If a product of poor quality that does not reflect the licensor's vision slips out from under the licensing director's radar, then the image and sales of the licensor can be negatively affected. Therefore, coordinating the work of many manufacturers located around the world that produce a range of product types is a tremendous task and responsibility.

■ **Figure 3.7a**
Licensing directors are responsible for making sure that product lines meet quality expectations and fit within the design concepts of their company's primary line, as with Jessica Simpson's apparel and accessories license.

■ **Figure 3.7b**
In 2005, Camuto acquired the master licensing rights for Jessica Simpson. It is one of the most successful celebrity-licensed lifestyle brands in the world, generating more than $1 billion in retail sales annually.

Summary

From locating vendors to collaborating with manufacturers, sourcing is the process of taking a product from its conception stage to the sales floor. In some companies, designers and their assistants locate the places from which to purchase piece goods. Larger companies may employ buyers to source fabrics and related products for the items in the designer's line. The career options that focus on sourcing fabrics and findings necessary for producing collections include fashion production planner, or raw goods buyer, and piece goods buyer. Production managers, who act as contacts between buyers and vendors, advise on the delivery status of purchase orders. Sourcing managers work with overseas or domestic producers to figure out product specifications and negotiate contracts. An import production coordinator is involved in all aspects of the production process and is often the link between the overseas factories and the design and buying teams.

Today's global market has inspired many companies to combine sourcing merchandise from overseas with importing and licensing. As international distribution continues to develop, manufacturers employ sourcing, importing, exporting, and licensing directors—all who understand licensing regulations, as illustrated in Box 3.3.

Although education and field experience are important qualifications for a career path in sourcing, the qualifications that are key to success are flexibility, organization, and communication. Knowledge of import and export laws, branding regulations, foreign languages, and different cultures is important to those working within all aspects of the global industry. If you are interested in sourcing as a future career, you must have the ability to work effectively when under pressure and possess excellent negotiation skills. Sourcing is an ideal profession for the curious, creative, and detail-oriented person. It is an exciting and satisfying journey to take a design from dream to reality.

THE JOB SEARCH

Box 3.3 Licensing Manager

Description:

Support Vice President of Licensing and Business Development in the management and growth of this high-end special occasion misses' garments licensing division to achieve company's brand expansion goals.

Responsibilities:

- Manage licensees in the development of the company's branded product extensions.

- Drive product development process across multiple licensees, with emphasis on maintaining and enforcing calendars and critical deadlines.

Box 3.3 *(continued)*

- Serve as brand ambassador to licensees; responsible for communicating and enforcing brand guidelines to ensure alignment across all licensed product categories.

- Hold regular meetings with licensed partners to review status of business, including reporting, product development, promotional initiatives, and opportunities for growth.

- Schedule, coordinate, and recap recurring business and product development discussions with licensees.

- Responsible for analyzing financial reports from licensees, including sales information, projections, quarterly and annual forecasting.

- Ensure compliance and maintain information as it relates to contractual requirements.

- Conduct in-depth market research and provide industry analysis to identify new licensing opportunities and potential partners.

- Partner with licensee and marketing team to create materials for trade shows, market presentations, and PR events.

- Support head of department with special projects and new business development.

Desired Skills and Experience:

- 5 years' experience in licensing, marketing, and/or brand management in fashion-related field

- Outstanding communication, presentation, strategic thinking, and analytical skills

- Ability to interact and report on business with cross-functional teams and across all levels of management and proven ability to manage others

- Self-starter with positive, can-do attitude, and ability to think creatively

- Strong leadership and problem-solving skills, adaptability/flexibility, and initiative

- Ability to prioritize and manage multiple tasks in a dynamic, fast-paced environment

- Proficient in Word, Outlook, Excel, and PowerPoint

- BA or BS degree required

- Salary commensurate with experience

Key Terms

assistant importer

assistant piece goods buyer

chargebacks

collection

contractor

country of origin

exports

fashion production planner

findings

findings buyer

first cost

globalization

global sourcing

import production coordinator

imports

landed costs

letter of credit

license

licensee

licensing director

licensor

market representative

merchandiser

piece goods buyer

purchase order (PO)

sourcing

sourcing manager

stock-keeping unit (SKU)

store-owned foreign buying office

trimmings

trimmings buyer

vendor

volume driver

yardage

Online Resources

www.forbes.com/sites/walterloeb/2014/04/25/j-c-penney-must-fix-its-sourcing-to-fix-its-business/

www.kurtsalmon.com/en-us/Retail/vertical-insight/976/Reshuffling-the-Global-Apparel-Sourcing-Deck#.VCScSf5OXd0

www.pinterest.com/internationalap/

online.wsj.com/articles/apparel-retailer-gap-forges-ahead-in-myanmar-1402091240

theapparelagency.com/paris-sourcing-recap-0214/

www.magiconline.com/sourcing-at-magic

www.sourcingjournalonline.com/sourcing-trends-2103-year-review/

Discussion Questions

1. How many different components, or parts, make up the clothes and accessories you are wearing today? Determine the fabrics, trimmings, and findings that were sourced to assemble each garment. How likely is it that all of these parts have come from the same producer or even the same country?

2. Research to discover how many licensing agreements your favorite designer shares with manufacturers. Generate a list of three key designers and the licensing arrangements they have by product and manufacturer. Do the manufacturers produce similar lines for other fashion companies?

3. Why do piece goods buyers rarely source fabrics and findings from the United States? Construct a list of six reasons for the movement in outsourcing.
4. Which countries host the largest or greatest number of manufacturing companies for fashion products? In what specific merchandise classifications, fabrics, or production processes does each country specialize? What are some reasons for specialization? Develop a spreadsheet to answer these queries.

Profile: Sourcing Expert Vince Camuto

Vince Camuto has built a fashion empire through his creative inspiration, love of people, and focus on licensing. With the Camuto Group's track record of success internationally and new growth initiatives in place, fashion icon Vince Camuto shows no signs of scaling back on what has been an illustrious career filled with many accolades and accomplishments. As founder and chief executive officer of Camuto Group, this fashion legend continues to lead his Greenwich, Connecticut–based company with style, hands-on involvement, and an entrepreneurial spirit that has defined his career and illustrates his persona.

From a retail perspective, Camuto's style and philosophy is reminiscent of the legendary Sam Walton, the people-friendly merchant who founded Walmart. Like Walton, Camuto believes in hiring the best people, maintaining the highest level of integrity, and talking to customers in his stores. And they both share the commitment to deliver value to their customers.

"There are three things that are very important in our business: integrity, integrity, and integrity," says Camuto. "Then you need the visual design and sourcing capability to be successful." Another key aspect of Camuto's leadership style is his commitment to people and supporting a collaborative spirit across each of the different divisions and departments. "We are very schooled at picking the right people and putting the right teams together," emphasizes Camuto. The company mantra states:

The Camuto Group is founded on the principles of integrity and quality, and the people are the company's core asset. Talent is nurtured and developed and passion is paramount to the company's success. Empowering the team has enabled Camuto Group to make bold strides in the marketplace while never compromising on principles or quality.

Certainly, the Camuto Group's employees, and visitors as well, are regularly reminded about the company's mantra, with the following etched into the glass of its conference rooms: "There's no limit to what we can accomplish if we don't care who gets the credit." It's followed by the words "Determination. Passion. Loyalty. Integrity. Love. Pride. Creativity. Perseverance. Inspiration. Honesty."

"Vince is very involved from the top-level oversight and retail," says Leah Robert, executive vice president, licensing and marketing, Camuto Group. "He brings everyone together on every project. This business is such a passion for him, and it translates throughout the organization." Robert adds: "Vince has an uncanny ability to know what colors are going to be big next season or what silhouettes are important, and that translates across all classifications and lifestyle categories with a clear idea of what brands stand for."

Robert says that Camuto is always talking to customers and getting feedback. "He walks into a store and immediately starts talking to the floor

(continued on next page)

(continued)

manager," she says. Since it was officially founded in late 2001, the privately held Camuto Group has grown from a shoe line at Dillard's into a global fashion apparel trendsetter with its own retail stores, a robust licensing business, and state-of-the-art sourcing and distribution capabilities. Camuto Group, which serves as a licensor, licensee, and retail supplier, is much more diverse than what industry perceptions might suggest. It also has more growth potential than might otherwise be common knowledge. But none of that seems to concern Camuto, who is still the ultimate merchant and fashion expert, driven by the desire to design the next popular style his customers have come to expect season after season.

In fact, that's how Camuto started his new company after selling Nine West in 1999 and taking some personal time to travel and spend time with his family. "I was contacted by a friend and partner, Alex Dillard, who thought that something was missing in his former brand's quality and look that we had achieved prior to when the company was sold," recalls Camuto, explaining that after Nine West was sold, a lot of the sourcing was shifted from Brazil to China. "I had no preconceived idea about how to get back in the business," admits Camuto. "But we went back to Brazil to source and spearheaded several brands under private labels such as Antonio Melani, Gianni Bini, and four or five others." Camuto says he and his wife Louise started slowly building the brands for Dillard's, and he quickly found himself back in the business in a big way with additional partners and opportunities.

Today, Camuto Group has evolved to be much more than just stylish women's shoes, although Camuto will always have a special fondness for the business that launched his career more than 50 years ago. Camuto Group's portfolio consists of almost 20 brand names across various retail tiers and multiple categories highlighted more recently by men's apparel, as well as fragrances, home fashions, and infant products. The portfolio includes Vince Camuto, VC Signature, Louise et Cie, Two by Vince Camuto, Jessica Simpson, Tory Burch, BCBG

Maxazria, BCBGeneration, Lucky Brand, Sanctuary, Arturo Chiang, Gianni Bini, and Antonio Melani.

Perhaps one of the biggest opportunities of his career came in 2005, when Camuto acquired the master licensing rights for singer/actress Jessica Simpson. Since then, Camuto has built the property into one of the most successful celebrity-licensed lifestyle brands in the world, which now generates more than $1 billion in retail sales annually. "We thought Simpson was wholesome, very American, and like America's next-door neighbor," recalls Camuto, who credits Simpson as being a very hard worker who is immersed in the entire development process. The Jessica Simpson brand now includes more than 30 categories and counting, with several new collections including baby apparel, lifestyle products, and homewares set to launch this year, according to Robert.

A bridal collection is also being explored, she says. "Our strategy is to keep it all authentic to Jessica Simpson," explains Robert. "A family focus is where she is right now, and her customer is maturing, which is allowing her to go beyond the previous categories." Camuto has explored the possibility of other celebrity licensing initiatives, but remains uncommitted. "Many celebrities—including eight in last six months—have come to visit us and they all want to be another Jessica," says Camuto. "But if you do one thing once, you don't necessarily have to do it again. It would be very difficult to duplicate, and we would have to go upper end and look at what happened to all the other people who tried to do that."

Other key objectives for Camuto Group in 2014 and beyond are to expand the Vince Camuto brand, Louise et Cie and Two by Vince Camuto; add to its retail stores; and strengthen its multichannel initiatives. "An affordable designer brand is very important to consumers," believes Camuto, which is why the company will be focused on building such brands, particularly the Vince Camuto brand. One recent example of expanding the brand into new categories was the launch of Femme, a

(continued)

woman's fragrance, in November 2013, which is sold in Macy's.

Camuto Group product is currently in more than 60 countries, with plans to expand in South Africa for brands such as Vince Camuto and Jessica Simpson, and to add Lucky brand shops-in-shops within Edgars department stores. It will also extend to China through a joint venture with China Ting Group Holdings. In addition, Camuto Group is aggressively expanding its own retail stores, according to Robert. "We currently have 50 stores globally and will double that by year-end," she says. Last May, Camuto Group entered the United Kingdom with a store on Kensington High Street, and Camuto believes there are strong growth opportunities for the Vince Camuto brand there. "When we go to London, we see the same stores that were there 20 years ago, which is fine, but it's the same old, same old. I think the young

consumer is looking for what's next," says Camuto. "The retail stores really tell the story and drive the awareness level by putting the brand, such as the world of Jessica Simpson, together," says Robert. Camuto says the primary goal for the future is "to put our efforts into growing the company; to focus on what we have and continue to build the Vince Camuto brand and bring it to where it should be. "We don't have to be a big company," he adds. "We are a private company, and we will stay private. We have great people, and we want to enhance the quality and look of our brands." With Camuto's distinguished career and many accomplishments, it's easy to believe in the future of this fashion icon and his company.

Vince Camuto: Fashion Icon by Tony Lisanti, www.licensemag.com/license-global/vince-camuto-fashion-icon

chapter 4

Production

Some prospective employees find the construction and manu-
facture of fashion products to be the most interesting part of the industry. Others are drawn
to the more quantitative tasks, such as buying, costing, and production planning. Many are
fascinated with the technical and computer-oriented aspects of the fashion business. Still
others enjoy the creative and artistic parts of the fashion industry. Whether construction,
manufacturing, numbers, computers, or creativity appeals to you, there is a career path in
production that relates directly to each area.

The basic stages of the production process can be mapped as follows:

- Sourcing parts and producers for the product

- Securing bids for piece goods, findings, and trimmings

- Costing out the product

- Ordering product components

- Scheduling production

- Creating the production pattern

- Grading

- Marker making

- Spreading and cutting

- Assembling/constructing the product

- Controlling the quality of the product

- Packing and shipping

- Producing and shipping reorders

Production, or manufacturing, of **end products**, the products that will actually be purchased by the customer, is an area that offers diverse career opportunities. Many technological and management concepts relative to the fashion industry have created or affected career tracks in this area. These include computer-integrated manufacturing, electronic data interchange, mass customization, supply-chain management, and radio-frequency identification technology. These manufacturing trends are examined later in this chapter. First, an exploration of career options relating to these concepts, in both domestic and overseas production, includes employment opportunities in the following positions: product manager, production planner, production manager, traffic manager, production efficiency manager, quality control manager, pattern production (pattern grader and marker maker), and spreader and cutter.

Product Manager

Depending on the size of the company, a **product manager**, or *product design manager*, may be responsible for all of the products within a company's product line in a small firm, or for a specific product category in a line for a large company. Product managers often work with one foot in the creative part of the business and the other foot in the production part of the business. On the creative, design-focused side, product managers monitor market and fashion trends related to their assigned product lines. If a team of product managers is responsible for a variety of the company's product categories, it works to integrate the products for a consistent and cohesive fashion look. Product managers are also responsible for comparison shopping the lines of competitors. They compare assortment, quality, price, and trend representation. They will also shop merchandise lines outside of their product categories, making certain that their product lines will blend in terms of the color, style, and fabric trends being shown for the season in all departments.

For example, the product manager of the handbag division of Kate Spade & Co. may review the new line for trend representation, fabric selections, and key colors for the season. She may then meet with the product managers of Kate Spade's jewelry, scarf, glove, knitwear, footwear, apparel, and home goods categories to ascertain that all categories have color, pattern, fabric, and fashion trends in common. The goal is to create a clear and forward fashion image for the company as a whole, as illustrated in Figures 4.1a–d. The product manager will also examine the product lines of other manufacturers that appeal to Kate Spade's target market, such as handbag, footwear, accessories, and apparel lines that compete for Spade's target customers. The product manager reviews competitive lines by looking at product line similarities and differences, pricing, and product voids. **Product voids** refer to merchandise categories in which there are few, if any, items to fill consumer needs and desires. The product manager's objective is to guide the product line to higher sales by creating a timely fashion presence that fits with trends, meshes with the company's total image, and fills product voids.

■ **Figure 4.1a**
What began 20 years ago as a line of simple, boxy nylon bags has transformed into an iconic New York City lifestyle brand.

■ **Figure 4.1b**
Looking to quadruple retail sales to $4 billion, Kate Spade & Co. is modeling itself on Ralph Lauren's empire: a global lifestyle brand selling everything from apparel to home goods.

■ **Figure 4.1c**
The company is offering a range of price points to attract millennials on one end and luxury shoppers at the other.

■ **Figure 4.1d**
Kate Spade & Co. is licensed for luggage, shoes, sunglasses, fragrance, jewelry, watches, legwear, electronics cases, bedding, and stationery, with more product categories likely to come.

On the production side, the product manager works with sourcing personnel, production managers, and quality control directors, among other departments involved with the manufacturing of the product lines for which they are responsible. The product manager monitors the manufacturing of his or her product line(s) from start to finish by checking deliveries of product components, overseeing timelines as the products move through the manufacturing process, assessing quality, and assuring on-time delivery to the retailers. The effective product manager has a dual perspective on the product line—the creative viewpoint of fashion trends and a cohesive fashion image, and the business viewpoint of quality and timely production—both combining to place the right products in the consumers' hands at the right time.

Qualifications

The qualifications for this career are as follows:

- *Education.* A bachelor's degree in fashion merchandising, fashion design, product development, production, apparel manufacturing, or a related field is commonly a requirement.

- *Experience.* A sales representative for a manufacturing company may climb the career ladder into the position of product manager. An assistant in a trend forecasting firm may leave that sector of the industry to move up to a product manager position. Large firms have assistant product manager positions, for which product manager positions are the next step up the career ladder.

- *Personal characteristics.* Successful product managers have the ability to analyze their firm's market for opportunities and threats. Assessing competition, communicating fashion trends, and investigating retail trends require the personal attributes of curiosity, observation, and creativity, as well as strong skills in communication, organization, and presentation. They also have an in-depth knowledge of the manufacturing processes for their particular product categories.

Career Challenges

Many small companies do not employ product managers; instead, designers are responsible for evaluating competitors and determining fashion trends for the line. As a result, the number of positions in this area is limited to mid- and large-sized firms. Product managers are "under the gun" when it comes to being correct on the fashion colors, styling, and themes that will be featured in product lines. If, for example, rhinestones are the key fashion trend the product design manager chooses for the season, and it turns out to be trend a company's target market does not buy, then the product manager may be job hunting. Additionally, product managers face great challenges with manufacturing products abroad in terms of quality, fit, and deadlines. Because there is much at stake when a company produces the wrong product or ships the right product too late, product managers must conduct detailed research to make accurate decisions, which makes this position exciting and never dull.

Production Planner

The majority of large manufacturing firms have production planners on staff. **Production planners** estimate the amounts and types of products a company will manufacture, based either on previous seasonal sales or on orders received by sales representatives on the road and in the showroom. There are two primary methods of production planning: cut-to-order and cut-to-stock. **Cut-to-order** is considered the safest method of projecting manufacturing needs. It entails waiting until orders are received from buyers and then working within tight timelines to purchase product parts, construct product lines as ordered, and ship them to the retail accounts on time. Which types of fashion companies prefer the cut-to-order option? This technique is most often used by designer firms that feature higher-priced, high-fashion merchandise. For these companies, forecasting the sales of products that reflect new fashion trends is more difficult. Also, the costs of being wrong may be much higher than for less expensive, less fashion-forward merchandise because of the more expensive fabrics and, often, more detailed workmanship these high-fashion companies include in their products.

Cut-to-stock involves purchasing fabrics and other product components before orders are acquired. Production planners using the cut-to-stock method examine several variables before projecting manufacturing needs. They look at the economy and how, when, and on what consumers are spending their money. They investigate what the competition is doing, including new companies entering the market and targeting their customers. They study sales histories of products in the line, focusing on sales by style, color, size, and price for each season. They analyze the strength of new lines by discussing sales potential with the design staff and sales representatives.

What are the advantages of the cut-to-stock option? It enables production to be spread out over a longer period. This permits the manufacturer to keep factories in production mode throughout the year (Figure 4.2), rather than working around "peaks and valleys." Cut-to-stock also allows for a longer **lead time**, the amount of time needed between placing a

■ **Figure 4.2**
Garment workers sew at the American Apparel factory in downtown Los Angeles.

Production planning and control (PPC) is one of the most important departments in the garment manufacturing process. Production planning refers to the prearranged process of turning raw materials into finished goods, while control refers to the procedures put in place to assure timely results, quality products, and anticipated costs. There are six primary functions of PPC:

- Scheduling jobs or tasks for the line styles

- Planning material needs (e.g., fabric thread, zipper)

- Determining which styles and quantities will be loaded into production and when

- Selecting facilities and planning manufacturing processes

- Estimating costs of production

- Delivering goods, following up, and executing improvements to the process

Precision in PPC results in on-time shipments and the most economical use of resources, often because labor and appropriate supplies and equipment are available for each order. Garment manufacturers cannot afford to lose time or materials in the production process.

Late fees or product returns can result when products are not delivered as promised. In the highly competitive apparel industry, that's too risky. Buyers will quickly find other companies to replace manufacturers who cannot deliver, or who do not deliver on time. In addition, raw material prices rise consistently, and poor planning can lead to missed opportunities and higher costs. Approximately 60 to 70 percent of the cost of a garment is in the fabric,

according to smallbusiness.chron.com. Styles are changing rapidly as customers want new looks regularly, not just at the start of each season. To keep up with changing trends, buyers are making smaller orders more frequently with shorter lead times between ordering and delivery. Manufacturers who purchase materials at the right price and the right time and can meet short lead times have a distinct competitive advantage. As a result, the planning phase of each production piece must be as accurate as possible.

What types of problems does effective PPC avoid? If the cutting room falls behind in its production schedule, for example, the sewing and finishing lines must wait. This can lead to backlogs on the production line and, as a result, missed deadlines for shipment. To avoid lost time in the production process, the production planner must oversee each step of the production process daily. Anticipating problems and keeping the entire production line updated on any delays allows time for plans to be made and implemented to pick up any slack. In addition, PPC adds to the bottom lines of the manufacturer and the retailer in that the necessary materials are purchased in the right amount at the best possible prices. PPC—profitable, prompt, and consumer-driven—brings the manufacturer and buyer together and remains one of the most important departments in the garment manufacturing process.

Sources:

smallbusiness.chron.com/production-planning-garment-manufacturing-80975.html

www.onlineclothingstudy.com/2011/12/functions-of-production-planning-and.html

https://www.youtube.com/watch?v=Lnpm2T9OcKQ

production order and receiving a shipment of the products. With international production gaining importance, lead times have become longer for manufacturers using overseas factories. Which types of firms find the cut-to-stock alternative to be most efficient and cost effective? A manufacturing company that produces a significant number of basic products, such as a T-shirt company, has the ability to project sales more closely than does the producer of more expensive, fashion-sensitive goods (refer to Box 4.1).

Qualifications

Whether the production planner uses the cut-to-order or cut-to-stock option, the education, work experience, and personal characteristics needed for successful employment in this career track are similar, including the following:

- *Education.* A bachelor's degree in fashion merchandising, fashion design, product development, apparel manufacturing, or a related field is commonly required.

- *Experience.* Work experience with a manufacturer is needed, possibly beginning in the showroom and later moving into product development or purchasing. An understanding of how products are constructed, the materials they are made from, and the manufacturing processes required to bring them to fruition is critical.

- *Personal characteristics.* The successful product planner has strong quantitative abilities, effective communication skills, excellent time management, and top organizational skills.

Production Manager

Production managers, also referred to as *plant managers*, are responsible for all of the operations at production facilities, whether domestic or overseas locations, contracted or company owned. The job responsibilities of production managers include:

- Supervising or completing the estimation of production and employee costs scheduling work flow in factories

- Ensuring product quality control

- Hiring, training, and motivating production employees

Think about the number of employees, tasks, and potential problems associated with cutting, constructing, pressing, and shipping a product line. This is a challenging career track, but one that pays well and is critical to the success of a company. Box 4.2 is an example of a classified ad for a plant manager position.

Production assistants often support production managers with detail work, scheduling, and record keeping. Assistants may track fabric, trim, and findings deliveries; help with developing production schedules; and communicate the workflow of the factory to production managers. They also follow up on outgoing shipments, often keeping customers informed on the progress of their orders and expediting deliveries when needed. Additionally, production managers may have the assistance of traffic managers. **Traffic managers** supervise workflow on factory floors, monitoring products from start to finish. They anticipate problems that may stall production, whether in materials, personnel, or equipment. The goal of the traffic manager is to make certain that the factory employees have all they need to manufacture products with efficiency and in good quality.

Qualifications

The qualifications for a production manager, production assistant, and traffic manager are similar. The production assistant and traffic manager positions usually precede that of production manager.

Box 4.2 Plant Manager

Plant Manager—Textile Manufacturing and Production Company

Location: Dallas, Texas

Base Pay: $50,000–$80,000 annually

Industry: Fashion, Apparel, Textile, Manufacturing, Industrial

Required Education: Two-year degree

Required Experience: More than five years

Relocation Covered: Yes

Job Responsibilities

- Manage production facility of approximately 15 employees, consisting of supervisors, drivers, and production crew

- Manage day-to-day operations of the production process, including quality control and productions checks

- Hire, train, review, promote, and discharge employees as required

- Manage service technicians and maintenance crews as necessary

- Meet operational efficiencies by implementing process improvement and monitoring work flow and production

- Create and continuously promote a safe work environment by ensuring that all staff understands and adheres to safety-related policies and procedures

- Maintain appropriate safety and waste disposal records/logs

- Resolve day-to-day issues for production facility

- Monitor and order supplies

- Develop and maintain operational budget

Job Requirements

- Management experience within a production/manufacturing facility environment

- Excellent management skills with the ability to delegate responsibilities and tasks

- Solid understanding of budgeting and plant operations

- Associate's degree or higher

We offer a competitive salary, a comprehensive benefits package, incredible growth potential, and learning opportunities. If you have more than five years of management experience within a production/manufacturing facility environment, please apply for immediate consideration.

- *Education.* A bachelor's degree in fashion merchandising, fashion design, product development, apparel manufacturing, or a related field is commonly required.

- *Experience.* Hands-on experience in the industry, which may include work experience in computer-aided pattern design, grading and marker making, product costing, and quality control, is required for this position. The ability to produce flat sketches and specification drawings using a computer is helpful. A production assistant position is often posted as an entry-level position with the potential of moving into a production manager opening. Larger manufacturers offer assistant traffic manager positions as a starting place.

- *Personal characteristics.* Knowledge of raw materials and manufactured processes, design and product development, and production technology is required. An understanding of textiles, product construction, the capabilities and limitations of production equipment, and the principles of pattern assembly is essential. The ability to work as part of a team, as well as independently with little supervision, is critical to success. Good communication skills, both oral and written, are also required. Because apparel production workers represent many nationalities, the ability to speak Mandarin or Spanish, for example, is an asset. An appreciation of cultural diversity is essential.

Career Challenges

What are the challenges for production managers, assistant production managers, and traffic managers? All of them face the obstacles of tight deadlines, sometimes worsened by external factors that are difficult to foresee or control. Manufacturing equipment breakdowns, delayed textile shipments, defective zippers, or thread in the wrong color are types of problems that can halt the workflow of the manufacturing facility and cause the manufacturer to miss shipping commitments. This can be a high-stress area in which to work. Effective communication and excellent follow-up skills are essential to making it in this career path.

Production Efficiency Manager

Some large manufacturing firms offer the position of production efficiency manager. These companies are usually quite large and conduct global manufacturing activities. **Production efficiency managers** are responsible for monitoring the speed and output of the manufacturing facilities and for managing waste (Figure 4.3). Production efficiency managers often work closely with quality control managers to ensure that products meet quality standards while costs are under control. For example, the production efficiency manager of a handbag company may find an accessory firm to purchase leather scraps left over from the cutting tables to use them for belts.

Quality Control Manager

Quality control managers, or *quality control engineers*, develop specifications for the products that will be manufactured. They are responsible to see that those standards are met during all phases of production, identifying quality problems and working with manufacturing personnel to correct them. The quality control manager works with such issues as fit, fabric performance, construction difficulties, packaging and shipping needs, and production pace.

Production efficiency managers are responsible for monitoring the speed and output of the manufacturing facilities.

In large companies, a manufacturer's factories may be located worldwide. The quality control manager frequently travels to several manufacturing sites, coordinating production and deliveries, while checking to be certain that quality standards are being met at all locations. Because quality problems can run the gamut from the original product specifications to a defective button-holer machine, the quality control manager collaborates with personnel in various company divisions—from the design staff to plant employees.

Qualifications

The qualifications for production efficiency managers and quality control managers are related, with similar requirements in education, work experience, and personal characteristics:

- *Education.* A bachelor's degree in fashion design, fashion merchandising, textiles, production, or a related discipline is needed.

- *Experience.* Knowledge of product construction, textile technology, and manufacturing capabilities is required. Some quality control managers enter the field from design, merchandising, and/or production backgrounds.

- *Personal characteristics.* Personal characteristics that enhance the work of quality control managers include organizational abilities, effective time-management skills, and communication skills. Effective quality control managers are strong problem solvers with good follow-up skills and are detail oriented. This position requires people skills to gain the commitment of factory workers to produce high-quality products.

Career Challenges

Production efficiency managers and quality control managers face the challenge of working with a wide range of constituencies, from designers and pattern makers to plant managers and workers located in the United States and abroad. It is a significant challenge to communicate with so many people on such diverse levels in, possibly, global locations in different time zones. Strong communication skills and superior organizational abilities are keys to being successful in these two career tracks.

Pattern Production

Career paths in the area of pattern production include pattern maker, pattern grader, and marker maker. The career track of pattern maker is explored in Unit 2.

Marker makers and pattern graders share common characteristics: a superior level of accuracy, an understanding of how textiles perform, and an ability to adjust to increasing technological advances in pattern production. Pattern development, fit, and production require sharp focus and strong attention to detail (Figure 4.4). If a single pattern piece is one-quarter of an inch too large, then the apparel or home furnishing product will likely not flow through the production process. If by chance it does, the consumer will likely purchase a product that does not fit correctly or look attractive. If details and accuracy are in your realm of expertise, pattern production offers career options for you.

Pattern Grader

Working from the **master pattern**, the pattern that evolves after adjusting and perfecting the sample pattern, **pattern graders** develop the full pattern range of sizes offered by the manufacturer. For example, the master pattern may be graded in misses' dress sizes 12 to 20 or sizes 6 to 14, depending on the garment style, the company, and its target market. By enlarging or reducing the pattern within a figure-type category, all of the pattern pieces of a particular design are developed for each size. Pattern grading is technical and precise work. It is often work that must be done at a fast pace under the pressure of production deadlines. Although

■ **Figure 4.4**
If a single pattern piece is one-quarter of an inch too large, the garment will not likely flow through the production process. If by chance it does, the consumer will not purchase a product that does not fit correctly or look attractive.

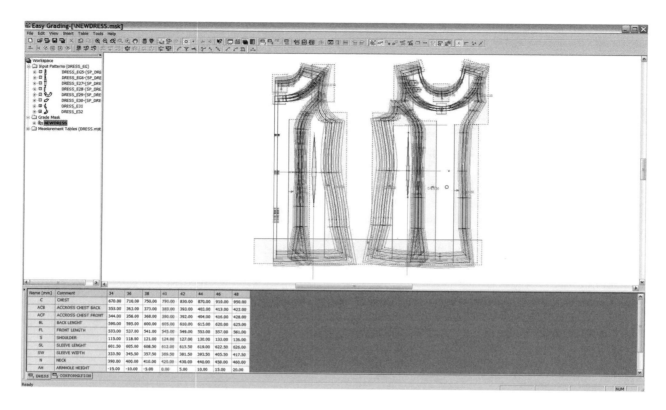

Figure 4.5
A pattern that has been graded into a size range using CAD software.

most large manufacturing companies use computers to do grading work quickly, many smaller companies cannot initially afford this technology and/or prefer the hands-on skills of a grader. Figure 4.5 depicts a pattern that has been graded using CAD software.

Qualifications

Pattern graders should have the following background in terms of education, experience, and personal characteristics:

- *Education.* A bachelor's degree in fashion design, apparel production, or a related field is a minimum requirement.

- *Experience.* Effective skills in pattern making, drafting, and product construction are necessary. Experience in pattern draping is a plus. An understanding of pattern grading technology and related work experience are needed.

- *Personal characteristics.* Strong attention to detail, the ability to work independently and under tight deadlines, and quantitative skills are job requirements for successful pattern graders.

Marker Maker

After the pattern is graded, it is time to develop a marker. A **marker** is the layout of pattern pieces on the fabrication from which the pieces will be cut, as illustrated in Figure 4.6. There are two main purposes of a marker: (1) a good marker minimizes fabric waste; and (2) it generates an accurate end design. Fabric prints and patterns, textures and naps, and sheens and matte finishes must be taken into consideration when creating a marker. Think, for example, about a corduroy jacket. If the fabric in the back of the jacket is cut in a different direction from the front, the front and the back will appear to be two different colors. **Marker makers** manipulate and trace the pattern pieces, by hand or by computer, into the tightest possible layout, while keeping the integrity of the design in mind. In some cases, a marker is generated in hard copy, or print; in other cases, it is computer-generated and stored in the computer.

Qualifications

The qualifications required for a marker maker are as follows:

- *Education*. A bachelor's degree in fashion design, apparel production, or a related field is a minimum requirement.

- *Experience*. Effective skills in pattern making, drafting, and product construction are necessary. Experience with marker making technology is often required.

- *Personal characteristics*. Like pattern graders, marker makers must have strong attention to detail, the ability to work independently and under tight deadlines, and strong quantitative skills. Additionally, marker makers must have the ability to "see" the product in its final form when determining pattern piece layout.

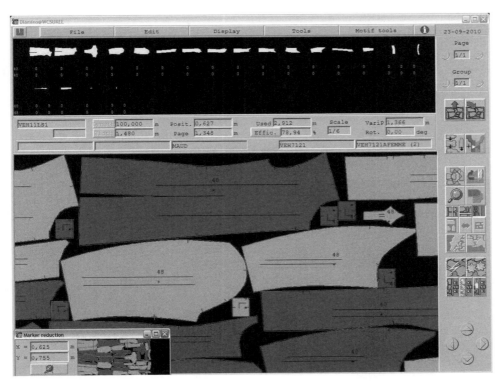

■ **Figure 4.6**
A marker is the layout of pattern pieces on the fabrication from which the pieces will be cut.

Spreader and Cutter

After the marker is developed, it is ready to be placed on the fabric as preparation for cutting the pattern pieces. A **spreader** lays out the selected fabric for cutting. The spreader guides bolts of material on a machine that lays the fabric smooth and straight, layer over layer. In mid- to large-sized companies, a machine (as shown in Figure 4.7) does this function. In smaller companies or computerized factories that require fewer employees, this job may be done by cutters. A **cutter** uses cutting machines to cut precisely around the pattern pieces through layers of fabric, often several inches in thickness, as shown in Figure 4.8. Although firms with advanced technology may use water jets or lasers to cut out garments quickly and accurately, some companies specialize in merchandise classifications that require hand cutting. A firm that produces beaded eveningwear or a couture design house that creates bridal wear may choose to have fabrications manually spread and cut in consideration of the delicate nature and high cost of the fabrics.

For the spreader and the cutter, vocational training or training with the manufacturer are usually considered adequate. In addition to these positions, there are a number of skilled or semiskilled workers on the production assembly line. These employees run the sewing machines, press or steam the final products, and package them for shipping, among other tasks. The production picture is a broad one with a variety of personnel opportunities.

Trends Affecting Careers in Production

At the start of this chapter, five trends in the production of apparel and home soft goods products were mentioned: computer-integrated manufacturing, electronic data interchange, mass customization, supply-chain management, and radio-frequency identification technology. Because these trends will undeniably shape the requirements for production careers in the fashion industry of the future, a brief discussion follows.

As technology develops at a rapid pace globally, the ability to link computers together has introduced amazing advances in production. Computers are being tied together, referred to as **computer-integrated manufacturing (CIM)**, to communicate throughout the entire

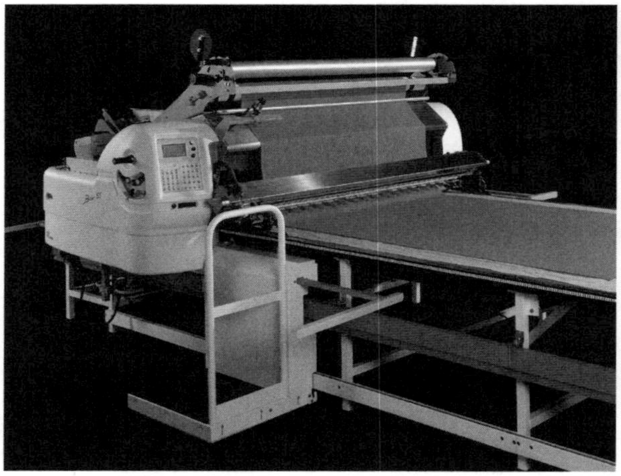

■ **Figure 4.7**
The spreading machine lays the fabric smooth and straight, layer over layer, in anticipation of the next step—cutting.

■ **Figure 4.8**
A cutter uses an electronic cutting machine to cut precisely around pattern pieces through layers of fabric.

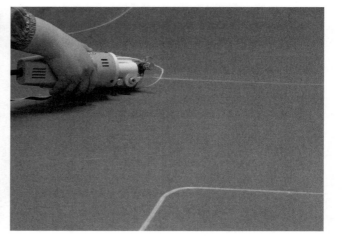

product development and manufacturing processes, from design to distribution. Computer-aided design and computer-aided manufacturing are linked to form a system in which design and product development activities move smoothly into pattern making, grading, marker making, cutting, and product construction activities. Examples of manufacturers and retailers using CIM include Talbots, Zara, and H&M (Figure 4.9). A related trend is **electronic data interchange (EDI)**, which refers to the electronic exchange of computer-generated information between one company's computer system and another's. Through EDI, manufacturers and retailers share data about the styles, colors, sizes, and price points that consumers are buying or those that are not selling and require markdowns.

Yet another strategy to gain market share is **mass customization**, a process that allows manufacturers or retailers to provide individualized products to consumers. Consumers desire products that can be personalized through fit preferences, color selection, fabric choices, or design characteristics. A solution to the fit preference is a scanner that takes a customer's measurements digitally, creating what is referred to as a **digital twin**. **Body-scanning** software defines and captures all of the measurements necessary for actually producing the garment or shoe. This data is forwarded online to the manufacturer, whose production technologies ensure an exact fit. Nike provides a Web site, www.store.nike.com/us/en_us/pw/nikeid/1k9, to give customers the opportunity to design their own shoes. They can select from a variety of athletic shoe styles, choose colors, and add design details from an assortment of options. Figure 4.10 provides an image of the Nike custom shoe process. Figures 4.11a–c depict the body-scanning process utilized by Brooks Brothers.

■ **Figure 4.9**
H&M uses computerized information systems to develop costing reports and specification sheets; later, shipping and sales data are analyzed.

NikeiD gives its
customers the
opportunity to design
their own athletic shoes,
selecting from a variety
of styles, colors, and
design details.

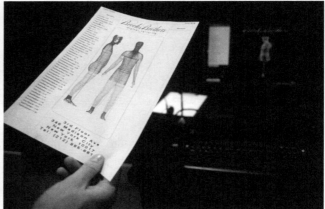

■ **Figures 4.11a–c**
The body-scanning
process utilized by
Brooks Brothers for
digital tailoring.

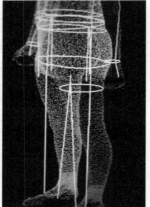

In the fashion industry, manufacturers and retailers continue to work to decrease the amount of time required from design and the purchase of raw materials to production and distribution of the final product into the consumer's hands. This goal requires a partnership among the supplier, manufacturer, and retailer in which open and honest communication is the key to success. Top-selling products can be reordered and received faster. Modifications of these products give the consumer more options through preferred merchandise assortments. This activity of sharing and coordinating information across all segments of the soft goods industry is referred to as **supply-chain management (SCM)**. SCM comprises all of the activities required to coordinate and manage every step needed to bring a product to the consumer, including procuring raw materials, producing goods, transporting and distributing those goods, and managing the selling process. The goals of SCM are to reduce inventory, shorten the time for raw materials to become a finished product in the hands of a consumer, and provide better service to the consumer.

Referred to as Quick Response in the past, "SCM goes beyond Quick Response in that SCM companies share forecasting, point-of-sale data, inventory information, and information about unforeseen changes in supply or demand for materials or products."[1] As SCM strategies

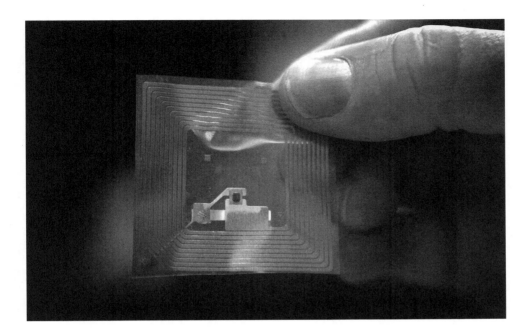

■ **Figure 4.12**
RFID technology refers to tags that are called the next-generation barcode.

grew, new technologies also increased to provide companies with tools for communication and integration. One such tool is radio-frequency identification technology.

Radio-frequency identification technology (RFID) is referred to as the next-generation barcode, because its primary functions are to increase SCM through the tagging of containers, pallets, and individual items so that they can be accurately tracked as they move through the supply chain. "However, unlike barcodes, RFID tags do not rely on line-of-sight readability. In fact, multiple RFID tags can be read simultaneously; they have memory and, therefore, can store and update data, and they provide fully automated data collection."[2] This technology has proven to be so effective that major global retailers, such as Walmart and Target, are requiring all suppliers to apply RFID tags to pallet and case shipments. With these major retailers requiring RFID technologies of their suppliers, RFID equipment, tags, and accessories are becoming more affordable and available to a broader range of companies (Figure 4.12).

Summary

Within fashion firms, large and small, there is a vast range of employment opportunities in the production sector, whether the firms manufacture their lines domestically, overseas, or both. Career tracks exist in production for those interested in fabrics, numbers, or technology. Careers that relate directly to manufacturing include product manager, traffic manager, production planner, production manager, production efficiency manager, and quality control manager. After the designer has created the line, development of the actual product before it goes into production is facilitated by the pattern maker and marker maker. Grading, spreading, and cutting are three phases of production in which computers are quickly impacting job opportunities. Additionally, several technological trends will undeniably impact the requirements for production careers in the fashion industry of the future. These include computer-integrated manufacturing, electronic data interchange, mass customization, supply-chain management, and radio-frequency identification technology.

Endnotes

1. Burns, L.D., and N. O. Bryant, *The Business of Fashion: Designing, Manufacturing, and Marketing*, 4th Edition. New York, Fairchild Books, 2011.
2. Ibid.

Key Terms

body scanning
computer-integrated manufacturing (CIM)
cutter
cut-to-order
cut-to-stock
digital twin
electronic data interchange (EDI)
end product
lead time
marker
marker maker
mass customization
master pattern

pattern grader
product manager
product void
production assistant
production efficiency manager
production manager
production planner
quality control manager
radio-frequency identification technology (RFID)
spreader
supply-chain management (SCM)
traffic manager

Online Resources

www.latimes.com/business/la-fi-american-apparel-made-in-usa-20140810-story.html#page=1

www.interviewmagazine.com/fashion/the-row/

www.apparelnews.net/news/manufacturing/

www.fashionindustrynetwork.com/group/garmentproduction

www.lectra.com

www.wwd.com/markets-news/textiles/the-american-way-7309282?navSection=package&navId=7313534

www.americanapparel.net/aboutus/verticalint/

www.wrapcompliance.org/

www.apparelsourcingshow-us.messefrankfurt.com/newyork/en/for-attendees/welcome.html

www.apparelnews.net/accounts/login/?next=/news/2014/sep/04/more-services-jump-bring-apparel-production-back-l/

Discussion Questions

1. Consider apparel and home soft-goods production a decade from now. What education, experience, and personal qualities will the production manager of a large domestic manufacturer in home furnishings need? Develop a classified advertisement to recruit a qualified candidate for this position.

2. Select three of the following production trends discussed in this chapter: computer-integrated manufacturing, electronic data interchange, mass customization, supply-chain management, and radio-frequency identification technology. Locate and copy articles that provide illustrations of each of these technologies being implemented in fashion companies for discussion in class.

3. Practice "futuring" by researching manufacturing trends and innovations in technology, not presented in this chapter, which will impact apparel manufacturing over the next decade. Construct a chart of the top-five innovations (e.g., software programs or hardware inventions, processes of production, new locations for manufacturing), their creators, and briefly describe the impact these advances will have on soft-goods manufacturing.

Profile: Laser Cutting Shapes

Laser Cutting Shapes is a textile cutting service located in Columbus, Ohio, which provides laser-cutting services for textile and industrial fabrics. Laser Cutting Shapes works with an array of fabrications, to include woven and nonwoven fabrics—organics such as silk, wool, cotton, and leather, and artificial materials such as polyesters, nylons, acrylics, neoprene, rubber, pleather, etc. As a partner of Eurolaser in Germany, Laser Cutting Shapes uses the fastest and most precise CO_2 laser systems to cut the most intricate details for the fashion industry. Two of Laser Cutting Shapes' most unique projects are laser-cut acrylic mannequins and a laser-cut vinyl tent for Design Miami, the paramount international fair for limited-edition design. In addition, Laser Cutting Shapes has laser-cut designs for Zac Posen and Michael Angel.

Why the interest in laser-cut fabrics by designers and manufacturers? The major benefits of laser cutting include the following:

- Creative, unique, and proprietary fabric designs can be developed out of most fabrics.

- Shorter lead times can be accomplished with laser cutting. At Laser Cutting Shapes, the general lead time for the average project is five to ten days.

Profile Figure 4a Zac Posen's laser-cut creation.

Profile Figure 4b Michael Angel's laser-cut neoprene dress.

(continued)

Profile Figure 4c Laser Cut Fabric's tent panels for Design Miami.

Profile Figure 4d Dress by Marchesa; Laser-cut fabric by Laser Cutting Shapes of Columbus, Ohio, USA.

- The laser beam seals the edges while cutting due to the high temperature, which reduces or completely eliminates fraying. For most textiles, serging, or sewing of the edges, is not required with laser cutting.

- Material waste is minimal due to the efficiency of fabric layouts and laser cutting. Laser-cut lines can be extremely close, almost next to each other.

- Software compatibility is easy for designers. Designs are accepted in vector format for laser cutting and bitmap formats for laser engraving. Typical formats are Adobe Illustrator, PDF, AutoCAD files, etc.

- Intricacy, quality, and accuracy of complex designs that cannot be completed with scissors or blades are consistently implemented through laser-cutting technology. Repeatable, precise, and detailed cuts are the cornerstone of laser cutting.

Courtesy of Laser Cutting Shapes, www.lasercuttingshapes.com

chapter 5

Resource Management: Sales, Finance and Accounting, and Human Resources

In the offices behind the fashion line, and behind the scenes, three departments are critical to the success of the fashion company. The people in these departments work in a world of sales reports, financial documents, and personnel files. The company divisions examined in this chapter have a common thread: resource management. These resources are the money upon which the company operates and the employees who run the company; they are represented by three company divisions: (1) sales, (2) finance and accounting, and (3) human resources. To begin, we examine the sales division and the career opportunities within it.

Sales

You likely know people who are natural-born salespersons. You may even be one of these people with the enthusiasm, drive, and persuasive skills to consistently sell products, services, or ideas. These people enjoy the thrill of the chase and the excitement of the closing. The best salespersons are skilled at, almost instantly, building a rapport with customers. Through observation and active listening, sales gurus can determine the customers' needs and desires and then, by emphasizing the benefits of particular products, effectively explain how the products will fit those needs. The finish line is in sight when the customer's concerns are alleviated and the sale is closed. As a grand finale, additional products or services are offered to build the sale. If you have ever purchased an automobile, a cellular phone, a sofa, or a suit from a sales pro, then you know the feeling of a smooth sale. In this section, sales careers in the wholesale sector of the fashion industry are explored. These include employment opportunities in the following positions: manufacturer's representative or company salesperson and merchandise coordinator.

Manufacturer's Representative

A **manufacturer's representative** is also referred to as a *manufacturer's rep*, an *independent rep* or *sales rep*. For the purposes of this chapter, we use the general term of *manufacturer's rep* and, later, discuss the differences between a company salesperson and a manufacturer's rep. No matter what this person is titled, his or her job is to sell a wholesale line(s). If he or she is self-employed, then the manufacturer's rep is, in essence, often a business owner. Manufacturer's reps sell the product line, or lines, of one or several manufacturers to retail store buyers. Reps who choose to sell several lines usually work with noncompetitive product lines and manufacturers. This type of manufacturer's rep is classified as a **multiline rep**, or *multiple-line rep*. For example, the manufacturer's rep may represent a handbag line from one manufacturer, a jewelry line from another vendor, and a glove line from yet another manufacturer. Such a rep can call, for instance, on the accessories buyers of retail stores and offer a selection of products. Occasionally, manufacturer's representatives decide to sell lines that are seasonally opposite, such as swimwear and outerwear. This way, the reps have better opportunities to generate sales income year-round. The manufacturer's rep who prefers to sell solely one manufacturer's line as an independent salesperson rather than as a company employee is a **single-line rep**.

The main task of a manufacturer's representative is to sell the products manufactured by the company to the buyers of retail operations. The manufacturer's rep holds meetings with prospective clients (i.e., retail buyers of brick-and-mortar stores or Web sites) in order to engage the buyers into purchasing the products and to support them in selling the products to the ultimate consumer. Next is a list of the manufacturer's rep's job responsibilities:

- Solicit orders from new and current clients in a specific geographic area

- Provide samples, catalogs, and illustrations of the company's product line

- Handle product inquiries of clients and address product-related issues

- Arrange special events, such as employee training or a trunk show, or product launches for new merchandise

- Collaborate on marketing and advertising strategies to increase sales

- Nurture partnerships and build new key accounts to maintain excellent customer relations and repeat business

- Survey clients, analyze data, and prepare proposals for new and current clients

Typically, employers look for fashion sales representatives who have strong sales and marketing skills. Sales representatives are increasingly using social media to communicate effectively with retail buyers and the ultimate consumer, as examined in Box 5.1.

SOCIAL MEDIA STRIKES

Box 5.1 How Manufacturer's Reps Can Use Social Media to Generate Sales

Social media is the perfect tool for manufacturer's reps of fashion brands to engage their customers online. A recent study[1] found that salespeople using social media on the job outperformed their peers who were not using it by an incredible 73 percent. They also exceeded their quotas 23 percent more often than their counterparts who were not using social media. Both social media and fashion are all about self-expression. Customers recognize that the way they dress reflects their emotions, personality, and how they want to be viewed by others—just like their tweets or Instagram posts. Fashion and social media—it's a perfect fit. Here's a look at social media strategies that can be applied to any fashion rep's business:

- *Super-size your audience.* Connect with your retail buyers *and* their customers, your ultimate end users who buy your line from the retailers' store and wear the fashion items all over town. Be available and credible, because clients-to-be do research before they walk into a showroom or talk to a sales rep. Make initial connections on LinkedIn and create a link to the manufacturer's Web site to give them more content to peruse.

- *Keep the goods coming.* Social media users don't take nights and weekends off. Neither should a media director. Facebook pages that are frequently updated with captivating posts are much more likely to generate likes and attract new fans. To keep fresh content that is needed for regular posts and interactions, think about asking Facebook users to contribute new material with a special theme, such as stories of where they wore—and what they did while wearing—your fashion line. For example, Tiffany & Co.'s Facebook page asks fans to post their love stories with photos of their engagement and/or wedding rings. There's also a place for the story-telling strategy on Twitter.

- *Provide customer service extrordinaire.* Facebook and Twitter give your customers constant accessibility and *personalized service*. Delivering personalized service is nothing new to a seasoned salesperson, but scaling this with social media is key to building sales productivity and effectiveness. Today's customers expect reps to do their homework and to reach out at the right time with the right message. Successful salespeople do not annoy prospects before they are ready to hear from them. There simply are not enough hours in the day to be in touch with everyone all the time, so the smart salesperson strives to provide immediate customer service when its needed. The days of waiting "forever" for a representative to be available to take the buyer's calls are over. A tweet is much simpler and quicker. Do you offer your buyers Twitter or Facebook customer service?

(continued on next page)

- *Instagram and Pinterest are your two new best friends*. Both sites provide a visual experience for your clients. Every user can instantly post photos of his or her looks from your lines; you can post looks from your new line with the speed of light—well, the speed of fashion anyway. Bring your fashions to the masses.

- *Reach out (virtually, that is) to bloggers*. Contact bloggers who relate to your line and suggest a giveaway (that sample line can come in handy here) to boost blog visits and your line's visibility. The resulting positive press can mean a whole new crowd of customers—buyers and wearers.

- *You're too square to be hip*? If you're over 45, you may want to call in reinforcements: the Youth Squad. Check out examples of a youthful approach at OscarPRGirl, a site that uses the persona of a PR girl who reports from inside the Oscar de la Renta fashion house as its moderator. Think about your target market, and find someone who is like them to help you with

your social media. It's a great job for a fashion intern from a nearby college or university.

- *Social media is a way to start a conversation with your buyers and customers and to make new friends*. It is also key to getting ahead of your competition. Post on Facebook, tweet on Twitter, create a board on Pinterest, take an Instagram, and then tally up your sales. It is the power of social media.

Sources:

blogs.hbr.org/2013/04/how-sales-reps-can-succeed-in/

blog.hootsuite.com/social-media-for-sales

www.clickz.com/clickz/column/2155088/salespeople-social-media

www.forbes.com/sites/markfidelman/2013/05/19/study-78-of-salespeople-using-social-media-outsell-their-peers/

www.inc.com/bob-marsh/6-tips-for-using-social-media-to-boost-sales.html

The manufacturer's representative usually works within a given territory, as negotiated with the manufacturer, such as the East Coast, Florida and Georgia, or Canada. In their territories, manufacturer's reps travel to the buying offices of retail companies, the locations of small store operations, and trade marts to sell their lines to retail buyers. **Trade marts**, also called *apparel marts*, house temporary sales booths and permanent showrooms leased by either the sales representatives or the manufacturers. **Market weeks**, also called *trade shows*, are scheduled at apparel and trade marts throughout the year in conjunction with the introduction of the new, seasonal lines presented by manufacturers. Although apparel marts are located across the United States, some of the larger ones are situated in New York City, Dallas, Los Angeles, Chicago, and Atlanta.

In Figure 5.1, manufacturers' product lines are featured on the runway at MAGIC in Las Vegas, one of the premier trade shows. Manufacturer's representatives arrive at the apparel marts a day or two ahead of the market opening to set up booths or showrooms, as in Figures 5.2a and b. When the market opens, it is show time. The manufacturer's reps show the line to buyers with whom prearranged appointments have been set or to buyers who stop by, hoping to find new lines that their customers will purchase. Market weeks are key times for representatives to gain new retail clients, meet with current accounts, and secure a part of the retailers' buying dollars.

Company Salesperson

What is the difference between the general title of manufacturer's representative and the specific title of company salesperson? Many large manufacturing firms hire company salespeople. The **company salesperson** is a sales representative who is employed and paid directly by a particular firm and who carries just one line, that of the employer. Like manufacturers' representatives,

■ **Figure 5.1**
Manufacturers' product lines are featured on the runway at MAGIC in Las Vegas, one of the premier trade shows.

■ **Figures 5.2a and b**
For market week, the sales reps set up booths or showrooms with the new lines and other materials, such as company brochures, USBs containing line sheets, and displays that will help sell the new merchandise.

company salespeople travel to retail buying offices, retail stores, or trade markets to show and sell their company's line. They often receive employee benefits, such as health insurance and vacation pay. Employers of company salespeople may also cover some of the expenses that manufacturers' representatives must incur, such as trade show fees, the cost of sample lines, and retail advertising contributions.

Showroom Salesperson

As depicted in Figure 5.3, which features Desigual, the majority of large manufacturers in the apparel and accessories industry have showrooms in New York City, Dallas, Chicago, Atlanta, Los Angeles, and other major metropolitan areas where large fashion trade markets take place. **Showrooms**, unlike typical apparel and accessories retail stores, rarely sell merchandise from the floor. Items are generally for display only, to allow the buyers to see pieces that would otherwise be visible only in a catalog or online (Figure 5.4).

Showroom salespeople, also called *showroom representatives*, are a type of company salesperson. They work at a manufacturer's or designer's showroom, where they meet with visiting retail buyers, present the latest product line to them, and assist with placing their purchase orders.

Qualifications

The education, work experience, and personal characteristics needed for successful employment as a manufacturer's representative, company salesperson, and showroom salesperson are similar and are listed next:

- *Education.* A bachelor's degree in fashion merchandising, fashion design, product development, business administration, marketing, or a related field is most often a minimum requirement.

■ **Figure 5.3**
Company representatives for firms like Desigual travel to retail buying offices, retail stores, or trade markets to show and sell the company's line.

- *Experience.* Sales, sales, and more sales are the key experiences needed for a career as a manufacturer's representative. Working as an assistant to a manufacturer's representative is an excellent route to understanding the responsibilities of this career and to building a network of industry contacts. Working in a showroom as a receptionist and then moving into sales is yet another option. Working on a retail sales floor or selling advertisements for the campus newspaper provides important knowledge and skills in sales. In essence, all types of sales experience provide a foundation for future employment as a company salesperson. In addition, an understanding of accounting and computers is also necessary, as is a willingness to travel.

- *Personal characteristics.* Self-discipline, self-motivation, good follow-through skills, perseverance, organizational abilities, a contagious enthusiasm, and the ability to handle rejection are key attributes of top manufacturer's reps. Successful reps are highly competitive and believe in the products they sell. They have excellent communication skills, both written and oral. Knowledge of fashion industry trends and manufacturers' competitors is critical. Understanding how products are constructed, the materials from which they are made, and the manufacturing processes helps reps educate their clients—retail buyers, in this case—about the product.

Career Challenges

Many manufacturers' reps are faced with the uncertainty of not knowing how much their next paychecks will be. In this career, income is primarily based on sales performance. Sometimes,

external factors beyond a rep's control may decrease the amount of money the rep receives. Unshipped orders, late deliveries, and incorrect shipments can reduce the remuneration reps expect based on merchandise they sold.

Company salespeople must work under the guidelines of their employers. In some cases, new accounts, trade market participation, and travel plans must be approved by the administration. This position is not as autonomous as that of the manufacturer's representative. When working with a single company, if the product line for a certain season is not strong, the company salesperson does not have another line to rely on for income. If competitive lines become stronger in terms of securing the retail buyers' orders, the company salesperson faces the challenge of staying afloat during a tough sell period or securing a position with a new employer.

Manufacturer's reps can incur some expenses in the process of doing business. Some manufacturer's representatives are required to purchase their sample lines, often at a discounted price, from manufacturers. A **sample line** includes a prototype of every style within the line. Each prototype is tagged with fabric swatches, color options, sizes available, and its wholesale price, also referred to as **cost price**, or *cost*. Depending on the size of the product line, a sample line can cost a manufacturer's representative thousands of dollars. Some manufacturers buy back the sample lines, possibly to sell at factory outlets. In other cases, reps may sell sample lines independently. Additionally, there are costs associated with showing lines during market weeks. There are travel expenses; rental fees for booths, showrooms, and fixtures; as well as trade organization dues. Manufacturer's representatives who have large businesses may employ administrative and sales assistants. As independent contractors, manufacturer's representatives are business owners who share the risk, potential, and challenges associated with being their own bosses.

Merchandise Coordinator

In the early 1990s, the number of specialty stores began declining, and large department stores began increasing in size and number of units. Many of these massive department stores did not offer the customer service that most specialty stores provided. In the department stores, there were fewer sales associates. The few sales staff members in the department stores were often part time, seasonal, or floaters, a term for sales associates who moved from department to department as needed, leaving little time for the retail sales staff to get to know the products and customers in order to provide excellent customer service. As a result, some of the large manufacturers were compelled to find a way to assist the department stores and, ultimately, help their firms to achieve higher sales volume. These manufacturers, among them Liz Claiborne, Ralph Lauren Polo, and Fossil, developed a new career path in the fashion industry, that of merchandise coordinator.

Merchandise coordinators assist with a manufacturer's line in retail stores and are employed by the manufacturer, rather than the retailer. Merchandise coordinators are hired to service the manufacturer's key retail accounts in a specific geographic area (see Figure 5.5). **Key accounts** are the large retailers, in terms of sales volume, carrying the manufacturer's line. Today, specialty stores have made a comeback as customers seek personalized service. Key accounts can include boutiques, specialty stores, Web sites, and large department stores, depending on the amount of inventory of a particular manufacturer's product line they carry. Merchandise coordinators travel to the retail sites to work with the owners, buyers, management personnel, sales staff, and customers. Most of these retail sites can be visited by car, as they are frequently in large metropolitan areas.

In most cases, it is not the merchandise coordinator's primary responsibility to sell the line to the buyer or customer; coordinators may write **reorders**, fill-ins on merchandise that is selling well. Another service that merchandise coordinators may perform is moving merchandise that has been shipped and is waiting in the stockroom to the sales floor. Reorders

■ Figure 5.5
The merchandise coordinator works with management and sales staff members of the key retail accounts in the territory.

and stock placement on the floor are commonly referred to as **inventory replenishment**. **Visual merchandising** is another job responsibility of merchandise coordinators and may include changing displays, straightening racks, and arranging shelved goods to present the best possible visual image to the customer. In essence, merchandise coordinators are somewhat like dedicated store owners, except the "stores" are the manufacturers' departments in the retailers' stores. Some retailers collaborate with merchandise coordinators on promotional events. For example, the merchandise coordinator may be featured in an advertisement as the line's representative, and customers are invited to meet the merchandise coordinator for personal assistance with line purchases.

Career Outlook

The future for merchandise coordinators is bright. This career track has been so successful for manufacturers that many large companies have added merchandise coordinator positions. Ralph Lauren Polo employs merchandise coordinators for children's wear, misses' sportswear, and menswear, among other divisions, in New York City, St. Louis, Chicago, Atlanta, and other large cities. Another example, Jones Apparel Group, Inc., employs about 100 merchandise coordinators who are trained by its apparel designers to make product recommendations to customers. Box 5.2 is a sample classified advertisement for a merchandise coordinator of footwear with a major online retailer.

THE JOB SEARCH

Box 5.2 Web Site Merchandise Coordinator of Shoes

Detailed Description:

Do you love shoes? Have a passion for fashion retail? The Shoes team is looking for a meticulous and tenacious self-starter to coordinate our merchandising process. The Merchandise Coordinator we are looking for is someone who is highly organized and obsessed with providing excellent customer experiences while continually improving existing processes. This position is a great opportunity for someone with talent, energy, and a love for fashion to join a fast-paced, growing e-business.

Responsibilities:

- Drive smooth execution of Shoes merchandising process from beginning to end
- Collaborate with merchandisers, vendor representatives, designers, and photo studio managers
- Streamline current processes and create efficiencies where needed
- Work cross-functionally to ensure accurate, on-time inputs for promotions
- Coordinate photo shoot samples and create shot lists
- Monitor featured items for receiving and stocking
- Assist with creation and accuracy of keywords, trends, and special features, and content and accuracy of features and site flips
- Produce and distribute weekly merchandising update reports
- Prioritize appropriately when process inputs may be at risk
- Provide support for special projects as assigned

Qualifications

Successful merchandise coordinators may meet or exceed the following job criteria:

- *Education.* A bachelor's degree in fashion merchandising, fashion design, product development, business administration, marketing, sales, or a related field is commonly required.

- *Experience.* Hands-on experience in the industry, which may include work experience in retail or wholesale selling, is required for this position. Many companies will hire new college graduates with strong selling skills and an enthusiasm for the manufacturer's line.

- *Personal characteristics.* Knowledge of the product line and marketing is required. An understanding of sales, visual merchandising, textiles, and product construction is helpful. The ability to work independently with little supervision and guidance is critical to success. Strong communication skills, both oral and written, are also required.

Career Challenges

Merchandise coordinators walk a fine line between several parties—the manufacturer, the manufacturer's sales rep, the retail buyer, the retailer's sales staff, and the customers. This career requires strong attention to the goals of all parties. Merchandise coordinators are constantly challenged to find ways to help retailers generate sales, while keeping their focus on their manufacturer's profits. There may be many client stores in a merchandise coordinator's territory, requiring carefully scheduled travel plans and exceptional time management. Additionally, they have to complete many tasks in each retail location. It is a fast-paced job, but it is an excellent position for someone who enjoys sharing the retailers' and manufacturers' worlds.

Once the fashion line is sold, the finance and accounting department begins the detailed process of billing the retailer, posting payments, reconciling accounts, etc.—the functions needed to keep the manufacturer's business afloat. Next, the finance and accounting activities and careers in a fashion business are explored.

Finance and Accounting

You may wonder, "Why would anyone choose a finance and accounting career in the fashion industry, rather than any other career path in the field?" Accounting had an image problem that is now in the past. Although the bean counter stereotype may have been the field's old image, it no longer represents an accurate picture of this career track (see Figure 5.6).

Several career tracks in finance and accounting are at the top of the career ladder in large fashion firms. Accountants are focusing more on analysis, interpretation, and business strategy. Many designers, such as Isaac Mizrahi and Diane Von Furstenberg, have learned through tough times that a focus on the accounting side of the business could save a company.

What are the advantages of a career in accounting? Accounting is a field that provides adaptability to many functions (e.g., purchasing, manufacturing, wholesaling, retailing, marketing, and finance). As the collectors and interpreters of financial information, accountants develop comprehensive knowledge about what is occurring and close relationships with key decision makers, and they are increasingly being called on to offer strategic advice. As a result, career options and promotional opportunities are readily available in the area of accounting. In this section, finance and accounting careers in fashion wholesale businesses are explored. These include employment opportunities in the following positions:

■ **Figure 5.6**
The image of accounting has changed; no longer considered bean counters, good accountants are critical to the success of a fashion business.

- Chief financial officer

- Controller

- Senior, intermediate, and entry-level accountants

- Accounts receivable and payable personnel

Chief Financial Officer

The **chief financial officer (CFO)** directs the overall financial plans and accounting practices of an organization. This executive oversees finances, accounting, budget, and tax and audit activities of the organization and its subsidiaries and is responsible for determining the financial and accounting system controls and standards. This includes ensuring timely financial and statistical reports used by management and the board of trustees. The CFO holds the top finance and accounting position within an organization.

Qualifications

Following are qualifications for a chief financial officer:

- *Education.* A bachelor's degree in accounting, finance, or a related field is a minimum requirement. In some companies, a master's degree in business administration, accounting, or finance is required. Most firms require that the CFO have a certified public accounting (CPA) or equivalent certification.

- *Experience.* A minimum of ten years of administrative experience in finance and accounting is often required.

- *Personal characteristics.* Successful CFOs have strong managerial abilities, effective oral and written communication skills, a quantitative aptitude, and organizational expertise. They have the ability to synthesize and summarize financial data for constituencies of the company, from management to stockholders. They are skilled at making strategic projections for the company based on an in-depth knowledge of the company's financial transactions.

Career Challenges

The CFO commonly works long hours, often more than 50 per week. CFOs are generally required to travel extensively to attend meetings of financial and economic associations and visit subsidiary firms or divisions of the corporation. They work in a leadership position of high visibility, one that requires a broad range of business and people skills (Figure 5.7). Interpersonal skills are important, because this position involves managing people and working as part of a team to solve problems. A broad overview of the business is also essential. Being able to shift from problem solving in financial issues to concerns with personnel in moments takes practice, focus, and skill. Financial operations are increasingly being affected by the global economy, so CFOs must continually update their knowledge of international finance.

■ **Figure 5.7**
Jean-Jacques Guiony, chief financial officer at LVMH Moët Hennessy Louis Vuitton, presents financial reports to the management team.

Controller

A **controller**, also referred to as a *comptroller*, is responsible for a company's financial plans and policies, its accounting practices, its relationships with lending institutions and the financial community, the maintenance of its fiscal records, and the preparation of its financial reports. This position may be the top level in a midsize company or report to the CFO in a very large company. If there is no CFO, the controller is, in essence, the top gun in accounting. Controllers direct the financial affairs of organizations by preparing financial analyses of the companies' operations for management's guidance. In some companies, they have the final responsibility for providing effective financial controls for the organization. In others, the CFO has this responsibility.

Although most people recognize that the controller works with the company's finances, many do not realize that the position requires working effectively with people, too. In large firms, controllers may supervise a staff of accountants in several accounting divisions. They are responsible for evaluating the performance of accounting, determining training requirements, and, in some firms, recommending that personnel be hired, promoted, or removed from the accounting divisions. The essential functions of the controller are as follows:

- Develop, analyze, and interpret statistical and accounting information to evaluate matters that affect the fiscal health and operating effectiveness of the organization

- Maintain the company's system of accounts to include records on all company transactions and assets; consolidate all budgets within the company

- Establish major economic objectives for the company and prepare reports that outline the company's financial position in the areas of income, expenses, and earnings based on past, present, and future operations

- Coordinate and direct development of the budget and financial forecasts, develop policies and procedures for financial planning and control, and analyze ways to achieve company efficiencies

- Oversee tax planning and compliance

- Revise and update internal and external reports

- Evaluate and recommend insurance coverage for protection against property losses and potential liabilities

- Allocate funding to support management decisions on projects with the highest priorities

- Ensure the adequate allocation of funding to the various business departments

In large firms, there is often a position for an assistant controller as well.

Qualifications

The necessary education, experience, and personal characteristics for employment as a controller may include the following:

- *Education.* A bachelor's degree in business administration (e.g., accounting, finance, control, or marketing) or a related field is a minimum requirement. Some firms require a master's degree in one of these disciplines. Major companies often require the controller to complete postgraduate studies in a finance or control area and obtain CPA certification or an equivalent licensure.

- *Experience.* For this executive position, many corporations require a minimum of five to seven years of relevant experience in financial management.

- *Personal characteristics.* The person in this key financial position must have very strong analytical skills, effective computer skills, and excellent communication abilities, both oral and written. In an international company, skills in a foreign language may be required. For example, Adidas requires its controller to have fluent written and spoken English and German language abilities.

Career Challenges

Review the career challenges of the CFO, as they are similar to those of the controller: long hours, the necessity of shifting quickly from one issue to another, and the need for a deep understanding of the financial needs and personnel of the business.

Senior, Intermediate, and Entry-level Accountants

Senior accountants are responsible for establishing, interpreting, and analyzing complex accounting records of financial statements for management, which may include general accounting, costing, or budget data. They also analyze variances in monthly financial reports, forecast finances, and reconcile budgets. Preparation of tax and audit schedules quarterly is often part of the senior accountant's tasks. **Intermediate accountants**, or *midlevel accountants*, prepare and maintain accounting records that may include general accounting, costing, or budget data. An **entry-level accountant** maintains records of routine accounting transactions and assists in the preparation of financial and operating reports. This involves helping with the analysis and interpretation of accounting records for use by management. This position is a great starting place for college graduates.

Qualifications

The following list of qualifications is applicable to most accounting positions:

- *Education*. A bachelor's degree is required, preferably in accounting or finance. Intermediate accountants have completed a bachelor's degree in accounting, finance, or business, followed by two to four years of relevant accounting experience.

- *Experience*. Work experience, such as an internship with an accounting firm or in the accounting department of a company, is a door-opener to the accounting profession. Experience in fashion, whether in retail sales or merchandising, provides an advantage to the accountant interested in employment with a fashion firm. Three to five years of general accounting experience is usually required to obtain a senior accountant position. Proficiency with computer programs, such as Microsoft Excel and Word, is required.

- *Personal characteristics*. Strong communication (both written and oral) and analytical skills are needed. Accountants must be detail oriented, organized, and capable of prioritizing their own workloads, as well as the workloads of other accounting staff, to complete multiple tasks and meet deadlines.

Career Challenges

Most accountants generally work a standard 40-hour week, but many work longer hours, particularly if they work for a large company with many divisions. Tax specialists often work long hours during the tax season. People planning a successful career in accounting must be able to analyze, compare, and interpret facts and figures quickly. Accountants must stay up to date on accounting software. Because financial decisions are made on the basis of their statements and services, accountants should have high standards of integrity, as they carry a legal responsibility for their reports.

Accounts Receivable and Payable Personnel

What do the terms *accounts receivable* and *accounts payable* mean? **Accounts receivable** refers to the amount of money owed to a business that it expects to receive for goods furnished and services rendered, including sales made on credit, reimbursements earned, and refunds due.

Accounts payable is defined as the monies owed to creditors for goods and services; it is often the amount owed by a business to its suppliers or vendors. An **accounts payable manager** arranges and oversees the completion of all accounts payable work by examining records of amounts due and making sure invoices are paid and discounts taken on time. The **accounts receivable manager** does the same for funds owed to the business. Developing written reports and suggesting improvements in processes to increase effectiveness of the accounts payable and receivable units are key responsibilities of both positions.

Qualifications

The qualifications for personnel in the accounts receivable and payable department managers of an accounting division are as follows:

- *Education.* To secure a position as an accounts receivable or payable manager or supervisor, a bachelor's degree in accounting or finance is a minimum requirement. Some firms will hire a candidate with an associate's degree as an accounts receivable or payable clerk, an entry-level position.

- *Experience.* The accounts receivable or payable manager position usually requires four to six years of relevant accounting work experience. Two to four years of relevant work is expected for the position of accounts receivable supervisor. Work experience should be in general accounting procedures and related computer programs; however, those interested in obtaining employment in the accounting division of a fashion firm should gain work experience in retail or merchandising.

- *Personal characteristics.* Strong attention to detail, strong organizational skills, and a high quantitative aptitude are critical to success in this position. Excellent communication abilities are necessary, because these accounting managers work with employees in all facets of the business.

Career Challenges

Accounts receivable and payable personnel deal with a continuing cycle of financial analyses that must be accurate and completed within tight deadlines. There are several times of the year, such as when preparing for a board meeting or preparing tax returns, when the accounts receivable staff works many hours of overtime. To some, the work is never-ending, as it is difficult to see the end of a project when many are ongoing every year.

Human Resources Development

Human resources (HR) refers to the department in charge of an organization's employees, which has responsibilities including finding and hiring employees (Figure 5.8), helping them grow and learn within the organization, and managing the process when employees either leave or are fired (Figure 5.9). **Human resources development (HRD)** refers to the activities of recruiting, training, maintaining, motivating, and managing—in essence, growing—the people who work for a business or organization. Viewed as a group, all of the employees or staff within a company are known as **personnel**.

One of the primary responsibilities of HRD is gauging the staffing needs a company has and will have, then deciding whether to use independent contractors or to hire employees to fill these needs. HRD is also responsible for recruiting and training the best employees,

■ Figure 5.8
A human resources
manager interviews a
prospective employee,
often using a position
description and job
requirement listing
to formulate the right
questions.

supporting them to be high performers, dealing with performance issues, and ensuring that personnel and management practices conform to various regulations. Tasks also include overseeing the management of employee benefits and compensation, as well as employee records and personnel policies. HRD includes employment opportunities in positions such as human resources manager, hiring manager, and others.

Human Resources Manager

Human resources managers, or *human resources directors*, identify human relations issues in the workplace and meet with supervisors and managers to determine effective solutions. They also provide guidance and counsel to managers, supervisors, and employees on a variety of issues, including conflict resolution, interpersonal communications, and effective group interaction. Another responsibility is negotiating contracts with vendors for programs, such as health insurance, and then managing the relationship between the vendor and the company. In addition, HR managers prepare annual operating budgets and monitor costs to ensure compliance with budgetary guidelines.

In small to midsize companies, HR managers recruit, interview, and select employees to fill vacant positions. They may plan employee orientation seminars to help new employees meet company goals. They work with other departments to make certain that policies and procedures are applied consistently and available training and development opportunities are accessible to all. HR managers are ultimately responsible for ensuring a safe and comfortable work environment for all employees. A list of job responsibilities for an HR manager follows:

- Promotes the ongoing role of HR and establishes department goals and action plans

- Monitors and reports on progress in the HR division

- Provides coaching, training, and professional development opportunities for company personnel

- Identifies and proactively raises organizational issues and trends; diagnoses processes, structures, and approaches; recommends alternatives for improved effectiveness

- Clarifies present and future skills and competencies needed by employees

In midsize to large companies, there is often an assistant human resources manager position.

Qualifications

The following is a list of qualifications for human resources managers:

- *Education*. A bachelor's degree in organizational development, human resources, or a related field is a minimum requirement. Some firms specify a master's degree as a preferred qualification.

- *Experience*. Seven to ten years of related experience in HRD is usually required. On-the-job experience in several HRD areas, such as interviewing, hiring, and training employees; planning, assigning, and directing work; appraising performance; rewarding and disciplining employees; and addressing complaints and resolving problems, is required for this supervisory position.

■ **Figure 5.9**
HR managers are responsible for firing employees whose work does not meet company standards.

- *Personal characteristics*. Successful HR managers have the ability to maintain a high level of confidentiality when dealing with highly sensitive issues or information. They must be able to present information effectively and respond to questions from groups of employees, administrators, customers, and the general public. Strong leadership skills, effective interpersonal relationship skills, and conflict resolution abilities are important characteristics. HR managers must also have excellent written and oral communication skills, the ability to manage multiple projects simultaneously, excellent decision-making and analytical skills, and strong coaching and consulting skills.

Career Challenges

The HR manager has the big responsibility of overseeing all of the personnel needs for a company. It is challenging to stay on top of all of the government hiring regulations, the firm's current and future employment requirements, internal company conflicts, employee satisfaction, and personnel budgets. The HR manager is a budget manager, a negotiator, an evaluator, a communicator, and a motivator. It is a huge task to manage and respond to all of the employees in a company; yet, ultimately, this is the HR manager's job.

Hiring Manager

In some companies, the HR manager is responsible for recruiting and hiring employees. In larger firms, there may also be a **hiring manager**, who is responsible for making the decisions on whether a job opening will be filled and who will fill it. A job opening comes about in one of two ways: either someone has left the position or a new position has been created. The hiring manager reviews the job description and the budget for it and then posts the job on internal and external listings, such as a classified advertisement in newspapers and trade publications and on Web sites that feature job listings. The hiring manager is often the first company representative to review the applications of potential candidates. Once applications are reviewed, or screened, the hiring manager schedules interviews with select applicants. The applicants may need to interview with several other people in the organization. It is the hiring manager's job to determine with whom these interviews will be and then to schedule them. It is also the hiring manager's responsibility to know which types of interview questions are appropriate and legal to ask. Once job candidates are located and interviewed, the hiring manager is responsible for recommending the top applicant for the position, offering the position, negotiating its terms to the applicant, and then following up on the hire.

Qualifications

What does a hiring manager need in terms of education, experience, and personal characteristics to succeed in this career track? A list of qualifications follows:

- *Education.* A bachelor's degree in organizational development, business administration, human resources, or a related field is a minimum requirement. Some firms specify a master's degree as a preferred qualification.

- *Experience.* Five to seven years of experience in HR is usually required. On-the-job experience in interviewing and hiring employees is required for this position. Some hiring managers begin as an assistant to the HR manager. If interested in a hiring manager position with a fashion-related firm, then work experience in a fashion company is a bonus. For example, candidates who worked part time during college in fashion retailing are likely to have insight on the skills needed for various positions in this type of company.

- *Personal characteristics.* Successful hiring managers are good at reading people and asking the right questions to discern whether a person is prepared and able to handle a specific job. Strong communication skills, the ability to manage multiple projects simultaneously, and excellent decision-making skills are necessary qualifications to be successful in this position.

Career Challenges

The hiring manager is held accountable for finding the right people for the positions the company needs to fill. If poor job and personnel matches are made and if there is excessive employee turnover, management turns to the hiring manager. It can be difficult to find excellent employees, particularly in certain geographic locations and if the positions require specialized skills or the organization is offering less than competitive salary ranges.

Summary

Fashion manufacturers employ or contract employees whose primary job is to sell the manufacturer's product line: the manufacturer's representative, the company salesperson, the merchandise coordinator. A manufacturer's rep is an independent salesperson who may represent the lines of several manufacturers. A type of manufacturer's rep, the company salesperson is employed directly by a particular firm and carries only the product line of the employer. The merchandise coordinator is employed by the manufacturer and works in the retail stores, servicing key accounts in a specific territory. Sales are critical to a fashion company's success. No matter how exceptional the product line is, there has to be a sales force behind it. With each season, with every trend, and with the ever-changing customer, there is a new opportunity to sell fashion. The sales results generated by the manufacturer's reps are turned over to the finance and accounting division.

Accounting employment opportunities in the wholesale businesses of fashion include the positions of chief financial officer; controller; senior, intermediate, and entry-level accountants; and accounts receivable and payable personnel. The chief financial officer holds the top accounting position in a large company, directing its overall financial plans and accounting practices. In smaller companies, the controller may hold the top position. Senior, intermediate, and entry-level accountants are responsible for many functions, ranging from analyzing and interpreting complex accounting documents to maintaining records of routine transactions. Accounts receivable, the amount of money owed to a business that it expects to receive, and accounts payable, the amount owed to creditors, are accounting departments. Every industry needs strong accounting personnel and practices to succeed, and fashion companies are no exception. Rated as one of the most desirable professions available, the accounting job track offers good compensation, autonomy, and significant employment demand.

Relating to employment demand, human resources development (HRD) focuses on recruiting, hiring, training, maintaining, motivating, and managing personnel, a company's greatest resource. Building and maintaining a strong workforce are critical to the success of every fashion organization. If supporting people to be their best in an optimal environment is your dream job, then HRD offers a range of opportunities.

Endnote

1. "Social Selling: Leveraging the Power of User-Generated Content to Optimize Sales Results," Aberdeen Group Report, February 2013. Accessed at http://www.slideshare.net/linkedin-sales-solutions/social-selling-impact-aberdeen-report-2013.

Key Terms

accounts payable

accounts payable manager

accounts receivable

accounts receivable manager

chief financial officer (CFO)

company salesperson

controller

cost price

entry-level accountant

hiring manager

human resources (HR)
human resources development (HRD)
human resources manager
intermediate accountant
inventory replenishment
key account
manufacturer's representative
market week
merchandise coordinator
multiline rep

personnel
reorder
sample line
senior accountant
showroom
showroom salesperson
single-line rep
trade mart
visual merchandising

Online Resources

education-portal.com/articles/
Fashion_Sales_Representative_Job_
Description_and_Information_About_a_
Career_in_Fashion_Sales.html

fabcounsel.com/fashion-contracts-
you-need-for-manufacturing-and-
sales-2/www.fashion-schools.org/
fashion-sales.htm

www.forbes.com/sites/
markfidelman/2013/05/19/study-78-
of-salespeople-using-social-media-
outsell-their-peers/

Discussion Questions

1. What constitutes a successful sale? Recall a good and a bad sales experience you have had as a customer or salesperson and determine why each was positive or negative and why.
2. Major fashion companies may require their accountants to have worked for one of the Big Four accounting firms in the United States. Research to find the names and backgrounds of these firms and determine why this experience is important. Which of the Big Four is most appealing to you? Why?
3. Develop a list of the activities that a small apparel manufacturer conducts that may require accounting assistance. Payroll, for example, is one of these; purchasing materials for the finished products is another. You may be surprised at the length of your list.
4. Go online to locate an example of a fashion manufacturing company with a human resources department that uses social media vehicles to connect with employees and consumers. Find and print illustrations of the company's online activities in recognizing employee efforts, building a team mindset, and informing employees on industry trends.

Profile: Interview with Buyer Juan Carlos Gaona on the Keys to Success for a Sales Representative

Interview with a Buyer by Gail McInnes, fashionmagnet.ca

Juan Carlos Gaona is the owner of Magnolia, a stylish boutique in Toronto. Next, Gaona shares thoughts on the process he takes when he is selecting lines to carry in his store.

What steps do you take when buying a line?

1. *Introduction:* Someone tells me about a few lines.

2. *Research:* I go to their Web sites and browse through their present and past collections, looking for what they stand for, and what is their overall style, price points, and aesthetic. (If a designer contacts me directly and I am interested, I ask for previous look books and line sheets.)

3. *Collection preview:* I go and see the collection they intend me to buy, and see how it works—both in the store and with the other labels we carry. Also, I do a quality check (I am immediately attracted to lines that pay as much attention to the inside as the outside). If they put on a fashion show, I try to attend to see what they are about as a whole and also I try to get guests' feedback.

4. *Collection edits:* I put together a mock order with what I feel are their stronger pieces, or what defines the brand. Here is where the main decision comes. If I can get their "stronger looks" from other designers I already have, I don't pick them. Same goes if their pieces don't look good with the other collections in-store.

5. *Final order and first season:* If I decide to add the label to our inventory, I place an order and see how they do, not only in terms of sales, but I look for their real values: quality (sampling and production can be very different), delivery timing, hanger appeal, sizing, fit, and real customer feedback. This defines entirely if they will be carried further ahead. I can personally love one label, but if customers have issues (e.g., pricing, quality, originality, fit, etc.), then it will only collect dust on our racks.

How would you advise manufacturers' reps or sales reps to approach retailers to carry their lines?

When sending a request to a retailer (especially a boutique type), try to make it as personal as possible, do some research, ask for the name/contact for the buyer/manager. There is nothing that makes me laugh more than e-mails (directed to info@magnoliaonline.ca) with the greeting "Dear info." True story, and, sadly, very common.

Why do you believe working with the sales rep is important?

I was at an appointment and the sales rep asked me if I was interested in carrying another line. I declined to even look at it, since I was about to go over budget. I had an appointment with them next week, so I came back. The mannequins at the entrance of the showroom were styled impeccably. I asked what they were wearing; obviously it was the line they had offered before. I loved it so much, I decided to risk it and went a little over budget with it. It has become one of my bestsellers. Moral: Sales reps know the tricks, they have a better relationship with the retail world, and they know by heart what their clients (and their clients' clients) want.

What are common mistakes sales reps make when approaching a retailer to buy their lines?

1. *No market research:* One of the biggest and most common mistakes. Thoroughly investigate your retailer, their vision, customers, prices, sizing, labels, etc. before offering your line. I've had people sending me look books of lingerie,

(continued on next page)

(continued)

bathing suits, sleepwear, and shoes; needless to say, I don't carry any of that.

2. *Less-than-spectacular look books:* Companies need to realize 90 percent of your chances (especially on a higher-end market) are based on first impressions; you need your look book to be your strongest selling point. That is what will make me curious or excited about your label as a whole and your particular collection that season.

3. *Too many adjectives:* When introducing a line, the use of too many adjectives is also a big mistake to me. Let the clothes speak for themselves; let the customers hear what your line has to say, before you try to put words in their minds.

4. *Cocky attitudes:* Some reps have contacted me to tell me their lines are what my store needs to make it big or that it's a mistake not to have them. Some have treated me with very poor manners until they realize I am the buyer. That speaks tons about you, both professionally and personally.

5. *Unannounced visits:* People have come through the door with their collection in a suitcase. Nothing wrong with that, you do what you can. But coming in unannounced during a time when the retailer has customers is very disrespectful.

6. *Double dipping:* If you already sell across the street, you should not approach another retailer in the area. It is one of the unspoken rules of retail, and sometimes it's actually illegal to do that (another reason to have a sales rep that can help you with distribution areas and these little inside things).

7. *Bad-quality samples:* If your samples are not finished the right way, it makes buyers anxious. At an appointment there's only so many times you can hear "this (e.g., color, sizing, length, closure, lining, zipper, etc.) will not be like this in production" without wondering if the dress you're looking at will still look like a dress when it's delivered.

How should the sales rep follow up with the retailer?

Take into consideration that buyers and retailers get harassed every season by tons of people. Be persistent, but learn the difference between being persistent and being pushy (no means no, not maybe). Buyers are very busy during showroom season, so it's very common if they take a day or two to return your call or e-mail. Don't call the next day every hour to see if they've read your materials or to ask what they think. I find this to be one of the most recurrent problems my buyer friends have.

How should the sales rep respond to buyer feedback?

If you can't take the good and the bad, don't ask for feedback at all. Life lessons are not free. The knowledge of a buyer has usually cost them one way or another. Be sure you have some sort of a relationship before asking for someone's expertise.

Source:

fashionmagnet.ca

Careers in Fashion Design, Product Development, and Fashion Promotion

Unit 2 looks at the field of fashion design and product development from two perspectives, those of the manufacturer (Chapter 6) and the retailer (Chapter 7). The move into outsourced production, the customer's need for speed in purchasing new looks, and the proliferation of technology in design and manufacturing have come together to generate new career opportunities in fashion design and product development. In Chapter 6, Designing Apparel and Accessories for the Manufacturer, careers related to designing apparel and accessories for the manufacturer are discussed. There are several relatively new positions, in addition to those of the fashion designer, assistant fashion designer, and pattern maker, among them are the career paths of the technical designer and specification technician.

Some retailers purchase fashion merchandise from manufacturers or wholesalers at markets where all of the retail buyers are selecting from the same product lines. Other retailers create exclusivity in their inventory offerings by developing and manufacturing their own products, or by collaborating with a manufacturer who will supply exclusive products that fit their customers' needs. Many large retail operations own a product development division that functions as a design and production source exclusively for them. In addition, many manufacturers are either specializing in creating and/or manufacturing product-developed goods specifically for their client retailers. As a result, Unit 2 examines design and product development for and by the fashion retailer. The career paths in this field, as discussed in Chapter 7, Product Development by the Manufacturer and Retailer, include the following: director of product development, merchandiser, sourcing staff, product development designer, project manager, colorist, textile technical designer, product development pattern maker, and quality control manager.

Whether the fashion product is created and manufactured by the retailer or purchased from a manufacturer, it must be marketed to appeal to the consumer. In Chapter 8, Promotion for the Designer and Manufacturer, we examine the promotion division of a manufacturer that does just that—markets the designer and/or the line of the manufacturer to the retail buyer and ultimate consumer. Promotion career opportunities in the primary level of the fashion industry, as examined in Chapter 8, include fashion stylist, public relations director, advertising research and promotion positions, social media director, and fashion event producer.

In the next unit (Unit 3), Chapter 9 explores promotion for the retail operation. As a result of the growth of social media and Internet marketing, career opportunities are exploding in promotion and public relations. Although there is some overlap in promotion tasks for the manufacturer and retailer, this growth and their differing goals and responsibilities warrant examining each separately and from their individual perspectives.

Unit 2 explores the growth of design and product development divisions in the retail sector of the fashion industry, which has added another area of job opportunities for the fashion design and product development professional. He or she is no longer limited to the manufacturing or wholesale levels of the industry. As fashion lines have become more prolific, more competitive, and more available via e-commerce, differentiating a line and highlighting it in the consumer's eyes have become essential and challenging tasks. As a result, promotion and public relations have become critical keys to the success of designers', manufacturers', and retailers' lines. The central line from the movie *Field of Dreams*, "If you build it, they will come," doesn't reflect the work of fashion designers and product developers today. For them, it is: "Build it well, promote it well, and they will come."

chapter 6

Designing Apparel and Accessories for the Manufacturer

Either a creative individual or a team of creatives came up with the design concept for your favorite shirt, jeans, or iPad case. The season after you purchased this product, a new and exciting version of this apparel or accessory item was introduced. How do these designers do this season after season, year after year? From all around the world, fashion designers share their trend and consumer knowledge, as well as their imaginations, personalities, and aesthetic preferences, as they develop their creations. They put themselves out there each fashion season. Think about Betsey Johnson, who has a love for detail and design that is evident in everything she has done in life and in business for nearly 50 years. She says, "Making clothes involves what I like, and color, pattern, shape, and movement, and I like the everyday process and the people, the pressure, the surprise of seeing the work come alive walking and dancing around on strangers."[1] Fashion design is about knowing your customer, as described by footwear designer Manolo Blahnik (Figure 6.1): "About half my designs are controlled fantasy, 15 percent are total madness, and the rest are bread-and-butter designs."[2] Fashion design is about creativity, self-expression, and change—always change. Karl Lagerfeld (Figure 6.2) explains this: "Fashion keeps me designing: the love of change, the idea that the next one will be the right one, the nonstop dialogue."[3]

Fashion design is the development and execution of wearable forms, structures, and patterns. Just as fashions have changed over the years, the field of fashion design has changed dramatically. The move into outsourcing (or overseas production), the customer's need for speed in purchasing new looks, and the rapid evolution of technology in design and manufacturing

■ **Figure 6.1**
Manolo Blahnik.

■ **Figure 6.2**
Karl Lagerfeld.

have generated new career opportunities in fashion design. There are several new positions in addition to that of the fashion designer, assistant fashion designer, and pattern maker. Among them are the career paths of the technical designer and specification technician. In this chapter, all five career paths are explored, beginning with the fashion designer.

Fashion Designer

■ **Figure 6.3**
Ralph Lauren.

Working as a **fashion designer**, an artist dedicated to the creation of apparel and accessories, can mean supervising a team of design assistants, working under the label of a big-name designer or manufacturer, freelancing for a line or group of lines, or designing and producing a line under your own name. Although the first two options may not appear to be as alluring as the others, they may be less stressful and, quite possibly, more lucrative. Designing and manufacturing your own label takes a great deal of money, time, dedication, and hard work.

There are as many different ways designers embark upon a fashion career as there are styles of design. Ralph Lauren started with a small tie collection that he sold to Bloomingdale's (Figure 6.3). Helmut Lang opened his own clothing store because he couldn't find "the right" T-shirt. Michael Kors (Figure 6.4) built a following of customers by selling his designs in an NYC boutique. Nicolas Ghesquière (Figure 6.5) is a globally recognized fashion designer who is currently creative director for LVMH's Louis Vuitton, replacing Marc Jacobs. He

learned the job hands-on as an assistant at Jean-Paul Gaultier and later as creative director for Balenciaga. The paths in fashion design are diverse, but most people find that the best foundation for a design career is a college degree and the work experience needed to truly know what it takes to be a fashion designer.

Fashion designers often choose to work in a specific area of fashion, such as the merchandise categories of men's, women's, and children's apparel, or accessories. Accessory designers create such items as handbags, belts, scarves, hats, hosiery, and eyewear. Jewelry designers work in the areas of costume jewelry or fine jewelry using precious stones and metals (Figure 6.6). Footwear designers create different styles of shoes and boots. Although most fashion designers specialize in a specific area of fashion (e.g., knitwear, wovens, fur, children's wear, handbags), a few work in all areas. Regardless of the merchandise category in which a designer works, the steps in the design process are very similar.

From conceiving the initial design to producing the final product, the design process can take between 18 and 24 months. Listed next are the general steps the fashion designer takes to place a new collection or a full line in the retailers' hands:

1. Researching current fashion and making predictions of future trends. Some designers conduct their own research, whereas others turn to fashion industry trade groups or trend forecasters, who publish trend reports that project the particular styles, colors, and fabrics for a season, as examined in Chapter 1.
2. Sketching preliminary designs. Many designers sketch initial designs by hand; more designers use computer-aided design (CAD) software to transfer these hand sketches to the computer, or to draw first sketches, as discussed in Box 6.1.
3. Attending trade shows or visiting manufacturers to peruse fabrics and procure samples in order to decide which fabrics to use
4. Determining a color palette
5. Designing the styles to be part of the new collection or line, knowing that some of these will later be eliminated due to cost or merchandising decisions

■ **Figure 6.4**
Michael Kors.

■ **Figure 6.5**
Nicolas Ghesquière.

■ **Figure 6.6**
Alexis Bittar.

6. Costing out styles to make certain they fit within the price range of the line
7. Creating a prototype or sample of the garment and then trying the sample on the fit model for design adjustments
8. Creating the full collection or line of samples and reviewing the full line to determine which styles to keep or delete
9. Having sample lines constructed to market to retail buyers in the showroom or at trade markets
10. After buyers have placed their orders, distributing the garments to retail operations and identifying top-selling items for the next collection

Qualifications

The qualifications for a fashion designer are presented in the following list:

- *Education.* A bachelor's degree in fashion design or product development is commonly required. Supplementing a fashion design degree with a business, marketing, or fashion merchandising degree or minor gives a job candidate an edge.

- *Experience.* A fashion designer needs basic skills in drawing, pattern making, clothing construction, and CAD. Fashion designers are expected to present a portfolio of work at interviews. Industry experience is necessary. Many fashion designers started out as interns, pattern makers, or design assistants for more experienced designers. Salaried designers as a rule earn higher and more stable incomes than do self-employed designers. However, a few self-employed fashion designers who have become very successful earn many times the salary of even the highly paid salaried designers. The largest concentrations of fashion designers are employed in New York and California. Designers with many years of experience can earn much greater than the average national salary, in addition to bonuses or commissions for exceptional seasonal sales.

- *Personal characteristics.* A strong eye for color and detail, a sense of balance and proportion, aesthetic appreciation, and knowledge of historical fashion are important competencies for a designer. Fashion designers also need effective communication and problem-solving skills. Strong sales and presentation skills and knowledge of the business end of the fashion industry are vital to a successful fashion design career.

Depending on the size of the design firm and the designer's level of experience, fashion designers have varying levels of involvement in different aspects of design and production, as shown in Box 6.2, an interview with fashion designer, Malie Bingham. In large design firms, fashion designers often are the lead designers who are responsible for creating the designs, choosing the colors and fabrics, and overseeing technical designers who turn the designs into

---

CASE STUDIES IN CAREER EXPLORATION

Box 6.2 A Day in the Life of a Corporate Fashion Designer

By Melissa McGraw, www.thefashionpotential.com

Do you aspire to work in the fashion industry? Do you have dreams of spending your days out shopping for inspiration or sitting in your office coming up with designs that will land in Barney's or Bloomie's? While there may be a glamorous side to being a fashion designer, there is also the not-so-glamorous (but equally rewarding, nonetheless) side of the job that you may not be aware of. Who better to explain it than menswear designer, Malie Bingham? She gives a brief timeline of one of her days here:

9:00 a.m. Coffee time!

9–10:30 a.m. Answer e-mails from factories overseas and explain or rework any outstanding issues they have on tech-packs in order to get either knit downs, hand looms, or samples in (depending on time of season).

10:30–11 a.m. Meet with sourcing team to discuss timeline and any issues relating to fabric development.

11–11:30 a.m. FedEx delivers proto samples (prototypes/samples) from the factory. They all have to be checked for mistakes before handing them off to technical design team for fittings. (We have specific days for fittings with models.)

11 a.m.–12 p.m. New e-mails are sent to factories giving my design comments of proto samples.

12–1 p.m. Lunch!

1–3 p.m. Design meeting with sales team to review current line that is under development. We show CADs (computer-aided designs), hand looms and knit downs, etc. Sales team members give their comments about what they need, why they hate some things, etc. We get new directions for styles that are needed asap.

3–6 p.m. Finally, get back to work! Either "CAD" anything needed to complete line, do sketches, or work on tech packs to complete whatever group I'm currently working on. At same time, the afternoon mail will have come in and I will need to approve lab-dips, trim cards, fabrics, wash panels, etc.

6–7:30 p.m. Time to go home!

Of course, this is a very general description of one day out of *many*, but you can get the idea. Besides all the work listed above, squeezing in time for trend research, sketch inspiration, and shopping can prove to be quite a challenge.

Source:
www.thefashionpotential.com/2012/04/a-day-in-the-life-of-a-corporate-fashion-designer/

a final product. (Technical designers are discussed later in this chapter.) Large design houses also employ their own pattern makers, who create the master patterns for the design and sew the prototypes and samples. Designers working in small firms, or those new to the job, usually perform most of the technical, pattern making, and sewing tasks, in addition to designing the clothing. A few high-fashion designers are self-employed and create custom designs for individual clients. Other high-fashion designers sell their designs in their own retail stores, specialty stores, or department stores.

Yet other fashion designers specialize in costume design for performing arts, film, and television productions. Although the work of costume designers is similar to that of other fashion designers, it is different in that costume designers often perform extensive research on the styles worn during the period in which the performance takes place, or collaborate with directors to select and create appropriate attire. They sketch the designs, select fabric and other materials, and oversee the production of the costumes for television and film. Costume designers are discussed in Chapter 13.

Career Challenges

A fashion design career is not for the meek. Fashion designers must be able to work in a high-pressure environment with an assortment of personalities—with the common goal of meeting tight deadlines. Those entering this occupation must be willing to work as part of a team. Designers are expected to handle criticism, and critics in this field can be brutal. Successful fashion designers know how to learn from a critique while maintaining their individual styles. Many designers tend to have sporadic working hours, often needing to make adjustments to their work days (or work nights) to accommodate company deadlines (e.g., market week timing, fashion show plans, production due dates). Constant interfacing with suppliers, manufacturers, and co-workers throughout the world requires excellent communication skills and patience. Most fashion designers can expect frequent travel. Finally, they must stay on top of consumer and fashion trends, competition, and how their lines are performing at retail. As trend reporter and marketer Jason Campbell states, "Spotting trends is an ongoing exercise."[4]

Assistant Fashion Designer

In the fashion design field, as well as any other career field, you have to start somewhere. This is where assistant designers, or design assistants, come in. **Assistant fashion designers** support designers by helping them create new materials, styles, colors, and patterns for fashion brands and labels. Like fashion designers, design assistants usually specialize in a particular line, such as woven garments, knitwear, footwear, or accessories. The design assistant uses product knowledge and, in some firms, strong apparel and accessories construction, pattern making, and computer-aided design skills to create prototypes or to modify existing garments. The assistant designer may also be responsible for managing parts of the design process, for example, making certain products arrive on time by working closely with factories and suppliers.

The duties of an assistant designer typically include the following:

- Assisting with the design and development teams to execute the seasonal concept direction, line plan style needs, margin requirements, and completion of product

- Communicating with vendors and other departments under the direction of the designer, such as sourcing fabrics and trimmings

- Participating in meetings with vendors, sales representatives, representatives of other company departments, and retail clients, as determined by the designer

- Communicating technical and creative ideas to the designer, using sketches, fabrics, and trims

- Assisting the designer in creating the product collections at the beginning of each season

- Preparing development creative packages and specification packets under the direction of the designer, such as clear and detailed technical sketches

- Assisting in the preparation of seasonal product review meetings

- Creating new artwork for trims, appliqués, and such for items in the collection

- Supporting the design and development team by preparing necessary visual tools (e.g., sketches, presentation boards, fabric swatches, and color standards)

- Checking for quality by inspecting products during the design process and, when a product is completed, ensuring that samples are constructed accurately and on time

With experience, the assistant designer may take part in seasonal market research to help the design team develop a new product range and forecast trends for the following season. Some companies hire interns, and it is often the assistant designer's responsibility to supervise and guide them. Although the assistant designer usually works in a studio, he or she may have the opportunity to travel and visit manufacturers or go on research trips to art galleries, trade shows, or particular places or countries that inspire a design theme (Figure 6.7).

■ **Figure 6.7**
Although the assistant designer usually works in a studio, he or she may have the opportunity to travel and visit manufacturers or go to trade shows.

Qualifications

The qualifications required for an assistant designer position vary with employers, but there are two common prerequisites: training in pattern making and experience in **computer-aided design (CAD)**. CAD is increasingly being used in the fashion design industry. Although most designers initially sketch designs by hand, a growing number translate these hand sketches to the computer or draw completely on the computer. CAD allows designers to view apparel styles on virtual models and in various colors and shapes, saving time by requiring fewer adjustments of prototypes and samples later. A listing of qualifications commonly required for an assistant designer follows:

- *Education.* A bachelor's degree in fashion design and/or product development is commonly required, to include coursework in pattern making, illustration, and CAD. Training in draping, tailoring, and specialized merchandise categories (e.g., swimwear, menswear, or children's wear) is a plus when it matches the employer's product line.

- *Experience.* The assistant designer should have computer skills in design-related software, such as Adobe Illustrator, Excel, Kaledo, and Photoshop. Working on CAD updates and color, color cards, fabric swatches, and tech pack updates requires strong computer skills. Experience in design or product development with some background in fit, fabric development, finishes, and construction details is often required. Experience often separates the candidate who receives the job offer from other applicants. This can begin in the form of volunteer work, such as costuming for a community theater, as well as an internship with a design or manufacturing firm during college years.

- *Personal characteristics.* Excellent organizational and verbal communication skills are needed. A high level of attention to detail and accuracy is important. The abilities to follow instructions, anticipate what will need to be done, and work as part of a team are mandatory. A strong aesthetic sense and abilities in color, proportion, and fit are critical skills for the assistant designer.

Technical Designer

Technical design is a career path that evolved from the manufacturer's move into outsourcing. As the majority of apparel and accessories production relocated from domestic production factories to overseas manufacturing facilities, these offshore manufacturers began producing a wide range of products across several categories. Many of the products were new to the manufacturers. Someone was needed to oversee what the factories were doing—the measurements they were using, the construction techniques that were being applied, the dates products were going through the different stages of production, and more. A specialist was needed to provide product specifications and to communicate with the various contractors. Technical design was born.

Technical design (also called *tech design*) refers to using drawings, measurements, patterns, and models to develop the "blueprints," or technical plans, needed for the manufacturing of products. Technical design includes determining specifications of trim colors, construction, and components of products as needed by the manufacturer. Fashion is a perfect fit for technical design because the manufacturer's work with overseas contractors mandates strict oversight of specifications to ensure consistent quality, good fit, and standardized sizing. In addition, technical design impacts manufacturing efficiency and cost effectiveness through reduced errors and quicker turnaround.

Today's technical designer essentially does parts of the job that designers used to do when companies were smaller and production was completed domestically. In years past, the technical design position did not exist because companies had their own production facilities. Their products were similar and used the same types of construction, and these processes were often standardized in-house. As production crossed borders and oceans, the designer needed help—badly. The technical design position provided the designer with time to focus on design again.

A **technical designer** is the liaison between the designer and the factory, and is responsible for working closely with the designers to communicate their specific product requests to the factory overseas. An apparel technical designer's focus is on the fit, construction, and quality of the garment, more than the actual design of it. Technical designers are, in essence, the architects of fashion products. They work with flat measurements, construction, and pattern corrections from the first sample to production. They are responsible for creating the prototypes, or samples, and patterns, and they work with the manufacturers and suppliers during the production stages. Technical designers may also work with the sales team to figure out how they want the fit executed, depending on the trend for that season. In Box 6.3, a day in the life of a technical designer is explored.

CASE STUDIES IN CAREER EXPLORATION

Box 6.3 A Day in the Life of a Technical Designer

The day-to-day tasks for one technical designer may be very atypical for another technical designer at a different company, but they all have the same goal at the end of the day: to produce a well-fitting garment at a marketable price. Next, an insider's view of the daily work as a technical designer follows.

My mornings usually start off with reading e-mails from the factories to see what issues or questions they might have or what they need from us. From there, I begin my day and focus on my priorities. I may be sending comments or production tech packs out to the factory, doing a fitting with the design team, and/or correcting a pattern. We also have meetings with the sales staff to go over new styles or a meeting on production issues that need to be solved with the production team.

Most technical designers work very closely with the factories, and, sometimes, we get the opportunity to fly over to meet the people we speak to overseas on a daily basis. Unfortunately, these days it's very rare to see that happen, due to the economy, but I think once the industry picks up, we will be able to experience that once again.

The working hours can be very exhausting, but each position is quite different. My hours do not allow for any personal time. I am always one of the first to arrive, and the last one to leave, with about a 10-minute lunch that requires me to swallow food whole while still reading e-mails. It's tiring, to say the least. That is why it is very important to like the people with whom you work; in this respect, I have been very fortunate.

Source:
http://www.39thandbroadway.com/interview-technical-designer/

Responsibilities of the technical designer vary with each company, as with any industry. Some companies require the technical designer to be more involved with design and computer work in such programs as Adobe Illustrator and Kaledo, whereas others require the technical designer to work heavily with patterns. The general responsibilities of the technical designer are as follows:

- Managing the fit process of production garments from first sample fitting through stock delivery

- Ensuring that garments adhere to the company's quality and fit standards

- Conducting fittings and issuing all fit corrections

- Resolving construction and fit issues to ensure consistent fit and quality

- Generating complete and accurate production specifications and corrections

- Organizing and tracking production samples

- Interfacing with manufacturing to identify any issues that may prevent timely fit approval

- Monitoring/resolving any problems with samples

- Providing care-labeling instructions

- Conducting stock review

- Communicating daily and troubleshooting with overseas offices

- Overseeing adherence to design and production calendar, responding to change as appropriate, and, if applicable, partnering with design and manufacturing team to ensure timely delivery of line

Box 6.4 provides a list of basic training, or objectives, for the technical designer.

Qualifications

The qualifications for the position of technical designer are as follows:

- *Education.* Technical designers are typically required to have at least an associate's degree, likely a bachelor's degree in fashion design or product development. Basic training includes computer skills in common programs (e.g., Microsoft Excel) and program-specific skills (e.g., Adobe Photoshop, Illustrator, and Kaledo).

- *Experience.* Pattern making and CAD experience are expected. Many technical designers are hired from the position of specification technician. An internship with a fashion design firm and work in the technical design department can help open the door to a position in this area. A strong portfolio of a job candidate's best work is the ideal way to showcase his or her creativity and can go a long way toward convincing potential employers that the candidate would be an asset to their business.

- *Personal characteristics.* An understanding of numbers, business, and technology can be very helpful to a technical designer, as are an eye for detail and strong interpersonal skills, because this position often requires working with a cross-disciplinary team. Technical designers often work within specialized niches, gaining field-specific knowledge as they continue to climb the professional ladder. As companies continue to outsource their work, often expanding overseas in the process, there will also continue to be a growing demand for technical designers.

Specification Technician

The typical duties of a **specification technician**, or a *spec tech*, are to attend the fittings of the sample garments, take measurements, and compile these measurements into packets to hand off to production. These packets are referred to as **spec packs**, or *tech packs*. They contain detailed information taken from the designer's sketch, translated into measurements in order to ensure desired fit and styling details, such as the placement of pockets, the length of zippers, the size of buttons, etc., as illustrated in Figure 6.8. Spec tech is usually an entry-level position,

CUSTOMER :								SEASON :	
DESC. OF SAMPLE :	SS KNIT SHIRT POLO							DATE :	
STYLE : KN21								MODIFY:	
QTY : (PCS)								VENDOR:	

DESC.	S	M	L	XL	1X	2X	3X	TOLERANCE
CHEST (1" BELOW ARMHOLE)	38	41	44	47	52	55	58	+ / - 1/4
SWEEP	38	41	44	47	52	55	58	+ / - 1/2
BACK LENGTH (FROM COLLAR SEAM DOWN)	25.5	26	26.5	27	27.75	28.5	29.25	+ / - 1/4
FRONT BODY LENGTH (FROM HIGH POINT)	26	26.5	27	27.5	28.25	29	29.75	+ / - 1/4
ACROSS SHOULDER	16	16.5	17	17.5	19	19.5	20	+ / - 1/4
ARMHOLE (CURVE)- HALF	9	9.5	10	10.5	11	11.75	12.5	+ / - 1/4
SLEEVE LENGTH (FROM CENTER BACK)	17	17.5	18	18.5	20	21	22	+ / - 1/4
SLEEVE OPENING (ON THE HALF)	5.5	6	6.5	7	7.25	7.5	7.75	+ / - 1/4
NECK OPENING	19.25	20	20.75	21.5	23	23.75	24.5	+ / - 1/4
COLLAR HEIGHT (CENTER BACK)	2.5	2.5	2.5	2.5	2.5	2.5	2.5	+ / - 1/8
FRONT NECK DROP	3.25	3.5	3.75	4	4.25	4.5	4.75	+ / - 1/8
BACK NECK DROP	1	1	1	1	1	1	1	+ / - 1/8
FRONT PLACKET WIDTH	1	1	1	1	1	1	1	+ / - 1/8
FRONT PLACKET LENGTH	4.5	4.5	4.5	4.5	4.5	4.5	4.5	+ / - 1/8
SLIT HEIGHT AT BOTTOM	2	2	2	2	2	2	2	+ / - 1/8
HEM HEIGHT	1	1	1	1	1	1	1	+ / - 1/8

■ Figure 6.8
Spec packs contain detailed information taken from the designer's sketch, translated into measurements in order to ensure desired fit and styling details, such as the placement of pockets, the length of zippers, the size of buttons, etc.

because the primary responsibility of the spec tech is to measure the product. Spec techs are usually promoted to technical designers after they gain a few years of experience, depending on their abilities and progress. The qualifications for a spec tech are equivalent to those of a beginning technical designer.

Pattern Maker

Pattern makers play a key role in the design and production processes. They are responsible for translating the design concept into a pattern for the actual garment. Pattern makers develop a **first pattern**, which is used to cut and sew the **prototype**, or first sample garment. The first pattern is made in a **sample size**, the size used for testing fit and appearance in addition to selling purposes. Although sample sizes vary by company, they are generally as follows:

- For juniors, sample sizes are 5, 7, or 9.

- For misses, they are 6, 8, or 10.

- For women's wear, sample sizes are 18 or 20, depending on the line and its target market.

- For menswear, sample sizes are 34 for trousers and 38 for tailored suits.

- For infants' apparel, size 3–6 months is the sample size.

- For toddlers' apparel, size 2 is often the sample size.

- In children's wear, it is usually a size 7.

Pattern makers may use three different techniques to develop the first pattern: draping, flat pattern, or computer-aided pattern making. With the **draping method**, pattern makers shape and cut muslin or the garment fabric on a dress form, or model, to create a pattern, as shown in Figure 6.9. Draping is the preferred strategy for soft, flowing designs. It allows the pattern maker to adjust the design as it evolves three-dimensionally, as with a piece of sculpture. When the designer approves the look, the pattern maker removes the muslin from the form and then draws the pattern on heavy paper.

Alternately, the **flat pattern method** uses angles, rulers, and curves to alter existing basic patterns, referred to as **blocks** or *slopers*. The term "block" is used to describe a pre-pattern template for which additional manipulation is required at the end to generate a pattern (e.g. changing the bust dart, adding seam allowances) for a variety of other garments. Finally, computer-aided pattern making is utilized by many large firms that can afford the expense of the equipment and software programs. With **computer-aided pattern making**, pattern makers can manipulate graphics of pattern pieces on a computer screen or make patterns manually using a **stylus**, a computerized pen, or a **puck**, a mouselike device.

■ **Figure 6.9**
With the draping method, pattern makers shape and cut muslin or the garment fabric on a dress form or model to create a pattern.

Another tool in computer-aided pattern making is the **digitizer**, a program integration feature used to make or alter patterns. Pattern makers and technical designers can copy and paste measurements to a design, as well as grade patterns. With a digitizer, they can also import appliqués, screen graphics, and embroideries from other programs for pattern placement. The digitizer can also be used to create or alter markers. Whether draped, created by flat pattern, or developed on a computer, the first pattern must accurately reflect the style, proportion, and fit the designer had in mind when conceiving the product.

Qualifications

Following are the qualifications for a pattern maker:

- *Education.* A bachelor's degree in fashion design, product development, apparel manufacturing, or a related field is commonly required.

- *Experience.* Preparation for the career of pattern maker includes knowledge of flat pattern making, computer-aided design, and, depending on the manufacturer, draping. Many pattern makers begin their careers as an assistant pattern maker or a pattern grader.

- *Personal characteristics.* Pattern makers must have an understanding of mathematical calculations as they pertain to sizing and fit. They must have keen eyes for proportion and line, as well as the ability to achieve perfect fits. The successful pattern maker is a design technician with a critical eye for detail and accuracy.

Summary

What are the differences in the careers of a technical designer, pattern maker, and specification technician? A technical designer's responsibilities encompass most of the duties that a pattern maker and specification technician would have. If a company offers all three positions (technical designer, pattern maker, and specification technician), then the team works together, each member with a different focus. The pattern maker focuses on adjusting patterns, correcting and balancing them so the garment fits properly. The technical designer works with measurements. The specification technician prepares the spec pack.

Endnotes

1. myshoppingspy.com/london/betsey-johnson
2. www.brainyquote.com/quotes/quotes/m/manoloblah110627.html
3. karllagerfeldquotes.tumblr.com/page/14
4. www.vogue.co.uk/celebrity-photos/080208-karl-lagerfeld-famous-quotes/gallery.aspx#/imageno/11

Key Terms

assistant fashion designer
block
computer-aided design (CAD)
computer-aided pattern making
digitizer
draping method
fashion design
fashion designer
first pattern
flat pattern method

pattern maker
prototype
puck
sample size
spec pack
specification technician
stylus
technical design
technical designer

Online Resources

www.fashionista.com

www.businessoffashion.com

www.louisvuitton.com

www.karl.com

www.jimmychoo.com

www.hugoboss.com

www.viviennewestwood.com/

www.wwd.com/fashion-news/designer-luxury/all-eyes-on-nicolas-ghesquires-debut-at-louis-vuitton-7511207

www.nytimes.com/2014/03/06/
fashion/Nicolas-Ghesquire-Debuts-
Louis-Vuitton-Collection-paris-
fashion-week.html

www.dailymail.co.uk/femail/
article-2487213/Balenciaga-designer-
Nicolas-Ghesqui-replaces-Marc-
Jacobs-Louis-Vuittons-artistic-
director.html

Discussion Questions

1. Select one of each: a new and relatively unknown designer, a current contemporary designer, and a legendary designer of the past. Construct a report examining the following aspects of these designers' careers: background (e.g., birthplace, education, experience), career startup and path (e.g., internships, jobs, and current position), signature looks, licenses in other product areas, and future plans.

2. Select three well-known apparel manufacturers that would likely require a pattern maker to have exceptional abilities in one of each of the following skill areas: draping, making flat patterns, and computer-aided pattern making. Why did you choose these manufacturers?

3. Compare and contrast two classified advertisements for technical designers. How are the position descriptions similar and different? Among many other Web sites, you can locate classified ads for the fashion industry at www.wwd.com/wwdcareers, www.stylecareers .com, and www.fashion.net/jobs/.

Profile: Interview with Fashion Designer Malie Bingham

By Melissa McGraw, www.thefashionpotential.com

You were introduced to Malie Bingham in Box 6.2, when she described a day in the life of a corporate designer. This American Intercontinental University and Miami International University of Art & Design alumna, knitwear guru, and menswear specialist has worked in the fashion industry for more than ten years. Malie has worked for a large menswear corporation for about a decade, designing knit and woven tops in men's sportswear for designer and mass-market labels. Her designs are distributed throughout midtier department stores across the country.

Can you tell me a little about yourself?

I am a menswear designer in New York City. I specialize in knits and sweaters. I was born in Houston, Texas.

When did you realize you wanted to work in fashion?

I knew from a very young age that I wanted to be in fashion. Like many people, I started making Barbie clothes when I was really little. As a pre-teen, I spent hours at the mall and I knew that I had a very clear sense of which trends were coming. I started sketching things and, a few months later, I would see similar things in the stores. I actually used to mail my sketches to Esprit! It was very funny.

What was your path to where you are today?

When I first went to fashion school, I originally thought I wanted to be a pattern maker because I really enjoyed the construction of the patterns and draping the fabric, etc. However, once I graduated, I had a very hard time finding a beginning job doing

Profile Figure 6a Fashion Designer, Malie Bingham.

that. Everyone wanted years of experience! I did have computer CAD experience. In Atlanta, I was able to get my first job at a menswear company as a design assistant/graphic designer. This was how I fell into menswear, and I am very happy that I did. I wouldn't change a thing!

(continued)

What kind of skills have you learned from your experiences, and/or what skills do successful fashion designers have?

You absolutely have to know how to CAD. Everything is done on the computer. I would say that, although CAD skills are very important, a knowledge of fabrics is the next thing. You have to understand textiles and fabric in order to design.

What are your job responsibilities?

I design all of the cut-and-sew knits and sweaters for a major men's sportswear brand. This includes coming up with the design concepts and inspiration each season, developing fabrics each season, approving lab dips, designing the models for each garment, attending fittings, and getting all the salesmen's samples in the showroom on time.

What types of social media do you use for work? For which purposes?

I use Pinterest just to find inspirational pictures. There is also a Web site that is not available to the public called WGSN, which has trends and news for the industry.

What are a few of your favorite Web sites and blogs that are fashion-related?

Style.com, WGSN.com, and Etsy.com

What do you love most about what you do?

I love shopping and finding new inspiration. There is always something new out there and it keeps me constantly inspired and interested.

What have been your toughest challenges?

Pricing is very critical in the mid-tier market in which I work. We are always challenged to do more with less. This is why understanding fabrications is so important. The American consumer wants a deal and is used to getting coupons or sales. They rarely pay full price, which means my fabric price has to be much lower.

What advice would you give to aspiring fashion designers?

Get as much experience as possible working at different companies doing different things at the beginning of your career. Try menswear, women's wear, children's, or accessories. Try technical design or marketing. It is much harder to transition over as you get older because the industry is always looking at your experience. Do as many internships as you can! This will also give you the opportunity to really see what you like and what you don't.

Profile: Fashion Designer Vera Wang

From the moment she unlaced her competitive figure skates for the last time, Vera Wang set her sights on a life in fashion. In the 40-plus years since, hers has been a singular ride, one that took her first on a 16-year editorial stint at *Vogue* magazine, where she learned that no one disturbed the calm of Mr. Penn's set with chatter, to Ralph Lauren, where she experienced the creative joys of limitless resources, and finally, 25 years ago, to her own company.

Vera Wang, a design leader in bridal gowns, continues to be a leader in fashion and social media. She tweeted that, for her spring bridal collection, she was inspired by the "lightness of being." Vera Wang then went on to unveil her Spring 2015 bridal collection in a film available online and via mobile devices. Directed by fast-rising fashion filmmaker Gordon Von Steiner, the mini-film stars A-list models Caroline Brasch Nielsen, Elisabeth Erm, Nastya Sten, and Sophie Touchet. The new film is titled *Chasing Alix*. Shot on Long Island, the girls cavort in Wang's slinky bridal designs to the minimalist soundtrack of Son Lux's "Easy." "The opportunity to create a visual and expressive experience of the clothes, as interpreted by my fashion vision, is a whole new way for me to communicate with not only brides, but women everywhere," explained Wang. "In this instance, bridal becomes the artistic vehicle to advance my love of fashion in general. I hope they will enjoy this new experience."

Profile Figure 6b Fashion Designer, Vera Wang.

Sources:

www.wwd.com/fashion-news/designer-luxury/vera-wang-a-life-in-fashion-3068440

www.nydailynews.com/life-style/fashion/vera-wang-unveils-spring-2015-bridal-film-article-1.1755906

www.wwd.com/media-news/digital/wwd-week-intweets-4192014-7649472

chapter 7

Product Development by the Manufacturer and Retailer

To compare product development with fashion design in apparel, you may want to envision (1) an illustration and a completed sample of a garment (i.e., fashion design) and (2) an illustration, the sample, the garment hanging in a store, and the customer walking away from the store with the garment in a shopping bag (i.e., product development). So what exactly does product development consist of? **Product development** is the creation, production, and marketing of a product from start to finish. This is not a new process.

Manufacturers in many industries, from automobiles to household appliances, have engaged in product development for many decades. However, in the 1980s, it became widespread for large fashion retailers to develop products of their own instead of solely selling the lines of manufacturers. The Gap, for example, used to carry a variety of national brands, such as Levi's. Now it carries only Gap-branded merchandise that is designed and developed in-house. Forever 21, H&M, and Banana Republic are other examples of retailers carrying fully product-developed goods. In contrast, Macy's, Neiman Marcus, and Saks Fifth Avenue are examples of retailers that carry both manufacturers'/designers' lines and their own product-developed lines.

Product development may be the function of one department in a retail operation or a division within an organization. For example, Macy's, Inc., with corporate offices in Cincinnati and New York, is one of the nation's premier retailers, with fiscal 2013 sales of $27.9 billion. The company operates Macy's and Bloomingdale's brands, with about 840 stores in 45 states, the District of Columbia, Guam, and Puerto Rico, as well as macys.com and bloomingdales.com Web sites. The diverse workforce of Macy's, Inc., includes approximately 172,500 employees.[1]

Within Macy's there is a division called Macy's Merchandising Group (MMG). MMG is responsible for conceptualizing, designing, sourcing, and marketing privately developed and privately branded goods sold at Macy's and Bloomingdale's. These private brands, available "Only at Macy's," are developed to appeal to a certain customer lifestyle and are supported with marketing programs Macy's builds to create a precisely defined image. Some of MMG's 15 highly successful private brands include I.N.C., Charter Club, American Rag, Alfani, Bar III, Belique, Epic Threads, First Impressions, and Hotel Collection.

Regardless of the company and whether it is a manufacturer or a retailer, many steps need to be taken when developing a line, although the details may change depending on the type of product, on whether the line is to be produced overseas or domestically, or if the company has an in-house sample department. The general steps that are taken for each season, as described by product developer and professor Kirsteen Buchanan, are as follows:

1. Inspiration sources (e.g., fabrics, art and museum exhibitions, travel destinations, films, color palettes, and so on) are reviewed. Market research is conducted. The previous year's sales and markdowns are analyzed. Product categories are decided.
2. Trend forecasts are discussed. The preliminary line is planned. The company decides "what it believes in." Color stories are selected.
3. Fabrics and trims are researched, then selections are made. Prints are designed.
4. Concepts are developed, storyboards are created, and designs are sketched. Sample fabrics and trims are ordered. Labdips, colored samples of selected fabrics, are requested.
5. Merchandising meetings are held. The line may be edited from sketches.
6. Specifications are written, and technical packages are compiled.
7. Sourcing is completed. Samples, or prototypes, are constructed, and preliminary costing is requested.
8. Patterns and first samples are produced by a sample room or contractors. Often 20 to 50 percent more designs are made than those that actually will be manufactured. Factories advise on costs.
9. Samples are fitted, edited, and adopted into the line during a line review. The fitting process continues until the sample is approved or dropped. Costs are negotiated. Quantity may be an integral part of cost negotiations, or it may be determined when orders are generated. Quantities may be finalized and orders may be placed at this time, depending on factory lead time.
10. Samples, or prototypes, are produced. Private label goods may require only a meeting sample. Costs are finalized. Photo and production samples are requested.
11. For a private brand in a retail operation with decentralized buying, the styles will be "sold" internally to buyers who quantify the purchase. **Decentralized buying** refers to the process used by individual stores or groups of stores within a retail chain that have a buyer who selects from the company's primary buyer's purchases.
12. Production fabric and trim are ordered as soon as the factories receive orders.
13. Production goods are manufactured, and quality control is completed.
14. Goods are packed and shipped to the retailer.
15. Merchandise is received by the retailer and delivered to the warehouse or selling floors.[2]

Box 7.1 The Product Development Manufacturer Reaches Out

Manufacturers that offer product development to retailers provide innovation, flexibility, and cost control for retailers. Many are responsible for a traditional manufacturer's tasks, such as bringing innovative fabrics to the retailer or producing garments from a product sample; however, others may be expected to work closely with the retailer's strategic plans to build products that are best suited for creating customer/brand familiarity—from start to finish. Some product development teams employed by manufacturers identify important trends and develop innovative products reflecting those trends. Whether providing a selection of textiles or working on the creation of new designs, the retailer's target market and budget, or price points, are at the heart of decisions made by the manufacturer's product development team.

Social media is one of the newest ways that product development divisions of manufacturers are listening to the retailer's target market. It

has provided them with interactive outlets that offer direct engagement with their clients' target customers. Collaborating with the retailer, the product development manufacturer can announce new products on YouTube, Pinterest, and Instagram. They can have a dialogue on Twitter with the retailer's customers about which styles to produce. With more than one billion people on Facebook worldwide (Social Media Today), it is no surprise that fashion manufacturers are spending time and money on social media advertising and campaigns. Converse, manufacturer of the iconic high-top sneaker, leads the list as number 1 of the top 40 fashion companies dominating social media in 2014, with a total audience of more than 40 million active users.

Source:

fabcounsel.com/40-top-fashion-companies-dominating-in-social-media/

In the fashion industry, there are three key types of businesses that produce merchandise: manufacturers, contractors, and retailers. As discussed in Unit 1, manufacturers are companies that create, produce, market, and distribute product lines on a continual basis. This may be a designer who owns a company or a company that employs designers. Manufacturers may own their own factories or use contractors to construct their products. A growing area of product development is the manufacturer that establishes a product development division to service its clientele of retailers, as illustrated in Box 7.1.

Contractors, factories that make and finish goods, may be domestic, meaning in the United States, or offshore, such as those in China, India, or Taiwan (refer to Figure 7.1). **Retailers** are businesses that sell products to the ultimate consumer and may include the vast range of brick-and-mortar stores (e.g., department stores, mass merchants, specialty stores, boutiques, discount stores, and outlet stores), as well as catalogues, brick-and-click stores, and online stores. **Brick-and-mortar store** refers to retail operations in a facility, such as a building or a store in a mall. **Brick-and-click store** refers to a retail operation that offers products both through actual stores and online. Some retailers sell through all or several of these channels. JCPenney, Saks Fifth Avenue, and Nordstrom's, for example, sell their product lines through brick-and-click stores and catalogues. Nearly all of the large retailers are currently engaging in some form of product development. Next, the focus is on the product development and design activities of retail operations.

■ **Figure 7.1**
Many retail product development divisions hire contractors, factories that make and finish goods, for production.

Why Retailers Became Designers

There are four main reasons why retailers moved into the business of developing their own products or lines of products. First, retailers wanted to be able to satisfy specific customer demands. Sometimes, the retail buyers were unable to locate the products, looks, prices, or fit for their customers' needs. The second reason retailers went into the business of creating products is fashion exclusivity. **Fashion exclusivity** refers to a company having merchandise that is unique to that particular company (Figure 7.2). You may have remarked or may have overheard a customer saying, "Everything in the mall looks the same. I don't want to see myself coming and going." Retailers wanting to project fashion images that are unique to their particular companies established product development departments or divisions. Most important, product development provided higher profit margins. Retailers reasoned that by producing directly through contracted or company-owned factories instead of buying from manufacturers, they could make more money on each item, even while charging the customers less than they charged for nationally branded merchandise. Finally, retailers needed to reduce lead time between ordering new merchandise and receiving it on the sales floor. This trend is referred to as fast fashion.

■ **Figure 7.2**
Fashion exclusivity refers to having merchandise that is unique to a particular company, sometimes in a specific geographic territory.

Fast fashion is a phrase used to describe apparel and accessories trends that are designed and manufactured quickly and affordably to allow the mainstream consumer to take advantage of current fashions at a lower price. This philosophy of quick manufacturing at affordable prices is considered the "success story" of many large retailers, such as H&M, Forever 21, and Zara. Fast fashion is achieved through the retailers' understanding of the target market's wants, in that new variations of products the customer is buying are delivered to the sales floor as fast as possible.

In most cases, the product developer's first objective is a high-fashion-looking garment at a mass-market price. His or her second objective is often to create modifications of the items that sell and have these manufactured quickly. The product developer, buyer, and manufacturer collaborate to maximize sales and profits by satisfying customer needs. Fast fashion brings more product options to the consumer more frequently.

Initially, retailers who developed their own product lines ran into some roadblocks. There is a long tradition in the fashion business of knocking off the hot or successful designs offered by top designers, rather than creating new looks. A **knockoff** is a copy of another style, often of lesser quality and with minor modifications. Knockoffs of Hermès' Birkin and Kelly bags, carried by celebrities like Victoria Beckham and Sarah Jessica Parker, can be found at midpriced retail stores (Figure 7.3). Although the practice is less common today, retailers were historically known for creating private-label lines that were collections of knockoffs. **Private label** refers to a line name or brand that the retailer develops and assigns to a collection of product development goods. Because many of the retailers were knocking off products that were already on the market, the majority of the private-label products lacked fashion newness. Retailers also had to take responsibility for securing fabrics, avoiding fit problems, and shipping goods. Another obstacle was that many overseas factories required retailers to open letters of credit to pay for goods. As a result, retailers were faced with tying up large amounts of their operations' dollars in advance of shipping, rather than paying for merchandise 30 days after they received shipment.

As retail-driven product development matured, retailers began to build highly skilled design and merchandising teams to remove some of the roadblocks. Some major retailers do not attempt to develop products in certain specialized apparel categories because these areas are too precarious or too dependent on major brand names. A few of the product categories that retailers place in product development are basic apparel, because of ease of fit; jeans, because of the low risk and ease of entry into the market as a price-point alternative (lower and higher) to major brands; and product categories that have a lower level of competition from

■ **Figure 7.3**
Knockoffs of Hermès' Birkin and Kelly bags can be found modified at mid- to low-priced retail stores, or copied by counterfeiters.

major brands. Some retail operations prefer to leave development of highly specialized apparel, such as swimwear and hosiery, or categories that require major advertising investments, such as cosmetics and fragrances, to the major brand manufacturers. As styling in basic products makes it difficult to distinguish a major brand from a private label, some retailers have found that they are safer developing this type of merchandise. Other retailers choose private-label lines to create unique and exclusive products that are not available in the market. Retailers often evaluate the risk of trying to develop trendy, high-priced merchandise, knowing that customers often prefer a designer name attached to their investment purchases.

Types of Product Development Businesses

Several product development classifications have evolved as retailers increasingly engage in the customizing of product lines. These classifications include retail label, private label, private brand, direct market brand, and licenses. A **retail label** is a brand with the retailer's name on it, such as Neiman Marcus, Custom Interiors, or Barney's. A retailer may negotiate with a manufacturer to put its label on a group of items instead of or in addition to the manufacturer's label. Some of the items carrying a retail label may be **exclusives**, or items that only one retailer carries. In some cases, a retailer may negotiate to be the only one in a geographic region to carry a particular item or the only one in the country to carry a particular color or style. For example, the label may read, "Burberry Exclusively for Neiman Marcus."

Similar to a private label, yet with a greater level of market penetration primarily through advertising, a **private brand** is a name owned exclusively by a particular store that is extensively marketed with a definite image, such as Target's Mossimo brand, Macy's I.N.C. brand (Figure 7.4), and JCPenney's Stafford brand. A **direct market brand** describes a brand that is the name of the retailer. This is often a specialty store chain, such as Ann Taylor, IKEA, or Gap (Figure 7.5).

■ **Figure 7.4**
Macy's displays clothing from I.N.C., International Concepts Collection, which is a private brand, or label.

■ **Figure 7.5**
The Gap features a full merchandise assortment of its own direct market brand in the United States and now overseas with recent store openings in China.

CASE STUDIES IN CAREER EXPLORATION

Box 7.2 Retailer in Product Development: Macy's Product Development Executive Development Program

The Product Development Executive Development Program is a part of Macy's Merchandising Group (MMG); this group is responsible for conceptualizing, designing, sourcing, producing, selling, and marketing Macy's extensive and successful family of Private Brands. Our Private Brands include I•N•C, Charter Club/Club Room, Alfani, Style & Co., American Rag, Jenni, Hotel Collection, Tools of The Trade, and The Cellar.

In this role, you'll learn to identify emerging trends, conceptualize branded styles, partner with our 14 overseas offices, and negotiate pricing strategies with global and domestic vendors to create the next wave of private label goods. You'll also react to sales performance, analyze consumer trends, and anticipate market needs to promote the visibility of private label goods—and this is only the beginning of what it means to pursue a career in Product Development. This Executive Development Program takes place exclusively in New York, NY.

Job Description

- Collaborate with key partners from merchandising, marketing, stores, fashion research and development, and color analysis

- Analyze and competitive shop to gain market awareness

- Partner with MMG overseas offices on sourcing, development, garment fit, quality, sampling, sales, and price negotiation

- Contribute business and trend strategy ideas in Line Development meetings with the Design Team

- Participate in tactical meetings with vendors and manufacturers to develop business driving strategies

- Gain exposure to supply chain management including purchase order creation and agreements, order tracking, and collaboration with customs and Macy's Logistics team

- Manage the Product Development Time and Action Calendar for Design, Technical, Quality Control, Manufacturing, and Customs to ensure accurate and timely delivery of shipments

- Create and analyze selling reports to develop strategic recommendations based on merchandise sales performance, present top seller product summary in monthly meetings

- Partner with the Private Brands Marketing team to identify new packaging and branding needs

- Track advertising and marketing samples, and monitor marketing related sales trends

- Assist in preparation for Market/Buy Meetings by creating style placement packages and line presentation materials

Requirements

- Bachelor's degree, all majors welcome

- Solid academic performance—minimum 3.0 GPA preferred

- Proficiency on PCs and MS Office; excellent Excel skills critical

- Strong analytical skills and attention to detail

- Strong communication and presentation skills

- Ability to prioritize multiple projects to achieve productivity and business goals

- Ability to promote teamwork, solve problems, and manage complex relationships

(continued on next page)

Box 7.2 (continued)

- Experience in retail; sales, management, or buying exposure a plus

The Product Development career path includes tracks in Product Management, Brand Management, and Retail Divisions. Each path is outlined below.

Training Program

In the Product Development Executive Development Program, you'll gain the fundamental tools and strategies needed in your first position as a Product Assistant. This layered program includes formal training classes that supplement hands-on experiences; working directly with Product Managers, Designers, Buyers, Planners, and Vendors, you'll learn the key strategies and techniques needed to successfully manage a specific brand classification within the Private Brands Business. Training Program highlights include:

- *Product Development Lifecycle*: This dynamic class teaches the fundamentals of the product development lifecycle through the eyes of a specific business. You'll walk through the struggles, revisions, and successes of a Private Brands style. Conducted in a learning environment, experience on-the-job examples regarding business, strategy, partnerships, systems, and retail terminology.

- *Design and Technical Design Overview*: Experience the function of Design and Technical Design through guiding a style from the conceptual sketch stage to a tangible product sample. Learn to successfully navigate the dynamic and important collaboration between the product development and design teams.

- *Retail Math*: Taught by a Professor from the Fashion Institute of Technology with a seasoned career in retail, you will learn the fundamentals of retail math and how to analyze your business and utilize sourcing negotiations to maximize your bottom line. This course is taught in stages as you progress in your business and financial acumen.

- *Sales Reporting*: Learn how to build a report used to analyze your business and in turn maximize profitability. Focus on the use of sales tracking to address fast and slow turning merchandise to react to and anticipate the needs of the business.

- *Trend and Color Research and Development*: Gain exposure to our in-house trend research and developers, while gaining insight on how forecasts of style and color trend are translated and represented within our Private Brands.

Macy's, Inc. is an Equal Opportunity Employer, committed to a diverse and inclusive work environment.

Source:

www.macyscollege.com/Careers/ProductDevelopment/; Courtesy of Macy's, Inc.

Today, large retail companies and manufacturers/designers are major employers of product development staffs, as illustrated by Macy's Product Development Executive Development Program in Box 7.2. The career paths in this field include the following: director of product development, merchandiser, sourcing staff, designer, colorist, textile technical designer, pattern maker, and quality control manager.

Director of Product Development

A **director of product development** is ultimately responsible for the strategic planning of the division, specifying exactly what the company will make and market, as well as when it will do this. After selecting a general product category, such as junior T-shirts, the director of product development must narrow the focus. The fashion market is extremely segmented, with each brand filling its particular niche. It is not enough simply to decide to create a line of junior T-shirts, because that is far too broad a category to allow for effective line development. Instead, the director of product development will decide, for example, to create vintage-inspired T-shirts for fashion-forward, young female customers in junior sizes extra-small to large. A key product segmentation decision is specifying the target market niche, which can be accomplished only by knowing the customer well—who she is, what she likes, and where she lives, works, and plays.

Other product segmentation decisions that product development directors must make relate to the product, price, size, and taste level. Next, the director of product development will work with the staff to build a brand by creating an image or personality for the line. An image is the way the product developer wants the brand to be perceived, the way that will best attract the target customer. With the abundance of fashion products on the market, image may be the only means of product differentiation. Carefully defining target customers will allow brands to develop images and product lines that will appeal to them.

There are two main approaches the director of product development may take toward the branding of a line: a design-driven brand or a merchandising-driven brand. A **design-driven brand** is led by a designer who is expressing a personal artistic vision and sense of taste, such as Target's collaboration with Missoni. This type of brand appeals to customers who relate to the designer's particular style and flair and includes most brands with designer names. These apparel brands tend to be more original and creative. Design-driven brands also have the peculiar distinction of representing both a particular designer's viewpoint and a line of products. In the case of a manufacturer's line, such as Ralph Lauren's apparel and accessories, the brand has several faces, including English gentleman, East Coast aristocrat, African safari adventurer, and Western individualist, as shown in Figures 7.6a–c.

Merchandising-driven brands, or *void-filling brands*, do just that. These market-based brands search for a void in the market or an underserved customer and create a product to fill that void and appeal to that distinct customer. Styling decisions are based on careful monitoring of past sales successes and failures in conjunction with customer desires. Customer comfort and competitive pricing are of utmost importance to merchandising-driven brands. Many private labels are merchandising-driven brands.

■ **Figures 7.6a–c**
A few of the many faces of designer Ralph Lauren's lines: (a) English gentleman, (b) world adventurer, and (c) Western Americana.

Figure 7.7
Cross-shopping is when a customer purchases a wide variety of products in an array of brands at various retail outlets.

The director of product development has an important overall task. Retailers' brands must have a fashion image consistent with that of the customer the operation attracts. It is the director of product development's responsibility to make certain that the designed products add up to a marketable line that matches the retail operation's image. If, for example, a retailer of women's conservative career wear brings in a private-label line of Indian cotton bohemian blouses and skirts, the customer may be turned off by the confusing look of the inventory.

Market knowledge is as critical to the success of a fashion brand as is customer knowledge. The director of product development must examine the competition. **Direct competition** is any other brand producing a similar product at roughly the same price point, targeted toward the same customer or market niche. It is important for product developers to be attentive to what direct competitors are doing, if only to refrain from duplicating their products or brand image. These direct competitors are fighting to be the consumer's choice. Ideally, a company wishing to grow a brand will have such a great product and know its customers so well that customers feel they must buy it. In a broader sense, competition is any other brand vying for consumers' retail dollars.

Types of competition change as retailing venues change. Think about the Internet as a shopping mall of new competitors. As the face of retail changes, a brand's product line may be competing with brands online, at different price ranges and from global companies. Consumers are less loyal to retailers today, because there is no stigma attached to cross-shopping. **Cross-shopping** refers to the customer's inclination to purchase a wide variety of products in an array of brands from various providers—directly from the manufacturer, in a resale store, at a flea market, or a retailer of high-end designers (Figure 7.7). For today's consumer, it is cool to buy smart. Think about wearing a $60 BCBG top with $232 Baldwin jeans and $4.99 Target flip-flops; now, that's cross-shopping. The new consumer mentality puts added pressure on the director of product development, who must now be aware of price, quality, and look of products in all categories, not just one narrow market niche.

Qualifications

The qualifications for the position of director of product development include the following:

- *Education*. A bachelor's degree in fashion merchandising, fashion design, product development, or a related field is required.

- *Experience*. The director of product development holds an executive position that often requires five to seven years of successful work experience as a merchandiser or designer.

- *Personal characteristics*. Creativity, a strong marketing sense, and an understanding of consumers, quantitative skills, and networking abilities are key attributes for directors of product development. They are excellent communicators—orally, in writing, and visually. Also, the director of product development has other diverse characteristics: curiosity, leadership abilities, and the ability to work with a variety of constituencies, from designers to merchandisers to colorists.

A classified advertisement for a senior product development director is featured in Box 7.3.

Box 7.3 Senior Product Development Director

Employer: Growing Contemporary Sportswear Manufacturer

Location: Los Angeles, California

Type: Supervisor in Product Development

Job Status: Full-time

Duties and Responsibilities:

- Research and coordinate all phases of the development process—beginning with fabric and trim selection/development, following through to the sealed tech pack for bulk production

- Responsible to coordinate approval for all fabric/wash/trim/print/color details between design and vendors in a timely manner following the company product calendar

- Responsible for setting up costing sheets, coordinating, and following up costing communications with vendors

- Effectively update beginning of the month reports (BOM) and communicate any changes, corrections, or suggestions to the sourcing partner (technical designer) and design

- Research the market for innovations in materials and fabric wash/finish technologies

Knowledge, Skills and Abilities Required:

- Five to ten years' experience in an apparel development–based position working with domestic and international vendors

- BA, BS, or BFA in a related apparel or business major

- Very knowledgeable of apparel construction, fabrics, fabric washes, trims, costing, color approval process, and overall manufacturing processes for both women's wear and men's wear markets

- Highly organized with the ability to manage multiple projects/seasons at various stages of the development process at the same time

- Ability to work effectively in a team environment

- Very proficient in Microsoft Office, Kaledo, Illustrator, and Adobe programs, especially Excel

- Proven analytical and problem-solving abilities, with a keen attention to detail

- Ability to effectively prioritize and execute tasks in a high-pressure environment

- Good written, oral, and interpersonal communication skills

- Team-oriented and skilled in working within a collaborative environment

Career Challenges

The director of product development is the leader of the pack. It is a high-pressure job in which one must be a motivator, guide, and, sometimes, the "take-charge" person. It takes a strong person with vision to manage a team of executives. In the position of product developer for a manufacturer, this person is likely guiding product design for several retail clients. He or she will have to learn exactly who each retailer's customers are and what they want, likely without ever setting foot in their stores. This takes a great deal of research and superior communication skills. If this person is the director of product development for a retailer, he or she may have the opportunity for excellent customer knowledge, but less daily experience in the production end of the business. Maintaining strengths while building expertise in weak areas in the fast-paced world of fashion are challenges for the product development director.

Merchandiser

A merchandiser's responsibilities vary widely depending on company requirements. A product development **merchandiser** collaborates with the director of product development in deciding what to produce and then organizes and manages the entire product development process. Merchandisers are responsible for the development of a balanced, marketable, profitable, and timely line. In some manufacturing companies, merchandisers oversee the design function and may serve as liaisons between design and sales. They will create the initial line plan and project target wholesale costs by analyzing sales from previous seasons, fashion trends, and customer wants. As Figure 7.8 illustrates, merchandisers work closely with designers on seasonal themes and guide designers on the development of cost-effective and marketable styles. In some manufacturing companies, merchandisers may also have responsibilities in sourcing and marketing functions. In other companies, there is a sourcing staff to locate the suppliers and manufacturers for the product.

The merchandiser is responsible for constructing the **merchandising calendar**, the product development team's schedule. The goal of the calendar is to deliver the right product (i.e., correct style, quality, and price) at the right time. When creating a new line, developers carefully plan how often they want goods to flow into the stores. Once they complete the delivery schedule, merchandisers create a calendar by working backward from in-store delivery dates, listing all of the tasks in the product development cycle, with deadlines for each. Next, merchandisers develop detailed line plans. The **line plan** shows the number of styles in the line, the number and general types of fabrics and yarns to be used, the colors per style, the anticipated stock-keeping units (SKUs), and the approximate preferred costs. The line plan not only gives product developers guidelines from which to work and focuses their efforts in a distinct direction but also takes into account fabric and yarn minimums and lead times. Merchandisers often work on different phases of several seasons at once.

Typical responsibilities of the merchandiser include the following:

- Researching the market, including tracking market trends and attending trade shows

- Fashion forecasting

- Attending consumer focus groups

- Shopping the competition

- Scouting fabric and trim markets

- Analyzing past sales, markdowns, and market trends within the retail operation

- Developing the merchandising calendar and line plan

- Creating design concepts with the product developers

- Calculating cost estimates for new products

- Directing and participating in line presentations

- Choosing and quantifying which styles will actually be produced, sometimes prior to sales (referred to as **production authorization**)

- Sourcing, in some cases

- Fostering a creative environment so technical design and sourcing staffs can do their best work

Qualifications

To achieve a career as a retail merchandiser, consider obtaining the following qualifications:

- *Education.* A bachelor's degree in fashion merchandising, fashion design, product development, retailing, or a related field is required.

- *Experience.* The merchandiser is sometimes promoted from within the product development department or division, having worked on the sourcing or technical design staff, for example. Three to five years of on-the-job experience in product development is preferred. In some cases, highly skilled merchandisers from the retail side of the business may be hired for this position in a manufacturing firm, and vice versa.

- *Personal characteristics.* The merchandiser is an excellent communicator—orally, visually, and in writing. Thorough market knowledge, a keen fashion sense, strong analytical skills, creativity, and an astute marketing instinct are essential characteristics. Successful merchandisers are continually cognizant of the market environment and the target customer and make well-informed decisions quickly and confidently. In companies that manufacture the majority of their product lines overseas, fluency in the languages of the countries where production takes place can be very helpful.

Career Challenges

The merchandiser is a planner. You know—or perhaps you are—this type of person, with your schedule drafted months in advance, telephone numbers and addresses at your fingertips, and a to-do list in a constant state of addition and completion. The merchandiser thinks creatively and quantitatively. The product lines are viewed from many perspectives—what will be in fashion, how much will it cost to manufacture a product, which items will the customer purchase, and what is the competition doing. The successful merchandiser must be a sponge, soaking up all of the variables that affect whether a product will sell. When a line doesn't sell, the merchandiser may be held responsible for figuring out why it didn't sell and for making certain it doesn't happen again. Stressful? It can be.

Sourcing Staff

Sourcing—locating components and producers of the final product—was discussed in Chapter 3 as it relates to the primary level of the industry, manufacturers of fashion merchandise. Sourcing in product development for the retailer is much the same as it is for the manufacturer. The primary difference, in most cases, is that the retailer often finds and hires contractors to produce private-label lines, rather than building or purchasing factories to manufacture the lines. The sourcing staff of a product development team is responsible for finding the best possible fabrics, findings, trims, and manufacturers to make the designers' lines reality. Members of the sourcing staff may specialize in specific categories, such as belting or trims. They may also travel extensively to locate parts of the product or a manufacturer for the product.

The sourcing staff often works with a sales forecast to determine the amount of product components needed. A **sales forecast** is created by the product development director and merchandiser, in conjunction with the sourcing staff. It includes projections of sales by category, style, color, and size based on historical data and statistical analysis. This information may be used to place preliminary fabric and trim orders and block out production time in factories. As the sourcing staff must often place orders early, an accurate sales forecast is critical to deliveries made at the right time and in the right amount.

Qualifications

To become a member of a company's sourcing staff, one should have the following qualifications:

- *Education.* Usually employers require a bachelor's degree in fashion design, fashion merchandising, product development, project management, or a related field.

- *Experience.* In many corporations, sourcing personnel are promoted from the technical design staff or are hired with assistant designer experience from outside of the company.

- *Personal characteristics.* Sourcing personnel pay attention to detail and have efficient organizational skills and strong written and oral communication abilities. They are "born to shop," comparing quality, price, and availability in product parts and production requirements.

Career Challenges

Sourcing staff personnel face the task of finding the best product or product parts at the best price, in the right quantity, and in a timely fashion. Many are required to travel globally and frequently. Negotiations can be tough when working with people from different cultures, with or without an interpreter. The abilities to shop until you drop and then communicate effectively and negotiate successfully take a great deal of flexibility and stamina.

Product Development Designer

Product development designers (sometimes called *private-label designers*) are the creators of the product line for a manufacturer or a retailer. For example, Fossil manufactures a collection of watches under the Donna Karan label and has product development designers working on this collection each season. From a retail perspective, MMG at Macy's has design teams working on each of its company-branded lines, from I.N.C. to Hotel Collection. They are trend forecasters in their own right by determining what their customers will be ready for next. They go through the design process with each new season. Table 7.1 shows monthly activities for product development by season.

The **design process** refers to the conception of a style, to include its inspiration or theme, color palette, fabric selection, form, and fit. Product development designers must be adept at synthesizing a variety of fashion influences while acknowledging marketability and fulfilling customer wants and needs. An important designer trait is the art of compromise. These designers must balance the desired fashion look of a product and the highest possible quality standards with a price tag that is acceptable to the target customer.

After determining the style, color, fabric, and trend concepts, designers begin sketching individual styles, usually with a particular form, or silhouette, in mind that epitomizes the fashion trends for the upcoming season. They may repeat versions of this silhouette throughout the line. Some styles may be completely original, but sometimes designers will adapt a style from an actual garment found on a shopping expedition or in a magazine. Most lines include at least a few **carryovers**, updated bestsellers from a previous season. The designers will be careful to include important basics and to balance each group with the help of the merchandiser. Many companies ask for estimated costs from factories before samples are made, so that styles can either be dropped or adjusted when the line is still in sketch form. Oversampling is quite expensive, so the merchandiser will generally try to keep it under control. When a complete group of styles is finalized, all of the sketches are placed on a line sheet so the group may be seen at a glance.

Typical tasks of the designer may include the following:

- Shopping the retail market, sometimes with merchandisers or a member of the sourcing staff, for design ideas and knowledge of the competition; buying samples

- Shopping the fabric, yarn, and trim markets

Table 7.1 Product Development Activity Calendar

Activity	Fall	Holiday/Resort	Spring	Summer
Design/Development	January/February	April/May	July/August	November/December
Selling and Show Dates	February/March	June/August	September/October	January
Producing Orders Begins	May	August	November	February
Shipping Starts	July	October	January	April
Shipping Completed	September	Early December	Early March	Early May

- Attending trend forecasting meetings

- Developing **color palettes**, groups of colors, and **colorways**, combinations or pairings of colors

- Determining the styling direction of the line and creating concept boards or storyboards

- Shopping the print market and buying print paintings for textile development

- Developing styles through sketching garments by hand or on a computer

- Recoloring garments or prints

- Designing embroideries, screen prints, and appliqués

- Writing specification sheets

- Corresponding with factories or in-house sample departments regarding drapes, patterns, and garment construction

- Attending fit meetings

These tasks vary, often depending on the size of the company for which the designer works. Some of the larger companies may assign some of these tasks, such as writing specifications or developing color palettes, to more specialized personnel, such as technical designers or colorists.

Qualifications

Designers on product development teams are likely to have the following qualifications:

- *Education.* A bachelor's degree in fashion design, product development, fashion merchandising, or a related field is a minimum requirement.

- *Experience.* Employment as an assistant designer or technical designer is an excellent stepping-stone to the position of designer. These entry-level positions provide knowledge of fabrics, construction, and fit. Additionally, the designer needs prior experience in PC software, such as spreadsheets, imagery, and word processing. Many employers require designers to have CAD experience.

- *Personal characteristics.* Successful designers have excellent organizational skills and pay attention to detail. They can create an image of the final product, either on a drawing pad or on the computer. Because much business is conducted in Asian countries, foreign language skills in languages such as Mandarin and Japanese are a plus.

Career Challenges

The successful designer must know the retailer's customer well, because knowing the customer's likes and dislikes minimizes the designer's fashion risks. Designers must be able to multitask with the best, often working on two or more collections at one time. Working with color, silhouettes or forms, fabric, and trend themes, they are challenged to create collections. It may be difficult to find new sources of inspiration and to find a common theme to weave among the items in a collection. In addition, product development designers must balance aesthetics with price, a decision that sometimes compromises their vision of the initial design concept. They must constantly remember the customer for whom they are designing, rather than incorporating their personal tastes.

Colorist

A **colorist** in product development chooses the color combinations that will be used in creating the product lines. Colorists need a strong knowledge of textiles. They need to be able to ascertain, for example, how a print design will be produced, how the finished article will be used, how the fabric will react to dyes and finishes, and how big or limited the budget is.

Colorists frequently travel to trade and fashion markets and subscribe to color-forecasting publications to stay on top of current and future color trends. They observe what the customers purchase, or do not buy, to understand their needs and interpret their color preferences accurately. Colorists collaborate with marketing, buying, and technical staff members, as well as design colleagues, on color trends and preferences. They often conduct research for ideas and inspiration, in such diverse areas as historical costume, architecture, art, and global destinations. Color inspiration can come from anywhere. After determining a color palette for the season, the colorist produces boards, swatches, or other visuals to present the color ideas to the product development team.

■ **Figure 7.9**
An example of a dress design and the fabrics selected to construct it from Todd & Duncan and Pitti Textiles.

Colors and patterns are constantly changing in the fashion industry. Specific terminology is used to describe outcomes in this area of product development: labdips, colorways, and strike-offs. As soon as colors and fabrics have been determined, the design and color staff must decide whether any of the colors will be custom dyed in any of the fabrics. If so, original color standards must be sent to the dyeing mills or fabric companies so that dye formulations may be created. The mills will send **labdips**, small swatches of the dyed fabric, to the product development team for color approval before dyeing large yardages of fabric. Organizing and approving labdips may consume a significant amount of a colorist's time.

Printed fabric may be purchased from different companies, but sometimes a designer will want to include a print on the line that is exclusive to the company. This requires that the designer develop a print on the computer or by hand, or that the company buy a **croquis**, a painting of the print. It will be examined in terms of its repeat and colorways, or the color composition, will be decided. When these projects are finalized, the print image is sent to a printing mill. The mill will print a few yards of fabric, called a **strike-off**, and send it to the product developer (i.e., colorist or designer) for approval before it is made into a sample (Figure 7.9).

Qualifications

Following are the qualifications for a successful colorist:

- *Education.* A bachelor's degree in visual arts, fine arts, computer-aided design, graphic design, fashion design, textiles, or a related discipline is a minimum requirement.

- *Experience.* Technical designers, particularly those with experience in textiles, may move into the position of colorist. An understanding of how a textile will be used, what properties it needs in order to function optimally, and how the addition of color dyes or surface treatments will affect these properties is critical to the colorist's work. Two to five years' experience in design is often a prerequisite for this position. One of the paths to move into the position of colorist is to work as an assistant to the colorist. Some fortunate college students are able to secure internships in the color department of a product development division. Prospective employers often require the candidate to have a strong and relevant portfolio of work for review.

- *Personal characteristics.* The colorist must keep up to date with fashion and population trends—current and projected—while staying on top of new design and production processes. Flexibility, computer skills, the ability to meet deadlines, and effective business skills make colorists successful. They have an exceptional eye for discerning and recalling colors. A strong network of color expertise, from trade organizations to publications to peers, supports the colorist's own expertise. The successful colorist has the ability to identify color trends that evolve from such external influences as major art exhibitions, timely couturiers, and popular travel destinations.

Career Challenges

The colorist is part chemist, part artist, and part fashion forecaster. It takes a wealth of skills in many areas. This person must maintain extremely high standards and pay careful attention to detail. It is critical that the colorist be an effective communicator. Think about describing a specific color to someone and explaining it so effectively that this person can actually mix the paint for the exact color. It is not an easy task. Colorists most often work standard hours, but they need to be flexible to meet deadlines, especially prior to market week or production deadlines.

Textile Technical Designer

A **textile technical designer** creates new textile designs or modifies existing textile goods, altering patterns or prints that have been successful on the retail floor to turn them into fresh, new products. The textile technical designer will develop color alternatives for a modified fabric print or pattern or work with a colorist to accomplish this task. Most textile technical designers work on computers to create or modify designs. An example of a popular fashion product and textile design software program is Kaledo by Lectra, as shown in Figures 7.10a and b. Technical textile designers can work in several specialized areas, including wovens, knits, or prints. For example, a technical textile designer may work primarily with either sweater knits or woven shirtings. The textile technical designer who specializes in prints often uses a computer-aided design program to create a croquis.

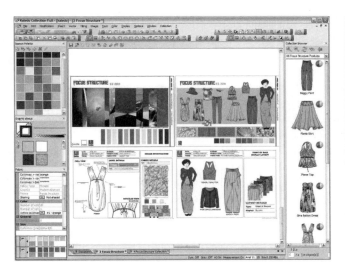

■ Figures 7.10a and b
Kaledo is a popular software program developed by Lectra, used for fashion production and textile design.

Qualifications

The following is a list of qualifications for the career path of a textile technical designer:

- *Education.* A bachelor's degree in textiles, textile technology, fashion design, computer-aided design, graphic design, fine arts, or a related discipline is a minimum requirement.

- *Experience.* Many textile technical designers begin in this position after college graduation. An internship in the technical design division of a retail corporation is an ideal way to open the door to this field.

- *Personal characteristics.* A textile technical designer has knowledge of textiles and their applications and usage, computer-aided design, and technical considerations as they relate to textile applications. An awareness of consumer wants and needs and an eye for color and patterns are essentials. The successful textile technical designer is simultaneously creative and technologically savvy.

Career Challenges

Textile technical designers live in a high-touch, high-tech world. They must understand the technical features of CAD and the production aspects of knit, woven, print, and textured fabrics. In addition, they must understand the feel, or hand, of a diverse array of fabrics and the application of each. Which types of fabrics are best suited for which products? How do these fabrics wear? What are the care factors for each? There is much to know in this field, in which new fabrics, computer technology, and manufacturing techniques arrive daily.

Product Development Pattern Maker

The **product development pattern maker** takes accurate measurements and develops a pattern, using either draping or flat pattern methods, which, if correctly developed, ensure that the designer's vision will be implemented. Specification lists, commonly referred to as **spec**

sheets, typically provide detailed measurements and construction guidelines. Designers may give pattern makers sketches and a few measurement specifications for guidance or may actually drape a garment to get the exact form they envisioned. Following the designers' approval, pattern makers develop detailed spec sheets. A spec sheet includes a technical sketch, all of the measurements and tolerances, type and yardage of fabrication, and trim information. Different companies have their own spec sheet formats, but all of them have similar components. Each item on the spec sheet can have a critical impact on cost and on production of the item. The components of a spec sheet are illustrated in Figure 7.11.

Some retail product developers have additional challenges. They often do not employ in-house pattern makers and do much of the manufacturing in faraway factories, where the factories' pattern makers do the work. They frequently have to complete whole spec packages to send overseas that tell factories every detail of what will be required to engineer a style. Spec sheets are often used to calculate estimated costing, so that items can be adjusted or canceled before a costly sample is made. If the company does not employ the technical staff to write specifications, it can contract with pattern-making and CAD companies that will write specs and prepare detailed spec sheets.

Qualifications

Following are the qualifications for a pattern maker on a product development team:

- *Education.* A bachelor's degree in fashion design, product development, or a related field is often required.

- *Experience.* If a position as a pattern maker's assistant is available, this position is often an entry for college graduates. Some technical designers and sample makers move into the pattern maker slot. Two to five years' experience is usually required for a key pattern-maker position. Effective skills in draping, flat pattern making, and CAD are necessary.

- *Personal characteristics.* The product development pattern maker is, in essence, an engineer. A keen attention to detail, the ability to construct almost every type of garment, and a passion for accuracy are necessary characteristics of successful pattern makers.

Career Challenges

Pattern makers must work with accuracy and speed on details. If a pattern piece is one-eighth inch smaller than it should be, the entire garment may not be able to be produced. Even if it can be manufactured, it may not fit, or it may have a design flaw. That is a large responsibility to bear. Many of the people who are interested in pattern making enjoy methodical and detailed work—engineering of sorts. What they often do not enjoy is the pressure of deadlines. With the influx of computerized pattern making, some pattern makers are finding full-time employment difficult to secure and are working in freelance capacities.

Quality Control Manager

The **quality control manager** of a product development team is responsible for the initial inspection of sample garments and the final inspection of stock garments from the manufacturer. The quality control manager checks fabric, fit, and construction for quality and adherence to

Dress Spec Sheet

NAME:			DATE:			
SEASON: **SPRING**		STYLE: **CHEONG SAM**	SIZE:	**14 PRETEEN**		
DESCRIPTION: **MANDARIN COLLAR, CAP SLEEVES, FRONT FROG DETAILS AND BACK ZIPPER CLOSURE**						
FABRICATION: **97% POLYESTER, 3% SPANDEX**						
ACCESSORIES:		TRIM: **1-19" INVISIBLE ZIPER, 2 FROGS W/ 15 LIGHE KNOTTED BUTTONS**				

		FRONT	BACK	TOTAL	COMMENTS
1	NECK DROP	2.75	0.25		
2	NECK – WIDTH	7.00			
3	NECK CIRCUMFERENCE	9.00	8.00	17.00	
4	SHOULDER – LENGTH	4.00			
5	ACROSS SHOULDER			14.50	
6	LENGTH *				
	a. HPS	32.00	32.00		
	b. CF/CB	29.25	31.75		
	c. Side			23.50	
7	ACROSS BACK		14.00		4" FROM CB
8	ACROSS CHEST	16.50	16.50	33.00	
9	WAIST – LENGTH *				
	a. CF/CB	11.25	13.75		
	b. HPS	14.00	14.00		
10	ACROSS WAIST				
	a. Relaxed	15.50	16.00	31.50	
	b. Extended				
11	HIGH HIP	16.00	16.50	32.50	3" FROM WAIST
12	LOW HIP	17.50	18.00	35.50	6" FROM WAIST
13	BOTTOM EDGE OPENING (SWEEP)	20.00	20.00	40.00	
14	HPS TO UNDERARM	9.50			
15	ARMHOLE CIRCUMFERENCE	8.50	9.50	18.00	
16	UPPER SLEEVE – WIDTH				
17	SLEEVE – LENGTH *				
	a. Overarm	3.50			
	b. Underarm				
	c. CB		11.00		
	d. HPS		7.50		
18	ELBOW				
19	SLEEVE HEM/CUFF OPENING				
	a. Relaxed	5.00	4.00	9.00	
	b. Extended				
20	DEPTH OF SLEEVE HEM			0.25	
21	CUFF HEIGHT				
22	DART				
	a. Placement – CF/CB to top of dart	3.50	3.50		
	b. Placement – HPS to top of dart	10.50	10.00		
	c. Placement – CF/CB to bottom of dart	3.50	3.75		
	d. Placement – HPS to bottom of dart	18.00	18.00		
	e. Dart – Length	7.50	8.00		
23	BINDING WIDTH/HEM			1.00	
24	BUTTON PLACEMENT	SEE FROGS			

REMARKS/OTHER SPECS/STITCHING: All measurements in inches; all graphs drawn at .125" = 1" scale

COLLAR STAND - FRONT/BACK 1"

YOKE SEAM - LEFT SIDE ONLY
  CF TO ARMHOLE L - 6.5"
  HPS TO YOKE TOP 3.25"
  HPS TO YOKE BOTTOM 5.5"

SIDE SLITS 2"

2 FROGS
  L - 2.25"
  W - .875"

FROG 'A'
CF TO TOP - .75
CF TO BOTTOM 2"
HPS TO TOP 3"
HPS TO BOTTOM 5.25

FROG 'B'
CF TO TOP 4.75"
CF TO BOTTOM 3.75"
HPS TO TOP 4"
HPS TO BOTTOM 6.25"

STITCH - SN .25" FROM EDGE -
ARMHOLE SLEEVE HEM,
SIDE SLIT

SN AT EDGE - YOKE

SN - HEM

BAR TAC - TOP OF SLIT

* Circle method for measuring   Abbreviations: high point of shoulder (HPS), center front (CF), center back (CB), single needle (SN)

■ **Figure 7.11**
Example of a spec sheet for a dress.

product specification guidelines. In a large company, this person is responsible for training the quality control staff and for developing specific guidelines and standards for the department.

Qualifications

The background and characteristics of a successful quality control manager in the retail setting are as follows:

- *Education.* An associate of arts degree in fashion design, product development, or a similar field is required. A bachelor's degree is preferred.

- *Experience.* Knowledge of textiles and clothing construction is required. Two to four years of experience in quality control are expected as a prerequisite for this supervisory position. The quality control manager must have a solid understanding of garment construction, garment specifications, and spec sheets.

- *Personal characteristics.* The quality control manager should possess an excellent eye for detail and a commitment to high standards. Bilingual skills may be necessary, depending on the location of the manufacturing facilities. Excellent communication and people skills are important.

Career Challenges

The quality control manager must maintain excellent standards and oversee every detail of production from beginning to conclusion. It can be a high-pressure job with little recognition. The product development team, the retail personnel, and the customers assume that products will be made correctly and will perform well. When this is not the case, the white-hot spotlight shines on the quality control manager.

Summary

Product development describes the processes needed to bring a product, or product line, from conception and manufacturing to marketing and sales. In this chapter, product development conducted by both the manufacturer and the retailer is examined. The three main reasons retailers moved into the business of developing their own product lines include satisfying specific merchandise needs of their customers, creating exclusive products unique to their particular companies, and generating higher profit margins. Several product development classifications have evolved as retailers and manufacturers increasingly engage in the customizing of product lines. These classifications include retail label, private label, private brand, direct market brand, and licenses.

As a result of this move into product development, large manufacturing and retail companies are major employers of product development staffs. The careers in this field include director of product development, merchandiser, sourcing staff, designer, colorist, textile technical designer, pattern maker, and quality control manager. The director of product development is ultimately responsible for the strategic planning of the division, specifying exactly what the company will make and market, as well as when it will do this. The merchandiser collaborates with the director of product development in deciding what to produce and then organizes and manages the entire product development process. The sourcing staff of a product development team is responsible for finding the best possible fabrics, findings, trims, and manufacturers to make the designers' lines a reality. The product development designer is the creator of the merchandise lines. The colorist chooses the color combinations that will be used in creating the product lines. Using this color direction, the textile technical designer creates new fabric designs or modifies existing textile goods by altering patterns or prints that have been successful on the retail floor to turn them into fresh, new products. The pattern maker uses draping, flat pattern, or computer-aided pattern-making methods to develop a pattern that uses these textile options and implements the designers' vision. The quality control manager reviews the final product for fit, durability, and overall quality. Together, the product development team brings exclusive merchandise developed specifically to appeal to an exclusive target market from conception to reality.

Endnotes

1. www.macysinc.com/AboutUs/
2. Kirsteen Buchanan, Stephens College, Columbia, Missouri, 2013.

Key Terms

brick-and-click store
brick-and-mortar store
carryover
color palette
colorist
colorway
contractor
croquis
cross-shopping
decentralized buying
design-driven brand
design process
direct competition
direct market brand
director of product development
exclusive
fashion exclusivity
fast fashion
knockoff

labdip
line plan
merchandiser
merchandising calendar
merchandising-driven brand
private brand
private label
product development
product development designer
product development pattern maker
production authorization
quality control manager
retail label
retailer
sales forecast
spec sheet
strike-off
textile technical designer

Online Resources

retailinginfocus.wordpress.com/tag/forever-21/

corporate.target.com/careers/career-areas/product-design-development

www.careerthreads.com/CareersProductDev.html

www.forbes.com/sites/barbarathau/2013/12/06/why-uniqlo-chose-a-forever-21-veteran-to-lead-its-u-s-business/

www.wwd.com/fashion-news/fashion-scoops/banana-republic-marimekko-team-up-7387037

www.forbes.com/sites/lydiadishman/2013/06/12/can-private-labels-restore-j-c-penneys-profits/

www.wwd.com/fashion-news/fashion-features/first-lady-michelle-obamas-lesson-in-fashion-7973141

Discussion Questions

1. What are your predictions for the future of private-label merchandise by retailers? Will it increase, decrease, or remain the same, and why?
2. This chapter mentions that a few of the product categories retailers place in product development include basic apparel, jeans, and product categories that have a lower level of competition from major brands. Provide specific examples of brands in the latter product categories (those with less competition from national brands), and identify retailers that have succeeded in these merchandise classifications.
3. Develop a line plan for a small private-label jean line. Specify the season of the line, then identify the number of styles, colors, size ranges, and price points that are in your line. Provide word descriptions and visuals for the line, such as magazine clippings, Internet images, or sketches.

Profile: Interview with Technical Designer Nicole Narain

By Amanda Irel Sajecki

Nicole Narain is a young lady who is succeeding in New York City's fashion industry. As an FIT graduate with a degree in Fashion Design, specializing in intimate apparel, Nicole landed a position as an Assistant Technical Designer at Yummie Tummie.

Using all of her personal drive and diligence, coupled with her natural creativity, Nicole is proof that you don't have to be born into connections to make it in NYC's fast-paced, high-stakes fashion industry. We recently sat down with Nicole to bring you some tips and tricks to pursuing your dream career.

(continued)

When did you first become interested in design?

I used to try to make costumes for my Barbie dolls and have runway shows with them. Something tells me it started there.

What inspired you to pursue a degree in fashion design?

I'm really lucky to have amazing and supportive parents. They always encouraged me to pursue my passions in life. I was able to take fashion illustration classes in my high school. I had a lot of fun in that class. I practiced fashion illustration every chance I had.

How did you decide the specific area of fashion in which you studied?

When I went to F.I.T., I had to pick specialization for my last semester of the associate's degree, and a specialization for my last year and a half for the bachelor's degree. When it came time to pick one for my bachelor's degree, I looked at everything I had studied and I realized I had never studied intimate apparel. We had a "Boned Bodice" project coming up, but that was it. I really wanted to learn something new. It just so happens that I fell in love with it.

What are the top five pieces of advice you can offer to someone applying to a fashion school?

1. If you are applying to be a design major, know how to sew. I can't stress this enough.
2. Know that you're entering a very competitive environment.
3. You don't always get in right away, but that doesn't mean you won't get in.
4. Learn to live without sleep.
5. Become an early bird. The early bird is always first to get the better dress form.

How were you able to transform your studies into a career?

My school's major focus was not on drawing great designs, but creating them. We learned how to sew and drape different fabrics, and what different fabrics are used for. We learned how to alter patterns. There was a lot of learning from mistakes as well. Currently, I am an Assistant Technical Designer. A technical designer has to know what works and has to instruct factories on how to create the desired garment. My entire four years of studies were a great preparation for this.

What inspires your current designs?

One of my favorite sources for inspiration are fairy tales.

How much of your own design can you incorporate into your current job role?

None. It's not a technical designer's role to do any of the actual designing; however, there are designers that design in a technical way. They can be the most creative because they know all the different possibilities on how to construct what they want.

How do you stay inspired? Where do you look for inspiration?

Inspiration can be found everywhere and anywhere. The only trick about inspiration is what inspires you. For me, it can be as simple as what I have to work with. I like searching for fabric and different trims. Once I have that, I get to play around with them on my dress form and see what I create.

Who is the designer you most admire?

Alexander McQueen is my biggest idol.

What does it take to "make it" in the industry?

You can "make it" in any industry as long as you work hard, put yourself out there, and just don't ever give up, even when you feel like it's just not going to happen and you should give up.

Any plans for the future of your designs?

You'll have to stay tuned.

Source:

www.thefashionpotential.com

chapter 8

Promotion for the Designer and Manufacturer

Picture a new fashion designer who has recently been featured in magazines, in blogs, on Twitter, and on television. As if it happens overnight, the former Mr. Unknown becomes a significant name and face to fashion industry professionals and fashion followers. When you peruse a fashion magazine, such as *Vogue*, *In Style*, or *W*, you are inundated by promotion in the forms of glossy and, sometimes, eyebrow-raising advertisements of fashion brands such as Kate Spade, Cynthia Rowley, Versace, and Gucci. You may also see editorial pieces on celebrities who wear these designs or about the designers themselves. Examples of fashion promotion include the home decor article about the pink Manhattan apartment designed by Betsey Johnson (Figure 8.1) and the one featuring her custom-made Kentucky Derby hat (Figure 8.2).

Through a major television series, *Mad Men*, costume designer Janie Bryant placed the spotlight on the late 1950s and 1960s-era apparel—and the online and brick-and-mortar retailers of vintage clothing—through her selection of sleek and structured suits for men, curve-hugging dresses and cardigans for office secretaries, and glamorous gowns and furs for women to wear to swanky dinner parties (Figures 8.3a and b). Magazine articles, advertisements, and editorial pieces, all of these forms of promotion, resulted from the "Mad Men" fashion trend. **Promotion** refers to the endorsement of a person, a product, an idea or cause, or an organization. The ultimate goal of promotion is to encourage the growth, exposure, and development of an individual, product, idea, or company by advancing it to a higher position in the public's mind.

■ **Figure 8.1**
Part of the Manhattan
apartment designed
by Betsey Johnson
and featured in fashion
and shelter magazines
worldwide.

■ **Figure 8.2**
Betsey Johnson in her custom
Kentucky Derby Hat.

Let's look back at the promotional steps that could have led up to some of Janie Bryant's wardrobing choices for *Mad Men*. The designer/owner of a vintage-look line hired someone to write a press release about her line and to photograph the selections that the designer wanted the costumer to buy. These were sent to Ms. Bryant, the television stylist. She was intrigued and ordered 1960s-look garments and accessories, which were shipped to the wardrobe studio. With this great news, the designer contacted the promotion director of the public relations firm representing her company, who then contacted magazine editors and pitched this story. Numerous print and Web articles featured the designer, the retail stores that carried her line, and her Web site; orders piled in. All of these activities fit into the field of promotion.

The major tasks for a director or manager in promotion involve (1) understanding the significance of public relations, (2) recognizing the costs and uses of various advertising vehicles, (3) never underestimating the importance of selling, (4) creating a network of contacts in the field of promotion, (5) finding hooks, or topics of interest, for each media source, and (6) organizing sponsorships and partnerships, especially via the Internet, for fashion businesses and events. Promotion directors work diligently to find themes or topics that the media will want to cover and to tie these into the businesses of their clients. For example, a promotion director may work for a major apparel manufacturer/designer, such as Nicole Miller. When Nicole Miller introduces her new home accessories lines of bed linens, pillows, photograph frames, and dinnerware, the public relations director may schedule her to appear at some key retail stores around the country. In conjunction with these retail partner arrangements, the promotion director will contact the media and fashion organizations in each city to generate news coverage of the designer's appearances in the retail stores.

■ **Figure 8.3a**
In *Mad Men*, costume designer Janie Bryant placed the spotlight on apparel from the late 1950s and 1960s through her selection of sleek and structured suits for men and glamorous gowns and sheath dresses for women.

■ **Figure 8.3b**
Today's interpretation of Joan's *Mad Men* signature look.

The interrelationship between these promotional tasks illustrates the teamwork and versatility required by the industry: from glossy magazines through advertising and feature stories to visual media with its videos of backstage happenings before shows and events and front-of-house press dossiers and seating plans. The term **promotion product** can refer to an item, such as a press release or an advertisement, or an event, such as a fashion show or music video.

Career opportunities in fashion promotion exist in the industry sectors of apparel and accessories; home furnishings and accessories; publishing, art, and music; image and style consultancy; photography, illustration, and digital visual imagery; and styling of all kinds, from music groups to television and theater celebrities, broadcast media and DVDs, to the Internet. General areas of study provide a strong foundation for future employees in all career tracks within the fashion promotion industry. An understanding of merchandising and marketing will be used consistently in all fashion promotion career options. Knowledge of computer-aided design and graphics provides an employee in this area of the industry with the skills to communicate a design concept through drawings and board presentations. Knowledge of public relations and advertising is a key component of all promotional careers. Journalism skills prepare the fashion promotion candidate for fashion writing, whether in commentary scripts, advertising copy, press releases, or editorial features in consumer or trade publications.

Consumer and Trade Publications

What is the difference between consumer and trade publications? A **consumer publication** is readily available to the layperson, the general customer. The consumer may subscribe to the periodical, online or in print, or purchase it at a store. Nearly all consumer lifestyle publications feature some type of fashion content (e.g., *People, Town & Country,* and *Travel*); some are devoted exclusively to fashion and interior design. Examples of fashion consumer publications include *Vogue, In Style, House & Garden, W,* and *Elle*; the list goes on and on (Figure 8.4). Most magazines with a nationwide readership are headquartered in New York City.

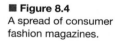
■ Figure 8.4
A spread of consumer fashion magazines.

PLUS:
DAPHNE PLAYS DEAD
EYE: Daphne Guinness was covered in a shroud at a party in London.
PAGE 9

WWD

TUESDAY, JULY 5, 2011 ■ WOMEN'S WEAR DAILY ■ $3.00

Turnaround Time

The showing of Christian Dior haute couture is always a hotly anticipated event. That proved true on Monday afternoon, but under wildly atypical circumstances. Studio director Bill Gaytten and first assistant Susanna Venegas gamely pulled out all the stops while working to invoke the famed aesthetic John Galliano brought to the house. The result, as seen in this look, was graphic, colorful and at times fun, yet ultimately proved too daunting in this most exacting of fashion arenas. For more couture, see pages 6 to 8.

PARIS
Couture Fall 2011

PHOTO BY GIOVANNI GIANNONI

OPPORTUNITY KNOCKS

Survey: Fashion's Job Market Rallies

By ARNOLD J. KARR

IT'S TIME FOR FASHION COMPANIES TO PONY UP.
The recent recession sharply curtailed opportunities for better jobs, higher salaries and improved benefits, but those doors are opening up once again. And smart managers need to reconsider what they have to offer if they want to attract and retain top talent.

That's among the inescapable conclusions of the 2011 Salary Survey and Job Market Report released today by 24 Seven, the New York-based talent recruitment firm, in connection the American Apparel & Footwear Association.

The hottest, most in-demand jobs include apparel design, social media-related posts and luxury brand management and sales. Visual merchandising and graphic design posts are expected to become more prosperous career paths as well.

One thing is clear: retaining talent isn't getting any easier. Job candidates, especially younger ones, are aggressively pursuing new opportunities, and many are finding them. A full 31 percent of the more than 2,000 respondents to the survey have been in their jobs less than a year, and just over half — 51 percent — said they are actively searching for a new job, versus 36 percent who are taking a "passive" approach to job hunting and just 13 percent who aren't testing the waters.

Nearly seven in 10 — 68 percent — are considering a career move in the next year. Among all those surveyed, a higher base salary was the most popular reason for looking for a new job (67 percent), but better growth potential (57 percent) and improved quality of life (39 percent) also scored high.

The survey strongly suggested that mobility yields substantial financial benefits. Those who've moved into a new job within the past 12 months
SEE PAGE 12

IN WWD TODAY

Jason Wu Strides Forward PAGE 12
ACCESSORIES: The designer collaborates with Melissa Shoes on a footwear line. ▲

Saks Builds Wear PAGE 4
FASHION: Saks Fifth Avenue is aiming to reinvent the former bridge market by renovating its fourth-floor Wear department.

Prada Exercises Option PAGE 2
FINANCIAL: Prada raised another $321 million by exercising the overallotment option of its initial public offering.

■ **Figure 8.5**
Women's Wear Daily is a print and Web news vehicle that focuses on different merchandise types each day of the week and often features broader fashion news, such as general retail trends in sales or mergers and acquisitions in the fashion industry.

In contrast, **trade publications** are designed for readers who are interested in or employed in specific professions or vocations. These magazines and newspapers are promoted to people in a specific career field. Other publications provide information about a wide range of merchandise classifications to retailers, designers, manufacturers, and buyers. The top publication in women's apparel and accessories is *Women's Wear Daily*, a print and Web news source that focuses on different merchandise types each day of the week and often features broad-scope fashion news, such as general retail trends in sales or mergers and acquisitions in the fashion industry (Figure 8.5).

Fashion Stylist

A **fashion stylist** is the person who does most of the work before the cameras start shooting, whether for a magazine, film, television series, fashion show, or a personal client. **Fashion photostylist** is the term used to specify the stylist who works with photography. Whether styling for a photograph or a fashion show, a stylist must be aware of the latest trends and bring great resources and a strong personal style to every event. **Fashion shoots**, photography sessions of models and fashions, are a team effort, and the stylist's role is critical to its success. Stylists are responsible for selecting and assembling the garments and accessories needed for the event and preparing the people involved in the event, such as the models, dressers, makeup artists, hairstylists, and lighting designers. Stylists must make decisions in minutes, quickly determining, for example, how various items of apparel are to be combined and accessorized to show each off to the best features. Stylists also handle a myriad of details, ensuring that the right sizes and colors are available for each model. If the models are celebrities, the appropriateness of the apparel to each of their images becomes an additional factor. Stylists must be diplomats to win the cooperation of everyone involved in an event. In addition to magazine work, stylists may find employment with advertising agencies, working on print ads or television commercials. Figure 8.6 features a fashion stylist working with a model in a photography studio.

■ **Figure 8.6**
A fashion stylist working with a model in a photography studio. The garments are created by Jennifer McKelvie from Tyvec building wrap material.

Qualifications

Do you have what it takes to pursue a career in fashion styling? Following is a list of qualifications for a fashion stylist:

- *Education.* A bachelor's degree in fashion design, fashion merchandising, fashion journalism, fashion communication, photography, visual arts, or a related field is preferred.

- *Experience.* An internship with a photographer or stylist is an excellent way to build one's résumé for employment in this industry. Some fashion stylists begin in visual merchandising or as an assistant to a stylist. Fashion stylists are often chosen based on the look of their "books," large volumes of tearsheets, or samples of work, from published print or Internet work to Polaroid or digital images that illustrate work they have done with different photographers and/or models. Digital portfolios and computer-aided design skills are beneficial.

- *Personal characteristics.* The attributes of successful fashion stylists include having a network of professionals in photography, hair and makeup design, and the modeling industry; a keen eye for detail; the ability to apply visual art principles to print work and photographs; effective verbal, written, and visual communication skills; strong time-management skills; and the ability to work well under pressure, whether with deadlines or uncontrollable factors, such as poor lighting during an outdoor shoot or models who miss their flights.

Career Challenges

Fashion stylist positions are often only available with large companies or as freelance work. It is a growing, exciting, and potentially profitable career track. Fashion stylists face many challenges, including quick decision making and coordinating a multitude of details. Because stylists must ensure that the correct apparel is available for the right models, they must do a great deal of preplanning for the expected and the unexpected, such as broken zippers, a late hairstylist, or models with attitude. "Plan ahead and be prepared for anything" is a motto for successful fashion stylists. Stylists must also work with all types of people and be able to motivate everyone involved in the shoot. It is not enough to have the vision; it is as important to have the skills to implement the vision.

Public Relations and Advertising Directors

Public relations directors are responsible for finding minimal or no-cost ways to effectively promote the designer or company they represent. They develop proposals that will put their clients in a favorable spotlight and persuade the media to feature press about the client. Public relations directors work with all types of media representatives, from television and radio producers to newspaper, magazine, Web site, and blog publishers. Some public relations companies specialize in fashion and represent designer and manufacturer clients. In addition, many of the designer firms, such as Gucci, Salvatore Ferragamo, and Tod's, have in-house public relations staffs.

Some of the activities that public relations directors develop include social events such as fashion shows, book signings, and parties; events that raise awareness for a fashion company or designer while generating funds and appreciation for a philanthropic cause; press coverage for

■ Figure 8.7
A fashion student works on an original design for the Vogue Knitting Magic of Mohair competition.

designers who are presenting new collections; and competitions for fashion students to submit original designs that will be produced by a major manufacturer (Figure 8.7).

While the public relations director is seeking out nonpaid ways to promote his or her company, the advertising director is determining how and where to spend money on promotional activities that will generate business and brand-loyal customers. **Advertising directors** develop and implement a company's paid promotional strategy for the purpose of increasing visibility, image, and, ultimately, sales. **Advertising** refers to a type of promotion that is a paid, nonpersonal communication delivered through mass media. Public relations and advertising directors generally work under the supervision of the promotion or marketing director.

Qualifications

Public relations and advertising directors should meet the following criteria:

- *Education.* A bachelor's degree in marketing, public relations, promotion, advertising, business administration, fashion merchandising, fashion design, or a related field is a minimum requirement.

- *Experience.* To move into the director position, one usually needs a minimum of eight to ten years of fashion public relations or advertising experience and must have an array of excellent contacts within the fashion and lifestyle media fields. Additionally, prospective public relations and advertising directors must compile portfolios of work samples to present at job interviews.

- *Personal characteristics.* Exceptional writing and oral communication skills are essential for public relations and advertising directors. They need to be creative, with a specialty in finding new ways to look at what may be perceived by others as old topics. They are described as possessing "excellent pitching skills," the ability to sell one's ideas in a persuasive and articulate manner. Budget management skills are also essential.

Career Challenges

Successful public relations and advertising directors are great salespeople, frequently selling (and reselling) a person's or company's image, ideas, and products. This person must have the ability to stay positive and enthusiastic in a world of repeated rejection. With so much going on in the fashion world, public relations and advertising directors are competing in a world of many vying for the attention of newspaper and magazine publishers, online publishers, and television producers. Finding creative ways to pitch stories and build relationships with ever-changing media representatives are challenges these directors face.

This career path is not all about selling, creating, and networking though. Public relations and advertising directors must have a head for numbers to meet the responsibility for finding cost-effective ways to promote the company. At some point in their careers, public relations directors will likely be confronted with countering negative publicity. In such cases, they must have the skills to work under the pressures of time and stress, quickly developing plans that will put the company in a favorable spotlight and persuading the media to feature positive press about the company.

Advertising Research and Promotion Positions

The major source of revenue for a Web and print publication is the sale of advertising space. Those who like to sell may find their niche as **advertising sales representatives**, the people who sell advertising for consumer and trade publications, such as *Glamour*, *Women's Wear Daily*, or *Lucky*. Other positions in fashion publications include those in advertising research and promotion. Many publications offer positions for those who prefer research. An **advertising research assistant** helps sell advertising space in a publication by supplying facts that advertisers will want to know, such as the number of issues sold, the top locations in terms of sales volume, and the profile and buying power of the publication's readers. These facts indicate the publication's ability to reach potential customers for the advertiser. The **advertising promotion staff**, yet another source of job opportunities, develops presentations to help sell advertising space to new and existing accounts. These people often have skills in persuasive writing and creative projects.

A related job option in advertising is that of **media planner**. Media planning is a statistical and mathematical process through which planners determine prices, including quantity discounts, for a media buy that may include several venues, such as radio, television, Internet, and newspaper. They determine how advertising budgets are best spent to generate the most exposure and sales.

Qualifications

Following is a list of qualifications for a career in advertising research and promotion:

- *Education.* A bachelor's degree in advertising, journalism, business administration, marketing, fashion merchandising, or a related field is required.

- *Experience.* Working in retail sales is a great way to get started while still in school. Selling is selling, whether it is for an apparel retailer or a newspaper publisher. Some students gain direct sales experience selling advertisements for college publications, such as the yearbook and programs for athletic events and theatrical performances. Some enter the advertising industry through copywriting and/or research jobs with newspapers or publishing firms and then move into the advertising sales representative position. Others gain experience at the retail level through a position in a store's advertising department, writing copy for advertised items, or laying out the actual advertisement.

- *Personal characteristics.* The ability to sell one's ideas is key to success in advertising. An understanding of budgets and accounting is necessary. With a high level of attention to detail, successful advertising professionals are focused on accuracy and fact checking.

Career Challenges

Advertising research and promotion personnel must gather data from all types of sources and then compile this research to tell a story—why their media vehicle is the best choice for advertisers to spend their promotional dollars. This job is not an easy one, because it combines the abilities of acquiring and interpreting data with strong writing skills. Advertising is a creative, numbers-based, and fast-paced field. Advertising research and promotion staff members need to stay up to date on all facets of the competition: their target markets, companies that advertise in their publications, and their advertising rates. As competition in this industry is constantly evolving, this is a time-consuming task.

Social Media Director

With the high-speed growth of Internet marketing, fashion public relations is jumping into social media with both feet, and a new career path has evolved—that of the social media director. **Social media** refers to the tools and social Web sites of the Internet that are used to communicate online with others. **Social Web sites**, such as Facebook, LinkedIn, Twitter, Pinterest, Vine, and Polyvore, function as online communities of Internet users. **Social networking** is the grouping of individuals into factions with similar interests. The Internet is filled with millions of individuals who are looking to develop friendships or professional alliances, to gather and share firsthand information and experiences about fashion and news, to find employment, and to market products. Twitter.com indicates that, in 2014, it had 225 million active monthly users sending 500 million tweets per day. To say that Twitter has a global reach is an understatement, as 77 percent of these accounts are outside of the United States. Box 8.1 highlights Diesel's use of Twitter to make customers an integral part of the company's fashion show. Although the fashion show was located in Venice, Italy, planes, trains, and gondolas were not needed for fans to be there.

The integration of Facebook, Twitter, Instagram, and the like into our daily lives has led to the development of the career position of social media director. The **social media director** develops, manages, and oversees the implementation of public relations programs in the social media venue. This includes creating content and generating coverage for social media efforts in all forms. Primary responsibilities of the social media director include the following:

- Managing and initiating strategic and creative planning of public relations campaigns through social media projects

Box 8.1 Diesel Tweets Venice

After one year with the company, fashion designer Nicola Formichetti made his Diesel debut with a big splash at the label's Autumn/Winter 2014 show in Venice. When Formichetti, the Artistic Director for Diesel, decided to debut his first full collection for the label in Venice, he knew that only so many people would be able to attend in person. To share the otherwise exclusive gathering more broadly as it happened, he gave fans around the world a view from the front row and a look behind the scenes on Twitter. Formichetti stated: "This event in Venice is intimate, but it's not about being exclusive. On the contrary, while we are not live-streaming it, we want to do something different and more contemporary and are supporting Twitter."

Formichetti and the Diesel staff organized groups of live-tweeting fashion influencers, pre- and post-show Q&As, behind-the-scenes Vine videos, and Twitter Mirrors backstage so fans would feel as if they were watching the show live at the Arsenale. Vine artist Jordan Burt created Vine videos to give fans a look behind the scenes, from fittings to interactions with the models. To capture all of the excitement, Diesel placed Twitter Mirrors backstage among the models and in the Twitter Lounge with VIP guests. The Twitter Mirrors tweeted photos with sneak peeks of hair, makeup, and design teasers that even invited guests hadn't yet seen.

Fashion editors with big followings were enlisted to tweet about the event from their seats. The editors, including Anna Dello Russo, fashion director of *Vogue Japan*; Eric Wilson, fashion news director of *InStyle*; Franca Sozzani, editor-in-chief of *Vogue Italia*; Imran Amed, editor-in-chief of *Business of Fashion*; and Joe Zee, creative director of *Elle Magazine*, took turns taking over the @Diesel account to answer fan questions, as did bloggers Suzie Bubble and Chiara Ferragni. Fans tweeted questions ranging from which models would walk the runway to which trend the editors believed was the biggest to come out of the show.

Diesel wanted to give fans not only a peek behind the curtain at what went into the preparation and creation of the show, but also a glimpse of what it was like to get to Venice. The fashion editors and industry influencers took to Twitter to document their travels to the show, giving Twitter users a feel for the ambience of Venice by live-tweeting their experiences leading up to the show—everything from their water taxi rides to the rush they felt when the first model walked the runway.

Whether you are part of an established brand, an up-and-coming designer, or a fashion blogger, your audience is on Twitter. It is a great way to make real human connections with customers, designers, editors, models, and others. This social media event showed great results for Diesel, which had 15 times its average daily follower growth on the day of the show.

Sources:

blog.twitter.com/2014/diesel-shows-fashion-on-twitter

www.fashiontimes.com/articles/4424/20140402/diesel-use-twitter-promote-fall-runway-show.htm

www.dazeddigital.com/fashion/article/19485/1/diesel-aw14

- Integrating projects with marketing, advertising, and promotional divisions

- Managing public relations agencies contracted by the company, if applicable

- Cultivating and developing productive relationships with social media contacts

- Managing press interviews with company executives

- Working to innovate and integrate the use of technology/social media into all public relations efforts

- Managing department resources—personnel and fiscal

Qualifications

Future social media directors should work to acquire the following qualifications:

- *Education.* A bachelor's degree in marketing, computer information systems, public relations, advertising, business administration, fashion merchandising, or a related field is a minimum requirement.

- *Experience.* To move into the director position, one usually needs a minimum of five to seven years of fashion public relations experience with an emphasis on social media. Broad knowledge of social media tools, current and future, is expected, as is a knowledge of traditional fashion press. A comprehensive understanding of competitors and their social networking outreach is a plus. Additionally, the candidate for a social media director position must present a portfolio of proposals.

- *Personal characteristics.* Excellent leadership and management skills are necessary tools. Successful social media directors are described as possessing excellent "futuring" skills, the ability to anticipate the next big thing in social networking. Budget management and human resource skills are also essential.

Career Challenges

The social media director is faced with the challenges of updating the social networking efforts of the company by the minute, hour, or day. The work must be ever-changing yet consistent. Conveying the company's image accurately and person-to-person through an online presence is critical. In addition, new online communities and media vehicles for people to connect to one another are popping up constantly. Anticipating which new social media will be the latest universal tie-in and which current one is the next to go out of favor are critical decisions for the social media director. Finding new topics and interesting ways to engage social media views is yet another significant challenge for the social media director.

Fashion Event Producer

Have you ever visited a pop-up shop? Viewed a fashion show production? Attended a trunk show? Participated in a bridal show extravaganza? If so, you have seen the handiwork of a **fashion event producer**, or *fashion event planner*, also referred to as a *special events coordinator*. Fashion event producers increase the visibility of design houses, brands, products, or fabrics by coordinating fashion events that provide positive exposure for the company.

Fashion Events

Fashion event producers coordinate and implement many occasions to promote an image, an idea, an organization, or a product. As discussed in the next section of this chapter, trunk shows in the designer salon of a department store, for example, may spotlight a new designer line. Another way to create exposure is through tearoom modeling for a women's organization or a community group at a country club or restaurant. A newer development in the fashion event sector, one that takes the fashion show or trunk show a step further, is the pop-up shop.

Whether you call them **pop-up shops** or pop-up stores, these projects are like hide-and-seek boutiques that pop up within other retail locations or at vacant retail spaces with few preliminary announcements. They quickly draw crowds, are open for a limited period, and then disappear or morph into something else. The designer's or manufacturer's goals for the pop-up stores are to add freshness, exclusivity, and surprise to their images and product lines, and to sell merchandise. Whether it is tagged mass exclusivity or planned spontaneity, it is working. In Box 8.2, Marc Jacob's Daisy fragrance is promoted by a pop-up shop that uses social media as currency. Figure 8.8 shows an example of a pop-up shop.

SOCIAL MEDIA STRIKES

Box 8.2 This Time in a Pop-up

Pop-up shops are not a new thing, especially during Fashion Week, but Marc Jacobs' fragrance division had a slightly different twist on promotion during spring 2014. Called the Daisy Marc Jacobs Tweet Shop and located in Manhattan's Soho district, this pop-up sold its wares to the sweet, sweet tune of zero dollars. It accepted a new kind of currency, the social kind—a tweet, Instagram, or Facebook post tagged #MJDaisyChain—in exchange for goods. The barter system has clearly gone high-tech. While posting photos to Instagram costs shoppers nothing, it gives Marc Jacobs an instant explosion of collective social marketing across social media platforms.

The shop opened in conjunction with the release of a new print campaign for Daisy. It did smell like fun with its lounge, a Daisy photo booth for selfies, refreshments, and Wi-Fi. On the walls, there were Daisy-themed artwork and a large projection highlighting the latest tweets and photos posted with the hashtag. The wall was refreshed every 30 seconds. Fragrances and Marc Jacobs accessories were on hand for shoppers to nab via tweet, Instagram, and Facebook. As a grand finale, the most creative social media posts won Marc Jacobs accessories throughout the day, ranging from perfume and necklaces to even purses (the best Instagram photo of the day won a handbag).

This wasn't the first time that Marc Jacobs' fragrance division has created consumer interest with its product promotion. When Honey launched last year, its debut was coupled with a Google Maps–powered campaign that showed Jacobs' favorite hotspots across various cities. There was an interactive map featuring the designer's very own London hotspots: Kew Gardens, Portabello Road, Duck and Waffle, Big Ben, Dalston Superstore, Shoreditch House, Tate Modern, Southbank, and The Clove Club. There was also a place for fans to contribute their favorites. When users uploaded their own spots to the interactive map, they were entered to win fragrance and clothing prizes. To sweeten the deal, customers at designated malls could pay a visit to the Marc Jacobs Ice Cream Van, which was giving out free Marc Jacobs Honey ice creams, fragrances, and more. What more can you ask for? Tweets traded for Marc Jacobs' products, a directory of fashionable hotspots, and yummy ice cream. Count me in.

Sources:

mashable.com/2014/02/06/marc-jacobs-tweet-store/

fashionista.com/2014/01/marc-jacobs-is-opening-a-fashion-week-pop-up-that-accepts-tweets-as-payment#awesm=~oHRok1wWDo5bZF

allfacebook.com/daisy-marc-jacobs-tweet-shop_b128708

■ Figure 8.8
The Tommy Hilfiger Prep World pop-up cottage in New York's Meatpacking District.

Some of the fashion experiences that fashion event producers develop and participate in are discussed in the following sections.

Bridal Shows

Through **bridal shows**, or bridal markets, wedding product or service manufacturer's reps and retail buyers are able to get together to review the new season's offerings. The bridal market is often organized in a convention center with booths that feature each of the vendors and with a fashion show as the main event. These are usually staged in the Fall before the Spring wedding season.

Informal Fashion Show

An **informal fashion show** is one without extravagant staging and technical assistance, often taking place in a conference center, hotel, or restaurant, in which models circulate among the tables as refreshments are served. The apparel manufacturer may team up with another organization and use this activity as a drawing card for an internal sales meeting or as an external fundraiser for a philanthropic cause. Instead of commentary, printed programs are often left at the place settings or on chairs to enable guests to read descriptions, prices, and size ranges of the featured garments and accessories at their leisure.

Trunk Shows

Through a **trunk show**, a fashion event producer or a manufacturer's representative brings the vendor's full seasonal line to a retail store that carries that particular manufacturer (Figure 8.9). The planner or representative works with individual customers, educating them about the line and providing personal fashion consultations. The customers can then place special orders. Sometimes, a trunk show in an upscale department or specialty store may feature a well-known designer, as well as the designer's latest collection (Figure 8.10).

■ **Figure 8.9**
Through a trunk show, a fashion event producer or a manufacturer's representative brings the vendor's full seasonal line to a retail store that carries that particular manufacturer.

■ Figure 8.10
Designer Stella
McCartney greets
guests at her trunk show
and party at Bergdorf
Goodman in New York.

Party Planning

In some instances, fashion event producers can literally be paid to party—prepare and manage the party, that is. **Party planning** can involve a manufacturer, a designer, a PR director, or an organization hiring a fashion event producer to put together a celebratory event (Figure 8.11). For example, a textile manufacturer may employ a fashion event producer to coordinate such an event during Fashion Week for retail buyers—potential and existing clients. The event producer arranges to have the showroom open after hours for the party and sends out invitations to the retail buyers who registered to attend the show, offering them a private showing of the new product line during the party. He or she works with the sales manager of the textile production firm to schedule sales associates for this evening event and locates a new restaurant and wine shop to serve complimentary appetizers and drinks in exchange for publicity. The event producer decorates the showroom and locates a desk and hostess at the entrance of the showroom to greet and sign in guests and to secure their contact information for future emails. Door prizes provided by the manufacturer are incentives for guests to stay for the entire length of the party. The cost of the event is minimal; the visibility is great, as the textile producer showcases its business to the retail buyers. The freelance fashion event producer is then paid well for a job well done.

Educational Events

A fashion event producer or an employee hired by a fashion event producer may stage an **educational event** to inform an audience about a product. For example, depending on the manufacturer's product line, the presenter may demonstrate different ways to wear jewelry,

■ **Figure 8.11**
The fashion event, or party, planner coordinates Opening Ceremony's celebration of Fashion's Night Out.

sportswear, or evening wear. In home furnishings, a demonstrator may educate an audience of sales reps by showing how to configure a new sectional sofa for a number of different looks and space needs. The presenter hired by a manufacturer may have an audience of sales reps, retail buyers, or ultimate consumers; it depends on the company's objectives for the event.

Partnership Events

A **partnership event** is one in which a fashion firm collaborates with another company outside of the fashion industry, with the intent of drawing in more customers. For example, an apparel manufacturer and an airline may get together and hire a fashion event planner to conduct workshops on how to pack for travel and what to wear on an African safari. The fashion event producer plans and implements the events, which are part of a larger promotional plan that showcases both the manufacturer and the airline. Collaborating with companies outside of the fashion industry allows the fashion event planner to generate new contacts and, possibly, additional revenue.

Philanthropic Fashion Show

A fashion event planner may execute a fashion show that benefits a nonprofit or charitable organization through its ticket sales or donations. This is referred to as a **philanthropic fashion show**, or *charity fashion show*. Community leaders, local celebrities, or executives of the philanthropic organization often model the apparel and accessories, acting as a drawing card for the show. The fashion event planner may also solicit door prizes or auction items from benefactors to generate additional funds for the cause.

Fashion Shows and Technology

Technology has impacted the world of fashion shows. Designers are streaming their fashion shows online so that their fans from anywhere in the world can see their newest collections as soon as they hit the runway. Some fashion firms are combining digital media in promotion with technology in fashion shows. Designer of Balenciaga since 2013, Alexander Wang concluded his 2014 show with several models standing on a circular runway that rotated as other models walked around them, spinning faster and faster. Some of the audience members surely left the show asking the question: Was this a metaphor for fashion designers and their collections around the world?

Technology in fashion shows is helping designers connect with potential and current customers around the globe. In 2014, Valentino introduced its first-ever new collection outside of Paris in Shanghai, using a combination of digital marketing and exclusivity (items available only in China) to generate sales. Valentino's capsule collection of ready-to-wear and couture clothing, as well as accessories, was shown on a live webcast from Shanghai after being heavily promoted on Sina Weibo with the hashtag "Valentino Shanghai." Before the event, the brand featured a countdown on both its Web site and social media, as well as short teaser videos, to build anticipation. Immediately following the show, the ready-to-wear items were made available for purchase at Valentino's new Shanghai flagship store. In hopes of gaining Chinese sales at a time when China's affluent were increasingly traveling to boutiques abroad to purchase designer items, the new collection was only available in Shanghai for a few months before it was released to other locations, including New York, Milan, Paris, and Rome.

Burberry introduced itself to China through a multimedia, Broadway-like show, described as an "immersive, theatrical journey through the Burberry world of music, heritage, product and innovation." On a theatre-style stage dominated by a façade of London's iconic terrace houses and surrounded by digital images of iconic landmarks in Shanghai and London,

Box 8.3 Streaming, Pinning, and Winning

Once upon a time, Fashion Week was an exclusive event reserved for the fashion elite (Let them eat cake!), for which hungry fashion peasants were forced to wait for the photos and publications before they could see the coverage, images, and commentary—rarely live. However, technology has arrived, and democracy has come to Fashion Week. Fashion bloggers are now sitting in the front-row seats of the best shows, and fashion lovers around the world are participating in each amazing minute of Fashion Week via live streaming, blogs, Twitter, Instagram, Vine, Pinterest, and more. While using digital channels is not new this year, these social media platforms are being regarded as must-have marketing channels. The 2014 Fashion Weeks were full of live streaming and related social media, hashtag campaigns, social and digital lounges, and innovative digital partnership promotions.

Elle magazine, for example, gave Pinterest pinners a front-row seat to 2014 Fashion Weeks. Pinners watched fashion unfold as *Elle* pinned each look that came down the runway to their Runway Trends board during runway shows of Fall and Spring Fashion Weeks in New York, London, Milan, and Paris. *Elle*'s live pinning approach created a significant boost in pin virality and referral traffic. The Runway Trends board saw seven times more activity than other boards, with more than 16,000 repins and nearly 4,000 likes during New York Fashion Week alone. And, the live pinning was mutually advantageous, as referral traffic from Pinterest to *Elle*'s Web site increased by 13 percent throughout the week, as users clicked through to learn more about the designer's collections.

Sources:

business.pinterest.com/en/success-stories/Elle-magazine#sthash.DMfUvkZ1.dpuf

socialmediatoday.com/julie-blakley/1747436/digital-and-social-trends-seen-new-york-fashion-week

models danced through several musical numbers wearing Burberry trench coats and carrying umbrellas. In one scene, they took refuge from the rain, while holograms of falling raindrops were projected. Christopher Bailey, CEO of Burberry, describes the company "as much a media-content company as we are a design company."

Some fashion media companies are counting on and collaborating on the consumer value of a designer fashion show. During Fashion Week in New York, social media star Pinterest and publication powerhouse *Elle* magazine teamed up to "live pin" each look that came down the designer runways, as featured in Box 8.3. Was it a successful partnership? Elle's Runway Trends board saw seven times the activity as other boards, with more than 16,000 repins.

Whether the fashion event producer uses holograms, projected imagery, or a traditional stage, his or her basic responsibilities in fashion show production are the same.

Duties of a Fashion Event Producer

There are many ways to generate interest through fashion events. Because there is much work involved and, in many cases, a great deal of expertise needed, some manufacturers and designers hire freelance fashion event producers to execute them, whereas others have part- or full-time staffs to do this. So, what kinds of activities do fashion event producers perform? Here is a sampling:

- Locate and reserve the place after negotiating the price, terms, and dates for the event—to fit the client's needs and desires and to fit within the budget

- Determine staging, lighting, music, sound system, and technology needs

- Assemble merchandise to be featured

- Hire and fit models, arrange lineup, and supervise rehearsals

- Compile commentary, if appropriate, and recruit commentator

- Arrange for printing needs (e.g., tickets, signage, invitations, and programs)

- Arrange for seating, to include setup and breakdown of seats, tables, and staging

- Recruit backstage help, such as hairstylists, makeup artists, and dressers

- Recruit front-of-stage help, such as ticket sales, concessions, and ushers

- Locate caterers or sponsors for refreshments, if needed

- Handle publicity, which may include invitations, press releases, advertisements, television and/or radio interviews, social media, and other media-related activities

The job of fashion event producer is one of those "chief cook and bottle washer" positions that may have the planner initially doing a little bit of everything to pull the event together. Once the producer becomes more established in the industry, then he or she is able to hire others to handle parts of the larger projects.

Qualifications

This career requires the following qualifications:

- *Education.* A bachelor's degree in fashion merchandising, fashion design, promotion, special events planning, or a related field is required.

- *Experience.* Fashion event planners come from a wide range of industry sectors: retail, design, and manufacturing. Many work as assistants to fashion directors or coordinators in retail operations or manufacturer's showrooms before branching out on their own. Others initially work as assistants to established fashion event planners. Some large retail stores have special events departments through which starting, or assistant, fashion event planners can learn the ropes of fashion event planning and production. Through the positions leading up to becoming a fashion event planner, a large and useful network of contacts related to the fashion industry can be developed.

- *Personal characteristics.* Successful fashion event planners have the following skills and knowledge: an enthusiastic and creative personality, the ability to sell one's ideas and vision, accounting skills to develop and manage budgets, strong organizational and communication skills, and effective time-management abilities.

Career Challenges

The job tasks of fashion event planning require endless attention to detail to ensure trouble-free events. Fashion event planners need a strong sense of fashion, organizational skills, the ability to work well in stressful situations, and the communication skills to work with a wide range of people. Managing a major fashion event can be compared to coordinating a three-ring circus. Frequently, many people are involved and myriad details need to be considered. When combining these stresses with the need to keep events on budget and on time, fashion event planners must have the skills to remain calm and collected under pressure. This person needs nerves of steel and iron-clad organization skills.

Summary

Promotion refers to the endorsement of a person, a product, a cause, an idea, or an organization. The ultimate goal of promotion for the designer or manufacturer is to encourage the growth, exposure, and development of the designer, company, its lines, and its image by advancing it to a higher position with a greater number of consumers. The ultimate goal is increased visibility in positive ways that motivate consumers to buy, resulting in increased sales. Promotion career opportunities in the primary level of the fashion industry include fashion stylist, public relations director, advertising director, advertising sales representative and related positions, social media director, and fashion event planner. Although the public relations director, social media director, and advertising representative are usually employed by a large firm, fashion stylists and fashion events planners may choose a career with a retail company, manufacturer, or public relations firm, or decide to open their own companies. In all of these promotion careers, the goal is to sell an idea, an image, or a product—directly or indirectly. It is marketing in its truest form; it is creative, thought provoking, and profitable at its best.

Key Terms

advertising
advertising director
advertising promotion staff
advertising research assistant
advertising sales representative
bridal show
consumer publication
educational event
fashion event producer
fashion photostylist
fashion shoot
fashion stylist
informal fashion show
media planner

partnership event
party planning
philanthropic fashion show
pop-up shop
promotion
promotion product
public relations director
social media
social media director
social networking
social Web site
trade publication
trunk show

Online Resources

service.prweb.com/learning/article/public-relations-blogs-25-essential-pr-bloggers-you-should-be-reading/

www.fashion-tweets.com/

www.huffingtonpost.com/2014/02/04/twitter-fashion-week-_n_4718795.html

blog.twitter.com/2014/diesel-shows-fashion-on-twitter

www.prcouture.com

www.refinery29.com/best-new-fashion-designers#slide

www.refinery29.com/women-in-pr#slide

Discussion Questions

1. How does your favorite designer promote his or her products? Determine the promotional activities coordinated by the company's public relations director. Is the public relations director contracted from an outside firm? If so, what other companies does this firm promote? Are there similarities among its clients?

2. Which do you read more regularly—consumer or trade publications? Read an article from each type of publication and analyze the value of each as it relates to your future career goals.

3. Go online to locate three recent examples each of fashion designers' and manufacturers' use of digital media in promotion. Set up a spreadsheet to compare and contrast these examples. What are the similarities and differences among these?

Profile: Interview with Junior Public Relations Executive Chelsea Bommel

Interviewed by Michele M. Granger

Can you tell us a bit about your background?

I've known since high school (probably younger) that I wanted to pursue a career in fashion. I've always had a million subscriptions to fashion magazines, loved shopping and accessorizing, and helping style my friends and family. I would make inspiration boards in my room from magazines when I was around 10 (yes, some of them included pictures of Jonathan Taylor Thomas). Thankfully, the university I attended had an amazing fashion program, and I graduated college in May of 2011 with a Bachelor of Science degree in Fashion Merchandising and a minor in Marketing.

Profile Figure 8 Chelsea Bommel, Junior Public Relations Account Executive.

During college, I decided that I wanted to see more of the country and took a public relations internship in Los Angeles while attending the university. (I was the only student in our internship class who went to LA, of course I *had* to be different.) After college, my friend and I decided to move to New York City to pursue careers in the fashion industry. In NYC, I took an internship with *Lucky* magazine, where I learned about the publishing side of public relations. After my internship ended, I accepted an offer from a boutique public relations company, which became the basis of everything I know thus far.

When did you realize you wanted to work in PR and why?

I realized that I wanted to work in PR after my internship with *Lucky* magazine. I loved the concept of shaping the growth of designers through strategic representation in the press. I wanted to be the reason that my client was on the cover of *Vogue*. And, hey, the idea of free samples wasn't a terrible lure either!

What is an average day for you?

This question always makes me laugh because, in PR (or the fashion industry in general), you really don't have a typical day. You can go into work with a full to-do list, but at the end of the day the only thing that you have done is to add to it. As far as day-to-day responsibilities, I am the contact between editors and our clients. I coordinate the transfer of any information about our clients' products, new collections, and samples to editors. I also pitch to top-tier regional and national publications in both long lead and short lead outlets. The information that I send out can be about new collections or trends that I have noticed in our clients' products that these publications have not yet written about or explored.

What was your path to where you are today?

Living in the Midwest didn't make it easy to get into the fashion industry. It took courage, determination, and a thick skin to get where I am today. I had seven unpaid internships before I got my first paying job. I worked long hours when I first got to New York City. I had a part-time job while interning at *Lucky* that barely paid the bills, but I knew if I pushed through it that I would find a job I loved! You also don't go into fashion public relations expecting to make the big bucks either. You have to be passionate about the work you are doing. Your clients are your top priority, and if you don't love and support the brands you represent, you are in the wrong field.

Working in the fashion industry definitely is not glitz and glamour all the time, especially when you are first starting out. Find a man in finance. Just kidding. Sort of. [A joke shared among many women in the fashion industry.]

What kind of skills have you learned from your experiences, and/or what skills do successful PR execs have?

You need great communication skills, both verbal and written. I suggest taking many writing courses throughout college. You also can't be afraid to break out of your shell. PR execs have to do *a lot* of socializing. You have to entertain editors, clients, stylists, and, sometimes, celebrities. I watch and learn from my senior peers daily, trying to gain as much knowledge as possible. You must also be very detail-oriented and a strong self-motivator.

What does your company do?

We are a boutique costume and fine jewelry public relations agency. We handle editorial and celebrity outreach. In a nutshell, we get our clients top editorial press, and make sure relevant celebrities are wearing our client's jewelry. Our LA office handles all the celebrity and VIP requests. They are in contact with stylists who are dressing for top events, from red carpet affairs to music videos. The NY office is responsible for all editorial outreach.

What types of social media do you use at work? For which purposes?

These days, if you are not using every possible social media outlet, you can deem your business as outdated. Our company and fellow clients use

(continued on next page)

(continued)

Facebook, Twitter, Instagram, and Pinterest. Every social media site is used to show the press what our clients have received recently, whether it's within a publication, a celebrity wearing the client's jewelry, or an online post. Twitter and Instagram are great for tagging highly recognized editors, celebrities, stylists, bloggers, publications, etc. with hopes that their following will see the post and, in return, will follow our clients' accounts.

Social media is huge in PR, and only getting bigger and better. It's great for competitor analysis, staying up to date with recent news, knowing the daily life of your favorite celebrity, and so much more.

What are your favorite fashion Web sites and blogs related to PR?

StyleCaster—My go-to for style news and trends.

Women's Wear Daily (WWD.com)—If you are in fashion, you should be reading this every day. It's basically the daily ritual.

The Man Repeller—There is nothing better than reading a fashion Web site with humor. Leandra Medine, the founder behind The Man Repeller, has the best articles for fashion, trends, pop culture, and beauty.

Ashli with an Eye—One of my best friend's up-and-coming fashion blog. I'm envious of her new hobby, and she is amazing at what she does! I'm definitely one of her biggest fans, and I'm excited to see where she takes her blog!

Refinery 29—A Web site that is updated daily with news, trends, and shopping deals in fashion, beauty, and entertainment.

What do you love most about what you do?

There is so much that goes into the day-to-day of a PR girl, and you never know what just might be thrown your way, good or bad. I like the fact that the business keeps me on my feet. There is *always* something more you could be doing: a new relationship you could be nurturing or different angles to pitch your client. This means, no day is boring!

What have been your toughest challenges in PR?

Working with different and difficult personalities can be challenging. You may not enjoy working with everyone within your team, but you have to find ways to still work as a team. At the end of the day, in PR, we aren't saving lives; you have to pick your battles. I try to go into work every day with a smile on my face and an optimistic attitude!

What advice would you give to aspiring PR people?

Intern, intern, and intern. Most important, intern for a fashion publication, if you can. Being on the editorial side at *Lucky* helped me to connect the dots among different aspects of the business. It also taught me to have patience when dealing with the burgeoning sample closets when I need to get samples back.

Network! I can't stress that enough. It is something that you need to continually be doing throughout your career. Write down names, numbers, and email addresses of anyone in the industry you meet. You never know when a person's contact information can come in handy! And keep in touch with your contacts. They could be your foot-in-the-door to your next job or internship!

Is fashion art? With fashion runways and fashion exhibitions in museums

drawing larger audiences worldwide, the distinct line that once separated fashion and art is blurred. While a number of notable designers, such as Schiaparelli and Paul Poiret, have stated unequivocally that fashion is art and belongs in museums, Karl Lagerfeld dismisses the notion, stating "I am against museums and exhibitions in fashion. If you call yourself an artist, then you are second-rate" (Figure C10). Fashion designers, as well as art and fashion historians, remain divided.

Merriam-Webster Dictionary defines art as "something that is created with imagination and skill and that is beautiful or that expresses important ideas or feelings." Doesn't this place fashion in the same realm as art? When executed by the hands of certain designers, such as Alexander McQueen and Jean Paul Gaultier, fashion can be an application of imagination and skill, as well as an expression of important ideas and feelings. The exhibition "Fashion World of Jean Paul Gaultier: From the Sidewalk to the Catwalk" attracted record-breaking crowds around the world (Figure C15).

Many fashion designers concur that their creations are inspired by art. Vera Wang's breakout collection of 2005 was inspired by the brooding colors in Flemish paintings. It was the moment that *New York Times* fashion critic Cathy Horyn described as "when Wang went from being known as a designer of bridal and evening clothes to just Ms. Wang, designer" (Figure C1). Since then Wang's collections have continued to draw inspiration from artists and art collectors, such as Françoise Sagan, Peggy Guggenheim, and Niki de Saint Phalle (Figure C2). Other designers are inspired by fashion of the past—fashion they view as art. Hanging in a back office is a rack loaded with part of Ashley and Mary-Kate Olsen's huge collection of vintage apparel. "I couldn't believe what they did when I texted in a panic about having nothing to wear for my audition for *Gatsby*," says Carey Mulligan, the actress cast to play Daisy Buchanan for Baz Luhrmann. "I was hoping they'd send me some things from The Row, but then these huge boxes arrived—Ashley's entire collection of thirties vintage dresses." The designers study them for inspiration (Figure C6), in addition to lending them to friends and—of course—wearing them. "I look at The Met [Gala] as a time to, not wear a costume, but really find the beauty in couture and search through the fabulous old gowns," Mary-Kate says (Figure C5).

When you step into Alexander Wang's New York Flagship store, you see "The Cage," an enclosure Wang designed to give customers new ways to experience his designs through a series of curated artwork collaborations and integration into to his runway shows (Figures C3 and C4). For Fall of 2014, the installation combined a giant carved wave, Haydenshapes surfboard art pieces, sculpted sand, and Wang's accessories. Surfboards must be the cool new art medium, as designer Lisa Perry also featured artist-designed boards at The Breast Cancer Research Foundation's Paddle and Party for Pink (Figures C11 to C14).

Fashion functions for the purposes of protecting the human body from environmental elements and adorning it, a means of self-expression (Figure C16). It has an aspect of commerce, the potential for profit (Figures C7 and C8). While art is sometimes considered commercial, it is often viewed as less fleeting and more artist-centric than fashion. Perhaps, all can agree that art and fashion have a symbiotic relationship—two different entities that mutually benefit one another. Even Karl Lagerfeld acquiesced when he told the *New York Times* in 2008, "Art is art. Fashion is fashion. However, Andy Warhol proved that they can exist together." (Figure C9).

Sources:

www.byrdie.com/mary-kate-ashley-olsen-beauty-Inspiration

www.vogue.com/865448/mary-kate-and-ashley-olsen-balancing-act/

nymag.com/fashion/11/spring/71655/index1.html

www.byrdie.com/mary-kate-ashley-olsen-beauty-inspiration/slide9

www.blouinartinfo.com/news/story/805583/is-fashion-art-karl-lagerfeld-puts-the-debate-back-into-the-spotlight

www.brooklynmuseum.org/exhibitions/jean_paul_gaultier/

design-milk.com/thecage22-haydenshapes-surfboards-x-alexander-wang/

C1. Vera Wang attends the Metropolitan Museum of Art's 2013 Gala. (Chapter 6)

C2. Models on the runway at Vera Wang's Spring 2014 show at Lincoln Center. (Chapter 8)

C3. Models on the runway at Alexander Wang's Spring 2014 show at Pier 94. (Chapter 8)

C4. Kristen Wiig and Alexander Wang attend the Metropolitan Museum of Art's 2014 Costume Institute Gala featuring the opening of the exhibit "Charles James: Beyond Fashion." (Chapter 6)

C5. Ashley and Mary-Kate Olsen at the Metropolitan Museum of Art's Costume Institute Gala featuring the opening of the exhibit "Punk: Chaos to Couture." (Chapter 6)

C6. Models on the runway at The Row's Spring 2014 show. (Chapter 8)

C7. Models at the Coach Leatherware Fall 2014 presentation in New York. (Chapter 8)

C9. Karl Lagerfeld poses with a model on the runway of the Grand Palais fashion show. (Chapter 6)

C10. Karl Lagerfeld with models on the runway at Chanel's Fall haute couture show at the Grand Palais. (Chapter 6)

C12. Donna Karan and Lisa Perry attend the Breast Cancer Research Foundation's Paddle and Party for Pink. (Chapter 13)

C13. The Breast Cancer Research Foundation's Paddle and Party for Pink featuring Lisa Perry. (Chapter 13)

C14. Models at Lisa Perry's spring presentation at her Madison Avenue store. (Chapter 9)

C16. The $14.7 billion (2013) health and wellness spa industry has generated strong growth over the past decade, especially in day spas which make up the vast majority. (Chapter 16)

UNIT 3

Careers in Fashion Retailing

Unit 3 examines the retail level of the fashion industry in three function areas: marketing, management, and merchandising. In Chapter 8, promotion activities used by the manufacturer/designer to inform potential consumers (i.e., retail buyers and end users) about the company and its products are examined. The more a business can integrate advertising, publicity, sales promotion, and personal selling, the more promotion will be effective. Retailers use additional promotional efforts, such as window and in-store displays, Web sites, product labeling and packaging, and store signage, as other ways of promoting the product. Regardless of the type of promotion, the reason for choosing and constructing all promotional messages in all media venues is based on (1) the principles of marketing and (2) in-depth knowledge of the company and its consumer. In Chapter 9, Marketing for the Retailer, the marketing mix and marketing plans are explored, and career tracks that focus on marketing and promotion are introduced: marketing director and manager, product marketing manager, brand marketing manager, digital marketing manager, art director, and copywriter.

Chapter 10, Merchandising for the Retailer, illustrates the tremendous impact retail merchandisers, or buyers, have on their fashion retailing businesses in terms of exclusivity, image, and pricing. The major activities of the buyer in merchandising include locating and purchasing products, with the preferences of the consumer in mind, and then selling these products at a profit. Merchandising also includes extensive research on the department's or store's customers, trying to predict which types of merchandise customers will want to buy for upcoming seasons. There are a variety of positions available in the merchandising division of retailing operation, depending on its size and channels of distribution. The career options discussed in Chapter 10 include the general merchandising manager, divisional merchandising manager, buyer/fashion merchandiser, assistant buyer, planner, distribution manager/allocator, and merchandising trainee. The varied career tracks in merchandising for the retailer have several challenges in common—locating products that (1) appeal to the customer, (2) are priced right, (3) arrive at the right place when needed, and (4) sell to the retailers' customers.

In Chapter 11, Management for the Retailer, career opportunities in retail management—the division in charge of organizing and controlling of the affairs of the business as a whole or a particular department—are explored. This chapter focuses on management careers in fashion retailing that include a wide variety of retail venues, such as manager of an apparel store, manager of an Internet fashion operation, or assistant manager of a factory outlet. The specific career tracks in retail management examined in Chapter 11 include the following positions: regional manager; operations manager; retail store manager; manager-in-training (MIT); assistant and associate store manager; department manager; customer service manager; and retail operation entrepreneur, or store owner.

The 3 Ms of retailing—marketing, merchandising, and management—interrelate to facilitate a successful fashion retail operation. If one of the three is weak, then the company will likely have issues. For example, the buyers can purchase the top-selling, best-priced, and most customer-centered merchandise, and the store management team can be skilled and ready to sell it, but, if the store and the merchandise are not marketed well, the sales may not happen. Alternately, if the merchandise and the marketing are top-notch and ready to roll out, but the store management and staff are not motivated and customer service oriented, then the customers may not come to the retailer. It is a balancing act to keep this triangle upright, and one that pays off when it is done well.

chapter 9

Marketing for the Retailer

In the previous chapter, promotion was examined from the perspectives of designers and manufacturers of fashion products. In this chapter, we examine how retailers penetrate their markets and use promotion. Take, for example, H&M and how it communicates its business model of "fashion and quality at the best price" through the various advertising campaigns. H&M's promotions are produced internally at its headquarters in Stockholm, Sweden, by the marketing department, in cooperation with creative professionals located in the major fashion hubs of the world. The campaigns are designed to be clear and simple and to inform customers of what is new at H&M; the focus is on product, not celebrity models or a corporate message. H&M's advertising images do not aim to communicate any specific ideal, but rather a range of styles and attitudes. H&M goes one step further by featuring models with different looks, styles, and cultural backgrounds to advertise its products for women, men, teenagers, and children. The models "must portray the current fashion in a positive and healthy manner," H&M declares.

In contrast, Zara has grown with very little advertising and much word-of-mouth promotion. It is intentional and part of the retailer's business model, which has a mini-marketing department that does not engage in showy campaigns, as its competitors do. Instead, Zara saves on the expense of traditional advertising, relying on word-of-mouth and free media coverage of celebrities wearing its clothes, such as the Spanish queen-to-be Princess Letizia and Prince George's mother Kate Middleton, Her Royal Highness, the Duchess of Cambridge. Instead of promotion, Zara's Spanish parent company, Inditex, is well-known for its focus on real estate. The company invests heavily in the aesthetics, historical appeal, and locations of its shops.

Although its buildings may be expansive, Inditex is famously an introverted company when it comes to press. Despite being one of the world's three richest men and the primary owner of Zara, Mr. Amancio Ortego refuses to do press interviews. *Fortune* describes him in this way: "He's difficult to know, impossible to interview, and incredibly secretive."[1] With its marketing strategy built on "un-promotion" (i.e., without advertising and almost all forms of mainstream marketing), ultimate locations, and its exclusive, ever-changing lines, Zara is exploding. At the start of 2014, the company produced about 450 million items per year for its 1,770 stores in 86 countries.[2] You can read more about Zara and its marketing strategy in boxes throughout this chapter.

In Chapter 8, promotion career opportunities in the primary level of the fashion industry were explored, to include fashion stylist, public relations director, advertising director, advertising sales representative and related positions, social media director, and fashion event planner. The majority of these positions are also available at the retail level of the industry, with many of the same position requirements and similar career challenges. In this chapter, other career tracks that focus on marketing and promotion are introduced: marketing director and manager, product marketing manager, brand marketing manager, digital marketing manager, art director, and copywriter. The career path of graphic designer is often available in the promotion division of both the large designer/manufacturer and the retailer. This position is examined in Chapter 12 because of its significant relationship today with digital media.

As stated in the previous chapter, promotion involves the activities used to inform the potential consumer (i.e., retail buyers and end users) about the company and its products. The more a business can integrate advertising, publicity, sales promotion, and personal selling, the more promotion will be effective. Retailers use additional promotional efforts, such as window displays and in-store displays, Web sites, product labeling and packaging, and store signage, as other ways of promoting the product. Regardless of the type of promotion, the reason for choosing and constructing all promotional messages in all media venues is based on (1) the principles of marketing and (2) in-depth knowledge of the company and its consumer. Next is an examination of the foundation for retailers' marketing plans, the marketing mix.

The Marketing Mix: The Four, Make That Five, Ps of Marketing

Retailers look at methods of differentiating their business from those of competitors through the four Ps of marketing: price, product, placement, and promotion. A fifth P of marketing can be added—the people or consumers who are targeted as potential customers or product users, referred to as the **target market**. These market variables, referred to as the **marketing mix**, when combined, must reinforce the image of the company and its products to the potential and active customer. All five elements should complement one another in order to achieve the firm's marketing objectives. The best marketing plan for a company is one that directs resources or dollars toward products, place, promotion, and pricing, with the highest potential to increase revenue and profits among the people who are targeted as product buyers. Next, we examine how the components of the marketing mix are integrated into a strategic marketing plan and which career track manages each part of the plan.

The Marketing Plan

Determining a successful marketing plan, or marketing strategy, is key to directing the retail fashion business on implementation of the five Ps of the marketing mix and, ultimately, leading the retail fashion business to success. The effective marketing plan reaches customers and motivates them to buy. The **marketing plan** helps define and quantify user benefits, establishes the market size as well as potential customer interest, and addresses the competition. The

CASE STUDIES IN CAREER EXPLORATION

Box 9.1 Zara: Marketing 101 Around the World

At Zara headquarters, regional sales managers field calls from store managers around the world to learn what's selling, and then they meet with the designers and decide whether there's a trend. In this way, Inditex peers into the minds of fashion shoppers around the world. "The manager will say, 'My customers are asking for red trousers,' and, if it's the same demand in Istanbul, New York, and Tokyo, that means it's a global trend, so they know to produce more red pants," Zara's PR representative reports. In addition to learning which styles and colors to manufacture, Zara's trendspotters have learned a thing or two about global fashion tastes.

Customers have different tastes when they live in different parts of the world, right? Not necessarily, Zara has learned. In general, the company has seen that, when you find a fashion trend, it's global—whether in New York or Germany. Although there are more similarities, there are some differences. For example, Brazilian women like more brilliant colors, whereas in Paris the women buy more black.

Fashion has to be a bit sexier in Russia; in China, during the New Year, they want to wear red.

Most interesting, Zara's regional sales managers have concluded that neighborhoods share trends more than countries do. For example, the store on Fifth Avenue in Manhattan is most similar to the store in Ginza, Tokyo, which is an elegant area that's also a tourism center. And the SoHo district in New York City is closest to Shibuya in Tokyo, as both are very trendy and young. Within the United States, Zara has learned that Brooklyn is now a wildly trendy place for New Yorkers to go, whereas Manhattan is the mecca for tourists on the prowl for fashion goods.

Sources:

www.theguardian.com/fashion/2013/dec/15/inditex-spain-global-fashion-powerhouse

www.nytimes.com/2012/11/11/magazine/how-zara-grew-into-the-worlds-largest-fashion-retailer.html?pagewanted=all&_r=0

marketing plan serves several purposes. First, it helps the retailer determine how potential customers can become aware of the product or service. Second, it helps define the message the retailer wishes to convey about the product, service, or company. Third, it helps identify the methods that will best deliver and reinforce that message, and how sales will be achieved. Finally, the marketing plan addresses how the company positions itself relative to the competition. Now, imagine that you are writing a marketing plan for a boutique you plan to open in your community. Then, imagine developing a marketing plan for a company with about 6,000 stores located all around the world. Zara has done just this and is successfully getting to know and compare its customers globally, as illustrated in Box 9.1.

Marketing Director

Although a higher executive position of **chief marketing officer (CMO)** exists in some large companies of the fashion industry, the **marketing director** often develops, implements, and facilitates the marketing plan in fashion retailing. The key job responsibilities of a marketing director are as follows:

- *Develop the marketing plan.* Translate company objectives to brand portfolio objectives, strategies, and plans to facilitate company growth.

- *Monitor the marketing budget.* Plan and administer the firm's marketing operations budget.

- *Manage marketing suppliers.* Negotiate with media agents to secure agreements for translation of materials into other media. Develop and edit promotional materials according to specific market or customer requirements.

- *Oversee business development and corporate communications activities.* Coordinate external and internal communications and systems, as well as public relations efforts.

- *Oversee the marketing database.* Gather financial and traffic results of promotions, plus consumer demographics, to include spending patterns, patronage motives, and shopping incentives, etc.

- *Manage the marketing department.* Build and develop a successful marketing team. Manage day-to-day activity with PR and press.

Depending on the company, the marketing director may be promoted to the position of vice president of marketing or CMO. In some firms, a **marketing manager** position is just below that of marketing director in the executive hierarchy and has qualifications similar to those of marketing director.

Qualifications

If director of marketing is your career goal, certain educational goals, work experiences, and personal characteristics will help you open the door and then move upward in this career path.

- *Education.* A bachelor of science in marketing, fashion merchandising, or a related business administration or fashion field is required.

- *Experience.* A minimum of five to eight years of executive-level marketing experience in a fashion organization is required, as is experience with new media and Internet advertising.

- *Personal Characteristics.* The marketing director is detail-oriented and has the skills to manage projects from conception through execution. He or she must have excellent communication skills—verbal, visual, and written. Successful marketing directors have a hunger to learn and the ability to flourish in a dynamic, high-growth, and entrepreneurial environment. The effective marketing director is a self-starter with a hands-on approach to problem solving.

Career Challenges

The marketing director needs to maintain a high energy level despite long hours and frequent meetings with a wide variety of staff members and administrators. Marketing directors need exceptional skills in multitasking and prioritizing, because they are often managing several projects simultaneously, with different deadlines, budget, and objectives for each. Their responsibilities require excellent time management and negotiation abilities. Picture the marketing director walking a high wire while balancing a tray of drinks, and you will have an idea of the possible stress level involved in the position. Finally, the marketing director must be both creative and analytical, coming up with innovative and unique concepts while managing people and processes.

Fashion resides in a competitive, revolving marketplace. Retailers must be open to innovation and change in their product lines and, subsequently, the marketing plan. Next, the marketing position that focuses on the product, or the product line, is introduced—that of the product marketing manager.

Product Marketing Manager

The product life cycle must be understood in order for the retailer, and in particular the product marketing manager, to determine if and when to introduce new products into the existing product line. There are four stages in the product life cycle: introduction, acceleration, peak, and decline (Figure 9.1). There are no predictable time periods for products to reside in any one of the phases. In fact, the product life cycle of a fad item may last as little as four to six weeks. Fashion trend items can last for a season or a decade. The challenge for the **product marketing manager** is to anticipate when to get into a fashion style, color, or theme and when to get out. The time to introduce a new product is during the early life cycle of the current product when sales are strong and profit margins are higher.

Product Placement and the Product Marketing Manager

The P in the marketing mix called "place" is referred to as **distribution** and involves the product marketing manager in making sure that the product is available where and when it is wanted. Marketers can choose among many ways of moving products to consumers. They may choose among different types of outlets and store locations, as illustrated by Zara's location marketing strategy in Box 9.2. In contrast, with today's online access, many retailers are reducing investments in locations and turning to an online presence, not only to promote the business, but also to offer the sale of products to consumers on a global scale. Distribution also involves decisions such as how much inventory to hold, how to transport goods, and where to locate warehouses.

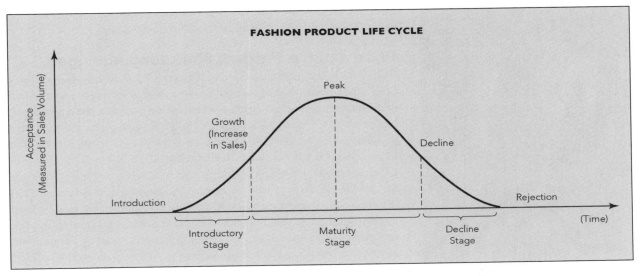

■ **Figure 9.1**
The product life cycle should be understood by the product marketing manager in order to determine when to introduce new products into the existing product line.

■ **Figure 9.2**
Actress Julianna Margulies and designer Narciso Rodriguez attend Kohl's Narciso Rodriguez collection launch party in New York.

Consumers are looking for products and services that are convenient for them to acquire exactly when they want or need them. In selecting the **channel of distribution**—the method selected for moving goods from producer to consumer—the product marketing manager gives careful consideration to using distributors that can provide good service at a reasonable price. The primary channel of distribution for the fashion retail industry moves from manufacturer to retailer to consumer. Some manufacturers, however, sell directly to the consumer through catalogs, Web sites, or factory outlets. An alternative, and less frequently used, channel of distribution in the fashion industry is the wholesaler. In this case, the manufacturer sells merchandise to a **wholesale** company, one that sells the goods to the retailer for subsequent resale to the consumer.

Price and the Product Marketing Manager

Pricing decisions impact almost every aspect of a business—the product's image, the company's sales, and the retailer's success. Pricing is a component of the marketing strategy. Covering expenses and making a profit are crucial, but pricing is also an issue of relationship to competitor's pricing, the product's positioning, and supply and demand—what the customer is willing to pay. Pricing is not just about numbers. The price of the merchandise sends a message about the perceived value of the product to customers regarding the product or service they are buying. As illustrated in Box 9.3, Zara's customers know that they will find new merchandise in the stores almost weekly, and they are confident that they can afford it. Zara controls its price structure through spin-offs of successful products with low or nonexistent start-up expenses (e.g., pattern development, sample construction, and fit perfection), as well as production in its own factories, which saves costs.

As shown in Figure 9.2, more high-end designers, such as Missoni, Narcisco Rodriguez, and Vera Wang, are introducing **diffusion labels**

Box 9.3 Price: Zara's Claim to Fame, Fast Fashion

Zara's marketing strategy is to quickly and consistently supply, and resupply, trendy and decently made, but relatively inexpensive, products that are sold in beautiful, high-end-looking stores in high-end locations. Twice every week, each store receives a tailored assortment, three to four units of a style per store. A little more than 50 percent of the stock will be designed and manufactured less than a month before it hits the store floors. Customers in Spain, Portugal, and Greece can buy the clothes as much as 30 percent cheaper than elsewhere in Europe or overseas markets, such as China and the United States. In the United States, Zara's prices are similar to those of the Gap, with a fashion T-shirt selling for about $30.

A traditional ready-to-wear company in the United States sends its designs to factories in countries with low labor costs, such as China and India. The garments are then shipped to the United States to be stocked in stores in fall, holiday, spring, and summer with smaller shipments throughout the year. In contrast, more than half of Inditex's manufacturing takes place in the factories it owns or those of contractors located near company headquarters or as far away as China and Bangladesh. Basic items, such as T-shirts, are manufactured in the distant locations. Fads, or trend items, are produced closest to home so that the manufacturing process, from start to finish, takes only two to three weeks. The winning formula is that higher labor costs in production are offset by greater flexibility, which results in higher sales volume, fewer markdowns, and faster stock turn.

In 2012, Inditex produced 840 million garments per year and had about 5,900 stores, 4,400 of them in Europe. Today, its Zara division has more than 2,000 stores strategically located in leading cities across 88 countries. Inditex's store number is always changing because it has, in recent years, opened more than a store per day, or between 300 and 400 stores annually. Inditex's top three competitors are Arcadia Group, which owns Topshop, among others, and has about 3,000 stores worldwide; H&M, based in Sweden, which has 2,500 stores; and Mango, also headquartered in Spain, which has 2,400 stores.

Sources:

www.theguardian.com/fashion/2013/dec/15/inditex-spain-global-fashion-powerhouse

www.nytimes.com/2012/11/11/magazine/how-zara-grew-into-the-worlds-largest-fashion-retailer.html?pagewanted=all&_r=0

www.inditex.com/en/brands/zara

(secondary lines) at lower prices exclusively to mass merchandisers to increase market share. These designers are offering less-expensive labels and distributing those labels through discount stores, such as Target or Kohl's.

In some retail firms, the product marketing manager may be in charge of brand marketing; however, more companies are adding the position of brand marketing manager to focus on the importance of creating and managing the brand of the product.

Brand Marketing Manager

Branding is defined as the sum of all the associations, feelings, beliefs, attitudes, and perceptions customers have with a company and/or its products. The American Marketing Association defines a *brand* as "a name, term, design, symbol, or any other feature that identifies one seller's good or service as distinct from those of other sellers." Fashion icons such as Louis Vuitton, Nike, and Gucci have brands that are recognizable and unmistakable. The brand is reflected in the name, logo (i.e., its color, font, and tag lines), and trademarks.

Reporting to the marketing director or CMO, the **brand marketing manager** strategically develops and executes multichannel brand marketing and promotional programs in order to drive brand awareness, support and reinforce the brand's character, and ultimately generate increased revenue. The brand manager monitors and measures customer activity that he or she works to create. Brand marketing managers use a variety of communication tools to send the messages of their brands, including PR, direct marketing, visual merchandising, and print. Because of the need for a consistent message and a variety of ways to spread that message, the brand marketing manager and team often work with other departments, such as digital marketing and PR. Following is a listing of the key responsibilities of the brand marketing manager:

1. *Develop a vision for the brand.* What does the business aspire to be? The vision should focus on a longer-term perspective. Brands take time to build and become recognized in the marketplace. The more solid the brand vision, the greater the chance the customer will understand and relate to the vision.
2. *Position the brand in relationship to the competition.* The brand should differentiate the business from the competition. Successful brands focus on what separates them from the competition. Brands are multidimensional in that they carry with them images and associations in the minds of the consumer.
3. *Create a personality.* Each brand has a distinct personality. Some take on a more comical approach, whereas others lend themselves to a more serious product or service. Desigual, a retailer and manufacturer, brands with humor, open-mindedness, and a free spirit (Figure 9.3), whereas Chanel conveys sophistication, luxury, glamour, and beauty. The more emotion a brand can communicate, the more memorable it will be in the mind of the market. TOMs shoes—with its "buy one to give one to a needy child" business model—provides an example of an emotional and memorable message that tells a story.
4. *Articulate the benefits.* The brand represents a set of benefits and value to the customer.

■ **Figure 9.3**
Managing a brand includes creating a personality for it. Desigual, a retailer and manufacturer, uses the following description for its brand: humor, open-mindedness, and a free spirit.

5. *Define the values the brand represents.* The brand represents a defined set of values established by the retailer. Clearly defining the value of the business can create long-term customers.

The message of the brand is then conveyed through the sum of its marketing materials—from its logo, business cards, and brochures to its signage, Web site, and advertisements.

The qualifications of the product and brand marketing managers are very similar to those of the digital marketing manager and will follow the discussion of this career path.

Digital Marketing Manager

The **digital marketing manager** works to further develop and manage a company's digital marketing presence and oversees the digital marketing strategy for the brand. This person is responsible for managing online brand and product campaigns to raise brand awareness. One of the digital marketing director's main goals is to devise strategies to drive online traffic to the company's Web site, blog, Pinterest boards, or whatever media the company uses to connect with customers. In addition, he or she evaluates customer research, market conditions, and competitor data, especially the ways competitors are using their Web sites and social media.

The digital marketing manager collaborates with the company's product and brand managers, as well as the social media director. Digital marketing managers work closely with the Web master to improve the usability, design, content, and conversion of the company's Web site. Next, Web site marketing will be introduced, and later, in Chapter 12, it is examined further.

Web Site Marketing

Web sites have become standard equipment for fashion retailers and their customers. The Web site can serve as an online retail store, a means to communicate information about the business, a promotional tool, a direct line to each current and prospective customer, and the hardest-working salesperson in the company. With 24/7 availability, most Web sites work to build the brand and customer list, while selling products any time of the day or night.

Following are questions digital marketing directors and Web developers ask when developing or redesigning a Web site:

1. What is the purpose of the Web site? Is the purpose to generate customer interest? Serve as an animated and informational brochure? Or function as an online retail store?
2. Who is the target audience?
3. How will customers find the Web site? Offline strategies, such as advertising, can drive traffic.
4. What do customers expect to find on the site? The ability to purchase? Pricing? Hours of operation? Location? Arrivals of new merchandise?
5. What can be done to cause customers to linger longer at the site?
6. How does the Web site compare to that of the competition? Just as brick-and-mortar stores compete for customers, Web sites compete as well. How are they designed? What are the messages?
7. How will the Web site be monitored? A good Web site host will provide a set of statistics that disclose number of visitors, when they visited, how they found the site, what they viewed, and whether they made a purchase.

Next, qualifications for product, brand, and digital marketing managers are presented.

Qualifications

- *Education.* A bachelor's degree in digital media or computer information systems is required for the digital marketing manager. A bachelor's degree in fashion merchandising, fashion design, product development, marketing, advertising, retailing, or a related field is required for the product or brand marketing manager.

- *Experience.* For the product, brand, and digital marketing managers, on-the-job experience in fashion retailing is necessary to develop a strong understanding of current brick-and-mortar and online marketing concepts, strategies, and best practices. Substantial digital marketing experience within a retail company is often required for the digital marketing manager. Students can gain work experience in their area of interest through an internship and/or part-time employment or volunteer work while attending college.

- *Personal Characteristics.* Effective visual, verbal, and written communication abilities are necessary for these positions. Organization and time management are also needed skills. The ability to sell the company and its image, as well as yourself and your work, is essential and is a critical component of the networking that all of these positions require. An understanding of the numbers, from budgets to consumer data, is required.

Career Challenges

One brand manager put it this way: "In marketing, there is no such thing as consensus." That is one of the digital, brand, and product marketing managers' greatest obstacles. They must work to bring the CEO, CMO, marketing director, and interdepartmental colleagues together in support of the marketing concept before the development of the marketing campaign can get off the ground. Multiple projects driven by time and funding constraints, long hours and late nights when projects are due, and negotiating with co-workers (repeatedly) are some of the challenges the digital, brand, and product marketing managers regularly face.

Creative Art Director

In some large retail companies, there are both a creative director and an art director. The differences are often internal to a specific company, but there are some general distinctions. In most cases, **creative directors** oversee art directors and other in-house art staff. The creative director often works directly with the marketing director (and, in some companies, the creative director *is* the marketing director) to ensure that the strategy, marketing goals, and branding expectations are being met. A creative director position is more managerial and reports to the CMO, while an art director position is more hands-on in the design process and reports to the creative director. The creative director conceptualizes and works on the visual components and production of a campaign, and the art director manages and oversees the visual design and production of projects. The creative director articulates the vision and selects and directs the talent (e.g., graphic designers, Web developers, and photographers), while the art director designs a project with a direction that is already set. The creative director usually goes into this position with at least 12 years of experience, while the art director can start with three to five years of experience.

Art Director

The **art director** produces or oversees production of artwork for advertising campaigns, magazines, television shows, films, Web sites, or products, often working with the other marketing divisions and reporting to the creative director. Art directors lead creative sessions for project kick-offs and, later, collaborate with product designers, graphic designers, copywriters, photographers, and others to discuss project requirements and concepts. They review and approve proofs of printed copy and art materials developed by creative department members. They may also coordinate and attend photo shoots and printing sessions to ensure that the images needed are obtained. All of these tasks are completed by the art director in line with the budget planned for the art department. The future for art directors looks bright with an anticipated 7.4 percent growth projection in employment by the year 2022, according to the Bureau of Labor Statistics (2014).

Copywriter

A **copywriter** is responsible for writing the words, slogans, and audio scripts that accompany promotional visuals—online and in print. A typical copywriting project includes the following activities:

- Discussing the core message and target audience

- Brainstorming visual and copy ideas with other members of the creative team

- Writing and presenting a few options to management

- Modifying copy to meet management's expectations

- Overseeing the production phase

The art director and copywriter are accountable for checking that all of the content being advertised is appealing, clear, reflective of the brand, truthful, and in compliance with codes of advertising practice.

Qualifications

- *Education.* For the art director, a bachelor's degree in art, fine arts, graphic design, and computer-aided design is commonly required. For the copywriter, a degree in journalism, English, writing, advertising, or a related field is mandatory.

- *Experience.* The art director should have a thorough understanding of art, photography, typography, and printing. The art director needs a broad range of art expertise, from the ability to sketch to computer-aided design. Excellent computer skills in relevant art and design software packages are must-haves for the art director. The copywriter should have a keen understanding of journalism, advertising, promotion, and publicity.

- *Personal Characteristics.* Both the art director and the copywriter should be highly creative and have excellent interpersonal and communication skills. They need to work well as part of a team with a range of people. Having an interest in social and cultural trends helps encourage creativity. The successful copywriter must have not only excellent writing skills but strong interpersonal skills as well. Both must be able to work under the pressure of deadlines and quantitative goals (e.g., how many sales the copy in banner advertisements or the images on billboards have generated). Both must also have a keen eye for aesthetics, detail, and accuracy.

Career Challenges

The art director and copywriter face two primary challenges: time and money. There is substantial pressure to be creative on demand, to be constrained by budget parameters, and to declare a product finished in order to be on time. In addition, the art director and copywriter need to be able to see other people's points of view and cope with criticism. This can be difficult when significant time and effort went into a copywriting assignment or a graphic design for an advertisement. It is also challenging to be highly motivated and creative on every project. Finally, positions in these two creative marketing areas are limited, and starting salaries are often low.

Customer Service and Customer Relationship Management

Rooted in understanding and quantifying consumer behavior, **client/customer relationship management (CRM)** marketing encompasses the ability to analyze significant amounts of data to understand consumer demographics, key market segments, and best practices for recruiting or retaining those customers. This information helps the marketing divisions of a fashion company leverage the brand to accomplish the following goals:

- To reach the most qualified customers

- To develop loyalty programs

- To determine the best media forms to reach the consumer

- To understand online consumer behavior to drive sales at the brick-and-mortar stores

As a result, the CRM department works closely with other members of the other marketing divisions. CRM team members know that promotion alone will not generate all of a company's sales. Customer service is an important element of most successful retail operations. As we communicate via e-mail, text messages, Web sites, Facebook, LinkedIn, Instagram, Twitter, and the like, face-to-face interaction between retailers and their customers becomes scarcer. With this shift in communication, retailers must find new and better ways to stay in touch with their most valuable assets: their customers. In Box 9.4, Zara breaks the rules again, applying old fashioned face-to-face communication in a new way—by asking customers what they like and do not like.

One of the ways fashion retail businesses differentiate from each other and compete with larger companies is by providing exceptional customer service. Working closely with customers to build lasting relationships is important in retaining lifelong customers. Nordstrom, for example, is committed to exceptional customer service. It implements a culture of motivated and empowered employees, each with an entrepreneurial retailing spirit. Nordstrom encourages sales associates to do all they can to make sure a shopper leaves the store a satisfied customer. Nordstrom's Web site includes a live chat room, which allows customers to chat online in real time with personal shoppers. In addition, Nordstrom has a hassle-free online return policy, and customers can return merchandise to any Nordstrom store.

Some retailers are making it a point to work on attracting, training, and retaining good sales associates who will provide quality customer service. When asked, most customers state they decided to buy from a particular fashion retailer because of the company's reputation, the level of customer service, the manner in which the retailer responded to complaints and requests, and the relationship they have with the salespeople.

Summary

Developing a marketing strategy, as well as constructing and implementing a marketing plan, is key to the successful penetration of the market. Analyzing the marketing mix includes an examination of the interrelationship of product, price, placement, promotion, and people (i.e., customers—past, present, and future) in a cohesive marketing plan. Thoughtfully pricing the product and placing it can help define and differentiate the marketing strategy and play a crucial role in the success of the business. As marketing and promotion gain importance, several career options designed to transmit messages to the target market about the company's image, product lines, and services have also gained importance. These career tracks include marketing director and manager, product marketing manager, brand marketing manager, digital marketing manager, art director, and copywriter. All work, autonomously and collaboratively, to determine the target market, select the right medium, and clarify promotional goals to reach and penetrate the market. Effective customer relationship management (CRM) is also part of the marketing plan.

Successful marketing identifies the reasons consumers choose to buy products from one company over another. Several global companies have accomplished this objective—from H&M, Forever21, and Zara to Nordstrom, Saks Fifth Avenue, and Macy's. And, they may be part of the reason why, according to Elizabeth Cline, the author of *Overdressed: The Shockingly High Cost of Cheap Fashion*, "Americans buy 20 billion garments a year—an average of 64 garments a person."[3]

Endnotes

1. Berfield, S., and Baigorri, M., "Zara's Fast-Fashion Edge," *Bloomberg Businessweek*, November 14, 2013.
2. www.bbc.com/news/business-26642277 (March 19, 2014).
3. Cline, E., *Overdressed: The Shockingly High Cost of Cheap Fashion*. New York: Penguin, 2012.

Key Terms

art director
brand marketing manager
branding
channel of distribution
client/customer relationship management (CRM)
chief marketing officer (CMO)
copywriter
creative director
diffusion labels

digital marketing manager
distribution
marketing director
marketing manager
marketing mix
marketing plan
product marketing manager
target market
wholesale

Discussion Questions

1. Evaluate the five Ps of marketing and assess why each is important to the company's marketing strategy. Rank them in order of importance, in your perspective, and explain why one is more important than another.

2. Construct a two-column chart and identify the differences and similarities between *marketing* and *promotion*.
3. Outline the advantages and disadvantages of the various advertising media. Consider newspapers, magazines, online advertising, radio, television, mailers, billboards, etc.
4. Discuss the importance of customer service. What constitutes good or valuable customer service—in-store and online? Examine each separately.

Online Resources

www.fortune.com/2013/01/08/meet-amancio-ortega-the-third-richest-man-in-the-world/

www.businessweek.com/articles/2013-11-14/2014-outlook-zaras-fashion-supply-chain-edge

www.reuters.com/article/2014/06/11/us-inditex-idUSKBN0EM0O920140611

www.marketingpower.com

www.hoovers.com

money.usnews.com/careers/best-jobs/art-director

Profile: Interview with Chief Marketing Officer Marivi Avalos Monarrez of Fashionbi

By Pulkit Rastogi, Founder and CEO of ilovefashionretail.com

Fashion is fickle and can change in a minute. That's why there is always a feeling of uncertainty one has to deal with when making decisions. One wrong decision and you can get stuck with the wrong merchandise or unsold dead stock. Most retailers make merchandising and marketing decisions based on intuition; however, you can also use market data to validate your gut instinct to be more confident about your decision making.

With correct data insights, you can predict more accurately what price points will work for your brand. With data, you can make informed merchandising decisions instead of guesses and know exactly what is a fad and what is a trend. We caught up with Marivi Avalos Monarrez, Chief Marketing Officer and Managing Director for Asia

Profile Figure 9a Pulkit Rastogi.

at Fashionbi, to learn more about how online fashion retailers can use data to their advantage—to optimize product mix and price-points, and to discount and merchandise their brands.

(continued on next page)

(continued)

Profile Figure 9b Marivi Avalos Monarrez.

Please tell us about yourself.

I have a Bachelor's degree in International Relations and a Master's degree in Fashion and Luxury Management. I've been a part of the Fashionbi team since the project started almost three years ago. I started as a Fashion Brand Analyst, then I was the Manager for Marketing and, recently, I was appointed CMO and Managing Director for our new office in Shanghai.

What does Fashionbi do?

Fashionbi is a company that serves the fashion and luxury business with marketing intelligence. Our mission is to empower the people in fashion with actionable data. We help them make smart decisions in the fashion and luxury industry; we give them the clear view to see how well (or not) their marketing strategies are paying off country by country, month by month.

We are able to do it because we have more than 3,500 brands from the fashion and luxury industry in our database, and our analysts are constantly doing market research and keeping track of the brands and companies' performance. More than a database, we are a team providing knowledge about the best practices and the opportunities for marketing with a strong focus in Europe, the U.S. and Asia.

How can fashion retailers use data to make buying decisions, such as "Will it sell? Why will it sell?"

There are many ways fashion retailers can use data:

- Picking the right assortment of products to sell

- Tracking the fashion trends in the market and act on them

- Understanding what customers want now

- Knowing what customers can demand in future; for example, what will sell during upcoming holiday season?

- Optimizing product mix, price and offer at a given time period

Apart from this, retailers should study market share, market size, and growth rate to understand who the major players in the industry are and who will be their real competitors.

We offer data insights in the form of Social Media Reports and Live Track Events. For example, a team of analysts monitor the performance of a brand during a specific period—let's say Fashion Week or a specific campaign. We then compare among the different social networks what brand sold and how many fans or followers reacted to the brand's marketing campaigns to sell the product. With Fashionbi's Key Performance Indicators, it is possible to understand which items from the latest collection are the most popular. It helps us to predict which products are going to be the bestsellers of the season.

Also, we study social media channels to determine from which countries new fans are coming. This can help the retailers create local strategies for their audience.

How can fashion e-commerce businesses use data to make smarter marketing decisions?

Data insights are extremely useful, I have to say. Through data insights, you can know if customers

(continued)

are visiting your Web site via mobile or a desktop, their demographics, and how much time they spent on a specific category/product/page of your store. This data helps you identify what is appealing (and what is not appealing) to them. If you are running a multi-brand store, you should know which brands create more customer engagement on your store's site and across your various social media channels.

How can fashion retailers and suppliers use data to determine what pricing points work?

The business of fashion retailing is all about buying the right products and making sure you're selling them at the right prices. Retailers can use data in their price position strategy. It can start at a very basic level; for example, who are your competitors and how are they pricing their products? All this data helps retailers sell what customers want, at a price that isn't undercut by competitors.

Do you think data-driven decision making is always better than intuition?

This just makes me think about the role of fashion buyers, especially those from Milan. They believe a person has natural skills to be a buyer, based on their sensibility for aesthetics and style trends—like you said, mainly from intuition and feeling. But the truth is that there is no black or white. Great decision making is having access to the knowledge, which is all the possible information that will help you to connect the dots.

Do you really think data can help in predicting future trends?

I do, especially because of the digital media. The online and offline worlds are getting more and more connected day by day. We wake up checking our smartphones and go to bed with our iPads. All of our behavior is being tracked and monitored.

That's fascinating. Is it possible for an online retailer to do data analysis for decision making in-house?

Yes, it is. The only problem, however, with doing all the data crunching in-house is the effort, time, and human resources required to not only gather data but also interpret what it means. If you have those kinds of resources to do all the data collection and analysis in-house, it's well worth a shot.

What are the sources of your data?

Everything—social media, financial reports, daily news, our in-house tools, and our exclusive members' network.

Can data from physical retail be applied to e-commerce businesses for decision making?

Absolutely. Data can help in decision making about how to link offline and online business in a smart way to give customers the shopping experience through all the possible channels.

Any advice for someone starting a fashion e-commerce business?

If you're a start-up, it's better to manage e-commerce in-house to control the prices. If you're running a multi-brand e-commerce store, it's important that you have few unique offers for your customers that no other retailer is giving in physical or e-commerce stores.

Source:

ilovefashionretail.com/fashion-e-commerce-2/how-online-fashion-retailers-can-use-data-for-decision-making-interview-with-marivi-avalos-monarrez-from-fashionbi, March 7, 2014

chapter 10

Merchandising for the Retailer

How simple is it to find a new pair of jeans to buy? All you have to do is go to the nearest discount, department, or specialty store, or order the jeans online at your favorite apparel Web site. Have you ever wondered how the dozens or even hundreds of pairs of blue jeans ended up at the retail store or Web site in the first place (Figures 10.1a–c)? Who decided which brands and styles of jeans the retailer would sell and which ones it would not? Chances are, a buyer indirectly influenced your wardrobe. Effective retail buying is so important to the success of retailers that they are finding innovative ways to include their customers in buying decisions.

Modcloth.com knows this and invites its customers to be part of its buying process. Sometimes, Modcloth's retail buyers adore certain designs and want to buy them for their customers, but the manufacturer/designer can only put them into production with a large quantity order in hand. For a retail company like Modcloth, it is difficult to make these big inventory commitments without knowing if customers will love the designs as much as the buyers do. Both the manufacturing and retailing sides of the business are looking for ways to minimize their risks.

Rather than looking into a crystal ball, Modcloth created "Be the Buyer," a program that invites the customer to be a virtual member of the ModCloth buying team. Potential designs are posted online, and using the "Pick It" button, customers can vote for their favorites. If a style gets enough votes, it will be manufactured by the designer and sold by ModCloth. When the item a majority of customers selects is produced and becomes available for purchase, the "Pick It" voters will receive an email inviting them to be among the first to buy the design. "Be the Buyer" participants can spread the word about the pieces they chose that won the vote-off by sharing links with their friends via Facebook, Twitter, or email.

■ **Figure 10.1a–c**
Have you ever wondered how the dozens or even hundreds of pairs of blue jeans ended up at the retail store or Web site for your selection?

Modcloth exemplifies how customers can be included in buying decisions, but the merchandise found in a fashion retail operation is ultimately selected and purchased either by the business owner or a buyer who is employed by the business owner. A buyer can work for a specialty chain (e.g., Gap, The Limited, or Charming Charlie), a department store (e.g., Nordstrom, Macy's, or Saks Fifth Avenue), a privately owned store or boutique, or an online retailer (e.g., Nasty Girl, Zappos, or Zuilily). In large operations, the buying tasks are performed by a team of merchandising specialists who have acquired in-depth knowledge of buying for a specific department or a group of related departments. In small operations, the buying function may be one of many carried out by the company's owner. Alternatively, the small business owner may employ a buyer to purchase merchandise for all of the departments in the retail operation.

Merchandising refers to all of the activities involved in the buying and selling of the retailer's products. The major activities in merchandising are locating and purchasing products, with the preferences of the consumer in mind, and then selling these products at a profit. Merchandising includes extensive research on the department's or store's customers, trying to predict which types of merchandise customers will want to buy for upcoming seasons. The selection of products available for sale in a fashion operation is commonly called its **inventory**, or *merchandise assortment.* Who are the people involved in selecting the merchandise assortment, and how do they do it?

In this chapter, merchandising positions for the retailer are explored. The career options that are discussed include the general merchandising manager, divisional merchandising manager, buyer/fashion merchandiser, assistant buyer, planner, distribution manager/allocator, and merchandising trainee.

General Merchandising Manager

A **general merchandising manager (GMM)** is the boss of the buyers' boss. The GMM leads and manages the buyers of all divisions in a retail operation. This key administrator is responsible for setting the overall strategy and merchandise direction of the retail operation. The GMM develops the buying and selling strategies that will, hopefully, maximize business performance and profitability. The GMM ensures that pricing decisions, promotional strategies, and marketing activities support the financial objectives of the merchandising team. To accomplish this, the GMM must understand not only the competitors' strengths, weaknesses, and strategies, but also the customers' demographics, wants, and needs, as well as merchandise trends in all departments.

GMMs set the merchandise direction to ensure a focused continuity on the selling floor. They work with the divisional merchandising managers and buyers to develop competitive merchandise assortments that appeal to customers at the right prices and at the right fashion level. They also assist the buying staff with securing the best merchandise exclusives, product launches, and deliveries available in the market, as illustrated by the product launch of Zooey Deschanel and Tommy Hilfiger's line, To Tommy from Zooey, in Figure 10.2. The GMM collaborates with the buying team on which manufacturers or designers, fashion items, and merchandise categories will be carried in depth by the retail organization.

GMMs manage, coach, and develop the buying staff, creating an environment that promotes the professional development of the divisional merchandising managers and buyers and enhancing

■ **Figure 10.2**
Two celebrities, Zooey Deschanel and Tommy Hilfiger, promote the new line they collaborated on, To Tommy from Zooey.

Box 10.1 General Merchandising Manager (GMM)—Junior Apparel Retail Chain

Job Responsibilities:

The general merchandising manager is a senior position with a private, regional, midsize retailer of junior apparel, shoes, and accessories. Responsibilities include:

- Developing and managing strategic plans

- Planning merchandise assortments

- Maintaining vendor relations

- Monitoring retail pricing, along with analysis of what competition is doing

- Promotional planning to achieve financial goals

- Identifying, recruiting, challenging, and developing buying staff

Job Requirements:

- Four-year college or university degree in business, fashion merchandising, retailing, or a related field

- Ten-plus years of experience in the apparel industry

- Excellent established vendor relationships in the apparel industry

- Negotiation skills

- Strategic planning skills

- Specialty store buying experience preferred

- 25 percent travel required

Other:

Position reports directly to the president. Excellent benefits including life, medical, dental insurance; 529, 401(k), profit-sharing plan; a generous merchandise discount; and possible annual bonus based on performance and net profit. Relocation assistance will be provided as needed.

---

morale among the entire buying team. While collaborating with the divisional merchandising managers in developing merchandise assortments that support the needs of the customers and the financial objectives of each merchandise division, GMMs are ultimately responsible for overseeing merchandise selection and procurement of goods by the buyers. Box 10.1 is a classified advertisement seeking to fill this position.

The number of GMM positions is limited, as these are top leadership slots available in midsize and large retail operations. Some companies offer GMMs supplementary packages, such as bonuses or stock options, based on increases in the company's sales volume and gross margin.

Divisional Merchandising Manager

Once you have mastered the buying side of the fashion world as a fashion merchandiser, you may be ready for advancement. Before a buyer becomes a GMM, the next step up the career ladder is to the divisional merchandising manager position. A **divisional merchandising manager (DMM)** works under the GMM and provides leadership for the buying staff of a division, or a related group of departments, such as menswear, women's wear, or home furnishings. DMMs coordinate teamwork among the buyers and delegate responsibilities to the buyers, assistant buyers, and planners. They collaborate with the buyers on future purchases, marketing and promotional efforts, merchandise expenditures, and inventory management. The main objective of the DMM is to keep profits up and losses down by maximizing sales and minimizing markdowns. They also study the fashion industry through shopping the competition, forecasting trends, attending markets, and working with buyers on the right fashion directions for the upcoming season. Box 10.2 is a classified advertisement seeking a DMM.

In general, DMMs oversee the work of the buyers in a particular department of the business. Specifically, their job responsibilities include the following:

- Developing merchandise strategies in support of the total company

- Managing, coaching, and developing the buying staff, to include assistant buyers

- Mentoring and fostering an environment that promotes the development of buyers and their businesses as a divisional buying team

- Setting the overall strategy and merchandise direction for the division

- Directing buyers to develop assortments that support the needs of the customer and the financial objectives of the merchandise division

- Ensuring that pricing, promotional strategies, and marketing support the financial objectives of the merchandise division

- Working with the planning organization to develop by-store assortment plans that support the overall plan for positioning key merchandise categories, selected trends, items, and vendors

- Working with the buyers to strengthen market relationships and knowledge of market trends

- Understanding competitors' strengths, weaknesses, and strategies

- Facilitating and promoting timely communication and cooperation between branch stores, merchandising functions, and resources

Box 10.2 Divisional Merchandise Manager of Men's Sportswear

Seeking a seasoned, creative, enthusiastic, and friendly individual to join our merchandising team as Divisional Merchandise Manager (DMM) of Men's Sportswear. The DMM of Men's Sportswear partners with the GMM in the development and implementation of merchandising strategies, new business initiatives, and key item strategies to drive top-line sales, sales per square foot, and profit growth for the Men's Sportswear department. This position has profit and loss accountability and responsibility for the merchandising, inventory control, and private label development for this evolving Men's Sportswear business. This role will also focus on overall direction, market penetration, assortment, and vendor mix to meet the needs of the demanding customer base, as well as the development and management of private label within the department.

Our Benefits:

In addition to a dynamic and friendly work environment, where dedication and hard work are recognized and rewarded and work/family balance is valued, the company also offers the following benefits:

- Relocation assistance
- Generous incentive compensation plan
- Generous associate discount
- Paid holidays
- Paid vacation, sick, and personal days
- Medical/dental/vision plans

- Short/long-term disability plans
- 401(k) retirement plan
- Employee stock purchase plan
- Flexible spending account
- Life insurance

Requirements:

- Bachelor's degree in business, retail merchandising, or related field is required
- Five to seven years of applicable corporate retail merchandising/buying expertise and leadership experience within the Men's Sportswear category
- Solid track record of success in growing and enhancing businesses within the Men's Sportswear category
- Experience working with various technologies including Retail Merchandising systems
- PC skills to include proficiency with Microsoft Office, Excel, and Outlook e-mail applications

- Merchandising skills, negotiating skills, retail math skills, and project management skills
- Ability to research and analyze large amounts of data
- Results-oriented personality; willingness to follow through, make informed decisions, complete tasks, and problem-solve
- Demonstrated abilities in learning new skills, change/variety in work, and creativity
- Should display a strong fashion sense and understanding of quality/value relationships
- Some amount of travel is required

Are you looking for a leadership role in the buying division? What does it take to be at the highest levels of the merchandising career ladder? While it takes intelligence, perseverance, and a high level of energy, the retail employer will expect a high level of qualifications as well. Because the GMM and DMM positions have similar education requirements, experience expectations, characteristics, and challenges, a list of the qualifications and discussion of career challenges for a top-notch GMM or DMM follows.

Qualifications

- *Education.* A bachelor's degree in fashion merchandising, retailing, retail merchandising, management, marketing, business administration, or a related field is necessary. A master's degree in these fields may be required.

- *Experience.* A minimum of ten years of retail management, divisional merchandise management, or extensive buying experience is often required for the GMM. Five to seven years of retail buying experience is typically required for the DMM position. For both, administrative experience in a full-line department store, specialty store chain, or e-commerce site is usually required for this key administrative position. Experience in multi-location retail stores as a merchandiser or with multiple delivery systems (e.g., brick-and-mortar, Internet, and catalogue) and product development is preferred.

- *Personal characteristics.* Strong leadership, organizational, and financial skills are necessary. The ability to change priorities and work topics quickly is a needed personal quality. Being able to manage teams and relate to all levels of employees is important. Excellent communication and negotiation skills are critical for the successful DMM and GMM, as are being able to plan ahead and be an analytical problem solver. In terms of personality, the best GMMs and DMMs are articulate, enthusiastic, and charismatic.

Career Challenges

As leaders of the merchandising staff, the GMM and DMM must understand the team of merchandising personnel and all of their merchandise classifications. Leading a group of diverse buyers working in a wide range of departments requires a great deal of multitasking and prioritizing. It is critical to be able to move quickly between buyers and their respective departments and be up to date on each of their areas. As leaders, the GMM and DMM are challenged to keep all merchandisers on the same path in terms of merchandise selection, price ranges, fashion trends, and similar variables. They need to know when to push or pull back buyers who are not meeting sales goals or buying into the designated fashion trend statements.

The GMM and DMM are often held accountable for the accuracy of the numbers the buyers submit, such as planned sales and inventories. In summary, these executives must specialize in a variety of areas—fashion, merchandising retail mathematics, vendor negotiations, and personnel management.

Buyer or Fashion Merchandiser

Are you someone who enjoys the thrill of the shopping hunt? Do you enjoy trend forecasting and being involved in product development? Are attending markets and purchasing the newest trends to sell to customers enticing job tasks for you? Do you have, or can you acquire, skills in retail mathematics? Then you may want to pursue a career as a buyer/fashion merchandiser. **Buyers**, or *fashion merchandisers* or *retail buyers*, are typically responsible for all of the product purchases for a company or particular department of a company within a certain budget. Buyers monitor the fashion trends and determine which seasonal items their customers will buy. They search for the items (often traveling to do so) that best fit the seasonal theme and their customers' preferences, primarily during market weeks at apparel markets (Box 10.3). They locate the right merchandise suppliers and negotiate prices, shipping, and discounts. They sometimes work with other departments in the retail operation, such as advertising and visual merchandising, on promotions and product placement.

The ultimate goal of a buyer is to recognize trends that fit with the target market in terms of taste and price, procure merchandise that reflects these trends, and translate them into a profitable business plan for the retailer. Buyers select and purchase products from designers, manufacturers, or wholesalers for retail sale to their customers. They use their fashion sense, knowledge of trends, and understanding of their target customers' wants to purchase desirable merchandise assortments at markets for their retail businesses (Figure 10.3). Due to the length of time it takes for a designer or manufacturer to fill orders, buyers often make their purchases three to six months in advance, or longer if they are high-fashion goods. Buyers must be effective at budgeting and planning their assortments so that a good selection of products is always available to the consumer. Buyers for larger retail operations usually specialize in a merchandise classification, such as men's tailored apparel or home tabletop fashions.

■ **Figure 10.3**
Collaborating with the visual merchandising department, the buyer plans visual presentation strategies for the stores to support seasonal trends.

CASE STUDIES IN CAREER EXPLORATION

Box 10.3 Buyer's Preparation for a Market Trip

What to Bring

Buyers should bring several copies of the following to the apparel mart for their initial visits:

- Tax identification number for business

- Bank reference (letter from bank)

- Business cards

- Resale license/permit

- Purchase order forms

To make filling out forms fast and easy, you may want to bring a rubber stamp or computer labels with the following information: business name; street and email addresses; phone and fax numbers; contact person; and tax identification number.

Preparing for Market

- Make travel arrangements well in advance. Ask about special buyer rates at partner hotels.

- Allow time for seminars, fashion shows, and comparison shopping.

- Review the directory of exhibitors, product categories, mart maps, and floor plans to help you organize your schedule for the market week. You can request a printed version of the directory or locate it online.

- Attend a new buyer orientation. During market orientation, you will learn the building design and layout, the showroom numbering system, the location of merchandise, how to use the market directory, and the locations of various buyer amenities, such as restaurants.

- You may want to save time by going directly from the airport to the mart. If you have any luggage with you, check it at the mart.

- Take time to walk the building and familiarize yourself with the product layout.

- Take advantage of free buyer lounges to network with buyers from other locations or to take a break.

Quick Tips for Covering Market

- Arrive prepared with open-to-buy figures by department. Have a buying plan—a general description of the types and quantities of merchandise to be purchased.

- Bring extra business cards to distribute to sales reps and retailers with whom you've networked.

- Make appointments with showrooms before the market begins.

- If possible, set aside at least one day for "just looking."

- Wear comfortable shoes for all-day walking and line viewing.

- Visit tried-and-true vendors first, allowing time to find new vendors and items. Be sure to shop the temporary floors to discover new trends and up-and-coming designers.

- Prepare a list of questions for each vendor you visit.

- Write orders as soon as possible to ensure on-time deliveries.

- Never pack uncompleted orders or line sheets in luggage you check with the airlines.

- If you are loaded down with line sheets, order forms or copies, samples, brochures, etc., send them home ahead of time via UPS or FedEx.

■ Figure 10.4
After developing the buying plan, the buyer analyzes market trends, calculates how much will be spent on new products, and then attends markets to preview apparel lines.

To get started, a buyer begins with an analysis of the numbers—sales, markdowns, and inventories by month for the past year or a few years. Next, the buyer develops a buying plan, usually six months to one year before the merchandise can be purchased by customers. The six-month **buying plan**, or *six-month plan*, is a financial plan that takes into account past and projected sales, inventory, markups and markdowns by department, and profit, or **gross margin**. After developing the buying plan, the buyer tracks and analyzes market trends, calculates how much will be spent on new products, and then goes to markets and meets with manufacturers to preview apparel that will be produced (Figure 10.4). Once the manufacturers' lines are reviewed, the buyer places orders for merchandise to arrive in the future, from one month for reorders to as much as one year in advance for new merchandise.

Being a fashion merchandiser or buyer is like being a product developer, with a twist. Instead of reinventing the wheel every season, the buyer takes the retailer's bestsellers from the previous season or year and finds the item with slight changes. The buyer may locate an item that was a bestseller with an updated color or new styling detail. The result is a new item with a good sales history for the upcoming selling season. A fashion merchandiser also makes decisions on new, fashion-forward merchandise. The buyer always wants fresh, trendy looks to welcome customers into the department.

This career path, however, is not all about shopping. The fashion merchandiser is accountable for the bottom line. The company wants to know whether the merchandise selected for customers to buy has made a profit. Fashion merchandisers are responsible for the financials of their departments and the resulting profit or loss. It is a daily task for fashion merchandisers to track the sales of merchandise and decide whether items need to be reordered

Box 10.4 Shoe Buyer for a Luxury Fashion Retailer

Job Responsibilities:

- Manage, update, and review open-to-buy

- Select/place seasonal market orders

- Project seasonal sales

- Review weekly sales reports, ensuring planned sales and inventory levels are achieved

- Place and confirm reorders as needed

- Manage return-to-vendors

- Review and follow up with deliveries

- Manage stock placement for new merchandise

- Update and manage purchase orders

- Place and confirm special orders as needed

- Manage inventory for store events

- Recap show and incentive results

- Make stock projections; review sales and net receipts

- Oversee stock balances

- Review sales results on advertising campaigns and catalogue styles

- Prepare and review fast/slow sellers report

- Prepare and review sell-through report

- Provide end of season (EOS) product analysis and final sales report

- Provide EOS final sale reports

Skills and Competencies:

- Ability to effectively manage merchandise coordinator

- Strategic agility

- Excellent organizational skills and drive for results

Job Requirements:

- Four to six years prior merchandising experience; luxury retail preferred

- Availability for frequent travel

- Strong knowledge of Microsoft Office programs (e.g., Excel, PivotTable, and Word)

or put on sale. They also spend time talking with vendors and negotiating the best wholesale prices so that higher profits can be achieved. Because most fashion merchandisers have worked their way through the ranks, they also know how important it is to communicate with the department and store managers and solicit feedback about what customers are seeking, buying, and rejecting. A career as a fashion merchandiser is a very exciting and rewarding one for a high-energy person, as shown in Box 10.4, which features a classified advertisement for the shoe buyer position with a luxury retailer.

CASE STUDIES IN CAREER EXPLORATION

Box 10.5 Renato Grant, Fashion Buyer of a Chain of Independently Owned Women's Wear Boutiques

How did you get into the fashion industry?

Most fashion buyers start out by working on the shop floor either as sales assistants or shop managers. I was no different and worked on the shop floor for four years. This allowed me to get a full understanding of all the designers and merchandise we stocked, from clothing, bags, and accessories to small jewelry items. It also gave me great insight into the many comments we receive, good and bad, directly from customers.

What are the highs and lows to your job?

There are many of both! As I love the fashion industry the highs outweigh the lows. I get to see all the latest trends at catwalk shows, trade exhibitions, and fashion showrooms. I travel extensively and get to order the collections I love for our stores, bearing in mind our customer profile, and I get to see the results of my opinions and hard work by the sell-throughs on each item I have ordered.

The lows can be the long hours I need to put in. Often, I'm on the shop floor very early in the morning merchandising, late in the evening organizing window dressing, and on weekends and during holiday periods when the stores are extremely busy. There is a lot of paperwork for buyers, lots of running from showroom to showroom, and sometimes when merchandise is delivered we have to return some to the designer as it can be different from what we have ordered, this is not what we like to do but is a part of the business. Dealing with customers directly also has its challenges. As I buy for my own stores, I am often on the shop floor listening to comments directly from customers (which sometimes can be

less than complimentary, especially if we do not have something available in their size).

Do you get to travel within your job?

Yes, extensively both at home and abroad. It's very important for a fashion buyer to stock fashion designers and brands that are not available on every high street. In order for us to do this, we have to travel to seek out these labels. We get to visit catwalk shows, tradeshows, exhibitions, and fashion showrooms around the world but particularly throughout Europe—London, Copenhagen, Berlin, Paris, Milan, Denmark—and New York and Los Angeles.

What does a typical day for you involve?

It really depends upon the time of the season and, if I am honest, there is no such thing as a typical day for me as each one has different challenges. If it's the buying season, then typically I will be traveling from showroom to showroom placing orders for the collections I want to stock, then returning to the store to catch up on the mountain of paperwork that always needs doing: returning goods to suppliers, paying invoices due, making sure my Web site has everything it needs and is constantly updated with new imagery coming through, handling PR and customer queries, making appointments, planning launch days, reordering stock, the list goes on! I have to make sure that the shop window looks fabulous at all times and the stock in store is correctly merchandised and priced.

Source:

Renato Grant / Boutique Buyers,
www.boutiquebuyers.com

The most important task performed by the buyer is selecting merchandise for the retail operation. This responsibility encompasses determining which goods are needed, calculating the size of purchases and from which vendors the goods should be bought, recognizing when merchandise should be ordered for timely delivery, and negotiating the prices and terms of a sale. From a planning perspective, the buyer projects sales and inventory levels by month for each department and, subsequently, determines the amount of funding to be spent on inventory. Another part of the planning process is determining merchandise assortments in terms of color, size, and style. The amount of money allocated for new merchandise purchases each month is referred to as **open-to-buy**. With open-to-buy as the lead factor, the buyer determines which lines will be carried in large quantities and which ones will be stocked in smaller quantities. Those manufacturers' lines featured as the greatest proportion of a retailer's inventory are called **key vendors**. Lines carried in smaller quantities are referred to as **secondary vendors**.

Buyers have a great number of responsibilities in addition to locating the vendors, selecting and purchasing the right amount of the right merchandise, and setting prices on the merchandise, primarily depending on the size of the retail operation. Box 10.5 illustrates the responsibilities of a buyer for a small chain of boutiques. In addition to purchasing goods, buyers often handle tasks that relate to merchandising in other departments in the company. For example, they may assign floor space for items or lines, select specific merchandise for visual displays and advertisements, and manage or collaborate with personnel in various areas of the business. A buyer may hold training seminars to educate management and sales staffs on the newest trends and product lines. In multi-unit retail operations, the buyer advises receiving or warehouse personnel on how many units, sizes, and/or colors of a style should be shipped to or transferred from one branch store or another. With the advertising department, the buyer determines marketing plans and promotional calendars for each month. Collaborating with the visual merchandising department, the buyer plans visual presentation strategies for the stores, to support seasonal trends (Figure 10.5). For example, the buyer may meet with the director of visual merchandising to discuss color trends, specific manufacturers' lines, and key fashion items that should be featured in windows and interior displays to give the retail operation a strong, fashion-forward look and, ultimately, sell products.

■ Figure 10.5
Buyers use their fashion sense, knowledge of trends, and understanding of their target customers to purchase desirable merchandise for their retail businesses.

Qualifications

Do you love to travel, enjoy searching for a specific item, and have proficient mathematical and analytical skills? You may consider the career path of buyer. What are the education and work experiences you will need to secure a position in this field? Which personal characteristics are significant to the success of a buyer? The answers to these questions are as follows:

- *Education.* A bachelor's degree in fashion merchandising, retailing, retail merchandising, or a related field is required. A minor or additional coursework in business administration and fashion design is very helpful.

- *Experience.* Two to five years of work in the apparel industry is required for a buyer, including retail or sales experience. Retail sales experience is very helpful, because understanding customer buying behavior is a key part of being a successful buyer. The common step into a buyer position is from assistant buyer. To move up the career ladder, buyers gain experience buying for a variety of departments, usually moving from one department to another of higher sales volume.

- *Personal characteristics.* Successful buyers love fashion and have knowledge of fashion history and trends, as well as an understanding of the fashion industry as a whole. They have good analytical, mathematical, and computer skills (e.g., Microsoft Excel), particularly in budgeting, planning, and inventory management. Successful buyers are good negotiators, possess excellent communication and organizational skills, are detail oriented, and are able to deal well with deadlines and stress.

The outlook for career opportunities in buying is very good to excellent. The number of new buyer positions available is expected to remain stable, and existing positions will become available because of internal promotions or transitions. One can grow on the job by being promoted to the buyer's position in a larger department with greater sales volume.

Career Challenges

There are many buyer positions available in the fashion industry; however, buyers excel by showing maintained profitability and growth within their departments and by making good buying decisions for their particular target markets. Because the numbers tell the story, buyers are under pressure to reach or surpass sales-volume goals while maintaining the planned inventory levels—every single month. If a line does not sell, the buyer is expected to negotiate with the vendor for returns, exchanges, or a reduced price to cover the cost of markdowns. Items planned for advertising can be a source of stress if they are not delivered as planned. The buyer has a multitude of tasks to juggle, and all of them require high attention to detail and quick turnarounds.

Assistant Buyer

An **assistant buyer** works directly for the buyer of a department or group of related departments. Assistant buyers primarily work with the six-month plan, open-to-buy, and inventory, taking cues from buyers. In some companies, they will accompany buyers to markets. They often work hands-on with the merchandise assortment, transferring items from one retail location to another as needed, and placing special orders. In most companies, the assistant buyer is in training for a buying position in the future.

Qualifications

Following are the education and work experience requirements for the assistant buyer, as well as necessary personal characteristics:

- *Education.* A bachelor's degree in fashion merchandising, retailing, retail merchandising, or a related field is usually required. Some companies will accept an associate's degree in these disciplines. Additional coursework in business administration and fashion design is very helpful.

- *Experience.* Two to three years of apparel industry experience, including retail or sales experience, is required. Experience in accounting and budgeting is extremely helpful. Some companies have an executive training program to prepare entry-level employees for a merchandising career, often beginning as an assistant buyer.

- *Personal characteristics.* Assistant buyers understand the fashion of today and yesterday— its history and current trends. To move up the career ladder, they must have both a sense of what is fashionable and of who the customer is. Additionally, they should have knowledge of retailing and sales and strong analytical, mathematical, and computer skills, particularly Excel, because their responsibilities include extensive work in budgeting, planning, and inventory management. Assistant buyers who are self-directed and motivated will advance quickly. Effective communication and organizational skills, attention to detail, an eye for accuracy, and the ability to work well under pressure are significant attributes.

College graduates who begin at the assistant buyer level and have the right skills, personal qualities, and ambition have a good chance of becoming full-fledged buyers within three to five years.

Career Challenges

Many assistant buyers describe their job responsibilities as "doing what the buyer does not want to do, or does not have time to do." The key word in the job title is "assistant," as this person is employed to help the buyer accomplish all merchandising tasks. Some buyers believe it is a part of their responsibilities to educate assistant buyers on all it takes to become a buyer; others do not. Some buyers do not want to retrain a new assistant and, consequently, prefer to keep their assistant buyers in this position. It can be a challenge for the assistant buyer to learn all of the ropes of merchandising and earn the support of the buyer to move into a buying position, but it can be accomplished. Anticipating what needs to be done and doing it well and independently are keys to succeeding in this position.

Planner

In large companies, a **planner** works in collaboration with a buyer to develop sales forecasts, inventory plans, and spending budgets for merchandise to minimize markdowns and achieve the retailer's sales and profit objectives. Using past sales data and sales projections based on fashion trends, planners construct merchandise assortments for specific departments. The merchandise assortment plan can include sizes, colors, styles, price ranges, and classifications. For example, a planner in a junior sportswear department may construct a chart, referred to as a planning module, for top-to-bottom ratios. In this **planning module**, the planner will project how many blouses, T-shirts, and tank tops to purchase and how many pants, shorts, or skirts need to be purchased for a given season. Today's junior customer, for instance, buys two to four times as many tops as she does bottoms. The merchandise assortment needs to reflect this proportion to be profitable. Using the planning module, planners recommend product flow (e.g., tanks, tees, and long-sleeved shirts) by department and by month or season. They also project markdown dollar budgets by month or season, based on actual markdowns during prior seasons, and assist buyers in determining how much money will be available to spend on new merchandise by providing seasonal buying budgets and monthly open-to-buy dollars by department and by season.

In addition to planning at the start of a season, planners in multi-unit retail firms review sales and stock performance by retail location as it compares to plans. They also ensure that key vendor plans are in place and that there is adequate inventory for the sales of major lines.

Box 10.6 Retail Merchandise Planner

Company Description: High-end Intimate Apparel Boutique in Miami, Florida

Job Responsibilities

- Regularly manage, update, and review open-to-buy plan

- Prepare detailed daily, weekly, monthly, seasonal sales analysis based on history and current trends in order to strategically forecast future orders

- Prepare replenishment orders as needed

- Place and confirm special orders as needed

- Develop and place seasonally appropriate merchandise assortment, while paying special attention to merchandise classification structure

- Serve as a direct liaison between vendors and the company

Required Qualifications, Skills, and Knowledge

- University or college degree in fashion merchandising, retailing, or a related field

- Three or more years of buying/planning experience in a small fashion company

- Excellent retail math skills

- Knowledge of Retail Pro software, Excel, and related computer programs

- Must be honest and accountable

- Must have strong analytical, financial, strategic, and planning skills

- Must be a team player who can work effectively in a fast-paced environment and possess ability to multitask

- Must be a go-getter, with a can-do attitude and a true excitement for business

- Must have a strong sense of style with a keen understanding and interest in fashion and trends

- Must have excellent communication skills

Throughout each season, the planner coordinates communication to and from stores with regard to merchandise performance and sales plans. A department manager in the retail store may, for example, contact a planner for additional types of items that have sold out in the store. The planner will transfer the preferred merchandise into this store from a branch store that has not sold the items as well. Box 10.6 is a classified advertisement for a planner.

In partnership with the buying staff, the planner's main goal is to accurately anticipate and control inventories at the retail locations to maximize sales, inventory, and profit. The planner works to keep all store locations in stock of key items by directing the distribution of goods through reorders and transfers of merchandise. If you enjoy working with numbers, are accurate, and want to move into buying, the position of planner is a great place to begin.

Qualifications

A listing of the educational background, experience, and personal characteristics needed for the job of merchandise planner follows:

- *Education.* A bachelor's degree in fashion merchandising, retailing, accounting, finance, or a related field is a prerequisite. Some companies hire candidates who have completed a two-year associate's degree in one of these fields for the position of assistant planner.

- *Experience.* Gaining retail sales experience is an excellent way for the future planner to start. The person who understands the customer's desires as they pertain to sales and inventory is a step ahead of job candidates without this work experience.

- *Personal characteristics.* Planners must be detail oriented with strong analytical skills. They must be quick, accurate, and able to work with advanced spreadsheet applications. Effective interpersonal and communication skills are important in this position, as is the ability to work well with all levels of employees of the organization.

Some larger retail organizations offer the position of planning manager. A **planning manager** provides leadership, direction, and support at the merchandise-division level to plan, distribute, and monitor inventory appropriately within the company's various retail locations to maximize sales. The planning manager supervises the planners and supports the buyer and DMM in the financial planning process.

Career Challenges

The planner is a number cruncher, and this may be a challenging job for the fashion graduate entering the merchandising field. Although being a planner is an excellent entry-level position for the future assistant buyer or buyer, it can be a tough tour of duty for those who are interested in working with the actual merchandise. The important thing to remember is that those numbers represent the merchandise, and there is much to be learned in the planner's position. Accuracy is a critical part of this job, as one decimal point off can equal thousands of the company's dollars.

Distribution Manager/Allocator

Have you ever thought about how merchandise gets to the retail floor for customers to purchase? A **distribution manager**, or *allocator*, is responsible for planning and managing merchandise deliveries received from vendors, as ordered by buyers, to the retail locations. In some companies, this position is referred to as *replenishment analyst*. The merchandise is held in a central distribution warehouse to be allotted to the right store, at the right time, and in the right quantities to meet customer demands and maximize sales for the retail stores. Figure 10.6 depicts an allocator assessing the inventory of merchandise of each store unit prior to distribution of the shipment.

Distribution managers oversee merchandise receipts from manufacturers, shipments to the retail stores from the distribution center, and shipments from one store to another via the distribution center. They arrange for the transportation of merchandise to the retail outlet locations and may work for catalog and Internet distribution centers, where they are responsible for keeping items in stock in the warehouse. Their main job is to be certain that merchandise is available when a customer stops by a store or orders an item over the phone, by mail, or via the Internet. Distribution managers have some of the responsibilities of buyers. They must study sales and inventory reports and then analyze the needs of each individual retail store to determine the correct quantities to distribute to the stores.

Qualifications

If you are detail oriented and organized, and enjoy working with merchandise and numbers (while not on a sales floor), this career path may be ideal for you, if you meet the following criteria:

- *Education.* A bachelor's degree in fashion merchandising, retailing, business administration, or a related field is usually required. Some firms hire employees with associate's degrees in these fields.

- *Experience.* One of the most important backgrounds for the distribution manager may be surprising. It is retail experience. Working on the sales floor, observing the flow of merchandise, and getting to know the customer provide a future distribution manager with a solid foundation for this career. An internship in a distribution department is an ideal door-opener. Merchandising experience, such as being an assistant buyer, is another way of going into distribution management.

- *Personal characteristics.* Good problem-solving skills, detail and deadline orientation, the ability to coordinate scheduling, and strong math skills are important personal characteristics for distribution managers. Effective communication skills are important as well.

Opportunities for distribution manager positions can be found throughout the industry with major retailers of all kinds.

Career Challenges

If merchandise is not on the selling floor, then it will not sell. A distribution manager, or allocator, is under pressure to push products out of the distribution warehouse to the correct retail store quickly and in the right amounts, after it is tagged correctly. During pre-holiday times, when there are huge amounts of merchandise receipts and many buyers calling to check on the distribution of their orders, this is particularly challenging. Speed, organization, and accuracy must go hand in hand in this career track.

■ **Figures 10.6**
An allocator assesses the merchandise inventory of each store unit prior to distribution of the shipment of soft goods.

Merchandising Trainee

One avenue by which college graduates often choose to move into a merchandising career track is through an executive training program. Many retailers, particularly larger ones, offer these programs, which help graduates work their way up to buying positions. For example, the executive training programs at Neiman Marcus, Saks Fifth Avenue, Macy's, Nordstrom, and Bloomingdale's prepare participants for jobs as assistant buyers and, ultimately, buyers for the company.

A **merchandising executive training program** is designed for new hires, former interns, college recruits, or current employees who have shown skills in merchandising, to prepare them for their first assignments as assistant buyers. Through on-the-job and classroom training, trainees gain the necessary skills needed for analyzing financial data, planning assortment selections, and developing vendor relationships to achieve business goals. The executive training program is a structured development program of classes, guest speakers, and projects. The trainee must show active participation and successfully complete all of the training assignments within the time frame of the program, which can range from six weeks to twelve months.

Qualifications

What do you need to know to become a merchandising trainee?

- *Education.* A bachelor's degree in fashion merchandising, retail merchandising, retailing, business administration, or a related field is often required.

- *Experience.* Retail sales experience and, possibly, an internship with a retail organization are work experiences that make a potential merchandising executive trainee appealing to a retailer. Many companies require trainee candidates to complete tests that reveal proficiency in the areas of mathematics, case study analysis, writing, and presentation skills.

- *Personal characteristics.* Merchandising trainees exhibit strong analytical abilities, effective computer skills, organizational skills, and excellent communication skills—written, oral, and visual. Effective time management, flexibility, and the ability to react quickly and calmly to change are also important attributes. Successful merchandise trainees are self-motivated, self-directed, and able to work effectively as part of a team.

Career Challenges

There are very few career disadvantages when starting as a merchandising trainee with a major company. You select the company of your choice, secure the trainee position, and the company prepares you for an entry-level executive position. These training programs are often referred to as a form of graduate education without the price tag. Although you do not earn college credits or pay tuition, you do receive additional education that can be applied directly to the company. Frequently, the tough part is making the cut or securing the position. Company recruiters often interview 1,000 candidates for fewer than 100 trainee openings. In some firms, trainees complete a general company training program and then are assigned to either the merchandising or management track, based on their performance in the program. For those trainees who have their hearts set on one track or the other, this may be a difficult assignment if it does not match their preference.

Summary

Merchandising encompasses all of the activities involved in the buying and selling of a retailer's products. The major responsibilities of merchandising personnel are to locate and purchase products, with the consumer's preferences in mind, and then sell these products at a profit. Merchandising career opportunities include the following positions: general merchandising manager, divisional merchandising manager, buyer/fashion merchandiser, assistant buyer, planner, distribution manager or allocator, and merchandising trainee.

General merchandising managers (GMMs) lead and manage the buyers of all divisions in the retail operation. They are the key administrators responsible for setting the overall strategy and merchandise direction of their retail operations. The divisional merchandising manager (DMM) works under the GMM and provides leadership for the buying staff of a division or a related group of departments. Buyers, or fashion merchandisers, are typically responsible for all of the product purchases for a company or particular segment of the company within a certain budget. Buyers monitor fashion trends and determine which seasonal items their customers will purchase. They search for the items at trade marts that best fit the seasonal theme and their customers' preferences and negotiate prices, shipping, and discounts. They then monitor sales and inventory, adjusting the prices of merchandise and the amount of money they spend on new items accordingly. The assistant buyer works directly for the buyer of a department or group of related departments (e.g., handbags, jewelry, and scarves). The assistant buyer helps the buyer with updating the six-month plan, open-to-buy, and inventory. The planner works in collaboration with the buyer and assistant buyer to develop sales forecasts, inventory plans, and spending budgets for merchandise to achieve sales and profit objectives. The distribution manager, or allocator, is responsible for planning and managing the deliveries of goods received from the vendors, as ordered by the buyers, to retail locations. A merchandising, or merchant, executive training program is designed to prepare new hires, former interns, college recruits, or current employees who have shown skills in merchandising for their first assignment in the merchandising division of the retail operation. There are many career tracks in merchandising for the retailer, and they have several challenges in common—locating products that appeal to the customer, are priced right, arrive at the right place when needed, and sell!

Key Terms

assistant buyer
buyer
buying plan
distribution manager
divisional merchandising manager (DMM)
general merchandising manager (GMM)
gross margin
inventory

key vendor
merchandising
merchandising executive training program
open-to-buy
planner
planning manager
planning module
secondary vendor

Online Resources

Discussion Questions

1. Consider a major department store and construct a diagram separating the departments into divisions that would be headed by three separate divisional merchandise managers. Bracket together the departments that would be covered by an individual buyer.
2. Visit a menswear store or the men's department in a large retail operation to study how the merchandise may be segmented into classifications. Develop the categories for the merchandise plan of a men's sportswear department, including merchandise classifications, styles, sizes, colors, and price ranges.
3. Assume that you are the buyer for a large home accessories department. How will you divide the responsibilities of the planner and the assistant buyer assigned to your department? Compare and contrast the duties of each.

Profile: Interview with Women's Contemporary Apparel Buyer for Zappos.com, Mandy Raines-Cordia

Interviewed by Michele M. Granger

When did you realize you wanted to work in fashion merchandising?

I knew from a young age that I wanted to work in the fashion industry. A family friend introduced me to the business when he was buying children's clothing and asked me what I would want to wear. When I discovered the job required traveling and shopping, I knew it was for me. If only I had known then that buying is a little more complicated than just traveling and shopping.

What was your path to where you are today?

I grew up in a small city where my passion for shopping and fashion led me to major in fashion merchandising and minor in business at a local university. Once I graduated college, I started out in the industry as a Merchandise Assistant for a television retailer. Since then, I've been lucky enough to hold a few different positions in the industry, including working on the wholesale side in sales and product development, buying for a small boutique, and working as an assistant buyer for a department store before landing my current buying role for a major online retailer.

(continued on next page)

(continued)

I learned along the way that my passion is for the nontraditional retailer, and the online space is where I feel the most at home. Growing up in a small town, my shopping options were limited. I love the Internet because it put anything and everything at my fingertips. I have bought several different categories over the years, from handbags to footwear, jewelry to housewares, and accessories to beauty, before arriving in apparel. I feel like a good buyer can buy anything, but it helps to be passionate about the category you are buying.

What are your position responsibilities?

Simply put, my job as a buyer is to have the right product, at the right time, at the right price. Buying is a lot of numbers and analysis (which is ironic because I never liked a single math class I took in school). I create sales plans and budgets for a group of brands, travel to market to select product based on customer demand (not my own personal demand), negotiate with suppliers, track sales and performance for these suppliers, manage inventory levels based on sales, research trends, report selling history and trends, strategize to optimize business, and the list goes on. As a buyer, you routinely collaborate with other divisions within your organization. I work very closely with marketing, legal, planning, and accounting, just to name a few.

Profile Figure 10 Buyer for Zappos, Mandy Raines-Cordia.

Do you use social media in your work? If so, for what purposes?

As an e-commerce buyer, social media has become an important part of my job. Social media has bridged the gap between brands/designers/businesses and the end consumer like never before. We use social media to increase site traffic, generate brand awareness, engage consumers, and build customer loyalty. I personally have more interaction with Pinterest and Instagram as a way to share trends and outfit inspiration through product placement.

What do you love most about what you do?

I have always been entrepreneurial minded and have wanted to run my own business. As a buyer, I have that feeling of running my own business without the personal financial commitment. I have the power to make the decisions I feel will grow and support the business. I am responsible for my successes, as well as the failures. I am held accountable for my decisions, but encouraged to take risks. It's exciting to see the product you selected do well and see a risk pay off. I love taking a struggling brand, growing it, and taking it to the next level.

(continued)

What have been your toughest challenges?

Life is full of challenges, and the fashion industry is no exception. I personally struggle with the fact that there will always be factors beyond my control that will affect my business no matter how prepared I think I am. I cannot control the weather, the economy, a supplier's manufacturing capabilities, company directives, or shipping mishaps—all impact my business. As a buyer, sometimes all you can do is adapt and adjust going forward. I work very hard to achieve my sales goals and have a hard time not taking lackluster sales personally. I have to remind myself to breathe and let it go. If I've done everything I can do, I have no choice but to let it go, learn from it, and be prepared for the next time.

What kind of skills have you learned from your experiences, and/or what skills do successful fashion buyers have?

I started out in the industry young and naïve, but I had a willingness to learn. I have learned so much through a wide variety of experiences, but here are a few things that have benefitted me the most:

1. Never stop learning. Learn from your mistakes, learn about the industry, learn about new innovations, and learn about current events as they will all impact your buying decisions.

2. Be able to build relationships through honesty and trust.

3. If you don't already have it, invest in some thick skin. It will pay dividends.

4. Communication skills are a must. You have to be able to effectively communicate the needs, strategy, and results of your business.

5. Never settle for the status quo. There will always be opportunity for improvement.

6. Never take a job for the money. The money will come and experience is priceless.

What advice would you give to aspiring fashion buyers?

Someone once told me that if you do a job you are passionate about, you will never work a day in your life. This is so true. My job is not a 9 to 5 job, and it's rare that I ever get to disconnect from email. It doesn't feel so glamorous when you are trekking New York City with a laptop and line sheets in a foot of snow in February when it's 20 degrees, and you realize your favorite designer boots are not waterproof in a puddle of slush. It's not glamorous, though it has its moments. You really have to love the industry and job to be a buyer, or you will feel like you are working every single day.

Second, as with anything in life, stay determined to reach your goals and dreams. You will encounter bumps along the way. You might get fired from your first job, you might work for a difficult boss, you might get passed up for a promotion, you might make the wrong decision on product a few times, and you will probably encounter situations where you will have to make difficult decisions. Never let a job, a boss, a missed opportunity, or the fear of change keep you from your goals. Everything happens for a reason, every challenge is a chance to learn, and every closed door is a new opportunity. Trust me on this one.

Source:

Courtesy of Mandy Raines-Cordia

chapter 11

Management for the Retailer

If you are a person who loves the retail experience, you may envision yourself running a specialty store, an exclusive boutique, a designer outlet, a Web site, or a large department store. You may be someone who thrives in a retail environment and craves the excitement of getting new merchandise onto the sales floor, assisting customers with purchases, motivating sales associates, and challenging yourself and your team to surpass last year's sales figures. If this describes you, a career in retail management may be your path to profit and pleasure.

Management refers to the organizing and controlling of the affairs of a business or a particular sector of a business. This chapter focuses on management careers in the retail sector of the fashion industry, such as manager of an apparel store, manager of an Internet fashion operation, or assistant manager of a factory outlet. There are several career tracks in retail management, including the following positions: regional manager, operations manager, retail store manager, manager-in-training (MIT), assistant and associate store manager, department manager, customer service manager, and retail operation entrepreneur or store owner.

Regional Manager

Regional store managers, also known as *area* or *district managers*, are responsible for directing the retail stores of a particular company that are located in a particular area of the country. An **international store manager** supervises store sales and staff performance in a different country, or group of countries, not in the company's country of residence. Whether in the United States or abroad, these regional managers are responsible for the smooth operation and profitability of the company, as well as the success of employees in the retail outlets located within a specific geographic area (often referred to as an area, district, region, or territory). They are the liaisons between the corporate office and the retail stores in their territories. They collaborate with their store managers and other employees by making store visits, communicating through e-mail or telephone, and facilitating conferences, in person or electronically.

During these meetings, store managers share their current sales, markdowns, and returns; point out items that are selling well and those that are not; and identify promotional programs or incentives for employees that are increasing sales or traffic flow into the store. If sales are declining, regional managers work with store managers to stimulate sales by implementing in-store promotions or working with the retail organization's headquarters on promotional campaigns. The four main goals of the regional store manager are to (1) maximize sales at a profit, (2) motivate store employees, (3) share successes from one store with another, and (4) communicate with the corporate office. Box 11.1 provides descriptions of Express' retail store management positions.

Qualifications

If regional store management is your career choice, the following educational goals, work experiences, and personal characteristics will help you get a foot in the door:

- *Education.* A bachelor's degree in fashion merchandising, fashion retailing, business administration, retailing, management, or a related field is a requirement.

- *Experience.* Retail sales and store management experience are mandatory work experiences. Buying, advertising, visual merchandising, human resource development, marketing, inventory control, and customer service knowledge are areas of experience that will move a regional manager candidate to the top of the list. Previous work success as an assistant store manager and store manager gives the job candidate an edge over the competition.

- *Personal characteristics.* Strong communication and leadership skills are required. The ability to speak effectively to individuals and groups is important. Accounting skills, human resources knowledge, motivation and conflict skills, and an understanding of retail law are important. Organization, cognitive thinking, and time management are personal skills that support the regional manager's tasks in coordinating stores in a wide geographic area.

Career Challenges

Because they are responsible for several retail locations, regional managers may find their work to be stressful and without time constraints. Regional managers are responsible for not just one store, but a significant number of retail units in the operation. This means they oversee all of the employees who take care of the customers shopping in each store. It takes a person with abundant fashion and retail knowledge, excellent communication skills, and business savvy to succeed in this career choice. Long hours and frequent travel are realities of the job.

Operations Manager

In major companies, an operations manager reports to the regional manager or, in a very large company, the national operations director of stores. The **operations manager** works with other administrators and store managers in developing marketing strategies and funding plans for merchandising and management personnel, as well as supervising stock replenishment, equipment and supply needs, and inventory control procedures. The primary objective of the operations manager is to develop and maintain effective programs to operate and control all of the retail units in the company, with a focus on superior customer service and cost control. For example, the operations manager may work to find a faster, less expensive way to move merchandise from the central distribution warehouse to store units.

Developing a company-wide training program to help all employees identify and report theft may be another activity of the operations manager, because another area of responsibility for the operations manager is security. Security can have tremendous impact on the bottom line—profit. **Security** refers to safekeeping of merchandise in the store, as well as the safety of employees and customers. Because inadequate lighting, unsafe equipment, and poorly placed fixtures can prove to be safety hazards for people in the store, this is an important focus for the operations manager. In large stores, a **security manager** may be employed to work directly for the operations manager, overseeing the safekeeping of merchandise in the retail operation and minimizing theft.

■ **Figure 11.1**
Security decisions
include determining
which equipment will be
used to deter theft.

The security manager works with the operations manager to determine which equipment will be used to deter theft, such as tags, security cameras, or perhaps a security employee disguised as a shopper. Security not only protects the physical inventory from outside theft but also monitors against internal theft or pilferage. **Physical inventory** refers to the actual merchandise within the retail operation, whether on the sales floor, on trucks for delivery to the stores, or in the warehouse waiting to be transported to the store units. **Internal theft** refers to merchandise or money stolen by employees within the company. To minimize internal theft opportunities, employees may be required to have personal purchases processed through the cash terminal by a store manager, rather than on their own. They may be required to store their handbags and packages in lockers and use a clear bag on the sales floor. Additionally, security management covers loss training for employees of the company (Figure 11.1). Seminars on how to spot a shoplifter, who to contact, and where to go for assistance when identifying a thief assist employees in safely combating **shrinkage**, or merchandise losses resulting from theft.

Qualifications

Next are the educational background, work experience, and personal characteristics needed to succeed in the position of operations manager:

- *Education.* A bachelor's degree in business administration, merchandising, operations management, retail management, retailing, project management, or a related discipline is required. In some larger retail operations, a master's degree is required.

- *Experience.* A minimum of five years' experience in the operations field is required. Operations managers must have experience in project management, logistics, system analysis and budgets, and forecasts. Experience in Microsoft Excel and other programs used within the retail operation is necessary.

- *Personal characteristics.* Excellent organization, communication, and leadership skills are necessary for this position, as are superior analytical and technical skills. Good decision-making and problem-solving abilities are required. The operations manager may be expected to travel extensively to store unit locations.

Career Challenges

The challenges for an operations manager are similar to those of the regional store manager. Being responsible for the operations and employee performance in a significant number of store units is a large workload. Extensive travel and long hours are common requirements for this position. The operations manager spends much time analyzing the costs associated with the stores and developing ways to save money and improve sales without compromising quality. This requires much attention to detail, strong analytical skills, and the ability to see the big picture that will result when changes are implemented.

Retail Store Manager

A **retail store manager** oversees the activities of a retail store's operation, from sales transactions and advertising to special events and the store's people—the customers and employees, including assistant managers, department managers, sales associates, and other staff. The retail manager is responsible for implementing the firm's retail marketing and sales plans, while ensuring the efficient operation of sales, operations, and security within a retail location. Store managers' primary responsibilities are overseeing sales promotions, transitioning merchandise from receiving to the sales floor, monitoring sales and inventory levels, managing personnel, and generating profits. They oversee the inventory, ensuring that the store has the right quality, type, and amount of merchandise available. They also make sure supplies are reordered on time.

Depending on the store's size, the store manager may be involved in some manner with all of the store's departments, from displays and advertising to merchandising and human resources (Figure 11.2). Store managers may have hundreds of employees or just a few sales associates to lead. Either way, they set a tone for the store and share a vision of success and expectations about customer service, promotions, and store goals with all employees. They work with a wide variety of individuals, from executives in the corporate office to the customer who has a complaint. The main objectives of the store manager include the following:

- Ensuring that the sales targets are reached and profits increased

- Handling customer service issues and complaints

- Implementing health, safety, and security regulations

- Assuring that the store is attractive, organized, and well-maintained

- Overseeing that strong employees are recruited, interviewed, trained, supervised, motivated, and retained

Box 11.2 provides a detailed listing of the supervisory and administrative responsibilities that the store manager of a large retail operation may have.

■ **Figure 11.2**
Seminars on how to
spot a shoplifter, who to
contact, and where to
go for assistance when
identifying a thief assist
employees in safely
combating theft.

CASE STUDIES IN CAREER EXPLORATION

Box 11.2 Listing of the Supervisory and Administrative Responsibilities of the Manager of a Large Store

Supervisory Tasks

- Oversees employees engaged in selling, cleaning, and rearranging merchandise; displaying; pricing; taking inventory; and maintaining operations records

- Ensures efficient staffing of employees through proper assignments of duties, while respecting break periods, work hours, and vacations

- Implements compliance with human resource regulations by implementing established benefits and record-keeping procedures

- Trains, supervises, advises, and monitors store employees

- Encourages employee advancement if an employee's skills and the organizational structure allow it; may be called on for assistance in preparing or executing training sessions for employees on store policies, procedures, job duties, and customer service

- Plans and conducts regular sales meetings for staff to discuss latest sales techniques, new

products, overall performance, and other topics the store manager believes will promote high team spirit and company pride

- Supervises department managers and sales associates, performs work of subordinates as needed, and assists in completing difficult sales

- Plans store layout of fixtures, merchandise, and displays with the regional manager, taking into account special and seasonal promotions, as well as store safety and security measures

- Inspects merchandise to ensure it is correctly received, priced, and displayed

- Maintains all safety and security policies of the company, including locking and securing of the store at closing time, balancing receipts, and making cash deposits

- Communicates and upholds all company policies, rules, and regulations, while maintaining a productive and pleasant customer and employee environment; recognizes employees positively for achieving the same and initiates disciplinary action where needed

- Answers customers' complaints or inquiries and resolves customers' problems to restore and promote good public relations; makes decisions on returns, adjustments, refunds, customer checks, and customer service, as required

- Coordinates and supervises store housekeeping, maintenance, and repair

- Maintains physical inventory as required

- Assumes general responsibility for the inventory of the store falling at or below the company's shortage percent goal

Administrative Tasks

- Handles staff schedules, sales reports, inventory reports, and personnel reports

- Prepares each employee's appraisal reports and conducts evaluation meetings after input from regional manager and director of the human resources department

- Coordinates the store's sales promotion activities and campaigns, in coordination with regional manager and according to established budgets

- Keeps abreast of developments in the retail sales area by studying relevant Web sites, trade journals, sales and inventory analyses, and all merchandising and sales materials; initiates suggestions for improvement of the business

- Coordinates merchandise and advertisements, and maintains the store's offerings

- Maintains a current knowledge of management principles and has the willingness and ability to make difficult decisions under pressure

Qualifications

Following are the educational goals, work experiences, and personal qualities that enhance one's opportunities to secure a store manager position:

- *Education.* A bachelor's degree in fashion merchandising, fashion retailing, business administration, management, retailing, or a related discipline is a requirement.

- *Experience.* Several years of retail sales and management experience are needed to become a store manager. Most candidates are promoted after successfully working as an assistant store manager. Additional work experience in buying, advertising, store planning and visual merchandising, human resources management, marketing, inventory control, and customer service areas are helpful in securing prime positions.

- *Personal characteristics.* Store managers must be good team leaders who are self-motivated, adaptable, quick thinking, and prepared to make and be accountable for decisions. They must enjoy a fast-moving, high-pressure environment. On an interpersonal level, store managers must be able to communicate clearly with a variety of people at all levels and be committed to the needs of the customer. They must understand relevant retailing and human resources laws, business accounting, and computer programs in word processing, spreadsheet development, and inventory control.

Career Challenges

Store managers should anticipate a lengthy work schedule, which includes weekends, nights, and holidays. Working six days a week is not uncommon. The position includes office work, but managers are expected to spend much of their time on the sales floor. The store manager is head of the day-to-day business in the store, with the support of and responsibility to higher management. This means that the store manager must respond to the requests of the regional manager. The store manager who aspires to become a regional manager—the next step up the career ladder—should anticipate relocating several times to gain experience in various stores within the company. Moving from one location to another with little advance notice can be a difficult process for some people.

Manager-in-Training

A **manager-in-training (MIT)** is just that: an employee who is being trained to move into a management position. Some large retail organizations offer an MIT program through which prospective management employees are trained for assistant manager or store manager positions within the company (Figure 11.3). The main difference between an executive training program and an MIT program is that most companies train the MIT on the job in one of the branch store locations, rather than in a training facility at company headquarters. L.L. Bean, J. Crew, Burberry, Brooks Brothers, and Sephora are examples of fashion companies with management training programs for new and/or existing employees. All of these companies were included in *Business Insider*'s "The 10 Best Fashion Retailers to Work For."[1]

■ Figure 11.3
Some large retail organizations offer an MIT program through which prospective management employees are trained for assistant manager or store manager positions within the company.

Qualifications

Here are the qualifications often required for admittance into a manager-in-training program.

- *Education.* A bachelor's degree in fashion merchandising, fashion retailing, business administration, management, retailing, or a related field is usually required. Some MIT programs require the candidate to have a minimum cumulative, or major, grade point average, such as a 3.0 or 3.5 (on a scale of 4.0).

- *Experience.* One to three years' experience retailing is often required for this position. Many MIT candidates obtain this experience through part-time employment and/or an internship in retailing during their college years. A college graduate can apply directly for placement in an MIT program, or a company employee may decide to apply for admission into the program.

- *Personal characteristics.* Excellent interpersonal skills that support a team environment are required. Effective oral and written communication skills are needed to work with a wide range of employees. Strong planning and organizational skills with a sense of priority for deadlines and attention to detail are necessary for the successful MIT. Most important, the best MIT candidates are dedicated to high levels of customer service and sales productivity.

Career Challenges

As with the executive training program, one of the toughest parts of the MIT position is securing the job. As many as 100 candidates inside and outside of the retail operation may apply for as few as 10 positions. Of those selected for the MIT openings, only a few are promoted to the position of manager. The job is challenging in that it is "trial by fire," learning how to do the job well, while on the job. Long hours, which are often scheduled on weekends, holidays, and nights, are required for this job. The MIT is often on call and must be ready to go to work if the manager or another key employee is unavailable.

Assistant and Associate Store Manager

An **assistant store manager** helps the store manager in all of the daily responsibilities of successfully operating a store. The assistant manager takes direction from the store manager and works closely with all of the other departments in ensuring that the store's mission and financial goals are met. In some companies, assistant store managers have specified responsibilities, such as scheduling employees, supervising sales floor moves, and monitoring sales and inventory levels. In other companies, they may support store managers in all store management duties. Figure 11.4 shows an assistant store manager assessing inventory plans for the store manager.

Some companies with large individual store units hire for a position that lies between the assistant store manager and the store manager. This position is called **associate store manager**.

Qualifications

There are several prerequisites in education and experience for assistant or associate store managers, as follows:

- *Education.* A bachelor's degree in fashion merchandising, fashion retailing, business administration, management, retailing, or a related field is usually required.

■ **Figure 11.4**
The assistant store manager helps the store manager by planning strategies for employees to take the store inventory.

- *Experience.* Retail sales experience, managerial experience, or in-house management training is usually required. Work experience with a variety of departments—from buying, advertising, and human resources management to marketing, inventory control, and customer service—make the job candidate more appealing to the employer.

- *Personal characteristics.* Effective interpersonal and communication skills are significant attributes for this position. Assistant store managers also must have knowledge of business accounting, personnel, and marketing. They are detail oriented, have strong organizational skills, and are flexible. They must be able to adapt to constantly changing work schedules. Most important, the assistant manager must be a strong team player, anticipating the needs of the store and, in particular, those of the store manager.

Box 11.3 is a classified advertisement for an assistant store manager.

Department Manager

A **department manager** oversees a specific area, or department, within a store. For example, a department manager may be responsible for men's clothing, junior sportswear, or women's accessories. For their assigned departments, department managers coordinate the sales associates in their areas, assisting with employee hires, scheduling weekly work hours, handling employee and customer complaints, and monitoring the performance of employees. They schedule regular meetings with the store managers, assistant store managers, and other department managers. During these meetings, department managers report on weekly sales, discuss promotions, and talk about concerns or opportunities in their respective areas. They also stay in close contact with the buying office, as they relay employee and customer feedback on merchandise and advise buyers on reorders or possible voids in stock to help generate sales.

Department managers also maintain the sales floor by setting out new merchandise, adding signage for promotions, recording markdowns, and executing floor sets. Changing **floor sets** refers to moving fixtures and merchandise on the sales floor of the department to create a fresh look and to highlight new or undersold merchandise. Department managers work with sales associates in keeping the department neat and organized so that customers can easily find exactly what they are seeking.

Qualifications

What does it take to become a department manager? It is an excellent starting place for the college graduate. A list of qualifications follows:

- *Education.* A bachelor's degree in fashion merchandising, fashion retailing, an area of business administration, or a related degree is often required. Some companies accept an associate's degree in these disciplines.

- *Experience.* Successful retail sales experience is the top requirement for a department manager position. The sales associate who has gained experience in floor sets, exceptional customer service, and visual displays is well qualified for a promotion to department manager.

- *Personal characteristics.* The department manager is detail oriented, well organized, and an effective problem solver with good interpersonal skills. This position often demands a flexible work schedule, including weekends, nights, and holidays.

Box 11.3 Assistant Store Manager

Purpose and Scope

The assistant store manager will ensure a consistently memorable customer shopping experience for the men's department while generating meaningful revenue and positive operating profit for the store.

Responsibilities

- Responsible for sales and profit performance in store; responsible for achieving store shrinkage goals and for the establishment and implementation of both new and existing loss-prevention procedures

- Works with the general manager to establish and achieve sales and margin goals, develop operating budgets, and monitor employee and store performance

- Partners with visual merchandising team in regards to merchandise presentation

- Responsible for training and supervision of store staff to maximize sales and profit performance

- Directs the execution of promotional strategies and programs, ensuring that they support retail sales, marketing, and profit objectives

- Regularly visits relevant competition to maintain an awareness of store-performance issues and market trends

Job Requirements

- Four-year college degree

- Three years of retail management experience

- Strong business acumen and skill set that enables the management and development of staff

- Strong communication and interpersonal skills

We are an equal opportunity employer offering dynamic career opportunities with growth potential and a generous company discount.

Career Challenges

The department manager often works long hours for fairly low pay. The department manager reports to several people, including the assistant or associate store manager, store manager, and buyer. Each may have a different perspective on how to run the department. The department manager is challenged with satisfying several bosses, who may have dissimilar priorities.

Customer Service Manager

It is likely that you have heard the saying "The customer is always right," but is this really true? Most retailers have specific policies concerning merchandise returns and exchanges, out-of-stock advertised merchandise, and returned bank checks. With the Internet as an emerging retail channel, e-retailers need another set of policies concerning returns, shipping costs, payment, and security. All retailers want to keep their customers satisfied to establish a loyal customer base, yet customer care policies often have to be implemented to ensure a profitable bottom line. A **customer service manager** assists a customer with an issue or complaint and implements the retail operation's policies and procedures for returns, exchanges, out-of-stock merchandise, product warranties, and the like (Figure 11.5). It is the customer service manager's responsibility to maintain company policies, while assuring that customers feel their problems are being heard and taken care of in a professional and timely manner. The customer service manager often trains the sales staff to effectively assist customers with concerns and teaches them the people skills needed to calm irate customers and find win-win solutions for all involved.

Some large business operations have a separate department organized under the customer service manager that has the sole function of servicing the customer. In addition, some retail organizations handle the customer service responsibilities informally through management or personnel who have direct contact with the customer. Which types of services are coordinated by the customer service manager? Businesses offer varying types of services, often reflecting the price ranges of their products. For example, a high-fashion boutique carrying expensive designer garments will usually offer a wide range of customer services from alterations to home delivery. However, discount retail operations, such as Sam's Wholesale Club, provide minimal customer services in an effort to maintain retail prices that are below those of its competitors. At Sam's, for example, the customer is not provided with dressing-room facilities, packaging, or delivery. Types of services the customer service manager may be responsible for when working for a high-level service retail operation are listed in Box 11.4.

Qualifications

Are you an individual who remains calm in any situation? Are you an active listener? Do people find you to be an effective negotiator and a fair decision maker? If so, then the position of customer service manager may be the career option for you. The qualifications of a customer service manager include the following:

- *Education.* A bachelor's degree in fashion merchandising, fashion retailing, business administration, management, human resources, or a related field is a common requirement.

■ **Figure 11.5**
A customer service manager assists clients and implements store policies.

CASE STUDIES IN CAREER EXPLORATION

Box 11.4 Responsibilities of the Customer Service Manager

- Customer product adjustments (e.g., returns, replacements, and exchanges)
- Deliveries of purchases
- Layaway availability
- Information on product care
- Technical advice
- Discounts
- After-sales service

- Replacement guarantees
- Personal shopping appointments
- Merchandise delivered on approval
- Credit service
- Alterations
- Special orders
- Training of retail personnel in customer service

- *Experience.* Three to five years of experience in retail sales, preferably management, are required. Evidence of superior customer service through sales awards and positive customer feedback is a plus.

- *Personal characteristics.* The effective customer service manager has exceptional interpersonal and communication skills and is trustworthy, personable, and outgoing. Being a capable negotiator and a good listener are also important skills. The customer service manager must have a thorough understanding of the company and its policies.

Career Challenges

The customer service manager works with all kinds of people. If you have ever stood in line waiting to return a purchase, you may have seen a few of the types. They can be demanding to the point of unreasonable and rude to the point of unbearable. Regardless of the customer's state of mind, the customer service manager has to remain calm, polite, and helpful. The hours can be long, and the starting pay can be low.

Retail Operation Owner

Perhaps you dream of owning your own retail business, as many fashion students and graduates do. Maybe you love the fashion industry and seek the challenge and freedom of working for yourself. The good news is that a great number of people open their own businesses each year. The bad news is that you must, as a store owner, do everything discussed in this chapter (and several other tasks as well). The retail **entrepreneur**, or *store owner*, is financially responsible for the company and oversees all aspects of the retail business. There are three types of business ownership: sole proprietorship, partnership, and corporation. A business owned by an individual is referred to as a **sole proprietorship**. A **partnership** is owned by two or more

■ Figure 11.6
The retail entrepreneur often trains an employee to create and install window and in-store displays.

people. In a **corporation**, stockholders own the company, which may be run by an individual or a group.

Before opening a business, the prospective owner or ownership group must develop a **business plan**, a document that details plans for the business concept and target market, location and space needs (i.e., facility or Web site), growth and exit strategies, sales and inventory, and financing needs, among others. Whether the prospective entrepreneur is purchasing an existing business or opening a new one, securing funding to own the business is often a critical first step. **Funders**, financing sources such as banks and the Small Business Administration, require a well-written business plan that justifies financing because of a good potential for profit, minimal risk, and long-range potential.

Once the business loan is approved and after a location is secured, the owner often attends to the merchandise selection for the business by identifying the trends customers will want and then buying, or overseeing the buying, of the merchandise that fits the target market. The retail owner is responsible for developing a budget for seasonal purchases to make certain that the company's finances are not overextended. Once merchandise is received, the store owner and employees inventory, price, and tag the merchandise, and place it on the sales floor. The entrepreneur or an employee will take on the responsibility of creating and installing window and in-store displays (Figure 11.6). Straightening the inventory, cleaning the store, and restocking fixtures and shelves are all tasks the entrepreneur handles personally or assigns to employees.

A retail entrepreneur often locates, hires, trains, motivates, and evaluates all employees. In a small business, the entrepreneur is a one-person human resources department. Scheduling employees to meet the needs of fluctuating customer traffic and fit within the payroll budget is often a challenge for small business entrepreneurs. In many small operations, the customer prefers to work with the entrepreneur, valuing the personal attention and expertise. Rather than leaving it to employees, the retail entrepreneur often functions as customer service manager, handling customer returns, exchanges, and complaints. The retail entrepreneur is also responsible for making promotion, technology, and social media decisions for the fashion retail operation (Box 11.5).

Qualifications

Are you ready to take on the ultimate challenge of owning your own business? Consider the following list of educational background, work experience, and personal characteristics needed for successful business entrepreneurship:

* *Education*. A bachelor's degree in fashion merchandising, fashion retailing, business administration, marketing, management, retailing, entrepreneurship, or a related field is beneficial.

* *Experience*. Three to ten years of experience in the fashion industry, working in as many areas of a fashion business as possible, are critical to the future retail operation owner. An

Box 11.5 Free People Manages Social Media

Free People, a specialty retail chain and sales leader of the Urban Outfitters family of brands, knows how to be social. The ever-changing FreePeople.com site features Pinterest-like boards called "Collections" that allow shoppers to collect and post items on boards around a particular theme, such as "Spring Break, Bohemian Beauty, and Scenes from the Office." Customers become a community as they follow and comment on other shoppers' boards. They can also upload photos of themselves wearing Free People attire and accessories. And, to keep the shoppers engaged, Free People sends a weekly email update on Collections and photos that are trending. Since the program launched, consumers have created more than 30,000 Collections and uploaded more than 20,000 images.

In addition, the retailer's presence on Pinterest, Facebook, Twitter, Vine, Google Plus, and YouTube is phenomenal. Free People has more than 34,000 pins on Pinterest, the digital scrapbooking site loved by both pinners and retailers. Extensive pinning—by the retailer and consumers—has helped Free People drive 3.52 percent of its Web site traffic from Pinterest. Recent data from BloomReach indicates that Pinterest users spent 60 percent more than Facebook's and Pinterest traffic. In 2013, Free People went a step further with Pinterest by launching a special collection of limited-edition holiday dresses. Pinterest users were able to preorder these dresses with a special link, ahead of the collection's full launch.

At blog.freepeople.com, the retailer entices fans through daily musings on music, inspiration, DIY, and—of course—fashion. On its Facebook page, at www.facebook.com/FreePeople, there are more than one million likes. With a multichannel app (developed in 2013) that brings all of the shopping and sharing experiences together on the iPhone, Free People continues to integrate commerce both in stores and online through its customers' smartphones. With the phone app, the company was able to plunge deeper into social media, looking beyond the likes and follower counts to tap conversations and target customers in a very personal way. It allowed the retailer and its customers to get the wealth of data available online (e.g., reviews, "you might also like," outfit suggestions, sizing, color options, etc.). What's next for retailers wanting to engage their customers even more? Free People is not only asking the question and acting on it, but it is also inspiring future retail managers to ask another question: Is there, or will there be, a shift in retailers' thinking in which e-commerce is the primary focus and the physical stores are secondary?

For the retail store managers, FreePeople's social media strategies can inspire new ways to reach out to their customers—from Pinterest and Facebook to blogging and posting customers' photographs on their store Web sites.

Sources:

www.forbes.com/sites/lydiadishman/2013/10/16/how-free-people-is-using-big-data-and-social-commerce-for-bigger-sales/

readwrite.com/2013/04/17/social-networking-for-marketers-pinterest-crushes-facebook-infographic#awesm=~ol7FiM2BOIXbNc

www.skyword.com/contentstandard/news/new-free-people-mobile-app-snags-10-percent-of-company-sales/

internship with an entrepreneur provides ideal on-the-job education. Many entrepreneurs recommend that future business owners gain experience in the type of business that they intend to open in the future. For example, if you dream of owning a bridal boutique, working in this type of specialty store will provide knowledge and experience you will need in the long term.

- *Personal characteristics.* Successful business owners are calculated risk takers. They are well organized, financially savvy, respectful of money, flexible, responsible, and willing to ask for and accept help.

Career Challenges

Each month, the retail business owner faces the pressure of paying employees, vendors, the landlord, utility companies, and more. It can be a huge burden for some people. Because there is no way to accurately determine how much profit the business will generate, it is a risky profession in which one must constantly search for ways to maintain or grow the business. The retail business owner is ultimately responsible for all facets of the business. In most cases, a store owner does everything, including taking the trash out! Being a store owner can be one of the most gratifying experiences, although it can be very stressful at times. Being solely responsible for all of the expenses incurred by the business can be overwhelming.

Summary

This chapter explores management career options in fashion retailing. It is difficult to envision how many people are required to get a single product from the retail sales floor into the customers' shopping bags. The administrative employees in this industry sector are referred to as retail management. Management is the organization and control of the affairs of a business or a particular sector of a business. There are several career tracks in retail management, including the following positions: regional manager, operations manager, retail store manager, manager-in-training, assistant and associate store managers, department manager, customer service manager, and retail operation owner.

The regional store manager is responsible for the smooth running and profit of the operation and the success of employees in the retail store outlets located within a specific geographic area. Working with the regional store manager, the operations manager analyzes sales and inventory performance and procedures for general business practices, such as customer service and store security. A store manager oversees all aspects of a retail store unit's operation, from advertising and special events to the customers and employees. Some large retail organizations offer a manager-in-training program in which prospective management employees train for assistant manager or store manager positions within the company. The assistant store manager supports the store manager in all of the daily responsibilities of operating a store successfully. In some companies, there is a step between the assistant store manager and the store manager: the associate store manager. A department manager oversees a specific area, or department, within a store. The customer service manager assists consumers with their needs and concerns. Finally, retail operation owners are financially responsible for their own companies and oversee all aspects of the retail business. They are the managers of all managers.

Endnote

1. Peterson, H., "The 10 Best Fashion Retailers to Work For," www.businessinsider.com, November 8, 2013.

Key Terms

assistant store manager
associate store manager
business plan
corporation
customer service manager
department manager
entrepreneur
floor set
funder
internal theft
international store manager

management
manager-in-training (MIT)
operations manager
partnership
physical inventory
regional store manager
retail store manager
security
security manager
shrinkage
sole proprietorship

Online Resources

www.businessinsider.com/best-fashion-retail-companies-to-work-for-2013-11?op=1

www.payscale.com/research/US/Job=Retail_Store_Manager/Salary

www.internetretailer.com/2013/11/26/worlds-top-10-online-apparel-retailers

about.nordstrom.com/careers/#/student-center/main

www.careersatsaks.com/AboutUs/MeetOurPeople.aspx

www.fashion.net/jobs/

www.macysjobs.com/opportunities/fieldassociates.aspx

www.stylecareers.com/

Discussion Questions

1. Using the Internet and/or by interviewing a professional in a regional manager position, investigate the advantages and disadvantages of this career. Find out about the size of the regional manager's territory, the number of management personnel with whom the regional manager interacts, and the prospects for promotion in this field.

2. Investigate one of the job responsibilities of operations and security managers by exploring the types of security systems that are available to deter theft. Compare and contrast both technological devices and common-sense techniques, such as placing small, easily pocketed items at the cash counter to minimize theft.

3. Using the Internet or your college's career services department, locate four companies with MIT programs and compare them. What are the requirements to enter each of the programs? What is the length of each MIT program? How many participants are in each program? What types of training and projects are included in the programs? Which types of positions can one expect to work in after successfully completing MIT training?

4. Assume that you plan to open your own retail business in several years. First, conduct research to identify the type of fashion business that will have the best opportunity for success by identifying market voids and consumer shifts in the location where you would like to work. Next, develop a list of the work experiences that will prepare you for ownership of this retail operation. Finally, construct a chart of the general steps you will need to take to get ready for the business opening.

How to Interview for a Store Management Position with a Luxury Fashion Retailer

Before going to a store manager interview at a luxury fashion retail store, there are four objectives you will need to accomplish:

1. You have to know your stuff. You may need to research some of this stuff: the company's background, its designer, the merchandise it carries, recent happenings in the company, and so forth.
2. You will want to be dressed to impress (more on this later).
3. You'll need to demonstrate your knowledge of the subject, whether your expertise is in cosmetics, jewelry, or apparel, and show particular interest in the brand(s) with which you'll be working.
4. You'll need to demonstrate that you are a people person with exceptional selling skills. The challenge is to grab the interviewer's interest and accomplish all four objectives in the time frame of a typical interview, about 30 to 40 minutes.

Next are steps you can take to land that job.

Step 1—Do your homework by taking a field trip.
Visit one of the store's other branches, if you can, so you are not recognized by the staff when you later show up for the interview. Not only is it important to see what the employees are wearing, but you'll also want to see how many people are on the sales floor and how they work with the customers. If you will be interviewing with an apparel retailer, try on something in the store to get a feel for how it fits, how it was designed and made, and how the fabric feels. Look at the various collections in the store, particularly the styles and colors for the season. When you get home, make notes of what you observed and then go online. One of the advantages of interviewing with a luxury retailer is that you can search the Web to view the brand's advertisements, fashion shows, and press and to peruse the collections and trends for the season. The goal is to be well-educated about the brand.

Step 2—Review who the company is seeking to hire.
Re-read the job description to make sure you have all of the information you need to know. If the job description mentions an event or style, research it and be prepared to talk about it during the interview. Use key terms from the job description in the interview. Think of this as speaking the same language as the brand.

Step 3—Network with those in the know.

Check out social media to find people who have worked at the store or who work there now. Search for the company name on LinkedIn, Facebook, and Twitter. Ask these former and current employees what the interview process is like and what you can do to prepare.

Step 4—Rehearse for the interview.

Write some sample interview questions, based on the brand(s) the store sells, the brand's reputation or image, and the company's view of customer service. Popular interview questions focus on working with tough customers, how you've handled sales quotas in the past, your favorite fashion trends from the current season, or how to deal with a fellow employee with a poor attitude. Next, practice interviewing with a friend or colleague and the career services office of your college or university. Most important, ask for honest feedback about your performance, and apply it.

Step 5—Look the part.

Select your interview outfit carefully, and wear something fashion-forward, yet appropriately conservative. High-end apparel can be expensive and, in many luxury retail operations, employees are encouraged to wear the brand's clothing on the job. Although that may not be possible on your budget, do what you can to dress the part. Be dressed to impress. Match the brand by looking at the brand's images online and thinking about what you saw during your store visit. How did managers and associates wear their makeup and hair? Replicate the look. Shop at resale shops, browse online, or borrow from friends to get the outfit that will impress your future bosses. Also, take extra care with your hair and makeup, ensuring that you're using a light hand and choosing the right colors to complement you and your outfit.

Five steps to prepare for that management dream job? You are ready. Now, show that confidence, share that knowledge, and prepare to receive that job offer!

Profile: Interview with a Fashion Entrepreneur in Paris, Erin Burke

Interviewed by Michele M. Granger

Can you tell me a little about yourself?

I am a freelance trend forecaster and my company is based in Paris. Born an American, I double majored in Fashion Merchandising and Product Development at university in the U.S., and did an internship at *Glamour Magazine* in the fashion and beauty department, as well as an internship at Cotton Incorporated's trend department. After working for a short time in product development for an accessories private label company and as a manager in retail, I took my dream position as a trend forecaster at Cotton Incorporated. This job took me all over the world doing trend research, buying, and presenting to global designers and retailers about fabrics, color, finishing, and silhouette. I led the denim presentations and eventually took on the role as account manager in Europe for denim.

When did you realize you wanted to work in fashion?

I went to school for sports medicine and quickly realized my queasiness around blood was a big stumbling block. I took a few different classes looking for things I was interested in, one of which was a New York Study Tour of Fashion. When we were at *Glamour Magazine*, everything that the woman talked about seemed so exciting, so I applied for the internship and got it and then continued to study fashion.

What was your path to where you are today?

Erratic! I wish I would have thought through where I wanted to go and what I wanted to do a bit more, but I kind of tried a lot of things and then found the ones that I liked and kept pursuing those things. I started in editorial and enjoyed parts of it, then trend forecasting and enjoyed the creative side of this a lot. My first real job was in product development, which was a little disappointing in that I spent most of my time on the phone with

Profile Figure 11 Fashion Entrepreneur in Paris, Erin Burke.

China—trying to get samples in and keeping those samples organized and very little time actually designing. Then I thought it would be interesting to open a boutique, but after working in retail management, I quickly knew that was not going to be good for my skill set. I finally got my dream job doing fashion forecasting, and that was an incredible experience, but it required a lot of travel. In the end, it was over 50 percent of the job and tons of public speaking. I learned to do these things well and am very proud and glad that I did, but they aren't the things I love to do. So I left to do some freelance focusing on the research, writing, and reporting while pursuing writing a book and working on some entrepreneurial ventures.

What kind of skills have you learned from your experiences and/or what skills do successful fashion business owners have?

Time management is one that has been hard for me. As a creative, I tend to go into a zone and I can continue to edit things and change things forever, so I always set timelines and allotted times for each piece of a project. Also being able to manage multiple projects at a time and do them well is hard, but important. After a while you learn to find a rhythm, but I still allot times in my calendar to make sure they all fit.

Public speaking was so hard for me, but I think it's important to be able to stand up in front of people and communicate your ideas succinctly. Nurturing your creativity and having a creative process is really important, and you really have to fight to protect those times. You can get so busy that when it comes to development and design, you have nothing fresh because you haven't been nurturing yourself creatively. For me, I write every morning to get the ideas out of my head and to use as a map. I also make sure once a week I'm doing something that feeds me creatively, whether that's painting or going to exhibits or reading in a beautiful space, just something to keep my creative flow enabled.

A strong sense of self and what you want is necessary. When I decided to do freelance, it was a tough transition. When you're working with one company, you know how the company works and what your role is. When working for multiple companies and doing a variety of projects, each one is very different, with different cultures and ways of working. It took me some time to navigate asking the right questions and developing a system of checking in at each step to make sure I was doing things the way my clients wanted. Also being able to say no to things that I didn't think served me or the other well—for whatever reason, I'm not that good at this area or I didn't want my name on something I thought was subpar or the company wasn't handling it's affairs in a legal way. Another aspect of this is being able to evaluate what people are asking for, and measure that on a scale of time and money and what you can deliver and being

honest with them and not selling yourself short. It isn't good business unless it is mutually beneficial. It's smart to say no to things that are not.

What does your company do?

I have done such a variety of things as a freelancer (sole proprietorship) over the last two years that I'm not sure there is a limit. Companies can just pick your talents and try to plug them into what they need.

I've done the big future concepts and research for trend companies, marketing profiles and interviews of consumers, analysis of runways, tracking street style, covering runways, trade shows, and events and then writing about the trends or interviewing designers, trend videos, trend seminars for universities, visual and research tours for retailers, trend presentations with color palettes and fabric inspiration. I think the sky is the limit on what is possible, but I am trying to hone into the five or so things I do really well and focus on those projects.

What are your responsibilities?

Everything is my responsibility! This is the hard part about doing things on my own. I have to do a lot of things I know nothing about (i.e. creating a company, dealing with legal aspects, negotiating contracts, managing projects, taking care of social media, taxes and visas). It's good to find a network of people that you can run ideas by and get advice before making mistakes. Of course, I've made tons of mistakes, but at least you can get a handle of the landscape before making them. I also keep up my professional relationships, do the research and production for all my projects, generate invoices, and then continue to seek out new projects.

What types of social media do you use for work? For which purposes?

I use Pinterest just to organize photos or save ideas, Tumblr as a practice in curation, Instagram more for social media and showing research and projects, Twitter for saving or sharing ideas and for researching trends in different places around the world, Facebook mostly as research and to keep a

(continued on next page)

(continued)

face with all my contacts (primarily personal ones), and then LinkedIn as a professional research and contacts bank.

What are six of your favorite Web sites and blogs that are fashion-related?

style.com

nytimes.com/video/t-magazine/

manrepeller.com

refinery29.com

viciouslycyd.tumblr.com/

trendcentral.com/

What do you love most about what you do?

I love coming up with new ideas and researching future concepts, then creating stories around them and dreaming how that will change fashion. I love the variety of freelancing and the freedom to travel and work in different places.

What have been your toughest challenges?

Working in Paris and dealing with bureaucracy in a foreign language have been brutal, also the tax implications and visa requirements are tough.

That has been really difficult and time consuming. Also, learning how to sell myself and put myself out there has been difficult. You don't even think about these things when you have a full-time job. Dealing with rejection and making clients happy while maintaining creative integrity. Not letting companies take advantage of you. There are a lot of people in fashion that will do work for very little money and, if you think you're good, you should never sell yourself short. People generally know that you pay for what you get. Don't sell yourself short, but also know when to make concessions for a good business relationship. These have been tough challenges for me.

What advice would you give to aspiring fashion entrepreneurs?

Do a lot of internships, study abroad, learn foreign languages, and take some business, law, and coding classes. When you are young, find good mentors in jobs and listen to them and learn from them. Take time to develop yourself, stay true to what you do well, and go after the things you are passionate about. And believe in yourself!

Source:

Courtesy of Erin Burke, owner of Louvre Studio and www.thecuriositeur.com

UNIT 4

Careers in the Ancillary Businesses: Digital Media, Styling, Education, and Retail Design

Unit 4 presents ancillary businesses that promote, educate, house, and generally provide support to the producers, retailers, future employees, and consumers of fashion goods. Some of these businesses focus on digital media and visual communication. Digital media incorporates technology in Web sites and promotion. Fashion visuals include such activities as fashion shows, photography shoots, and films or videos wardrobed by costume designers or stylists. Whether working as freelancers or within a company, these ancillary businesspeople primarily offer services rather than tangible products.

In a new Chapter 12, Digital Media and Visual Communication, the ever-growing career opportunities in digital media and visual communication are explored. There are many career opportunities in this area, including digital media artist, graphic designer, Web site designer and developer, journalist and writer, and blogger. Breaking into these career paths requires not only skills in writing and technology but also great persistence and patience. With the increase of technology, many of these industries are evolving rapidly. Inspiration, creativity, hard work, and mastery of necessary technical skills are keys to breaking into these industries. As fashion moves further to the online platform and blogging becomes mainstream, careers in the fashion digital media and visual communication industry are not only attractive but attainable.

In Chapter 13, Fashion Styling, Photography, and Costume Design, career options are presented as fashion services and examined from the career path perspectives of the fashion show and event producer, modeling and talent agency director, fashion photographer, fashion stylist, and costume designer.

In Chapter 14, Fashion Curatorship and Scholarship, career opportunities in education, to include museums, schools, and universities, are explored. Opportunities in the fashion or historical costume division of a museum discussed in this chapter include museum director, museum curator, assistant curator, collections manager, museum archivist, and museum conservator. Within the fashion scholarship segment of the industry, the fashion educator may instruct and/or conduct research in historical costume or many other facets of the fashion industry, from production to design and product development to merchandising and entrepreneurship among other areas of study.

Chapter 15, Visual Merchandising, Interior Design, and Retail Design, presents another segment of fashion ancillary businesses with its focus on environments—visual merchandising, retail design, and interior design—all of which work with physical spaces where fashion businesses may be located, whether in the production, retail, or ancillary levels of the industry. The primary career tracks discussed in Chapter 15 include architect, interior designer, visual merchandiser, store planning director, and mall manager. If an existing facility cannot be found, someone (the architect) may design the building to order. Another person (the interior designer) may design and oversee the installation of the interior—from the ceiling and lights to the floor coverings and furnishings. Yet another individual (the visual merchandiser) may select the fixtures and mannequins, and then set up the sales floor to entice consumers to come into the store and buy. If the retailer is in e-commerce, the Web site designer and developer creates the "store" exterior and interior, its Web site with its imagery, links, sound, and motion, which was examined in Chapter 12.

In Chapter 16, Beauty, Spa, and Wellness, a growth area of the fashion industry is presented. It requires a specific type of environment—the beauty, spa, and wellness industry. Chapter 16 first presents the careers of beauty merchandising and marketing professionals working in the manufacturing and retail levels of the industry. Next, the career of a makeup artist is examined, with views of this profession in theater, film, photography, and a salon or spa. Finally, the career of the director of a spa is explored, as growth is expected to continue in spa and wellness environments. As we have watched health services integrate medicine and natural homeopathic remedies, we will see beauty services integrated with health and fitness in the future. New careers will evolve for those who are interested in beauty, health, and longevity.

Follow me on bloglovin'

style defined **NYC**

Eyelet Dresses:

Our 5 favorite
for summer!

 VOGUE BUST *Fashion* INDIE GLAMOUR Z!NK DIE ZEIT

Terms & Privacy Policies

Terms of Use | Privacy Policy

chapter 12

Digital Media and Visual Communication

By Lauren E. Reiter, PhD candidate

Let's go to the Fall/Winter show of Chanel in Paris. Right now! We can, you know, and it won't cost us a dime for airfare or hotel. We don't need the required invitation; only a computer, tablet, or phone. Just click on www.nowfashion.com, an online magazine that publishes photos of the show in real time, or one of many other fashion Web sites that bring us both front-house and backstage imagery of the shows while they are happening. It's a brave new world, and it's no longer black and white (Figure 12.1). We no longer need to be in the physical environment of a retail store or runway to see the latest fashion creations. The digital media and visual communication industries are bringing us there and increasingly becoming serious forces to be reckoned with in every facet of the fashion world.

Careers in digital media, graphic design, Web site design and development, journalism and writing, as well as blogging, are all areas of growth in relation to technology and the online medium. Fashion magazines and books are transforming into online blogs and collections. Web sites and their design, as well as content, provide a platform for designers and retailers to brand themselves and showcase their products. Logo development, advertising, branding, and image creation and manipulation are all parts of what makes a fashion company successful. The retail industry no longer depends on brick-and-mortar stores for its sales. Retailers can be just as successful, if not more, by providing online commerce. Trend boards are no longer prepared by hand but are, instead, crafted and shared online. The globalization and digitization of the fashion industry has not only helped the fashion industry to become seamless in operation, but it has also opened up numerous fashion industry jobs that incorporate software mastery, computer expertise, and Web-based design skills and understanding. This chapter discusses the particular types of career paths within the digital and visual sectors of the industry and gives an overview of what it takes to be successful in such a promising area for future job seekers, to include the digital media artist, graphic designer, fashion journalist and writer, and blogger.

Digital Media Artist

Digital media artists, also known as *multimedia artists*, create animation and digital effects for various media outlets, such as television, movies, and video games. They work primarily in three-dimensional models and animations. The general responsibilities of a digital media artist include (1) creating basic designs, drawings, and illustrations for product labels, direct mail, or television; (2) developing drawn images to be scanned, edited, colored, and/or animated by computer; and (3) constructing two-dimensional and three-dimensional images to illustrate motion or a process, using computer animation or modeling programs.

Digital media artists are also expected to design complex graphics and animation. In addition to using personal skills of independent judgment and creativity, they use technological skills to develop brochures, multimedia presentations, Web pages, promotional products, technical illustrations, and computer artwork. You can see the results of their work in products, technical manuals, publications, film, and videos (Figure 12.2). Manufacturers and retailers in the fashion industry ask digital media artists to participate in the design and production of multimedia campaigns, such as those by Nordstrom and H&M.

The Job Market for Digital Media Artists

According to the U.S. Bureau of Labor Statistics (2014), 62 percent of digital media artists are self-employed. These types of jobs are expected to increase 6 percent by 2022. A slight salary change from annual salaries of $68,900 in 2012 to $73,200 by 2022 is expected. This industry is projected to become more difficult to break into, with fewer job opportunities in the next 10 years. The time to jump into this career path is now. Box 12.1 provides a listing of top digital media companies that employ digital media artists.

■ **Figure 12.2**
You can see the results of digital artists' work in products, technical manuals, publications, film, and videos.

Qualifications

If you have a passion for imagery, technology, promotion, and problem solving, then the career of digital media artist may be right for you. Following is a list of qualifications for the digital media artist:

- *Education.* Digital media artists are usually required to have a bachelor's degree in fine art, computer graphics, animation, or a related field. Those looking to expand their education can pursue a master's degree in fine arts, either art or design. It is desirable to have a degree comprising mostly studio work and experience, which can be obtained at most art and design schools, rather than a solely classroom-focused degree. Digital media artists are expected to have a base knowledge of computers and electronics, fine arts, design, communications, and media. All professionals, and those seeking an entry-level position in the industry, must have a well-developed portfolio to showcase their work and style.

- *Experience.* Most digital media artists begin their careers as entry-level artists in publishing, advertising, or motion picture companies, or design houses, until they prove their design and leadership skills. Professionals in this field may start out as an assistant in the graphic design or Web departments of a company before moving into the position of digital media artist. They may also find an entry into the profession by doing freelance work, sometimes while holding down a full-time job, until their work becomes well-known and they build strong portfolios.

- *Personal characteristics.* Expected personal skills include critical thinking, time management, active listening, coordination, and communication skills. Artistic ability with an equal skill level in technology is essential. Those in this field must have strong abilities in visual, oral, and written communication, as well as the capability to see detail.

Technology and the Digital Media Artist

Digital media artists must possess certain technology and software mastery, including digital cameras, stylus pens, tablets, computers, computer-aided software, such as Adobe Photoshop and Illustrator, and Autodesk. Professional development in software is necessary, including the following programs:

- ActionScript

- Adobe Systems

- Adobe AIR

- Code libraries

- Graphics software, such as ACD Systems Canvas, Ability Photopaint, After Effects, Fireworks, and Flash

- Video and editing software, such as Adobe Director, Adobe Premiere Pro, and Apple Final Cut Studio

■ **Figure 12.3**
Digital media artists often collaborate with graphic designers, using skills and software to create unique ideas and concepts in order to attract customers and convey a specific message.

- Web platform development software, including Adobe Flex, Adobe Systems Adobe Shockwave Player, Cascading Style Sheets (CSS), Extensible Hypertext Markup Language (XHTML), and Hypertext Markup Language (HTML)

Career Challenges

Challenges in the digital media industry include keeping up with the numerous software capabilities, as well as constantly being unique and fresh in design creation. It can often be difficult to find a job in this field and similarly difficult to become established as a successful freelance artist. Along with the design tasks, many digital media artists also handle business responsibilities, such as budgeting and scheduling, production coordination, and progress tracking. Working with both the creative and business aspects of a project or a company can be a challenging balancing act for most artists.

Digital media artists often collaborate with graphic designers, the next digital media career track to be examined (Figure 12.3).

Graphic Designer

Graphic designers use skills and software to create unique ideas and concepts in order to attract customers and convey a specific message. The main goal of a graphic designer is to plan, analyze, and create visual results to solve problems. The problem may be surpassing competition, attracting new customers, or creating a new image, such as Burberry did when, less than 10 years ago, it moved its brand from the matronly British trench coat to very cool— yet very English—gear worn by A-list celebrities (and their children).

Graphic designers find the most active way to get a specific message across in various forms of media, such as print, electronic, and film. Through the use of color, type, illustration, photography, animation, and various print and layout techniques, graphic designers develop the overall layout and production design of magazines, Web sites, advertisements, and other publications. Although it may seem advantageous to be well-versed in all areas, it is best to choose one area of graphic design and specialize in it. Advertising, Web, print, multimedia, and animation are all different areas of foci within graphic design. Graphic designers meet with clients or art directors to discuss concepts and pathways of what is wanted and to pinpoint the target consumers they are trying to capture. Graphic designers can design anything from imagery (Figure 12.4), logos, and product packaging to print and television advertisements and Web sites. Regardless of how innovative their ideas may be, graphic designers are under the direction of the client and must ensure accuracy and implementation of the specific requirements assigned to the project. Graphic designers most often have to present their work to clients or art directors and make the necessary changes before the final product is approved.

■ **Figure 12.4**
Graphic designers can design anything from imagery, logos, and product packaging to print and television advertisements and Web sites.

The Job Market for Graphic Designers

According to the U.S. Bureau of Labor Statistics (2014), the salary of graphic designers ranges from $26,000 to $77,000, with the average median salary being $44,150 per year. About 9,000 new jobs per year become available in graphic design. A projected growth of 7 percent is expected in graphic design jobs from 2012 to 2022, resulting in a highly competitive industry. A listing of key graphic design companies follows in Box 12.2. Online and mobile device graphic design is expected to increase greatly. Related careers to graphic designers include tech artists, animators, and flash designers.

Qualifications

The qualifications for a graphic designer in the fashion industry are as follows:

- *Education.* A bachelor's degree in graphic design is desired for this career, but an associate's degree can be sufficient for more technical jobs. A professional portfolio displaying relevant work is essential when looking for a job in this industry. Several schools require basic art and design classes before being formally accepted into a graphic design program. Accepted graphic design majors then will delve into more detailed curriculum, including computerized design, commercial graphics production, printing techniques, and Web site design.

- *Experience.* The career path for graphic designer usually takes one to three years of on-the-job entry-level training and matures to chief designer, art or creative director, or a similar supervisory position. Many graphic designers gain experience and then continue on to be freelancers or open their own graphic design companies.

CASE STUDIES IN CAREER EXPLORATION

Box 12.2 Examples of Graphic Design Companies

400	Interbrand
47 Media	Landor
Brand Engine	Minale Tattersfield
Brownjohn	Object 9
Chermayeff & Geismar	Pentagram
DDB	Studio 7 Design
Future Brand	
Giant Creative	Source:
Go Media	design.tutsplus.com/articles/22-great-graphic-design-agencies—vector-2541

- *Personal Characteristics.* The most important qualities associated with graphic design jobs include communication, analytical, artistic, creativity, time management, and computer skills. The effective graphic designer is a self-starter who is flexible and able to work independently. Strong problem-solving skills, smart business sense, and a sales ability are additional attributes that separate the top candidates from the group of job seekers. Graphic designers know how to combine ideas through art, imagery, and text to convey a message or emotion. Although graphic designers are mostly creative, they must also be detail oriented and able to take responsibility for their work.

Graphic designers frequently collaborate with Web site designers on imagery to be used for a logo, landing page, or any other visual component the Web designer is seeking to make his or her site the next most-visited one. An examination of the career of a Web designer follows.

Web Site Designers and Developers

Web site design and development are concerned with constructing Web pages and sites from functional, aesthetic, and marketing perspectives. The titles used to describe positions in Web site development are not standard by any means, and the terms "Web site designer" and "Web site developer" are often used interchangeably or for two very different jobs. In many companies, Web site designers are in charge of the look or appearance of the site, while Web site developers, also referred to as *programmers*, are responsible for the function and operation of the site. For our purposes, we use the term **Web site designers** as people who not only create Web sites but also focus on the ongoing visual aspects of the site. They develop the overall layout and images associated with the products or services offered by the site. Also in this chapter, we refer to **Web site developers** as the people who monitor the performance and function of the site, incorporating features such as e-commerce, online community, animations, interactive applications, and advertising hosting into the site. All of this is accomplished while ensuring that the site's design is optimized for the specific technologies supporting it. There are both creative and technical aspects associated with this career path. Both Web site designers and developers understand the ins and outs of a site from its appearance and content to its capacity, such as speed and weight of traffic.

Other job titles for career tracks relating to Web site construction include the following:

- **General web developers** deal with the construction and maintenance of a site, whereas other career paths, including programmers, designers, and Web masters, are more specialized.

- **Web programmers** deal with the coding and technical aspects of a Web site. They work with management to ensure that the basic construction of the site is acceptable.

- **Web masters** maintain the Web site and ensure that it is constantly in working order. If there are any glitches associated with the site, they address and resolve problems as they arise.

The Job Market for Web Designers and Developers

According to the U.S. Bureau of Labor Statistics (2014), the job outlook for Web designers and developers is very good as more and more commerce moves online. Specifically, online retailing is expected to continue to increase greatly in the next 10 years. Web designer and developer positions should increase by 20 percent by 2022. A listing of Web site design/development companies follows in Box 12.3. The average full-time salary of a Web designer or developer ranges between $34,000 and $105,000, with the average salary at $62,500 per year. Many designers/developers work on-site, but the ability to work from anywhere in the world is not only possible but a perk of this career track.

Qualifications

The qualifications for Web designers and developers vary with the type of position, but generally align with the listing of education, experience, and personal characteristics that follows:

- *Education.* An associate's degree in Web development is the common requirement to obtain a position as a Web developer; Web design is the specialized degree for a Web designer. However, to maximize corporate and freelance employment opportunities, job candidates are encouraged to obtain a bachelor's degree in computer science, programming, or a related field, with a support area in graphic design, in order to handle the look of the site more effectively.

CASE STUDIES IN CAREER EXPLORATION

Box 12.3 Examples of Web Site Design/Development Companies

Big Drop	Hudson Horizons
Blue Fountain Media	Inflexion Interactive
Cadre	Intechnic
Clikzy Creative	Isadora Design
Cofa Media	Kohactive
Comrade	Magic Logix
Cynexis	Southern Web Group
Dotcomweavers	Skuba Design
Dotlogics	The Creative Momentum
Forix Web Design	Source: www.10bestdesign.com/firms/
High Level Marketing	

■ Figure 12.5
Whereas a Web designer/developer tells a story with multiple tools from images and text to motion, color, and more, the fashion journalist tells a story using a single tool—words.

- *Experience.* Web designers and developers can advance to Web project managers over the course of their careers, with freelancing also being very common, as 25 percent of today's Web designers and developers are self-employed. Web designers and developers must be well versed in HTML, XML, Javascript, SQL, Photoshop, and Flash. Keeping up-to-date on these and other necessary languages and multimedia tools is imperative to remain relevant in the industry.

- *Personal Characteristics.* Web designers and developers meet with clients to discuss the needs of their business. They also must work well in a team and relay the information to others if there is more than one developer on the project, as well as agree on content and visual concepts. Web site developers write code, monitor the workings of the site once it is up and running, and remove any bugs within the site. Web site designers select graphics, audio, and video components to integrate them into the project seamlessly. Other needed personal attributes include patience and attention to detail, a customer service orientation, effective communication skills, and creativity.

Career Challenges

Web designers and developers must work well with their clients and fulfill the client's specific wants and needs. Communication issues and interpersonal relationship problems can develop in a position such as this one. Being able to successfully communicate program capabilities, limitations, and problems to nontechies can require much patience. Different sites have different needs and require different applications. As a result, a Web designer and developer must be well versed in applications, especially in commerce, gaming, or news. In order to meet clients' needs, Web designers and developers must understand not only the software but also which graphics and applications are appropriate for each project.

Whereas a Web designer/developer tells a story with multiple tools from images and text to motion, color, and more, the fashion journalist tells a story using a single tool—words (Figure 12.5).

Fashion Journalist

Overall, **fashion journalists**, or *fashion writers*, develop stories and materials, such as articles, advertisements, and product descriptions, for books, magazines, newspapers, and online Web sites and blogs. Job titles for fashion writers can vary from fashion journalist or fashion writer to technical writer or copywriter to, simply, writer. Although these titles are similar, there are differences from position to position and within differing businesses.

The journalist in the fashion industry has expertise in fashion and advanced writing skills, combined with the ability to communicate ideas and facts in interesting ways. Imagine reporting on the latest fashion trends from Paris or London (Figure 12.6). Yes, journalism can be a fast-paced and prestigious career, but when you imagine it, envision a little glamour and much hard work. A typical day may include writing or editing articles or stories; dealing with photographers, public relations specialists, and designers; and researching the next big designer, retailer, or fashion trend. A journalist needs the skills to write and report for various media, including news publications, magazines, television, blogs, and Web sites. The top journalists build a network of fashion who's who to secure the best, most exclusive interviews. Fashion journalism often focuses on design trends, beauty products, and marketing strategies, written to appeal to consumers. Journalists often follow the career path from assistant to a journalist, editor, or reporter to actual journalist or reporter, then to editor, analyst, or even professor.

■ **Figure 12.6**
The fashion journalist, possibly reporting on the latest fashion shows in Paris or London, has expertise in fashion and advanced writing skills, combined with the ability to communicate ideas and facts in interesting ways.

Technical writers translate highly technical information into easy-to-understand text. They may work with textile manufacturers, museums, beauty product developers, and similar companies to prepare informational and educational documents. **Writers** work on blogs, stories, books, and the like—fiction and nonfiction. Some writers focus on creative writing. There is some debate about the difference between the definitions of a journalist and a writer. And, there is some consensus that journalists want to be at the heart of the story, investigating and news reporting, whereas the writer has more freedom in creating, sharing, and not speaking only on facts. It is an ongoing discussion. To add to the ambiguity, some fashion firms and professionals use the terms *writer* and *journalist* interchangeably.

The Job Market for Fashion Journalists and Writers

Unfortunately, the job market for writers is a tough one because of strong competition within the field. However, a career in writing often spans several decades, and there is room to move around among different types of writing positions. With the meteoric rise of online publications, there are tremendous opportunities for writers with multimedia experience. According to the U.S. Bureau of Labor Statistics (2014), the median salary for a writer in 2012 was $55,940 per year, with an annual range of $27,000 to $117,000. Increasing numbers—currently about two-thirds of the writing population—are self-employed freelance writers or full-time bloggers, which are discussed in the next section. No matter what kind of writer you want to be, a love for writing and working well under pressure are imperative personal traits. In Box 12.4, a list of prospective employers for fashion journalists, writers, and bloggers is presented.

CASE STUDIES IN CAREER EXPLORATION

Box 12.4 Examples of Employers for Fashion Journalists, Writers, and Bloggers

Fashion writing jobs are available all across the industry, with firms such as online and brick-and-mortar retail companies, magazine and news publications, wholesalers, and designers, to name a few. These jobs can take many forms, such as blogs, social media (e.g., Facebook, Twitter, and LinkedIn), Web sites, and printed articles. Examples of employers include the following:

Anthropologie

Bloomingdale's

Chanel

Condé Nast (publisher of, e.g., *Allure, Glamour, Lucky, Vogue, GQ, Details*, etc.)

Hot Topic

Just Fab

LVMH

Magazines (e.g., *Elle, Harper's Bazaar, Alive*, etc.)

Rent the Runway

Swirl

TAG Heuer

The Jones Group

The Marcus Group Inc.

Qualifications

The qualifications for a fashion journalist, technical writer, and writer are similar and are presented as follows:

- *Education.* Many journalists and writers hold bachelor's degrees in journalism, fashion journalism, communications, creative writing, literature, or English. Fashion, marketing, and business are also viable options, particularly as support areas. Technical writers need a degree or a support area in writing, but they also need a firm grasp of the industry they are writing about.

- *Experience.* Being involved in writing before college graduation is advantageous, whether it is for the high school or college paper or the local community paper or radio station. Recently, the popularity of writing is rising, with freelance blogging as a way to get your foot in the door to full-time writing positions. It is essential to include a portfolio of examples of writing when applying for jobs and interviewing. If you do not have these samples, write some sample pieces before applying for an internship or some sort of free-lance experience. Journalists often follow the career path from assistant to a journalist, editor, or reporter to actual journalist or reporter, then to editor or analyst. Writers generally start with a position as an intern and then move to editorial assistant, proofreader, or fact checker.

- *Personal Characteristics.* Writers must be able to communicate ideas effectively and efficiently. A love of language is very helpful in keeping an interest in a career such as this. Attention to detail, grammar, sentence structure, and punctuation are also necessary. Knowledge of when to break the rules of language and grammar is also necessary. Writers must be able to sell stories, and those stories can vary among specializations. For example, some writers sell a brand, journalists sell a story, business writers sell a company, or PR professionals give concise information to the media and public. Journalists and writers must not only be able to tell stories, but they also must be master researchers and proofreaders. Graphic design and page layout skills are increasingly necessary as more writing jobs move to online platforms.

Career Challenges

Journalists and writers often deal with long, varying hours and an uncertain schedule. The work revolves around the writing project. Many must pay their dues before becoming a full-time writer; this includes working as a proofreader, fact checker, or research assistant for several years before advancing to a full-time writing job. Writers are often assigned their stories by their editors. Writers have to prove themselves through strong writing and research using correct sources and citations to build solid credibility in the industry before they can choose their own material. Full-time jobs in writing are often located in larger metropolitan areas, but it is possible through freelancing to have a career in writing almost anywhere, especially with the increase of technology. Approximately one in four jobs as a writer is part-time, and writers are often paid by the story and not an annual salary. Many writers move on to become authors of books.

The Fashion Blogger

■ Figure 12.7
Whereas a journalist
is often matter of
fact and tells a story
based on those facts,
a blogger uses a more
conversational tone and
often shares his or her
personal messages,
which is a dream job for
many people.

Fashion bloggers are much like fashion writers, but with a definitive online presence, a distinct personality, and an informal writing style (Figure 12.7). Fashion bloggers possess unique creativity in the telling of a story, the curating of an idea, the teaching of a skill, or the inventing of something new. Whereas a journalist must be matter of fact and tell a story based on those facts, a blogger uses a more conversational tone and often shares his or her personal messages. The blogger must catch the reader's attention in seconds, usually with the title of the blog post. The competition for bloggers is intense; all have the same goal in mind—to become a viral hit on the Web. Most bloggers are self-employed or freelance for several blogs. One commonality among bloggers is their overwhelming passion for a certain topic—in this case, fashion. In the world of fashion, there are three different types of blogs: the street style blog, the fashion blog, and the micro blog.

Street style blogs encompass fashion trend, environments, and styles seen on the streets. Whether an object, a group, or an individual, they can be action shots or posed, usually taken in the middle of a city. These shots are often accompanied by a quote or explanation of location of where the photo was taken and/or which designer the subject was wearing. One of the most famous fashion street style blogs is www.thesartorialist.com. The traditional **fashion blog** covers all areas of fashion and focuses on designers at all levels. It discusses and shares information about products, retailers, designers, and anything else related to clothing and accessories. One of the most successful fashion bloggers in this category is www.manrepeller.com, as featured in Figure 12.8. **Micro blogs** provide shorter stories that are easy to read and are accompanied by video clips and links that are smaller in size and easy for readers to share with one another. For example, www.bryanboy.com is an excellent rendition of this style of blog. In Box 12.5, a list of the top 10 independent blogs of 2014 is provided.

The Job Market for Fashion Bloggers

It is fairly easy to become an independent fashion blogger. However, pay is not guaranteed and can vary greatly. Blogging is a fast-growing art form, but it can often take years to become a profitable venture. Finding a full-time job as or with a blogger can be tricky. Some tips to set you apart from the competition include the following:

- Establish yourself as highly knowledgeable in the area in which you want to blog.

- Make sure you know the ins and outs of blogging (i.e., software, coding, permission rights, ethical implications, how to publish content, and how to track traffic).

- Establish your own blog and build an online presence. The best time to start your own blog is in college, when you can build a presence and be prepared to enter the blogging workforce upon graduation.

- Prove that you can bring something to other sites.

- Bring writing samples of blog posts to an interview in a portfolio.

Bloggers are generally not paid until they reach a point of success that they can start making money through advertisers who pay to be featured on their blogs. This happens once a blog has become so popular that it is driving high numbers of consistent traffic. Several tools are available online to help bloggers build up the necessary traffic. Important tools for successful blogging include templates, headers, RSS feeds, plug-ins and add-ons such as spam blockers, editors, and analytic tools that provide services, such as traffic statistics. In addition, other forms of social media, such as Twitter, Instagram, Pinterest, Facebook, and YouTube, should be tied into the blog to maximize repeat viewers and spread the word of the blog.

Qualifications

Some of you are managing your own blogs now; most of you are reading a few, or quite a few, blogs regularly. Can you actually make a living doing something you absolutely love as fun and leisure? You can, but it is important to recognize that it takes time, perseverance, and a focus on differentiating your blog from the masses of others. In addition to managing your own blog, there are three other options to consider: (1) contributing to another blog, eventually for a fee per story; (2) running your blog while working a paying job and building blog traffic and sponsors; and (3) applying to work as an intern or employee on the blogs of digital media teams of designers and retailers (e.g., Urban Outfitters, Free People, Kate Spade, Diesel, TOMs; if it is a fashion firm, it likely has a blog. Check out company Web sites for these positions.).

Whatever career path you choose, the following education, work experience, and personal characteristics will help you prepare to be a blogging professional:

- *Education.* In order to be a fashion blogger, you need to be a general expert in the fashion field and a specialist in distinctive areas of the field (e.g., a category such as bespoke men's suiting, vintage designer costume jewelry, or Birkin handbags). A bachelor's degree in fashion marketing or fashion design will set you on the right track to understanding the industry. Marketing, social media, and computer technology are excellent support areas of study for the future blogger.

- *Experience.* It is important for bloggers to not only be good writers and to be creative, but they must also be very software savvy. It is helpful if bloggers understand HTML, XHTML, and CSS languages to help them better manage their blog sites. Many online tutorials and programming classes are offered within universities that provide these services. It is a fact: Many bloggers have a day job that supports their blogging. Be sure to incorporate skills mastered in that day job and translate them to directly relate to blogging skills. For example, communication, writing, idea creation, editing, and so on are all imperative skills to be a successful blogger. It is always recommended for an aspiring blogger to maintain a personal blog and include that Web address in his or her résumé and cover letter.

- *Personal Characteristics.* Bloggers must possess a marathon mindset in order to be successful, which does not happen overnight. It takes much patience, hard work, and perseverance. Bloggers must also be considerate of those around them. Sources of content, images, and photos should be cited, and most content (photos, always) must be granted permission. It is vital to remember that whatever is said is available to the entire Internet world. It is critical to not use slander and to fully understand the repercussions of the possible backlash of the Internet populace. If you are a full-time blogger who has been hired for a specific company, then the company will often have specific rules and regulations for how the blog is to be run. In addition, the company may have an editing and approval process of content before publishing.

Career Challenges

Starting a fashion blog can be tricky. With so much competition, setting yourself apart from the rest can be very difficult. Several tips are provided to help a fledgling fashion blogger become successful (Box 12.6). Being a full-time blogger can come with much freedom, but income is unpredictable, and there are also often costs associated with the start-up phase of a blog. Another caveat relates to the matter of ethics. Bloggers have the freedom to write in an informal and conversational way, but a code of ethics must still be upheld in the business.

CASE STUDIES IN CAREER EXPLORATION

Box 12.6 Tips for Starting a Fashion Blog

- Start your blog on WordPress and ensure that it is self-hosted, not on a free blog site such as Tumblr.

- Get your own domain name and Web host.

- Know what sets you apart from the rest before you start.

- Start with a main theme and layout of your blog.

- Ensure your early content is the absolute *best*.

- Network around the internet. Share other bloggers' content and start conversations.

- Make sure your blog has a unique image and has your stamp on it.

- Take risks with content.

- The only way to get better at writing is to do *a lot* of it.

- Make your content **evergreen**—relevant for a long period of time, not just the present or immediate future.

- Be aware of your competitors; know who they are, and regularly study what they are doing.

- Promote your blog and make sure you have a comment section.

- Use professional content such as photographs and videos. You will need to be aware of copyrights and licenses.

- Understand **search engine optimization (SEO)**. This is your best friend when starting a blog; SEO is several different tactics used to ensure that search engine "spiders" are liking your blog and are moving it up in search engines. The matter of whether they like or not can be based on your traffic, content, etc.

- Understand your audience and traffic. WordPress offers tools to track your audience and to tell what was successful or not.

- Vary your blog posts to keep it fresh.

- Don't take breaks; post consistently.

- Don't give up; a successful blog will take time.

Summary

There are many career opportunities in the world of digital media and visual communication, which include digital media artist, graphic designer, Web site designer and developer, journalist and writer, and blogger. Breaking into these career paths requires not only skills in writing and technology but also great persistence and patience. With the increase of technology, many of these industries are evolving rapidly. Inspiration, creativity, hard work, and mastery of necessary technical skills are keys to breaking into these industries. As fashion moves further to the online platform and blogging becomes mainstream, careers in the fashion digital media and visual communication industry are not only attractive but also attainable.

Key Terms

digital media artist
evergreen
fashion blog
fashion blogger
fashion journalist
general web developer
graphic designer
micro blog

search engine optimization (SEO)
street style blog
technical writer
Web master
Web programmer
Web site designer
Web site developer
Writer

Online Resources

www.99designs.com

www.bloggerfreelance.com/10-things-a-blogger-resume-must-include/

www.aiga.org

www.cherrymultimedia.com

www.condenast.com

www.graphicartistsguild.org

www.indeed.com/q-Fashion-Journalism-jobs.html

www.intraligi.com

www.manrepeller.com

www.nymag.com/thecut

www.onedayonejob.com/jobs-internships/graphic-design/

www.pinterest.com

www.refinery29.com

www.thesartorialist.com

www.styleapple.com

www.stylecareers.com

Discussion Questions

1. In order to be a part of the digital media and visual communication industry, what core skills and tools are needed to be successful? How are they applied on the job for each sector?

2. All of the digital media and visual communication industries hold the ability to freelance or become self-employed. What are the most common and most important traits of a freelancer in this area?

3. Many of the sectors discussed in this chapter do not directly relate to a fashion degree. How can these specific jobs be related to the fashion industry? What can a student who is majoring in a fashion degree program do to increase his or her marketability to go into one of these career paths?

4. What is evergreen content, and why is it necessary when posting material to a fashion blog? Provide Web links or print copies of examples.

Robin Givhan is perhaps one of the most well-known fashion journalists in the world today. Being the only fashion categorical journalist to win a Pulitzer Prize for Criticism in 2006, Robin Givhan has made her mark not only in the fashion world, but also within the sphere of high-end journalism. Robin graduated from Princeton in 1986 with a bachelor's degree in journalism, and she later received a master's degree also in journalism from the University of Michigan. After graduation, Givhan went on to work for the *Detroit Free Press*, *Vogue*, and the *San Francisco Chronicle*. Starting in 1995, she worked on and off as Fashion Editor at the *Washington Post* for 10 years, until her departure in 2010. She has been a style and culture correspondent for *Newsweek*, *The Daily Beast*, and fashion critic for *The Cut*, as well as being named one of *Time* magazine's "All Time" 100 Fashion Icons.

Some of her most notable contributions include her coverage of First Lady Obama's first year in office, Dick Cheney's parka in 2005, and L'Wren Scott's abrupt and tragic suicide. In addition to her writing, Givhan has appeared as a guest on the Colbert Report and CBS News interviews, and she has contributed to various pieces of literature work, including *Runway Madness, No Sweat: Fashion, Free Trade and the Rights of Garment Workers* and *Michelle: Her First Year as First Lady*. Givhan is known for her opinionated understanding of the fashion culture and dress as it relates to business and culture. Her strong arguments and command of the English language has set her apart from the rest. Givhan announced in April 2014 that she would return in June to the *Washington Post* as its Fashion Critic and Writer. Her book, *The Battle of Versailles: The Night American Fashion Stumbled into the Spotlight and Made History*, is set to release in March 2015.

Excerpts of Robin's work include the following:

> The best collections this season have been those in which the designer's voice is akin to that of van Noten: clear and honest. Those such as Haider Ackermann, Junya Watanabe, Céline's Phoebe Philo, Chitose Abe at Sacai, and Jun Takahashi of Undercover do not stray from their

Profile Figure 12 Fashion Journalist, Robin Givhan.

> philosophy. They are lucky; they don't have to balance house codes not of their making with their own vision. They are not single-minded, but they have an underlying aesthetic—a passion—that doesn't waiver. For them, each new season doesn't negate the past (March 2014).
>
> Fashion is built on desire. It thrives on change. But it is only memorable when it has a soul.

Courtesy of Robin Givhan/*The Cut*

For the entire article and more examples of Robin Givhan's work for *The Cut*, go to http://nymag.com/thecut/2014/03/read-all-robin-givhans-fashion-month-reviews.html. For examples on *The Daily Beast*, go to: www.thedailybeast.com/contributors/robin-givhan.html.

By Lauren E. Reiter

Can you introduce yourself and tell us a little about what you do?

It was definitely an interesting journey from the start of college to today—I've been in NYC for almost 12 years! Going to school in the city (at Columbia) was definitely a big part of my career evolution, but I graduated with a bachelor of arts in history, not journalism. So, yeah, I clearly didn't have aspirations of working in the fashion world, not to mention a vested interest in that career.

I grew up in a very, very small town in Massachusetts, where fashion trends weren't really even part of the conversation. It was typically New England and Yankee, which sartorially tends to lean more towards cable-knit sweaters, khakis, and boat shoes than, say, Isabel Marant or Tim Coppens. Granted, my Mom put a premium on dressing up, so I was tricked out in sailor suits (!!) and bright colors, so I did get exposure to the sense of fun and occasion fashion can add.

Childhood digressions aside, after a stint doing retail at Ralph Lauren and some PR jobs, I landed an amazing gig at Refinery29, becoming employee #5. I was there for over four years, and I had the incredible experience of watching it grow from a small team in a Tribeca basement to a media powerhouse in the digital space. When I left there were over 100 employees.

Currently, I am working on a book proposal— actually a novel very inspired by my time at R29, sort of like Bridget Jones meets Gossip Girl (meets Nancy Drew!), as well as freelancing for various magazines like *The Hollywood Reporter* and *Gotham* and writing weekly men's style stories for *The Manual*. I also do editorial consulting and copywriting work. Recently I was in San Francisco working with Yahoo! on rebooting its Flickr property.

What made you want to go into blogging?

There's no real answer for this, to be perfectly frank. In the years after college, I slowly became interested in the fashion world, as well as culture through a style-centric lens. Writing was always a passion of mine (i.e., being crazy enough to write two theses), but I think that some people know exactly what they want to do professionally from the get-go, and it takes others a little longer to have that *aha!* moment. I became a magazine junkie, devouring everything from *W* to *V*, as well as titles farther afield from straight-up fashion—*Travel + Leisure, Elle Décor, Oyster.* And you have to remember that I was already a twenty-something when the real digitization of media began. At first, the Internet seemed like a fad, but of course the way we consume our information was altered forever. So, it was cool being a part of that culture, and I think Refinery was a vanguard of taking advantage of this space before the host of other style-specific sites. I always admired Refinery because of its alternative voice and the strong emphasis on up-and-coming designers and off-the-beaten-path style stories. I applied for the New York Editor position when the company was first expanding into city editions, and then I transitioned to Senior Editor, overseeing various markets and writing across a breadth of channels, as well as helping create a solid social media foundation.

What are one challenge and one reward you've encountered being in the blogging world?

On the reward side of the equation, I absolutely love being able to learn more about something that catches my eye (and get paid for it!). It's always exciting to see a little-known label at a Parisian boutique and then be able to get the backstory and write about it and bring it to readers. I also get pitched by interesting designers who are starting out and looking to get their name out there, so it's

(continued)

rad being able to see a now-successful company from its inception.

As for challenges, it's hard to keep up with everything and it takes a lot of time. If you're really dedicated to making your site work or your articles authentic, you have to dig deep for the backstory *and* be aware of a million things. It's not easy to find that beautiful Portuguese potter or a must-visit, hitherto unknown craft capital while keeping up with best dresses at the Met Ball.

If you could trade closets with one person, who would it be? And why?

Oh man, what a hard question! I think Derek Blasberg. I'm not sure if he'd want my closet, but I admire his aesthetic. He's created a sartorial persona for himself with a real signature, a cool mix of preppy and fashion-forward and dapper. I love how he mixes things together in unexpected ways without looking like he's trying too hard.

What other blogs or sites do you follow?

Slam X Hype and Hypebeast, Man Repeller, Candice Lake, Song of Style, The Manual, My Belonging, Stay Classic, The Blake Wright, Dappered, Daily Mail (guilty!), Street Etiquette, Mr. Porter, Net-A-Porter, Eye Swoon, The New Potato, The Sartorialist, Terry's Diary, The Coveteur, The Selby, A Hotel Life, Etsy, Quirky—there are too many to name!

Do you have any advice for dealing with advertisers and creating a business through fashion blogging?

If you have the resources, I always advise to hire an ad salesperson with experience in the .com field. Honestly, if you're a novice to this, it's tough to compete with more established sites with an entire ad sales team. If you don't have the money to front one, or can't (or don't feel comfortable) offer some sort of profit-sharing agreement in lieu of a salary, there are still obviously a lot of brands that would like to be in front of the eyeballs of your readers.

Offer giveaways or other promotions, email acquisition partnerships, product placement—I work a lot on pitching ideas for advertorials, when you can integrate a brand with your own voice and vision. Original photography really helps! Advertisers always welcome creative ideas, especially if they help create a compelling story. Alternatively, you could look for an agent that helps broker deals with the right advertisers for your site. Don't forget to build up your social media presence, too. Having a high number of engaged Instagram followers or Facebook fans is important in selling your reach to brands.

Besides the runway, where do you draw your style inspiration?

I don't think anything beats the people I see everyday on the street! I live in the East Village in New York City, and you're always seeing the raddest outfits—at coffee, on the subway, at the dry cleaners, it's endless. I have no problem going up to someone and asking "Where'd you get that?!" Of course, Pinterest and Instagram are good sources for ideas, and surfing my favorite e-tailers (I especially love Need Supply and MR PORTER) is always a go-to.

What are your picks for the next up-and-coming social networks?

Learnist, Thumb.it, Chirp, Medium, Secret.

Lastly, what is one piece of advice you would give someone who wants to be a fashion blogger?

Don't go for the quick, easy win traffic-wise, whether it's in content or on social media. People recognize authenticity above all else, so you have to believe in what you're posting. Additionally, write about what you know or what you think is a hole in the market. Ask yourself: "Why can I do this better than anyone else?" and "Who is my demographic going to be?"

Courtesy of Kristian Laliberte

chapter 13

Fashion Styling, Photography, and Costume Design

If you have ever watched the Academy Awards or viewed with fascination the wardrobes of film characters, such as Sofia Coppola's *Marie Antoinette* or *Game of Thrones* warrior queen Daenerys Targaryen, you have been immersed in the world of a costume designer. Costume designers play a leading role on set and behind the scenes. They understand how to read between the lines, searching the script for clues that will inspire them as they research, create, and source costumes. Whether the performance takes place in the late 15th century during the Renaissance of Paris or stars Angelina Jolie as Maleficent, the right wardrobe helps bring the character to life for both the actors and the audience before the first word is spoken.

If you have ever been to a fashion show, trunk show, or retailer's grand opening, you have seen the work of a fashion show and event producer and, perhaps, a modeling and talent agency director, a stylist, and a fashion photographer. The models, caterers, entertainers, and workers did not simply arrive and know just what to do and where to be on their own. Fashion show and event producers, modeling and talent agency directors, stylists, and fashion photographers work with a wide range of activities, from small boutique and megastore openings to product launches, celebrity appearances, and trade shows. Lesser-known activities, including trunk shows, sample sales, and conferences, are also arranged and implemented by event planners. No matter what type of event is being held, it takes a huge amount of advance planning and on-the-job management to make that event a success.

In this chapter, companies or persons producing **fashion visuals** (e.g., fashion shows, photographs, films, costumes, and wardrobes) are examined as ancillary businesses. Some retail organizations, for example, hire a fashion show coordinator and a fashion photographer as employees. Many, however, contract these activities from outside companies or individuals. The companies and people who provide these fashion styling services are what this chapter is all about. In addition to the costume designer, the following career paths, as independent businesses, are explored: fashion show and event producer, modeling and talent agency director, fashion photographer, and stylist.

Fashion Show and Event Producer

A retailer, manufacturer, designer, or organization may contract an independent firm, the fashion show and event planning company, to do all or part of this work for a fee. In general, the **fashion show and event producer** manages fashion shows and special events for its clients. The company works with each client to determine the type of event, intended purpose, designated audience, and the budget. The company may be contracted to handle part or all of the advertising and public relations, which can include contacting the media and writing press kits, biographies, and letters. Fashion show and event producers are reaping press by supplementing, or even replacing, the traditional fashion show or special event with technology. Digital mapping, holograms, and video projection are launching the technology component of fashion productions. What is next? Only the imaginations of current and future fashion creators can tell (Box 13.1).

In addition, the fashion show and event firm may be responsible for the selection process for products and models. For example, a jury of selection may be configured to review fashion products for acceptance into a show. For the apparel industry, the planner may also recruit and select models, fit them in garments, and then choreograph and rehearse the presentation (Figure 13.1). The fashion event producer is often responsible not only for the site selection but also for the design and installation of staging, dressing rooms, seating, lighting, and music. Preparing and handling a reception following the show may be part of the fashion event company's contract as well.

Many fashion show and event companies do not solely produce fashion shows for their clients. Some of them design, organize, and coordinate other types of events, such as conventions, conferences, corporate meetings, and exhibitions for corporations and organizations. Fashion show and event producers may be responsible for every aspect of these functions, from marketing, catering, preparing, signage, and displays to locating audiovisual equipment, printing sources, and providing security. They may also be contracted to coordinate participants' registration, accommodations, and travel. Most significantly, they are often responsible for the financial side of events by working with clients to establish realistic budgets and then monitoring expenses and income for the ventures.

What types of activities are assigned to a fashion show and event firm? Although conferences and conventions, trade shows, and company training seminars are common events for the manufacturing and retail sectors of the fashion industry, the fashion show and event firm may also be contracted to coordinate company social gatherings and meetings, organize charity fundraisers, and direct the grand openings of new retail locations or the launches of new product lines. An area of growth in event planning is the wedding planning field. Today, engaged couples are spending thousands of dollars to hire someone to plan, implement, and manage the wedding event, from the engagement party to the honeymoon, as depicted in Figure 13.2.

CASE STUDIES IN CAREER EXPLORATION

Box 13.1 Fashion Show Marketing Tips for the Fashion Show Producer

How can the fashion event producer turn a fashion show into a highly anticipated event that people are clamoring to attend? Six easy steps to prepping and marketing a stellar fashion show are presented as follows:

1. *Live the brand*. When you're planning an event for a client, be clear on what the brand image is and what the message is that your client wants to send about it. Immerse yourself in the designer's or retailer's brand. Learn who the customer is, where she wears the clothing, and how she spends her time. Consider a representative for the brand—a specific model or an image that is used in all marketing efforts for the show. The spokesmodel should speak the brand's language, such as Victoria's Secret Angel, Adriana Lima, or Glamour Sales of Shanghai's Glam Dog, who was featured in a 2014 fashion show video with more than 2.6 million views and a 47 percent increase in sales.

2. *Recruit the right ambassadors and the best team*. Celebrities (local or otherwise) can draw a crowd. Target people who have the right attachment to your brand's message, whether they're the most recognizable or promotable through marketing. Select a support team that is well-trained and capable, and then trust the team. As the leader of the pack, it's the fashion event producer's job to delegate, but only after assessing how much a decision or task is potentially worth. Leaders keep their eyes focused on the bigger costs and opportunities. With so many things to do, hand over the smaller details to the trusted team.

3. *Use social media to source a crowd*. Advertise through social media, such as Facebook, Twitter, and Instagram. Send Evites. You may want to create a Facebook page specifically for your event. You will want to provide the specifics of the show (what, where, when, and how to get tickets, etc.) and insider information. Engage viewers in the event well before it happens. Think about profiling the models who will be in the show or highlighting the season's hottest trends. Ask some questions, such as "Which trend do you like best?" Be sure to reply to any comments and questions others post.

Create a dialogue. Use social media to expand your audience: target fashion design students, fashion business owners, and personal shoppers in your area.

Take, for example, Victoria's Secret's televised fashion show. Models were captured backstage on Instagram videos during the live taping. Social media peeks were used more as teasers than spoilers. The event producer showed viewers the process of building the fashion show. The goal was to bring them along—to show them the set, the stage, the garment racks, and make them integral to the event before the show hit the airwaves.

4. *Begin with press coverage in mind*. Before an event, plan storylines, or hooks, that will generate press interest. Photograph some of the merchandise to feature in press releases for the show. Rather than relying on simple vertical shots, try high-resolution photographs taken from several different angles. Get on a ladder and focus downward; take some images of the backs of outfits as well. Configure shots to convey the brand's personality, whether it's tailored and timeless or youthful and rebellious.

5. *Plan a pre-event party to get the buzz flowing*. Enlist a restaurant owner or caterer to provide refreshments and, possibly, a venue. Offer small door prizes, raffle off front row seating, and auction a garment that will be featured in the fashion show. Introduce the guests to your models, and share the designer's or retailer's background. Promote the pre-event party through your social media and other marketing activities, such as press releases, fliers, and advertisements. Be visible, consistent, and timely in your marketing message.

Sources:

www.entrepreneur.com/article/230304

smallbusiness.chron.com/market-fashion-show-39500.html

vsallaccess.victoriassecret.com/fashionshow/

www.creativeguerrillamarketing.com/guerrilla-marketing/first-glam-dog-digital-fashion-show-shanghai-glamour-sales/

www.youtube.com/watch?v=3bY323RknC8

■ Figure 13.1
The fashion event
planner may audition
and select models,
fit them in garments,
and then choreograph
and rehearse the
presentation.

■ Figure 13.2
An area of growth in
event planning is the
wedding planning field.

What are the typical tasks for a fashion show and event producer? In many ways, event management is similar to advertising and marketing. The fashion show and event producer views the event as a product or brand and then develops and promotes it in creative ways. The ultimate goal is to ensure that the attendees (the consumers) have a positive experience that leaves them feeling good about purchasing the product and supporting its sponsors, whether the sponsor is a business, a charity, or a club. Organization is critical in the planning process, especially when dealing with the management and coordination of services and supplies. Every physical detail needs to be considered, from the layout and design of the venue to lighting, sound, communications, videography, and other technical concerns. Catering services must be organized, along with less glamorous concerns, such as security, parking, and restroom facilities. Promotion, public relations, and advertising must also be planned and executed. Last, but not least, the performers, speakers, or participants need to be located, terms negotiated, and plans confirmed.

The fashion show and event producer must anticipate the costs of all of these aspects in advance, continually checking that the budget balances. Finally, management of the event is an organizational challenge in itself. The degree of the event's success is often a result of the level of planning and organization before the event. Following the conclusion of the event, the fashion show and event producer is responsible for formally thanking participants, ensuring that all income and expenses are reconciled, and evaluating the success of the event, noting corrections of errors to implement in the next event.

Qualifications

Is a career in fashion show and event producing for you? If so, you may want to work toward achieving the following educational goals, work experiences, and personal characteristics:

- *Education.* Top event planners typically have bachelor's degrees in fashion merchandising, business administration, marketing, event management, tourism or hospitality administration, or a similar field.

- *Experience.* Knowledge of marketing and press relations is invaluable. Work experience as an assistant or an intern in fashion show production or event planning is critical.

- *Personal characteristics.* An excellent understanding of fashion marketing, a great amount of energy and flexibility, and a high level of organizational and logistical skills are required for successful fashion show and event producers. Their presentation and communication skills should be excellent. Fashion show and event producers need the skills to motivate other people, along with the creative abilities to solve problems and make things happen. If you aspire to become a fashion show and event producer, be prepared to put in extra hours to ensure that the job gets done within its budget and on time. This work requires perfection, so the event planner must pay attention to every detail and be capable of handling last-minute disasters that may happen despite superb planning.

The event planning industry continues to grow rapidly, particularly in the areas of weddings, international conferences, and hospitality. Marketing and public relations are becoming even more important facets of the event planning business.

Career Challenges

The fashion show and event planner works in a high-stress environment. Lack of attention to a detail or two, a narrowly missed deadline, or an unexpected emergency can literally annihilate a major fashion show, trade show, or charity ball. If, for example, an event planner remembered everything but forgot to confirm catering arrangements, there may not be food and drinks at a charity ball. Another pressure for fashion show and event companies or freelancers comes with generating regular business events with repeat clientele to ensure consistent income.

Modeling and Talent Agency Director

Most models are recruited by modeling scouts or modeling and talent agency directors, who travel around the world in a tireless search for fresh faces. Models are often discovered in shopping malls, schools, clubs, concerts, or other obvious places where young people hang out. Some agencies also locate models through photographs sent by model hopefuls; another way is through an agency's open casting calls. Some prestigious agencies do not charge upfront fees to join the agency; rather, these agencies are profitable by taking a percentage of the models' earnings. Fees for administration and training are often deducted after the model has found paid assignments. Training can consist of full- or part-time courses that last for a few days to a few months. Topics for courses may include diet, health, image, grooming, runway turns and movements, photographic modeling techniques, and professional conduct with clients. Individual guidance on such areas as skin care, hairstyling, makeup, and overall appearance may be provided when the model first joins the agency. The **modeling and talent agency director** is ultimately responsible for locating and contracting new models, training them, and securing modeling jobs for them.

Modeling agency directors are often very involved with their models at the start of their careers. They will often find newly signed models an apartment and help them get settled into their new lives. Many modeling and talent agency directors have found that the beginning of a modeling career is a very difficult time for a young person. Most models are young, inexperienced, and far away from home. The agency director tries to support them through difficult times while teaching them to be safe and disciplined, show up to meetings on time, and treat modeling as a real job.

Modeling agencies hire for a variety of modeling positions. **Fit models** are used as live models to test how garments fit and for designers to drape, cut, and pin fabric and garments. Most companies rely on fit models, also referred to as *fashion house models*, to give them feedback on how a garment fits and feels, as well as where it needs adjustments. They may also model the finished garments for retail buyers in the company showroom and, in the case of couture, for individual customers. Box 13.2 provides information on the work and requirements of fit models. **Show models**, or *runway models*, present merchandise in fashion shows, whereas **photographic models**, also known as *print models*, are those hired for photographs to be used in promotional and selling materials, such as catalogues, brochures, or magazine advertisements. The modeling agency takes bookings from clients who need models to work at fashion exhibitions, trade markets, product launches, and so on.

What is the talent part of the modeling and talent agency director's job? In addition to locating and booking models, the modeling and talent agency director also finds and hires talent for film and media companies. For example, a movie producer from Los Angeles may choose Seattle as the location for filming. The casting director for the film may contact a modeling and talent agency to locate actors, extras, costumers, or hair and makeup professionals in the Seattle area. The modeling and talent agency director may also commission entertainment for special events, such as conferences, galas, benefits, parties, management and sales meetings, weddings, designer appearances, book signings, and so on.

Qualifications

What are the educational, experiential, and personal characteristics of a successful modeling and talent agency director? The list is as follows:

- *Education.* A bachelor's degree in fashion merchandising, marketing, business administration, visual arts, or a related field is a common requirement.

- *Experience.* Some modeling and talent agency directors once worked in the field, either as models or actors. Others gained work experience through employment with this type of company. Employment with a retailer in the fashion coordinator's office provides excellent opportunities to work with print and runway events. An internship with a modeling and talent agency is an excellent way to determine whether this business is for you and to get your foot in the door.

- *Personal characteristics.* Modeling and talent agency directors are constantly observing those around them, networking with industry professionals, and building relationships. The successful director is truly a people person. Business skills are critical, as this person often owns the company and must hire the right people to maintain a positive reputation and encourage repeat business.

CASE STUDIES IN CAREER EXPLORATION

Box 13.2 The Fit Model

After Fashion Week in New York City has officially ended, the amazing looks on the runway models will eventually trickle their way onto the sales floors and Web sites of retailers around the country. How does a runway-model size 0 translate into an average-person size 12? The fit models of the fashion world are the heroes who help make sure the new designs can actually be worn by the rest of us. Fit models are the behind-the-scenes fashion lifesavers for most of the consumer world, those who care about how clothes fit. There are few experiences more satisfying for a woman than finally finding "the one"—that one pair of jeans that actually fits like a glove and flatters her body. The perfect pair gently hugs but isn't too snug, isn't too short in the stride, and has room in the thighs. The cut and fabric have

enough give for walking or climbing stairs without the circulation being cut off in her legs. She can comfortably sit down without the back waistline opening into an embarrassing gap. Who does she thank for this masterpiece of perfect clothing? The department store buyer? The manufacturer? The designer? The person to thank is a fit model. Fit models are rarely seen outside of the design studio, but their presence is felt by anyone who is wearing a comfortable and flattering fit. A fit model helps make the customer happy and, as such, can make or break a manufacturer's line.

Expert fit models recognize the problems in a garment before they happen, prior to production. They know how a sleeve should fit, where the

(continued on next page)

Box 13.2 *(continued)*

buttons should be located, how the stitching should be, where the hem of the jacket should hit—qualities that sell a garment. It is the fit model's job to try on each piece to show the designer and the technical designer how it moves on a real person, instead of a mannequin. They discuss fit, comfort, and how the garment moves with the body. Wearing the sample garment, can the fit model comfortably hug a friend without the shoulders pulling? Can he or she reach for a box on a shelf without ripping an armhole? Do the buttons need to be moved so the blouse does not gap at the bustline? All of these questions and more must be answered before a garment goes into production. The manufacturer's bottom line depends on it. Poor-fitting clothes can cost a small retailer thousands of dollars and a national chain tens of thousands of dollars.

Each manufacturer dictates sizing standards for fit models; however, in general, sizes for female fit models are juniors' (size 5), misses' (size 8), contemporary (size 8), plus (usually around a size 18), and petite (size 8). Many large retailers and manufacturers prefer fit models who wear sizes in the middle of their lines, such as a size 12 for a line that runs from a 0 to a 20. Unfortunately for the consumer, not all companies use the same fit models, or even fit models with the same measurements, resulting in size variations among manufacturers. The two following classified advertisements for fit models were posted on the same day by fashion manufacturers:

"Size 8 fit model needed with these exact measurements: 33", 26", 36". Must be 5'6" to 5'8" tall and have a flexible schedule."

"Wanted: Size 8 fit model. Applicants must be at least 5'8". Measurements: bust-36", waist-29", high hip-35", lower hip-39"."

This isn't your average woman. According to a *Women's Wear Daily* 2011 report, since 2005, the average dress size in America has grown to size 14 from size 12. For size 14 and above, sizing is a whole different ball game. Sometimes, manufacturers have an existing style that sold well in small sizes that they want to produce as size 14

and above. The style that sold well in small sizes, however, doesn't always accommodate or flatter a larger size (e.g., strapless, one-shoulder, or inset waistline styles). While working with the fit model, the designer may add wide shoulder straps (to make it more bra friendly), raise the neckline (to ensure appropriate décolleté), and remove an inset waistline (to add comfort and a flattering shape). Throughout the restyling sessions, the fit model is there to help and guide the designer.

Fit models must know the slope of their shoulders, the placement of their waists, and every possible measurement. Male fit models should be aware of their chest, arm, shoulder, waist, inseam, and thigh measurements. A fit model must maintain his or her measurements within a half-inch to an inch or risk losing a job. Fit modeling is one of the few areas in the modeling world that allows for a long career if the fit models maintain their sizes and shapes.

One of the large retailers relying heavily on a team of fit models to size its apparel is New York & Company. It conducted a fit model study on backsides, for example, and revealed that there are several different types of bottoms on women: curvy, modified curvy, and rectangular. The company determined that it would be remiss not to fit those three distinct derriere categories, because they clearly exist in the customer base. A New York & Company fitting can include up to 50 people discussing how a garment fits the fit model. Once the sample garment has been fitted and approved, the specs for all sizes are determined, and the information is sent to a factory overseas. The garments are produced and shipped back to the stores. Welcome, perfect pair of jeans, and thank you, fit model.

Sources:

http://www.huffingtonpost.com/2014/01/05/plus-size-models_n_4544777.html

http://www.wwd.com/markets-news/intimates-activewear/more-choices-for-plus-sizes-3443993

http://culture.wnyc.org/articles/features/2011/feb/18/behind-stage-fashion-week-fit-models/

Career Challenges

The modeling and talent agency is only as lucrative as the people employed by the firm. If the modeling agency and talent director discovers and hires a new model who becomes a supermodel, then the director benefits financially from all of the model's jobs. Training, guiding, and managing new and often young talent can be challenging, as is maintaining a positive reputation in a field that is not always viewed as having high integrity.

Fashion Photographer

Thanks to our fashion-conscious society and the Internet, a fashion photographer can live just about anywhere. Fashion photographers used to locate to Paris, Milan, New York, or Los Angeles to earn a good living. Today, with the help of technology, this career dream is a possibility in almost any location. Successful fashion photographers are more than people who take good pictures. They can make products and their models look their best artistically. To succeed, a fashion photographer must possess the technical and artistic skills to ensure a professional, eye-catching, and distinctive photograph. Photographers work to develop an individual style of photography to differentiate themselves from their competition.

Fashion photography can be a highly creative and well-paid career, but it is a career path with limited opportunities and a focus on freelance work. A **fashion photographer** is in the business of taking pictures of models wearing the latest apparel, accessories, hairstyles, and makeup, or highlighting the newest home furnishings and other fashion products, primarily for commercial use. The photographs are used in a variety of media, including advertisements, catalogs, billboards, television, Web sites, and art venues. Often working to meet a client's requests, the photographers control lighting, tone, and perspective in their work, using a range of photographic equipment, accessories, and imaging software. Photographers must have a technical understanding of the medium, as well as an artistic vision. Key tasks of the fashion photographer include choosing and preparing locations; setting up lighting; selecting the appropriate cameras, lenses, film, and accessories; composing shots; positioning subjects; and instructing assistants. After shooting, they may process and print images or view and manipulate digital images using software such as Adobe Photoshop.

Some fashion photographers choose exclusive employment with a retailer, a publication (e.g., a magazine or a newspaper), a designer, an advertising company, a manufacturer, or a direct-mail company. Others may choose to freelance, with or without an agent, or open their own studios. These independent photographers make up the ancillary segment of the fashion industry. Most successful independent photographers develop positive reputations by accumulating considerable work experience in mail-order, editorial, or advertising work. Some photographers enter the field by submitting unsolicited photographs to magazines. There are many avenues for a fashion photographer to break into this business: freelance without an agent, freelance with an agent, or through one's own studio.

Photographers usually specialize in one of the following six areas: general practice, advertising or editorial, fashion, press, corporate, and technical. General practice, or social, photography refers to photographic services for local communities or businesses, with the majority of work in wedding and family photography. **Advertising photography**, or *editorial photography*, expresses a product's personality or illustrates a magazine story. It is usually classified as still life, food, transportation, portraiture, or landscape photography. Fashion photographers work with models and art directors in the apparel, accessories, or home products industries. They are often commissioned by art directors of catalogues and magazines. **Press photography**, also known as *photojournalism*, focuses on images directly related to news stories, both events and personalities. Corporate, also referred to as industrial or commercial, photographers produce images for promotional materials or annual reports. The **technical photographer** produces photographs for reports or research papers, such as textile durability analyses. Figure 13.3 is an example of technical photography.

■ **Figure 13.3**
An illustration of technical photography in the textile sector of the fashion industry.

In all areas of specialization in photography, the successful photographer has several work objectives:

- Maintaining a technical knowledge of cameras and related rapidly changing technologies, as photographers increasingly need to know how to use computer software programs and applications that allow them to prepare and edit images

- Developing an artistic understanding of light, distance, and perspective

- Cultivating a keen eye for aesthetic detail and inventive ways to communicate moods and ideas

- Building strong interpersonal skills to work with models and be sensitive to their moods so that they are comfortable in front of the camera

- Understanding studio lighting to bring out the best in skin tones and textures and colors of different fabrics

- Working well with natural light (or a lack of) for on-location shoots

- Establishing good relationships with stylists, art directors, modeling agents, and fashion editors

- Identifying and securing future assignments and clients

- Understanding the roles and responsibilities of an entrepreneur

Professional photographers often employ assistants to help the business run smoothly. **Assistant photographers** may deal with clients and suppliers; organize estimates, invoices, and payments; arrange props and assist with lighting; communicate with photographic labs and stylists; work with the photographer on shoots; and maintain the photographer's Web site and portfolio.

What are the benefits of a career in fashion photography? The attractions of fashion photography are obvious: exotic locations, plenty of foreign travel, and personal publicity in fashion journals and other magazines. There is also the chance to work within the world of fashion and design and to associate with the glamorous people who live there.

Qualifications

What do you need to know and do to secure a position in this field? Following are the qualifications required of a fashion photographer:

- *Education.* A bachelor's degree in photography or visual arts and a strong portfolio are usually essential. Freelance photographers need continuing education in technical proficiency, whether gained through a degree program, vocational training, or extensive work experience.

- *Experience.* Because entry-level positions for a fashion photography firm are rare, gaining a position as a photographer's studio assistant is a common way to enter the field. Some of the entry career paths for fashion photographers who are interested in freelance work or business ownership include working for periodicals, advertising agencies, retail operations, fashion designers, modeling agencies, catalogues, galleries, or stock photography agencies.

- *Personal characteristics.* Those fashion photographers who succeed in attracting enough work to earn a living are likely to be the most creative and adept at operating a business. They are also excellent at building and retaining relationships with other professionals. The independent fashion photographer needs to be extremely confident and have the persistence to solicit consistent work. Stamina is needed for working long hours, sometimes in uncomfortable conditions. Excellent communication skills and a flexible personality are needed, as the photographer must often have patience: it can take a long time to get the right shot.

The Portfolio

A photographer's most important tool is the portfolio, particularly for beginners who have not established a reputation. A **portfolio**, or *book*, is a collection of work that illustrates the job candidate's range of skills and outcomes. Box 13.3 presents tips from a well-known fashion magazine photo editor, a fashion and beauty photographer, and a photographers' agent for building a portfolio. Many photographers find that Web sites offer an inexpensive way to showcase a relatively large number of their images, but most industry clients will still need to see a traditional portfolio before they hire a photographer. Because magazine editors regularly receive many unsolicited portfolios, the fashion photographer must develop a portfolio that stands out in a crowd. Many fashion photographers find that at least 20 images and several tearsheets, if available, should be included in the portfolio. A **tearsheet** is a page that has been pulled from a newspaper, model book, or magazine. Tearsheets are excellent to include in the portfolio if the photographer has been published. The candidate for a photography job should be prepared to leave a copy of the portfolio with a potential client for at least a week (and include a self-addressed and stamped envelope if the photographer wants the portfolio copy returned). As technology progresses, more photographers are creating Web sites through which they can enable prospective employers to view their portfolios online.

Career Challenges

This is a tough field to enter, as it can take many years of experience at low pay to find opportunities to build a portfolio of work. Fashion photographers often pay their dues before establishing a strong reputation in the field. Some photographers find it frustrating to be directed by the retailer or designer on who will model or how and where to shoot print work. The individual's aesthetic sometimes must take a backseat to the employer's vision. Photographers are also challenged to constantly update software and related skills on the computer in order to alter or edit imagery.

Stylist

There are two types of stylists in the ancillary level of the fashion industry—the photo stylist and the fashion, or wardrobe, stylist. **Photography stylists** work with teams of people, such as photographers, designers, lighting technicians, and set builders. They set up the shoot for the

CASE STUDIES IN CAREER EXPLORATION

Box 13.3 How to Become a Fashion Photographer

A career in fashion photography doesn't have to be an impossible dream. With its huge audience, high paychecks, and glamorous international lifestyle, fashion photography may seem like one of the world's most sought-after professions. But for every fashion photographer who makes it through the door of a top magazine, a thousand others find their niches in fashion advertising, art photography, portraiture, or even paparazzi work. *Allure* magazine photo editor Clio McNicholl, New York fashion and beauty photographer Eva Mueller, and photo agent Gloria Cappelletti agree that breaking into the industry can be difficult, but they offer some tips for beginning photographers on building a portfolio, submitting work to magazine picture editors, and choosing a photo agency.

Building a Portfolio

A photographer's most important tool is the portfolio, and this is particularly true for beginners who don't have an established reputation. "Having been around, I know how hard it is to get in the door," says Clio McNicholl, who receives around 50 unsolicited portfolios a month at Condé Nast's *Allure* magazine. "If I don't know who the person is, I ask them to send me some promotional material. Generally, I only see people who are coming with a direct recommendation from somebody I know," she says.

Many photographers find that Web sites offer an inexpensive way to showcase a relatively large quantity of images. Despite the Web site's strengths, many hiring professionals want to see an old-fashioned book. Use the Web as your calling card, but have a portfolio to show when they call you in for a meeting. Many fashion photographers find the sharp, bright imaging of 4-by-5-inch transparencies show off their work best. Tearsheets (literally, pages ripped from a magazine) are great if you've been published, but good-quality 8-by-10-inch prints are also okay. Have at least 20 in your book; be prepared to leave a copy of your book for at least a week.

"I like to see a common thread throughout the book," states McNicholl, who says she can tell within three images whether she likes a photographer's style. She further states: "Tell a story: not necessarily having the pictures relating to each other, but I like to have some sort of sense at the end of it that I've seen that photographer's personality come through in the pictures." The images showcased in your portfolio should be thematically linked to the job you're trying to get—still-lives or product shots if you're going for an advertising gig, for example. Also, throw in one or two other images to demonstrate your range. Strong portraits are always a safe bet, because they tend to stay in the mind of the viewer. Once your portfolio is together, the next challenge is to get the picture editor to hire you.

Winning Over the Picture Editor

"Most people who cold call me haven't done their research, which is the world's biggest mistake," says McNicholl. "The single biggest thing that people should do is their research. Know what the magazine does, and see how you can apply that to what you do. And they should at least know the name of the photo editor." When you submit work to photo editors, remember that you are showing rather than selling. Editors rarely buy the specific image they see before them; they're looking for a photographer who can execute future commissions. You'll need to be persistent in sending out your work, and ruthless in editing what you choose to show.

The best way to grab an editor's attention is to show previously published work, but there is a downside. "Because there is such an oversupply of photographers, some magazines really take advantage of that fact," says Eva Mueller. "Some mags have a decent budget, but many magazines just cover the photographer's expenses." McNicholl says *Allure*'s rates start at $350 a day for unknown photographers, up to $130,000 for a fashion spread.

(continued on next page)

Box 13.3 *(continued)*

A photograph tells a story, as an article or an essay does. Celebrity portraiture, for example, should reveal an aspect of the subject's character, preferably one that is in harmony with an accompanying profile. Every month, fashion magazines all over the world buy hundreds of stock shots, which reflect topics commonly dealt with in feature articles—typically young women hanging out with friends, relaxing alone at home, or shopping in the mall. Presenting the stock shots you have done that have been purchased by magazines in your portfolio will help it stand out. When you're submitting your work, remember the following tips:

- Call the magazine ahead and get the name (with its correct spelling) and title of the person to whose attention the submission should be marked

- Label everything with your name and contact information

- Send working prints or transparencies, not originals

- Include a stamped, self-addressed envelope if you want the work back

Eve Mueller has a warning about dealing with magazines: "Another bad thing is not getting paid in ages. Some clients really take advantage of the fact that there are so many photographers: They make you pay for the whole shoot; they alter your pictures; and they don't tell you when they drop the story." There is a way to avoid time dealing with picture editors and to spend it on your work. That is to have a photo agency selling on your behalf.

Finding a Photo Agent

Photo agencies exist to liaise with clients and sell photographers' work for them. They benefit everyone, from start-out photographers, who may not have many industry contacts, to seasoned professionals, who are too busy to take care of business dealings themselves. Gloria Cappelletti, an agent with the Management Artists' Organization (MSO) in Manhattan, states:

> First of all, it's vital to be known, and an agency is in daily contact with clients and publications. That's the best way for a young photographer to be able to have a connection with them, because usually the photographer is busy taking pictures, and the agent is busy talking to clients. And that's the way it should be. Usually, the photographer doesn't have enough time to take care of everything.

Source:

Fashion Net, www.fashion.net/howto/fashionphotographer/

---

photographer, scouting locations and selecting appropriate props, fashions, accessories, and, perhaps, the models to enhance the shoot. The photo stylist often prepares backdrops, lighting, and equipment for the photographer. **Fashion stylists**, or *wardrobe stylists*, pull together outfits or wardrobes for their clients, to include executives, celebrities, fashion designer clients, and everyday people, from a new graduate entering the workforce to a new retiree moving into a more casual lifestyle.

Both types of stylists are responsible for bringing to life a photographer's, director's, or individual's vision and fashion image. For the photography stylist, this work shows up in magazines, catalogues, and Web site or newspaper advertisements. The fashion stylist's work may be seen in the wardrobes of clients—from sports celebrities to the cast of a television series to the new manager of the local bank, depending on the image, reputation, and skills of the stylist. Companies such as magazines, newspapers, retailers, advertising agencies, and music production companies often employ fashion stylists. Many stylists also choose to run their own businesses.

Typical work activities for the stylist are varied, from the shopping time to shooting the photograph or film. **Assistant stylists** are often responsible for contacting public relations companies, manufacturers, and retailers to locate the best assortment of merchandise to be used in a shoot. Next, they will borrow, lease, or purchase garments and props, and then they arrange to transport the selections to the studio or location to determine which combinations work best. Before the shoot begins, stylists work with hair and makeup personnel and dress the people featured in the shoot, adjusting the fit of apparel and accessories as needed.

Interning or apprenticing with a well-known stylist is an ideal way to learn the business, including inside information such as where the best military uniforms or 1940s evening wear is available, which tailor can do overnight alterations, and who can design and sew a sailor suit for a Chihuahua. Occasionally, a stylist has to deal with big egos, as well as big time constraints; it simply goes with the territory. Stylists have to avoid allowing their egos and tastes to interfere with a director's vision or a client's image. Box 13.4 features a classified advertisement for an Internet stylist.

Qualifications

If the vision of searching for the right look, pulling together wardrobes, and creating strong visual images sounds ideal to you, then the career of stylist is one to consider. It requires the following education and work experiences, as well as personal characteristics:

- *Education.* An associate's or bachelor's degree in fashion design, fashion merchandising, visual arts, photography, visual merchandising, or a related field is often required.

- *Experience.* Retail sales or management experience is helpful, as are internships with fashion publications or fashion stylists. Stylists may progress from editorial assistant work on fashion magazines, where there is constant contact with public relations companies, manufacturers, and retailers. The career path for a stylist may also begin with an internship or apprenticeship with an experienced stylist before moving into an assistant stylist position, and then to a staff fashion stylist.

- *Personal characteristics.* The fashion stylist has an eye for style and upcoming fashion trends, as well as a broad knowledge of historical fashions. Technical knowledge for creating sets and using lighting effectively is important. One needs to be creative, resourceful, persistent, and self-motivated. The fashion stylist should have good interpersonal, presentation, and communication skills. The ability to market one's self is critical. Aspiring fashion stylists should have the perseverance to work their way to the top. The most successful fashion stylists have extensive networks of contacts within the fashion industry to get the job done quickly and within budget.

With the influence of movies, television, and the Internet on the consumer, it is no surprise that stylists are often credited with setting fashion trends around the globe. A stylist may dress an actress in a funky retro gown or an amazing necklace to wear to a premiere. Once the image is splashed across the pages of fashion magazines and featured on television and the Internet, it can become a trend and put the stylist's name in the spotlight around the world.

Box 13.4 Internet Stylist

Full-time employee for large retail/product development company

San Francisco, California

Major Responsibilities

- Manage styling direction

- Execute each Web site's styling point of view for all in-house photography to include product lay-down and on-figure photography, and special lay-down and marketing photography

- Understand the marketing and merchandising seasonal objectives and executing site features based on those objectives

- Establish partnership with brand-styling team to promote styling and product consistency from the stores to the Web sites

- Obtain appropriate approvals from cross-functional partners to ensure consistency and translate the brand point of view appropriately for each Web site

- Create/manage a product style guide of all e-commerce sites

- Partner with creative team to co-lead and drive the styling direction for all e-commerce sites

- Create a relationship between the photography, stylist, and assistant stylist team to provide team synergy

- Manage operating practices

- Drive photography work flow by assessing the volume and photography set requirements

- Identify/document/present process efficiencies within the photography floor

Minimum Qualifications

- Minimum four years of experience with fashion styling and/or visual fashion retail experience

- Bachelor's of art or science degree in a related field

- Ability to balance creative with strategic deliverables

- Strong collaboration skills and ability to form effective partnerships across cross-functional team: photo studio, creative, merchandising, and marketing teams

- Extremely flexible, detail oriented, organized, and self-motivated with leadership skills

- Comfortable in a fast-paced environment

- Comfortable working with Excel, Photoshop, and related software, and databases in general

- Experienced in managing others

Career Challenges

The stylist may find this career filled with irregular work, long hours, limited budgets, and clients with conflicting personal tastes. It can be difficult to work for several bosses, from the client to the photographer or film director. This is a career track in which there is growing interest and strong competition for the minimal number of jobs that currently exist. It is challenging to get your foot in the door, and when you do, you have to be great. For those who are great, excellent remuneration, job satisfaction, and the opportunity to build a reputation are quite possible.

Costume Designer

A **costume designer** collaborates with film and video directors to design, consign, or construct apparel and accessories that fit with the mood, time frame, and image of the visual. Depending on style and complexity, costumes may be rented, made, bought, or revamped out of existing stock. The costumer's designs need to faithfully reflect the personalities of the characters in the script. Stage costumes can provide audiences with information about a character's occupation, social status, gender, age, sense of style, and personality. Costumes have the ability to reinforce the mood and style of a production and distinguish between major and minor characters. Costumes may also be used to change an actor's appearance or be objects of beauty in their own right.

The shapes, colors, and textures that a costumer chooses can make an immediate and powerful visual statement to the audience. Creative collaboration among the costumer, production director, and set and lighting designers ensures that the costumes are smoothly integrated into a production as a whole. Costuming also includes any accessories needed to project a character, such as canes, hats, gloves, shoes, jewelry, or masks. These costume props add a great deal of visual interest to the overall costume design. The costumer may also collaborate with a hair and wig master, hairstylist, and makeup artist. In European theater productions, these are often the items that truly distinguish one character from another.

Costumers begin their work by reading the script to be produced. If the production is set in a specific historical era, the fashions of this period need to be researched. To stimulate the flow of ideas at the first meeting with the director and design team (i.e., set, costume, lighting, and sound designers), the costumer may choose to present a few rough costume sketches. This is also an appropriate time to check with the director on the exact number of characters who need costumes, because any nonspeaking characters the director plans to include may not have been listed in the script.

It is the costumer's responsibility to draw up the costume plot. The **costume plot** is a list or chart that shows which characters appear in each scene, what they are wearing, and what their overall movements are throughout the play. This helps track the specific costume needs of every single character. It can also identify any potential costume challenges, such as very quick changes between scenes. Following the director and production team's approval of the preliminary sketches, the costumer draws up the final costume designs. The final designs are done in full color and show the style, silhouette, textures, accessories, and unique features of each costume. A summary of the responsibilities of the theater, film, video, and television costume designer follows:

- Research and utilize a broad range of cinematic, social, and historical references

- Read and analyze scripts

- Source costumes and materials

- Conceptualize, illustrate, and create costumes

- Oversee fittings

Catherine Martin (Box 13.5) received the Academy Award in 2014 for her work as costume designer for *The Great Gatsby*. For this film, Martin served as producer, production designer, and costume designer—a phenomenal undertaking. As the movie was shot in Australia, Martin and her team had to recreate 1920s New York at Sydney's Fox Studios. Everything from Gatsby's mansion—with its ballroom, pool, library, and grotto—to the Plaza's suite was created specifically for the movie. When it came to the costumes, some of the film's party scenes had close to 300 extras on set—each one outfitted in a unique costume. To give you an idea of just how many costumes that is, Brooks Brothers supplied 1,200 in total just on the men's side. Miuccia Prada helped out on the women's side, designing 40 background dresses, as well as some of Daisy's (played by Carey Mulligan) costumes.

Costuming may also include creating masks, makeup, or other unusual forms, such as the "dress of changing sizes" worn in Tim Burton's *Alice in Wonderland*, designed by Colleen Atwood and shown in Figures 13.4a and b.

■ **Figures 13.4a and b**
Costume designer Colleen Atwood's sketches for Tim Burton's *Alice in Wonderland*.

CASE STUDIES IN CAREER EXPLORATION

Box 13.5 Academy Award–Winning Designer Catherine Martin

Catherine Martin is a film, stage, and interior designer with four Oscars, five BAFTAs, and a Tony Award, among many other awards. Along with being honored as one of *Glamour Magazine*'s 2013 Women of the Year for her production, set, and costume designs, Catherine was inducted into the Rodeo Drive "Walk of Style" for her work on *The Great Gatsby*. Christened "CM" by Baz Luhrmann just a few weeks after they met, she is more commonly known by this distinctive moniker.

Martin is the wife and chief collaborator of Oscar-nominated director, producer, and writer, Baz Luhrmann. To the millions around the world who have seen the movies she's worked on, Martin is more likely to be known as the woman who made Nicole Kidman resplendent in red in the costumes for *Moulin Rouge!* (2001), for making us want to shimmy our way in beaded dresses into the lavish party scenes in *The Great Gatsby* (2013), and for collaborating on Baz Luhrmann's extraordinary contemporary reinterpretation of *Romeo + Juliet* (1996). The 20 years of experience of painstaking research she has undertaken for all of Baz's films, combined with her lifelong passion for fashion and the close industry relationships she has been able to forge at Baz's side (including Miuccia Prada and Karl Lagerfeld), have made her a force to be reckoned with.

Martin's profound ability to become deeply and authentically involved in the branding, brand message, and the very DNA of the projects she's involved in has allowed her to segue into the fashion world via brands such as Prada, Chanel, Tiffany & Co, and Brooks Brothers and through the creation of the Fitzgerald Suite at the Plaza Hotel in New York. Martin's passion for authenticity is the same quality that she brings to her burgeoning interiors business. Her design aesthetic for the home has resulted in elegant, timeless, and yet always functional creations that can both inspire and transport, from the chairs and bedding she has designed for leading

Box 13.5 Academy Award–Winning Costume Designer, Catherine Martin.

homewares brands like Anthropologie to her work with Designer Rugs and Mokum. Constantly inspired by the people she meets and the places she visits, Martin divides her time between Paris, New York, and Sydney, and she has two beautiful children, Lillian (10) and William (8).

Source:

Courtesy of Maria Farmer Public Relations

Costume designers typically work to enhance a character's personality through the way that character is dressed, while allowing the actor to move freely and perform actions as required by the script. The designer needs to possess strong artistic capabilities, a thorough familiarity with fashion history, as well as knowledge of clothing construction and fit. Professional costumers generally fall into three classifications: freelance, residential, and academic.

Freelance costumers are hired for a specific production by theater companies or production studios. A freelance costumer is traditionally paid in three installments: at hiring, on the delivery of final renderings, and on the opening night of the production. Freelancers are usually not obligated to any exclusivity in projects they are working on and may be designing for several theaters concurrently. A **residential costumer** is hired by a specific film company or theater for an extended series of productions. This can be as short as a summer stock contract or as long as several years. A residential costumer's contract may limit the amount of freelance work the costumer is permitted to accept. Unlike the freelancer, a residential costumer is consistently on location at the filming site or theater and is readily at hand to work with the costume studio and other collaborators. Residential costumers are more likely than freelancers to be associated with a union, as most theaters that can retain such a position have agreements with such organizations as the Actors' Equity Association.

Qualifications

If the career of a costumer appeals to you, following is a list of educational credentials and work experiences that will contribute to your success, and the personal characteristics you should acquire:

- *Education.* A bachelor's degree in theater costuming, historical costume, visual arts, fashion design, or a similar field is required.

- *Experience.* Some successful costumers begin in the career field through an internship with an experienced costume designer. Others gain work experience as assistant fashion designers or fashion stylists before moving into the film and theater industry. Interning in summer stock productions, volunteering to assist in off-Broadway or local theater productions, and working or volunteering at a costume rental agency are excellent ways for college students to acquire work experience. High school and college students can gain experience through costume, hair, or makeup work in school theater productions.

- *Personal characteristics.* A creative and resourceful personality is a plus. An understanding of historical fashion, clothing construction, and fit are necessities. Many costume designers find that the ability to sketch well is essential to communicating their ideas to directors and producers.

Career Challenges

The costumer is challenged with accurately interpreting the words and vision of the writer, director, or producer. In some cases, such as productions set in a different time or unique location, this takes a great deal of research. The costumer often works on a tight budget and an even tighter timeline. Costumes may require alterations, repairs, or replacement during the production. As costumers often work on several projects simultaneously, this career fits a person who can effectively multitask. Low pay and long hours should be expected at the start of this career track.

Summary

Fashion visuals include such activities as fashion shows, photography shoots, and films or videos wardrobed by costume designers or stylists. Some of these career tracks are examined as ancillary fashion businesses; others are viewed as company positions; all are viewed as offering fashion services. Some retail organizations, for example, hire fashion show coordinators and fashion photographers as employees. Many, however, contract these activities from outside companies. These career paths include the fashion show and event producer, modeling and talent agency director, fashion photographer, fashion stylist, and costume designer.

The fashion show and event producer manages fashion shows and special events for his or her clients for a fee. Special events include, but are not limited to, trunk shows, sample sales, weddings, meetings, conferences, training seminars, and trade markets. The modeling and talent agency director is ultimately responsible for locating and contracting new models, training them, and securing modeling jobs for them. Fashion photographers take photographs of models wearing the latest apparel, accessories, hairstyles, and makeup, or highlighting the newest home furnishings and other fashion products, primarily for commercial use. The photographs are used in a variety of media, including advertisements, catalogues, billboards, television, Web sites, and art galleries. Fashion stylists are responsible for bringing to life a photographer or director's vision for a fashion shoot, magazine layout, music video or film, television commercial, or print advertisement (Figure 13.5). The costume designer collaborates with stage, film, and video directors to design, consign, or construct costumes that fit with the mood, time frame, and image of the visual.

All in all, fashion media and visual career options are creative and growing entrepreneurial paths. As diverse as the careers of the freelance fashion show and event planner, modeling and talent agency director, photographer, stylist, and costumer are, those who follow them have something major in common. They are all entrepreneurs—owners of their own futures. As such, they require the business skills needed to estimate expenses and labor accurately, sell and market their services, and maintain and grow a client base. It is a creative, independent, and self-directed lifestyle that combines creativity with passion.

■ **Figure 13.5**
Fashion, or wardrobe, stylists pull together outfits or complete closets of clothing and accessories for their clients, to include executives, celebrities, fashion designer clients, and everyday people.

Key Terms

advertising photography

assistant photographer

assistant stylist

costume designer

costume plot

fashion photographer

fashion show and event producer

fashion stylist

fashion visual

fit model

freelance costumer

modeling and talent agency director

photographic model

photography stylist

portfolio

press photography

residential costumer

show model

tearsheet

technical photographer

Online Resources

fashionista.com/2013/04/great-gatsby-costume-and-set-designer-catherine-martin-tells-all

www.anothermag.com/current/view/332/Costume_Designer_Antonella_Cannarozzi

twitter.com/ChinaShopMag

www.clothesonfilm.com

www.ew.com/ew/gallery/0,,20311937_20468523_20916170,00.html

www.fashion.net

www.myfdb.com

Discussion Questions

1. By perusing trade publications and the Internet, develop a list of fashion show and event planning firms that are available to fashion retailers and manufacturers for contract. In what areas do these firms specialize? What career opportunities are available?

2. What are the requirements for a costume designer who wants to secure clients in the entertainment industry? Compare and contrast the licenses, union memberships, or other credentials that are required or are helpful.

3. What are the sign-on requirements for a major modeling agency? How does the director determine who receives a contract and who does not?

4. Select a costume designer for a well-known period film and describe this costumer's research and outcomes for the film's characters' costumes.

5. Compare and contrast the careers of the fashion stylist and the costumer. Clarify the differences and similarities. Can a person be both?

Profile: Interview with a Bridal Boutique Owner and Wedding Consultant, Stephanie Weiss of Ella Weiss Wedding Design

Interviewed by Michele Granger

Can you tell me a little about yourself?

I love what I do and have always been drawn to fashion. Growing up in a very small town, I studied my fashion magazines from front to back as a child. I now live in Springfield, Missouri, and have been married to my amazing husband for ten years. We have two beautiful daughters with a third on the way.

When did you realize you wanted to own a bridal boutique?

I worked as a bridal consultant right out of college, but wanted to gain more business and marketing experience. While I was a marketing director for a physicians' group, I visited Springfield, Missouri, to help my younger sister shop for her wedding dress. Unfortunately, we didn't have the best experience; not only was the customer service unsatisfactory, but the selection was limited and the consultants simply weren't listening to my sister. After a long day of shopping, my husband and I discussed the need for an upscale bridal boutique in the area that really focused on customer service. He said, "You should open a bridal boutique there," and the rest is history.

What was your path to where you are today?

After graduating from the University of Missouri with a bachelor's degree in fashion marketing and merchandising, I gained five years of bridal fashion and marketing experience to bring my dream to life. But a degree and years of experience cannot speak for what it takes to make your vision a reality. Ella Weiss Wedding Design is the concrete interpretation of my vision. To prepare for this, I created my own opportunities to learn everything I could about fashion and marketing so that one day I could successfully open my bridal boutique.

Profile Figure 13 Bridal Boutique Owner and Wedding Planner, Stephanie Weiss.

While in college, I witnessed every step of fashion from idea conception to runway at the renowned Paris Fashion Institute. After becoming a designer specialist for Neiman Marcus, I worked closely with Amsale, a couture wedding dress line. I traveled to New York City each season and met with the buyer of Neiman Marcus to choose the gowns that best fit the St. Louis target market. When these gowns arrived, I educated the sales staff on the new lines

(continued on next page)

and their selling points. This experience allowed me to gain valuable knowledge of bridal fabrics, designer lines, and the wedding industry in general. Finally, as a marketing director, I developed, implemented, and managed marketing promotions, sales plans, and advertising campaigns.

These vast experiences enabled me to operate a boutique in my own way. I truly understand the importance of relating to my customers and always giving them something extra. I noticed a trend of stressed-out, overwhelmed modern brides and wanted to change that through simplification, empowerment, and a lot of pampering. I can put my own stamp on wedding culture by placing the bride back on a luxurious pedestal. It is important to allow the bride's own sense of style and personality to shine through to ensure the vision of her dream wedding becomes a reality. I've developed a creative mind and an eye for detail to turn my boutique into a haven where brides know they will be taken care of. A vision of couture gowns, a refreshing atmosphere, and exceptional service embodies everything Ella.

What does your company do?

Ella Weiss Wedding Design is a full-service bridal boutique. Our goal is to put our brides at ease and pamper them from the moment they step in our doors. We help our brides create their entire wedding day look, starting with their perfect dress and then adding the finishing touches—the veil, headpiece, jewelry, and shoes. Because each gown is custom made for the individual bride, she has the freedom to personalize her dress, from the color to the length of the train, or by adding straps or buttons, etc. Once the bride has found her dress, we help her with bridesmaid dresses, flower girl dresses, and tuxedo rentals to complement her overall look and the style of her wedding. We offer in-house alterations to ensure a perfect fit. Ella

Weiss also offers in-house wedding coordinators who provide customized consulting, planning, and coordinating services that are personally tailored to each bride.

Why are you drawn to this career?

I love working with my brides. They are so happy and are planning for one of the biggest days in their lives. It's such a special moment when I've helped a bride find her perfect dress or worked with her for a year planning every detail of her day and being there to make sure everything goes smoothly. I am very detail oriented and a pretty good problem solver, so putting together the wedding itineraries and coming up with creative solutions to problems is right up my alley.

What is an average day for you?

No day is ever the same. I usually begin my day returning phone calls and e-mails; these could be appointments to schedule, questions about our designers or an existing order, etc. I have a continuous running to-do list that I constantly update. During bridal season, there are typically two to six fittings in a day. Appointments to help new brides usually take at least an hour. The majority of our brides like to come on Saturdays, but we see quite a few during the week as well. We have new shipments every day that either include a bride's gown or new inventory. Both types of shipments come with many steps to follow once they arrive: adding items to the inventory, tagging merchandise, steaming gowns and veils, calling the brides, adjusting our pending purchases, etc.

To stay in touch with our clients, we try to update our social media on a daily basis. We also try to maintain our e-mail marketing campaigns to keep promotions and new inventory advertised. Quickbooks and updating reports are also done on a daily basis.

(continued)

What kind of skills have you learned from your experiences, and how could they be applied in other careers in fashion?

This business has provided me with experience in buying, merchandising, sales, management, marketing and advertising—just to name a few. I feel like I could step into a wide variety of positions in the fashion industry with my background.

How do you get (and stay) inspired?

I get inspired every time I go to market and see the new and upcoming wedding trends. I love getting inspired from weddings I see on blogs or Pinterest.

What have been your toughest challenges?

I would say finding and keeping the right employees has been my toughest challenge. Someone who is hard-working, a good salesperson; someone who is mature and cares about my business is really

hard to find. Another struggle has been the fact that brides feel that they cannot afford to shop at my boutique, so they don't even visit the boutique or call to ask our price ranges, when we have dresses that start at $700.

What advice would you give to aspiring business owners?

I would definitely suggest working or interning at a company that is comparable to what you would like to open. Although I worked as a bridal consultant at Neiman Marcus, most of the business was conducted at the corporate office in Dallas. I wish I had worked or interned at a small business to see the ins and outs of the day-to-day business operations.

Source:
Courtesy of Ella Weiss

Profile: Fashion Stylist to the Stars, Micaela Erlanger

Micaela Erlanger began her education as a pre-med student, but fashion was always on her mind—starting at an early age. The Connecticut native remembers wearing a velvet party dress and patent leather Mary Janes to the emergency room when she had her tonsils removed. With a sewing machine gifted to her by her nanny, she created garments for the family cat. "I had an undeniable passion and interest," she says. After two years of pre-med, she transferred to Parsons the New School for Design, thinking she wanted to be a fashion editor. She quickly realized that the world of freelance styling existed through her internships. "I had this internship at *Cosmo*, where my job was to attend every shoot," she says. "Freelancers would come and do their thing, it was fascinating."

Soon after graduation, with a costume designing job in between, she began working with the late Annabel Tollman, stylist for Scarlett Johansson. "I worked with her six years and she taught me everything I know," Erlanger says. "She was an incredible talent and teacher." From learning about managing an entrepreneurial business to cultivating client relationships to shaping a discriminating eye, Tollman "taught me the things that can't be taught," Erlanger explains. She applies these lessons to her own list of clients, which today includes Olivia Munn, Winona Ryder, *Downton Abbey*'s Michelle Dockery, and *12 Years a Slave*'s Lupita Nyong'o. Although dealing with such varied women could be difficult, Erlanger explains, "It's about understanding who they are and their individual style, and translating that to the carpet."

Maybe it's who you know *and* how you can make them look. Erlanger's first client was Joely Richardson, whom she styled for the *Anonymous* and *The Girl With the Dragon Tattoo* press tours. Erlanger met Michelle Dockery when her makeup artist introduced them. Their first collaboration was a white and gold Alexandre Vauthier Couture gown for the 2013 Golden Globes. "Michelle was my first major client; her Globes dress was life-changing," says Erlanger.

Fast-forward to summer 2013, when Dockery befriended little-known Kenyan actress Nyong'o on the set of their action-thriller *Non-Stop* and offered to connect the star-to-be with her stylist. "Michelle said, 'When you're ready, I have the perfect stylist for you,'" recalls Nyong'o. Adds Erlanger, who first outfitted Nyong'o in white-and-gold Prada for the Toronto Film Festival: "The rest is history."

When Nyong'o first stepped out of the fitting room in the crimson Ralph Lauren gown that eventually sent the fashion world clamouring at the Golden Globes, Erlanger says she'll "never forget seeing it for the first time. We knew it was the one. Not only was it a bold color and striking silhouette, but there was a cape. That was an incredibly confident move that demanded attention." Later, Erlanger guided Nyong'o into a Prada plunging sky-blue dress that made the red carpet sing at the Oscars. "It was a total collaboration," Erlanger said. "She made that dress dance in the wind. It was the right look for the right person for the right occasion; that's when the magic happens."

(continued)

Red carpet events aren't the only places where Erlanger does her magic. "You have to think about the bigger picture," she said. Erlanger compared a succession of outfits worn by Nyong'o during awards season to a campaign of sorts. "It's an entire body of work. Everyone has different dimensions to their personalities, so we're never just going to repeat the same colors or silhouettte." Nyong'o, she says, "loves color and bold choices; it's about being super playful." Nyong'o's status as a fashion icon was bolstered when she was named the most beautiful woman of 2014 by *People* magazine. Nyong'o also landed a *Vogue* spread and a Miu Miu advertising campaign along the way, but she's the first to praise her stylist Micaela Erlanger for her rapid fashion accession. And, Micaela Erlanger says she's very happy with her work. "I love what I'm doing," she says, "and I want to continue to inspire, collaborate, and consult."

Sources:

www.vanityfair.com/vf-hollywood/lupita-nyongo-stylist

stylenews.peoplestylewatch.com/2014/02/28/lupita-nyongo-oscars-gown-stylist-micaela-erlanger/

www.hollywoodreporter.com/style/top-25-power-stylists-2014/micaela-erlanger/

chapter 14

Fashion Curatorship and Scholarship

In this chapter, Fashion Curatorship and Scholarship, we are looking at fashion through new lenses, which are focused on the education of fashion. **Fashion scholars** study, research, write, and teach students in a classroom or online about the industry (past, present, and future), its careers, and the skills needed to succeed in it. Fashion is an intersection of art (from impressionism to self-expressionism), history, and culture. Coco Chanel said it well: "Fashion is not something that exists in dresses only. Fashion is in the sky, in the street, fashion has to do with ideas, the way we live, what is happening." **Fashion curators** contextualize fashion works within their historical and socioeconomic frameworks. Curators educate people about fashion through accessing and archiving fashion artifacts and sharing many of these with the public. "Curating fashion," curator Judith Clark said, "is about the connections between fashion, history, and art history and capturing those connections through organization of the exhibition." Fashion curators are often part of a team responsible for preserving, researching, documenting, and displaying collections of fashion, textiles, and furniture. We begin our study of careers in fashion curation and scholarship with an examination of fashion careers available in museums and foundations.

There are many different sizes and types of fashion and interior-related museums and foundations throughout the world, and they hold a vast treasure trove of history. Museums can be large or small, public or private, and operated by colleges or universities, communities, the government, or a foundation. For example, many colleges and universities, such as Kent State University and the Fashion Institute of Technology (FIT), present design exhibitions in their museum facilities. Community or city museums feature collections and exhibits on fashion or topics related to soft goods associated with their locales, such as quilts, costumes, or apparel

CASE STUDIES IN CAREER EXPLORATION

Box 14.1 Foundation Pierre Bergé-Yves Saint Laurent

Yves Saint Laurent and Pierre Bergé opened their haute couture house in 1962. During 40 years of creating fashion, Yves Saint Laurent used what was considered traditional masculine styling to bring women self-assurance and power, while preserving their femininity. His designs are part of 20th-century history, reflecting women's emancipation in every domain, from personal to social to political. Yves Saint Laurent invented the modern woman's wardrobe: the pea jacket, trench coat, the first women's tuxedo (Le Smoking), the safari jacket, transparent blouses, and the jumpsuit.

In 1974, Bergé and Saint Laurent moved their company to 5 avenue Marceau, a *hôtel particulier* dating from the Second Empire that became Yves

Saint Laurent's *atelier*. It was here that Yves Saint Laurent would implement his design influence, until he ended his career in haute couture on January 7, 2002. On January 22 of the same year, at the Centre Georges-Pompidou, a retrospective show went back over Yves Saint Laurent's illustrious creation with more than 300 models, including his last collection, Spring/Summer 2002. From then until his passing in Paris at the age of 72 in 2008, Yves Saint Laurent devoted his energy to the activities of the Foundation Pierre Bergé-Yves Saint Laurent, which was approved by the state on December 5, 2002.

The Pierre Bergé-Yves Saint Laurent entity is not a museum but a foundation. The foundation has established three primary goals: (1) to conserve the

Box 14.1 Monsieur Yves Saint Laurent in Paris.

5,000 haute couture garments, 1,000 rive gauche styles and the 15,000 accessories, 35,000 sketches, patterns, and other objects associated with the four decades of Yves Saint Laurent's creativity; (2) to organize exhibitions of fashion, paintings, photographs, and drawings; and (3) to support cultural and educational projects. The Foundation Pierre Bergé-Yves Saint Laurent includes three types of space: public rooms for exhibitions, appointment rooms (for students, researchers, and journalists), and private rooms, such as the studio, which is open on occasion for tours. Rooms used for conservation of clothes, accessories, and sketches are also accessible by appointment.

The Foundation Pierre Bergé-Yves Saint Laurent opened its doors in 2004 with its debut exhibition: "Yves Saint Laurent, Dialogue with Art." In this exhibition, the relationship between art and fashion designer was visually communicated. Forty-two different haute couture outfits created by YSL between 1965 and 1988 were displayed, in conjunction with five paintings that inspired YSL. The artists included Picasso, Mondrian, Matisse,

and Warhol. In 2011, the foundation presented the exhibit "Saint Laurent Rive Gauche: La Révolution de la Mode." Desiring to dress all women, not only rich haute couture clients, Yves Saint Laurent opened his Saint Laurent Rive Gauche boutique in 1966 in Paris, the first ready-to-wear boutique to bear the couturier's name. In 2014, the Foundation presented its 21st exhibition, "Berber Women of Morocco," to share the richness of the Amazigh civilization, and to honor Berber women, weavers, and potters. The exhibition displayed the diverse and extraordinary beauty of Berber adornments.

Online at www.fondation-pb-ysl.net, you can view the production boards for each of St. Laurent's collections and sketches of the costumes he designed for the ballet, an overview of the design process by Berge, St. Laurent's biography, and photographs of his studio.

Source:

www.fondation-pb-ysl.net/en/Accueil-Foundation-Pierre-Berge-Yves-Saint-Laurent-575.html

and accessories. **Foundations**, institutions formally set up with endowment funds, present costume exhibitions, such as the Guggenheim Foundation in New York and the Foundation Pierre Bergé-Yves Saint Laurent in Paris (Box 14.1). And some world-renowned museums have costume collections, such as The Costume Institute of the Metropolitan Museum in New York City (Box 14.2), Musée des Arts Décoratifs' and Musée de la Mode et du Textile in Paris (Box 14.3), and the Victoria and Albert Museum in London (Box 14.4).

Museums are not only sites of exhibitions for public view, but they are also centers of research and conservation. Within museums around the world, there is also a variety of career options, many that are lesser known to the general public. The work is interdisciplinary, combining the study of fashion and textile history with hands-on skills in analysis, conservation, storage, and exhibition of textile and costume materials. Most towns and cities have museums, and staffing of the museums depends on their size. Larger museums employ a director and a team of curators, assistants, and technicians. In a small museum, the curator may take on the responsibilities of a museum director. Large or small, museums offer many career opportunities that fill the needs of a fashion student who enjoys learning about and preserving cultural references in history through costumes and interiors, and sharing them with others.

The following fashion careers in museums are examined in this chapter: museum director, museum curator, assistant curator, collections manager, museum archivist, and museum conservator. Additional museum positions are not examined in this chapter, because these positions are often limited to very large museums. These include the museum technician,

Box 14.2 Introduction to the Costume Institute of the Metropolitan Museum

The Costume Institute houses a collection of more than 35,000 costumes and accessories spanning seven centuries, from the fifteenth century to the present. The Costume Institute's curators organize one or more special exhibitions annually. In addition, two fashion-focused tours are available year round: "Fashion in Art," a tour led by Costume Institute docents that discusses costume history within the context of the Museum's collections of textiles, paintings, sculpture, and decorative arts, and "Costume: The Art of Dress," a tour that highlights historical costume throughout the Museum's galleries. Past thematic exhibitions have included "Jacqueline Kennedy: The White House Years," "Extreme Beauty: The Body Transformed," "Bravehearts: Men in Skirts," "Superheroes: Fashion and Fantasy," and "The Model as Muse: Embodying Fashion." Monographic exhibitions have featured prestigious designers, such as Alexander McQueen,

Yves Saint Laurent, Madame Grès, Christian Dior, Gianni Versace, Chanel, and Poiret.

Redesigned Costume Institute space was opened in 2014 after a two-year renovation as the Anna Wintour Costume Center with the exhibition "Charles James: Beyond Fashion." The fashion industry provides strong support for the work of the Costume Institute, including its exhibitions, acquisitions, and capital improvements. Each May, the annual Metropolitan Costume Institute Gala Benefit, its primary fundraising event, celebrates the opening of the spring exhibition. The benefit was introduced in 1948 and has been dubbed "the party of the year." The gala has become one of the most visible and successful charity events, drawing a stellar list of attendees from the fashion, film, society, business, and music industries.

Source:

www.metmuseum.org

Box 14.2 An exhibit at the Costume Institute of the Metropolitan Museum in New York City.

CASE STUDIES IN CAREER EXPLORATION

Box 14.3 Musée des Arts Décoratifs—Musée de la Mode et du Textile

The Musée des Arts Décoratifs was created after the success of the historic *Expositions Universelles*, and the Musée de la Mode et du Textile opened in the Marsan wing of the Louvre in 1905, moving in 1997 to over two levels in the Rohan wing. Located at 107 rue de Rivoli, its collections now contain some 16,000 costumes, 35,000 fashion accessories, and 30,000 pieces of textile. The artifacts total more than 81,000 works that trace the history of costume from the Regency period to the present day, and innovations in textiles since the seventh century. These collections are regularly enriched by generous gifts made by private donors, designers, and manufacturers. The museum presents theme exhibitions that change every year, such as costumes and accessories from the 17th century to the 21st century, textiles and embroideries, and important works by renowned couturiers, such as Paul Poiret, Madeleine Vionnet, André Courrèges, Christian Dior, Coco Chanel, Elsa Schiaparelli, Christian Lacroix, Yves Saint Laurent, and Alexander McQueen.

Sources:

www.lesartsdecoratifs.fr/english-439/mode-et-textile-740/

www.travelsignposts.com/Paris/sightseeing/musee-des-arts-decoratifs-musee-de-la-mode-et-du-textile

Box 14.3 Hussein Chalayan creations at the Musée des Arts Décoratif's Musée de la Mode et du Textile in Paris.

CASE STUDIES IN CAREER EXPLORATION

Box 14.4 The Victoria and Albert Museum

An example of a large and prestigious museum with a significant fashion collection is the Victoria and Albert Museum (V&A) in London, which has collected both dress and textiles since its earliest days. The collections cover fashionable dress from the 17th century to the present day, with an emphasis on progressive and influential designs from the major fashion centers of Europe. The V&A collections also include accessories such as jewelry, gloves, millinery, and handbags.

Research is a core activity of the V&A and is carried out in all of its departments. Some research concerns the identification and interpretation of individual objects, whereas other studies contribute to systematic research. This helps develop the public understanding of the art and artifacts of many of the great cultures of the world, past and present.

The conservation department of the V&A is primarily responsible for the long-term preservation of its collections. At the core of the V&A conservator's work is the development and implementation of storage, mounting, and handling procedures that reduce the risk of damage during movement and display.

Source:

www.vam.ac.uk

Box 14.4 The Victoria and Albert Museum in London.

who works in restoration and conservation; the development associate, who is in charge of generating revenue for the museum; the membership associate, who is responsible for increasing the number of members; the education specialist, who develops educational programs for visitors; the docent, who presents lectures or conducts educational tours of exhibitions; and the exhibit designer, who creates and installs displays.

Museum Director

Museum directors are responsible for managing collections of artistic, historical, and general-interest artifacts. In large facilities, museum directors manage the general operations and staffing of the institution and coordinate the public service mission of the museum. They literally run the business of the museum, with responsibilities for the human resources, public relations, budget development, and management of the facility. They work closely with assistants, curators, and staff to fulfill the mission of the organization. Foremost, the museum director is a steward of the artifacts held by the museum.

Increasing areas of focus for the museum director include public affairs, marketing, and development. **Public affairs** work includes collaborating with the community, the government, industry, and social and academic organizations to develop exhibitions and collections that appeal to and educate the community and its visitors. The museum director often acts as a guide for groups viewing the exhibitions, answering visitors' questions and giving talks in the museum to local organizations or school groups. Making the museum user-friendly and accessible by as much of the public as possible is a key objective of most museum directors. As a result, technology, including social media, has become an important marketing tool for the museum, as illustrated in Box 14.5, Social Media Strikes: Pinterest for Those with Museum Interest. Outside of the museum, directors may also be invited speakers at clubs or universities to present on the museum's collections or a specific installation. They may be asked to co-chair a gala or work with an outside sponsor on a public event planned to raise awareness or funds for the institution.

A leading museum cannot only influence the educational and civic well-being of a community, but it can also affect its fiscal health through revenue generated by tourists coming to see the museum. When visitors travel to a city to view its museum, they often spend money in the local restaurants, hotels, and stores, in addition to paying the museum admission fee and, possibly, patronizing its gift shop. Although directors work to attract visitors to a museum, they may also be asked to seek out and secure funding for the museum through national and state grants. Today, a significant part of a director's duties, perhaps shared by assistants, involves fundraising and promotion, which may include researching, writing, and reviewing grant proposals, journal articles, and publicity materials. Fundraising and promotional activities may also include attending meetings, conventions, and civic events.

Qualifications

The position of museum director requires knowledge and experience in diverse areas: museum studies, public relations, marketing, and human resources, to name a few. Following is a list of the educational qualifications, work experience, and personal characteristics that are needed for a museum director:

- *Education.* A bachelor's degree in fashion design, textiles, historical costume, museum curatorship, museum studies, heritage studies, art history, history, archaeology, or a related

Box 14.5 Pinterest for Those with Museum Interest

Pinterest is known as *the* social media channel for food and fashion. It's a visual delight and a treasure trove of information, with businesses, educators, and publishers using Pinterest to complement their other online material. Many museums have jumped on the Pinterest bandwagon. The Museum at the Fashion Institute of Technology is a perfect match for Pinterest. "The most fashionable museum in New York City" offers a rare level of expertise for Pinterest pinners. There are more than 100 boards featuring historical costumes sorted by century or decade, designer or inspiration, categories from handbags to hats, fashion illustrations and photographs, and much more. These images allow viewers to see artifacts of the collection that are rarely, if ever, exhibited. It's a peek behind the scenes and under the muslin covers of priceless fashion pieces from fashion icons like Charles Worth, Paul Poiret, Coco Chanel, and Elsa Schiaparelli. Check it out at www.pinterest.com/museumatfit/boards. You don't have to leave your apartment, stand in line, and pay admission—just sit back, relax, and start pinning your very own fashion archive.

Sources:

www.mashable.com/2014/01/29/pinterest-museums/

www.pinterest.com/museumatfit/boards

www.fitnyc.edu/museum.asp

field is expected. Many museums require that the director have a master of arts or fine arts or a master of science degree in one of these fields. Candidates with a doctoral degree in a related discipline have an edge in the job search.

- *Experience.* Applicants for the position of director must have experience in museum work, preferably as a museum curator or the director of a smaller museum. Management experience is essential, particularly in the areas of human resources and budget development and control. Many museums require that the prospective museum director have public relations and marketing experience; some view experience in the tourism and hospitality industries as a plus. Fundraising experience may be required or preferred. Computer skills are needed for information retrieval, maintaining the inventory of artifacts, and imaging of collection items.

- *Personal characteristics.* Museum directors are often passionate about history, community affairs, and education. The effective museum director is a strong leader and a visionary who is committed to generating public interest, and possibly funding, for the museum. The work requires a range of skills, including organizational abilities, time-management skills, and a high level of attention to detail. The successful director has strong oral and written communication skills, a heightened aesthetic sense, and excellent presentation skills.

Career Challenges

The museum director carries the weight of many responsibilities, from budget development and management of the facility to human resources and public relations. In human resources, the director supervises assistants, curators, and all other staff in the museum, as well as teams of unpaid volunteers. In public relations, the director must find innovative and inexpensive ways to promote the museum and generate funding through events and programs. It is challenging to sell an institution and its services, rather than a tangible product. The museum director has the role of being a jack-of-all-trades in a leadership role that often takes long hours and much multitasking.

Museum Curator

In large museums, **museum curators**, referred to as *museum keepers* in some countries, work under the supervision of the museum director. Curators direct the accession, deaccession, storage, and exhibition of collections (Figure 14.1). **Accession** refers to receiving new items and adding them to the collection; **deaccession** is the removal of items from a collection because of repetition of artifacts, the receipt of better examples, loss, or decay. Sometimes, when building collections, museums sell valuable pieces (often, duplicates in the collection) to raise money to buy items that they want more than the deaccessioned pieces. Curators negotiate and authorize the purchase, sale, exchange, or loan of collection items. They may be responsible for authenticating, evaluating, and categorizing the items in a collection. Curators also oversee and help conduct the museum's research projects and related educational programs.

In a large museum where there are teams of curators, each may be involved in one area of specialization, such as 18th-century fashions or Gothic furnishings. A large historical costume museum, for example, may employ different curators for its collections of textiles, accessories, menswear garments, and women's apparel. Some curators maintain their collections, some conduct research, and others perform administrative tasks. In small institutions with only one or a few curators, a curator may be responsible for many varied tasks, from maintaining collections to directing the affairs of the museum. The main role of the curator is to acquire objects and research, identify, and catalogue them, usually on a computer. Curators in large and small museums are also responsible for ensuring correct storage conditions. Other duties that they may be assigned include overseeing security and insurance and developing policies and procedures for the collections in collaboration with the museum director, if there is one.

Providing information to the public is an important part of the museum curator's job. This is accomplished through written reports, presentations, and exhibitions to the public. When assigned the task of a public exhibition, the curator either identifies or assists the museum director in identifying topics for public exhibitions (e.g., wedding gowns through the ages, 1940s costumes of women in film, Amish quilts, or menswear of the 18th century). After the subject of the exhibition is determined, the curator plans and designs the exhibition and selects the items to be displayed. In selecting items for display, the delicacy and rarity of some items will keep them from being included. If a museum collection does not contain all of the artifacts needed to implement the theme of the exhibition, then the curator may decide to borrow items from other establishments, companies, or private individuals. After the items to be displayed are confirmed, the artifacts are installed and correctly labeled, and related publications are developed. The curator may be responsible for writing signage copy, working with other departments in the museum to publicize the showing, and writing a program for viewers to follow. A trend in museum exhibitions is the **interactive display**, in which viewers can press a button to run a video or actively participate in the exhibition's subject matter. For example, a textile exhibition may include an instructional video and a work area where the viewer can weave a piece of fabric. Museums have added entertainment to their educational goals to engage the public. With such large undertakings, the curator often works with a staff of assistants and technicians.

Figure 14.1
Curators direct the accession, deaccession, storage, and exhibition of collections.

Although the range of museums has expanded enormously, from large museums with full-scale models being prepared for the public to visit and recapture past ages and small museums specializing in specific artifact categories (e.g., Victorian decor or 19th-century apparel and accessories), the curator's role has also expanded. Granted, most curators have the primary responsibility of collecting and displaying objects of historical, cultural, and scientific interest in order to inform and instruct. However, the majority of curators' work also includes regularly establishing policies and procedures to protect artifacts in their care. Most curators are called on to talk to museum visitors and answer their questions and to give lectures and visual presentations to local groups. Now, there is a new addition to the curator's job: fundraising and development. Writing grants and other publications, soliciting donors for gifts, locating sponsors for exhibitions, and attending conferences—with or without a museum director—help stretch limited museum budgets. Box 14.6 features a classified advertisement for a senior museum curator.

Training for museum curators covers three main areas: academic, museological, and managerial. **Academic curator training** refers to how to study and understand collections. **Museological training** for the museum curator covers how to care for and interpret collections. **Museum managerial training** for the curator focuses on how to run a museum, from personnel to finances to operations. Some large museums offer a type of internship or apprenticeship for the prospective curator, often referred to as the **curatorial traineeship**. If you do not secure one of these prestigious and limited positions, how can you open the door to a career as a museum curator?

Qualifications

Here is a list of educational goals, work experience, and personal characteristics you will need to become a museum curator:

- *Education.* A bachelor's degree in fashion design, textiles, historical costume, museum curatorship, museum studies, heritage studies, art history, history, archaeology, or a related field is required. Many top museums require that the curator have a master of art or fine arts or a master of science degree in one of these fields. Candidates with a doctoral degree have an advantage, particularly in museums with a widespread reputation for their collections or exhibitions.

- *Experience.* Preference is usually given to applicants with experience in museum work, which may be obtained on a voluntary basis. An internship in a museum, usually unpaid, is an excellent way to gain experience and, perhaps, college credit. Computer skills are needed for information retrieval, inventory of artifacts, and imaging of collection items. Promotion will probably be from a small museum to a larger one that will be more specialized. From there, curators can progress to directors. There are career opportunities for curators within private or national collections.

- *Personal characteristics.* Curators show a deep interest in the past and heritage and a commitment to education. In addition to an intellectual curiosity, they often have high levels of sensitivity and patience. The work is often time consuming and methodical, requiring strong organizational skills and attention to detail. The successful curator has strong oral and written communication skills, an eye for aesthetically pleasing displays, and managerial abilities that include human resources, as well as budget development and management.

Box 14.6 Senior Museum Curator of Costume

Employer: Educational Institution

Job Title: Senior Curator of Costume

Application Instructions:

Please provide the following documents: résumé/CV, cover letter, a list of three professional references with telephone numbers and e-mail addresses.

Responsibilities:

The Senior Curator of Costume assists the Director and Deputy Director in advancing the Museum's mission by developing the collection, organizing exhibitions, writing museum publications, and providing leadership for the Costume Department. The incumbent supervises the staff of the Costume Department, as well as the Textiles and Accessories curators. S/he works collaboratively with other senior staff on all museum-wide initiatives:

- Works closely with Director, Deputy Director, and other Museum staff on developing, researching, and organizing exhibitions in both the Fashion History Gallery and the Special Exhibitions Gallery

- Provides leadership for the Costume Department. Supervises staff of Costume Department, interns, and student aides. Also supervises the Textiles and Accessories curators.

- May write Museum publications, including but not limited to Museum books and catalogues, including the Masterpieces book

- Coordinates and project manages fashion history exhibitions

- Develops, researches, and conducts tours and specialized lectures on fashion to college classes

- Oversees schedule of tours and lectures using the Museum's collections, and supervises the curatorial staff in the development of such tours and lectures

- Supervises the curatorial staff in the preparation of materials for classes and classroom setups

- Performs and oversees regular collection maintenance, including assigning object locations in database

- Provides information relating to the Museum for students, faculty, staff, and visitors

Curators work closely with technicians, conservation officers, and restoration personnel who care for a wide range of artifacts and exhibits, from Egyptian jewelry to centuries-old pictures and wallpaper to costumes and accessories. The curator may work with assistants, as well as the conservation and restoration staff, to research and identify the source, material, and time period of artifacts. Establishing authenticity, providing as much information as possible about museum artifacts, soliciting new items, and clearing out unwanted items are key parts of the curator's job.

Assistant Curator

In mid- to large-sized museums, the curator may supervise one or more assistant curators. An **assistant curator** often serves as the registrar of the collection by coordinating the collection's accessions. Once the items are correctly identified, they are accurately labeled, properly catalogued, safely stored, and maintained. This task has a technical side, as the assistant curator has the responsibilities of cataloguing artifacts, entering related data into a computer, and processing collection imaging, including photography, digitizing, slide labeling, and responding by e-mail to requests for images. Some of these images may be used in the publication of collection materials, such as catalogues, postcards, and exhibition programs. The assistant also works with the curator to organize and present lectures and host outside groups. If the museum has an organized membership of donors and public attendees, the assistant curator may work on a computer to maintain a member database. Some assistant curators are assigned the responsibility of coordinating and managing student and volunteer staffs, as well as working with faculty and students on class activities and projects.

The qualifications and challenges of an assistant curator are similar to those of the curator. Qualifications are presented previously, and challenges follow.

Career Challenges

The museum curator and assistant curator work with creative projects, a detailed inventory, and budget management. It can be difficult for a creative person to work on projects that require a high level of accuracy, such as recording descriptions of new items in the collection, and quantitative analysis, such as overseeing the collection's budget. It can likewise be a struggle for the analytical person to construct an artistic display. The curator and assistant curator, however, must work in both areas. It is not easy to develop and install exciting and attractive exhibits with limited resources, but the curator must manage to stretch the museum's budget.

Collections Manager

Collections managers provide front-line supervision of specific museum collections. A collections manager usually takes one of two tracks to move up in the museum world: the curator or conservator track. Occasionally, the collections manager may prefer to take the archivist track. **Collections managers** are responsible for preparing, managing, and supervising the collections records; processing and cataloguing items in the museum collections; and maintaining and entering data into a computerized collections management system. They maintain and supervise the organization of artifacts in storage, making sure everything possible is being done to keep items safely preserved. They also supervise artifact cataloguing, keeping in mind that systems must provide access to the collections by the public, staff, researchers, and other museums. Collections managers may work with volunteers in the collections department by preparing instructions, assembling needed materials, training them in tasks, and reviewing their work. Additional duties may include overseeing the photography of the collection, handling the preservation of the collection, conducting research, and participating in exhibit development.

Qualifications

In the job search, the collections manager candidate is expected to have certain educational requirements, work experiences, and personal characteristics. An overview of these expectations follows:

- *Education.* A bachelor's degree in fashion, textiles, museum studies, archaeology, history, art history, or a related field is required. Some museums require or prefer the candidate with a master's degree in fine arts or museum studies for this position.

- *Experience.* Work experience, volunteer or paid, in museum activities is required. College students may want to secure an internship in a museum to gain experience. Some collections managers gain paid work experience in a starting position, such as a museum technician. Computer skills are needed for information retrieval, cataloguing of acquisitions, and imaging of collection inventory.

- *Personal characteristics.* Strong written, oral, and visual communication skills are needed. Collections managers must be organized and effective managers who are capable of leading and motivating a staff or team of volunteers. They must have strong attention to detail and accuracy, as well as knowledge of history, for cataloguing artifacts. An eye for effective displays and exhibitions is also needed.

Career Challenges

Working with volunteers requires the abilities to schedule, train, and motivate workers who are not being paid for the jobs they do. This can be a tough way to acquire the workforce that you need to get the job done. The collections manager is also challenged with maintaining high levels of accuracy and organization when dealing with collection artifacts. At any time, the collections manager should be able to quickly locate a single item in the collection.

Museum Archivist

With the curator's busy roles in accessing and displaying historical artifacts, public relations, and marketing, the position of museum archivist has become more important and prevalent in today's museums. Although some duties of archivists and curators are similar, the types of items they deal with are different. Curators usually handle objects with cultural, biological, or historical significance, such as sculptures, textiles and textile-related items, and paintings. **Archivists** mainly handle records and documents that are retained because of their importance and potential value in the future. Archivists analyze, describe, catalogue, and exhibit these important records for the benefit of researchers and the public (Figure 14.2). They preserve important records and photographs that document the conception, history, use, and ownership of artifacts.

Archivists are responsible for collecting and maintaining control over a wide range of information deemed important enough for permanent safekeeping. This information takes many forms: photographs, films, video and sound recordings, computer tapes, and video and image disks, as well as more traditional paper records, illustrations, letters, and documents. Archivists also solicit, inventory, and save records and reports generated by corporations, government agencies, and educational institutions that may be of great potential value to researchers, exhibitors, genealogists, and others who would benefit from having access to original source material.

Archivists maintain and save records according to standards and practices that ensure the long-term preservation and easy retrieval of the documents. Records may be saved on any medium, including paper, film, videotape, audiotape, or computerized disk. They also may be copied onto some other format to protect the original and make the records more accessible to researchers who use them. Some archivists work with the originals of specialized forms of records, such as manuscripts, electronic records, photographs, motion pictures, and sound recordings, and they determine the best ways of creating copies and saving the originals of these works. As various storage media evolve, archivists must keep abreast of technological advances in electronic information storage. **Archive technicians** help archivists organize, maintain, and provide access to historical documentary materials.

■ Figure 14.2
An archivist analyzes, describes, and catalogues the important records of artifacts for the benefit of researchers and the public.

Qualifications

If working with history and preserving it for the future sounds like a fascinating and fulfilling career to you, here is what you need to do and know to become a museum archivist:

- *Education.* A bachelor's degree in textiles; museum studies; costume and textiles; fashion and textile studies; history, theory, and museum practice; art history; or a related discipline is required.

- *Experience.* Archivists may gain work experience in a variety of organizations, including government agencies, museums, historical societies, and educational institutions. An internship or work experience as an archive technician is an ideal way to open the door to this career path. Experience in computer imaging, including photographs, illustrations, and films, is a plus.

- *Personal characteristics.* Archivists are methodical, detail oriented, and well organized. They often have inquisitive natures. They work to stay up to date on evolving restoration and preservation techniques.

Career Challenges

Education is never-ending for the museum archivist. Technological advances and new types of cleaning and restoration equipment help the archivist maintain collection items for longer periods of time, and the person in this position must constantly learn about the latest preservation techniques. The archivist is always working with details and must work methodically and with focus.

Museum Conservator

Museum conservators manage, care for, preserve, treat, and document works of art, artifacts, and specimens. Museum conservators are also referred to as *restoration and preservation specialists*. With regard to fashions or costumes, conservators acquire and preserve important visuals (e.g., photographs, illustrations, or sketches), costumes, accessories, furnishings, and other valuable items for permanent storage or display. Much of their work requires substantial historical, scientific, and archaeological research. Conservators use X-rays, chemical testing, microscopes, special lights, and other laboratory equipment and techniques to examine objects. Conservators' objectives are to determine the artifacts' conditions, their need for treatment or restoration, the best way to repair worn or damaged items, and the appropriate methods for preserving items. Many institutions prefer not to repair but to effectively maintain and preserve artifacts to minimize damage and deterioration. The conservator's work is performed under close supervision with an emphasis on saving and maintaining, or **stabilizing**, artifacts while developing the studies of historical preservation. Conservators may specialize in a particular material or group of objects, such as documents and books, paintings, decorative arts, textiles, metals, or architectural materials.

Qualifications

Qualifications for the museum conservator include the following educational goals, work experiences, and personal characteristics:

- *Education.* A bachelor's degree in museum studies, archaeology, textile science, art history, or a related field is a requirement. Larger, more prestigious museums require a master's degree in one of these areas.

- *Experience.* Museum conservators must have the knowledge, skills, and abilities required to perform basic preservation maintenance, repair, and treatment of historical artifacts. Consequently, training, coursework, or an internship with a museum or educational institution can provide the opportunity to learn these skills and remain up to date on the latest technology and restoration techniques.

- *Personal characteristics.* Museum conservators must have the patience and organizational skills to work methodically. They have the curiosity and ability of an investigator to piece information together. They are interested in science and keep current with restoration and preservation techniques.

Career Challenges

The challenges of a museum conservator's career are similar to those of the archivist. He or she is challenged to come up with the techniques, products, and equipment to restore and preserve artifacts. Although an interest in fashion is a plus, it is more important to have an understanding of chemistry, textile science, and technology. These museum employees are challenged to work methodically and accurately with safety and preservation of artifacts as key pressures. Next, an examination of the career opportunities in fashion scholarship is presented.

Fashion Educator

Starting with pre-college education, middle and high school teachers in the area of apparel and textiles often graduate from college and university programs with a bachelor's or master's degree in **Family and Consumer Science Education (FCSEd)**. They may be asked to teach courses in textiles, fashion, clothing selection and apparel care, clothing construction, interior design, consumer education, personal financial literacy, and careers in the fashion industry. Some FCSEd graduates choose employment with community colleges or **vocational schools**, providing training for students who elect not to participate in a four-year college degree program after high school graduation. In these programs, they teach a range of courses, such as commercial clothing construction, apparel alterations, pattern making, and retailing. Upon completion of these programs, the student may earn an associate's degree. There is also the opportunity for employment as a teacher in **trade schools**, those institutions offering fashion programs and providing certificates, rather than degrees, once the student completes the program. Trade schools offer programs in such areas as fashion design, illustration, retailing, and fashion merchandising.

Regardless of the type of school, educators in fashion programs are professionals who have many roles in addition to classroom instruction. Many make purchasing decisions about textbooks, supplies, and equipment, such as sewing machines, sergers, and dress forms. Some conduct research, write about their findings, and submit their reports for publication. Others seek out funding sources for their programs in the schools, sourcing and writing grants, and soliciting sponsors from the government or industry. Many participate in organizations and on committees that focus on pedagogical issues, curricula in schools and colleges, instructional methods, and job outlooks in fashion industry professions, among other topics.

Many fashion educators include **professional development** on their to-do lists. This includes continuing education, often toward a higher degree; internships in the field; conference participation; and memberships in trade and educational organizations. Educators in colleges and universities often have the **terminal degree**, or highest degree available (or its equivalent) in fashion, business administration, higher education, or a related field—with specializations in their areas of instruction. For example, a fashion design professor may have a doctorate in the field, industry experience as a designer, and a broad knowledge of fashion design. In addition to a general knowledge of the field, this professor is expected to have technical expertise in specialized areas such as computer-aided design, draping, pattern making, or garment construction. In addition, many universities require college-level teaching experience, often not only in the classroom but also through other delivery methods, such as guided studies and online courses.

If the college-level teaching position includes responsibilities for advising and instructing graduate students, the faculty member must hold a terminal degree and be approved as a member of the graduate faculty. Experience in research and publication is preferred to demonstrate professional potential in scholarly work. Terms of appointment for college faculty range between 9 and 12 months. They may be tenure track, instructor, or lecturer positions. With prior experience, tenure track positions can be secured at the levels of assistant or associate professor, primarily. Many colleges and universities specify the proportion of teaching and research that a position will hold, such as 50 percent research and 50 percent teaching.

Qualifications

The following is a list of the educational goals, work experiences, and personal characteristics that will assist the person seeking a career in fashion education:

- *Education.* Fashion teachers in middle and high schools need at least a bachelor's degree and teaching certification. Their majors in college may include FCSEd, education, fashion design, textiles, interior design, fashion merchandising, and similar degree programs. Many of these teachers choose to complete a master's degree in the field to attain a higher knowledge level and a higher salary. For the college or university educator, a master's degree in an appropriate discipline (e.g., fashion design, fashion merchandising, education, or business administration) is required as a minimum. Most colleges and universities prefer a teaching candidate with a doctoral degree in a related field; many require this.

- *Experience.* For some college and university teaching positions, the candidate must have a minimum of five years of professional industry experience. College teaching experience in specific areas (e.g., fashion design, fashion merchandising, or product development) may also be required by certain colleges or universities. In some cases, a record of juried, scholarly publications is either required or preferred. Prospective employers may require a portfolio that includes examples of one's own work and examples of students' work.

- *Personal characteristics.* Flexibility, creativity, and a passion for lifelong learning are qualities of the successful educator. The ability to work as a team member is critical, as is the ability to develop and maintain collegial and industry relationships. The effective teacher is often a constant student, participating in professional development activities to stay abreast of industry trends and career opportunities.

Career Challenges

Staying up to date on industry trends while staying on top of teaching responsibilities, such as preparing lectures and grading assignments, is a challenge. Many universities also require faculty to maintain a program of research, one that results in creative exhibits or publications, and to serve on college or community committees. This requires time management, organization, balance, and devotion to one's profession. Many fashion educators must wear several hats, from teacher and author to advisor and recruiter.

Summary

Museums offer a wide range of career opportunities, including museum director, curator, assistant curator, collections manager, archivist, and conservator. Curators administer the affairs of museum centers and historic sites. The head curator of a museum is usually called the museum director. Depending on the size of the museum, the curator may supervise one or more assistants. Whereas curators usually handle objects of historical significance, archivists handle mainly records and documents that are retained because of their importance and potential value in the future. The collections manager is responsible for preparing, managing, and supervising one or more specific groupings of artifacts in the museum. Museum conservators manage, preserve, treat, and document works of art and artifacts. On a related yet different career track, fashion educators teach, research, and contribute greatly to the fashion industry through career instruction and further studies.

Key Terms

academic curator training
accession
archive technician
archivist
assistant curator
collections manager
curatorial traineeship
deaccession
Family and Consumer Science
Education (FCSEd)
fashion curators
fashion scholar
foundations

interactive display
museological training
museum conservator
museum curator
museum director
museum managerial training
professional development
public affairs
stabilizing
terminal degree
trade school
vocational school

Online Resources

www.nytimes.com/2012/10/11/
arts/11iht-rartcurating11.html?_r=0

tmagazine.blogs.nytimes.com/2014/
06/27/duro-olowu-curate-art-show-
more-material/

www.fitnyc.edu/museum.asp

www.vam.ac.uk/page/f/fashion/

www.fondation-pb-ysl.net

www.guggenheim.org/new-york

www.itaaonline.org

www.kent.edu/museum

www.metmuseum.org

www.metmuseum.org/about-the-
museum/museum-departments/
curatorial-departments/the-costume-
institute

www.lesartsdecoratifs.fr/english-439/
fashion-and-textile/

www.palaisgalliera.paris.fr/en

www.nytimes.com/2014/05/06/
fashion/at-met-gala-fashionistas-
dress-up-in-tribute.html

Discussion Questions

1. Compare and contrast the work responsibilities of the museum conservator with those of the archivist. Using the Internet, research and report on the types of technological advances that may affect conservation and restoration of historic textiles.

2. After perusing classified advertisements online (e.g., www.HigherEd.com and www.itaaonline.org) for clothing and textile educators in colleges and universities, list the differences in education and work experience requirements for the following types of educator positions: tenure track, lecturer, and instructor.

3. Locate and list descriptions of six lesser-known museums around the world that specialize in decorative arts, apparel, accessories, and interior furnishing and accessories. What are their missions, educational programs, and preservation strategies?

4. Many fashion designers visit museums for design inspiration, construction ideas, and color ideas. Identify three well-known designers who use historical costume as a source of inspiration. Provide illustrations, such as magazine clippings, of current garments the designers have created that were inspired by historical costumes. Identify the time periods and designers of these historical costumes.

Interviewed by Michele M. Granger

Can you tell me a little about yourself?

During my fifteen years working in the New York City fashion industry, I quickly rose through the fashion ranks managing million-dollar accounts ranging from Amazon.com to Neiman Marcus and for companies that include Calvin Klein Jeans, Cynthia Rowley, Rocawear, Nicole Miller, and Joe's Jeans. I also played an important role in the successful launch of the Harajuku Lovers and L.A.M.B. handbag brands by Gwen Stefani.

In 2007, my entrepreneurial spirit went into overdrive and I co-created the popular women's Web site, Workchic. I also had the opportunity to become a guest writer/contributor/blogger for *Marie Claire*, Style Network, Shop it to me, and Shecky's, to just name a few. You could also find me giving out style advice on the ABC/HDTV weekly series *Mirror/ Mirror*. In 2010, I sold Workchic and created The Fashion Potential, which offers consulting services to fashion students and emerging designers looking to get ahead of their competition and launch their fashion careers the right way.

When did you realize you wanted to open a consulting service via a Web site?

I knew that if you didn't have a Web site, no matter what type of business you owned, it would put you behind your competition. I knew it was the wave of the future, and I had to jump on it.

What was your path to where you are today?

I started my career in fashion as an assistant buyer for a large department store three weeks after I graduated college in Pennsylvania. Over the next ten years, I worked in sales and product development for companies such as L.A.M.B., Calvin Klein, and Nicole Miller Handbags, to name a few. In 2009, I was laid off from my job, and my fashion career as I knew it changed overnight. It was a humbling experience. I went back to school at New York University to learn more about

Profile Figure 14a Fashion Career Consultant, Melissa McGraw.

e-commerce and digital marketing. I knew that if I wanted to get ahead in the fashion industry, I had to think outside the box. What was the next big thing? I was then offered an opportunity to work with a consumer products company that works closely with Amazon, so I could learn how e-commerce is changing how the consumer shops today. I am fortunate that I was able to expand my skill set even further and mentor those who are looking to launch their own fashion Web sites.

What does your company do?

The Fashion Potential teaches emerging fashion designers, fashion students, and professionals the insider tips and tricks they need to create a successful fashion career and brand. We teach you about the business side of fashion the right way. We provide the support, tools, and resources you need to save you the time, money, and headaches of launching your fashion career or label on your own.

Why are you drawn to this career?

I always knew I would be involved in the fashion industry from when I was a little girl. I graduated

(continued)

with a business degree, but knew that the fashion world suited me much better than finance. I landed my first job in New York City three weeks after I graduated from college and have been here ever since. I love the energy of the industry and seeing a product evolve from the ground up and thrive.

What kind of skills have you learned from your experiences, and how can they be applied in other careers in fashion?

I learned that, no matter what position you have in the fashion industry, you have to be able to multitask and to change. I like to be in control, but I quickly learned to go with the flow and not to sweat the small stuff. It really is an exciting and inspiring industry to work in. You can learn so many facets of business that you may not be exposed to in other careers. I took every experience—good or bad—and learned from it.

How do you get inspired?

What really inspires me is working individually with clients and fashion students. Even though I have been in the industry for a long time, I learn something new from each one of them. We teach each other. That truly is inspiring to me.

What do you love most about what you do?

I love being able to give back and mentor emerging designers and fashion students on what I learned in the fashion industry. It is so rewarding to see them carve their own unique niche in the industry no matter what path they choose.

What have been your toughest challenges?

When it comes to running your own Web site, it is not just about having a pretty Web site. There is more to it. You have to get people to want to visit it. That requires work—social media, online marketing, PR, sales. You have to learn how to manage your time wisely. Sometimes, I realize there are not enough hours in the day to get everything done.

What advice do you have for aspiring Web site entrepreneurs—from career consultants to prospective industry executives?

I realized when I created my first Web site that I created it without having a plan in place. I was in the "create first and think about it later mode." It led to spending too much time and resources without realizing it wasn't going to be a profitable and sustainable business model. Before you create the Web site, really think about the objectives of your Web site and how you are going to get traffic to it. Have a plan and budget in mind and stick to it.

Source:
**Courtesy of Melissa McGraw,
www.thefashionpotential.com**

Profile: Interview with Fashion Scholar Dr. Catherine Amoroso Leslie, Associate Professor and Graduate Studies Coordinator of the Fashion School at Kent State University

Interviewed by Michele M. Granger

Making it possible for all students to shine. Inspiring them. Connecting them to a world of possibilities. These are a few of the qualities students attribute to Professor Catherine Leslie—qualities that led to her receipt of the 2013 Alumni Association's Distinguished Teaching Award, the highest award at Kent State University.

Can you tell me a little about yourself?

I am an Associate Professor and Graduate Studies Coordinator at The Fashion School at Kent State University, a program of over 1,600 majors in Design and Merchandising. I teach the introductory class, Fashion Fundamentals, along with History of Costume, Historic Textiles, and the Capstone course for the Master's of Fashion degree. Since arriving at Kent State, I have prepared and taught more than 13 different courses. In 12 years of teaching, I have had over 5,500 students in my classes.

Kent State's fashion school is a very large program with over 1,600 majors in Design and Merchandising. I did not set out to teach in a large-format classroom, but have come to thrive in that environment. Fashion Fundamentals has about 220 students each semester, and it is taught in a large auditorium. I use the stage and the runway and embed video clips in every lecture. In some ways, I am putting on a performance for an audience of learners. I believe learning should be enjoyable and tell my students that their "brains will be so big at the end of the semester, they will not be able to fit through the door." That reflects my teaching philosophy; I want my students to learn and get excited about learning more.

When did you realize you wanted to work in fashion education?

I have been keenly interested in fashion, sewing, and needlework from when I was a young girl,

Profile Figure 14b Fashion Scholar, Dr. Catherine Amoroso Leslie.

learning to embroider at age six and sew on a machine by ten. As my mother and grandmother also sewed, I saw it as a means of creative expression, but did not recognize fashion as a career. I was also interested in teaching and learning, but was discouraged from being a teacher in favor of more lucrative work. I actually am pleased about that, because by having a career before becoming an educator, I was able to tap into my experience to be more confident and innovative in my classes.

(continued)

Being successful in one's work has a lot to do with knowing yourself and finding work that suits your interests, skills, and your nature. Through my positions outside of academia, I came to realize that I am much more project-oriented than process-oriented. I like things that have a beginning, middle, and end. Working really hard during the semester is okay, as long as I know that it will be over in December or May. Then we get our new pens, books, notebooks, and start again. That type of schedule suits me.

What was your path to where you are today?

My journey was not a linear one. It had to do with lots of different experiences, observation, and self data-collection. I think the most successful people are those who can put together ideas in unique combinations. But, that is challenging. Other people always have ideas of what one "should" do, but one must follow his or her heart. Only the individual can find his or her "thread of truth."

When I graduated from college, I took a position on Wall Street in New York City. I had to learn to adjust to the city as well as a high-pressure position, and to work with many different people and in many different situations. This taught me to be more assertive, more organized, and more resourceful. I had a decent salary, but not much for extras. I also needed a knockout wardrobe and could sew. I started to learn where the fabric and notions stores were and began to spend my weekends creating in my apartment. Being self-taught, I took Saturday courses at Parsons School of Design in draping, pattern making, and couture sewing techniques.

I thought I had all I needed to get a job in the fashion industry, but I was mistaken. There were positions, but without a degree, it would be years before I could come close to a comparable lifestyle. With entrepreneurial ambitions, I moved back to my hometown and started a dressmaking/custom design business, which I did for four years. I created wedding gowns, bridesmaid dresses, prom dresses, special occasion outfits, and custom clothing. My business supported me, and I was able to hire three

women who worked out of their homes. Yet, outside of wedding gowns, I found it a challenge to be compensated for the number of hours it took to do fine work. I worked long and hard in my studio, and I started to miss being with other people and having a "regular job."

I returned to school to earn a Master's degree in Apparel and Textiles. I landed a Graduate Assistantship where I worked in the Historic Costume and Textiles Collection, taught a textiles lab, and assisted with the History of Costume Course. It did not take long before I found that this was the combination that I was looking for, and started thinking of making education my career. I spoke to everyone I could about the best path to follow, and I came to the conclusion that to land a top-notch university position, I would need to earn a PhD. After that, I started at Kent State's Fashion School and have never looked back.

What kind of skills have you learned from your experiences?

My experiences have all contributed to abilities that I use in my work every day. An inherent interest in clothing, textiles, teaching, and learning keep me naturally enthusiastic about my work. Skills in communication, organization, and clarity of message learned in years of working in business directly translate to my position as a fashion educator. Through my journey, I realized that being an educator fosters my independent and individualized work style and ethic.

In my last business position, I had responsibility to develop, schedule, and deliver sales presentations to outside groups. I found myself engrossed in creating materials—a curriculum of sorts—and noticed that people were responding to my presentations and presentation style. From being a salesperson, I learned how to boil down information and not overwhelm my audience. I learned how to present, watch to see how it is received, and be flexible. I also learned to know my audience and to be very in tune with how things are going for the students. The best way to learn is to connect what

(continued on next page)

is known with what is new. I stay on top of the latest news and what my students are watching/seeing/talking about. I am a big proponent of humor.

I work very hard, most of it independently, so I have to be very self-motivated. My students see me in the classroom and in my office, but that is only part of the work I do. I tell people that professors do not have weekends during the semester. I spend most of my breaks and the summer working on research. Part of my position is to add to the "body of knowledge," and doing research, giving presentations, and publishing articles and books fulfills that aspect.

What are your position responsibilities?

From the outside, it may seem that a professor's position is mostly teaching, but we are evaluated under three main aspects: teaching, research, and service. I am the Graduate Studies Coordinator for our Masters of Fashion program, serve on university and professional committees, as well as do outreach activities like presentations to interest groups and consultations.

Do you use social media in your work? If so, for what purposes?

I use LinkedIn and encourage all my students to create a profile early and use it to network. Because of the number of students I have encountered and my natural tendency to connect with people and connect people with each other, I have over a thousand connections on LinkedIn. Once my students link with me, they can search my contacts for career advice and informational interviews, linking a professional with a student who is walking in their shoes. It makes me very pleased when my students go on to great things. I am very proud of their accomplishments and bright futures.

What are some of your favorite fashion Web sites and blogs?

In order to connect with my students and stay current with the ever-changing fashion industry, I check out the following sites on business, fashion, and entrepreneurial activity:

NRF.org

Shop.org

WWD.com

Refinery29.com

BusinessofFashion.com

Fashionista.com

Forbes.com

BusinessInsider.com

Mashable.com

FastCompany.com

CoolHunting.com

What do you love most about what you do?

I love to learn, I love to share, and I love connecting people with each other and with ideas. Even after 12 years of university teaching, my enthusiasm for all things fashion is contagious. I so enjoy getting to know my students, watching them grow, and soar. I am proud to have the opportunity to make a positive impact on individuals and our world. Fashion is a phenomenon, an industry, and a hobby. It continually keeps my interest. Fashion equals change.

(continued)

What have been your toughest challenges?

Initially, the challenge was how to develop interesting presentations to teach hundreds of students in an auditorium, but I came to enjoy it. I think the toughest challenge is the students who really are not interested in learning, who just see their education as a series of checkmarks on a list, something to get through. Their view of college in some ways makes me feel sad. If your entire goal is just to be certified with a college degree to get a better job, that's missing the point. Learning and being smart is something you have inside, and no one can take that away. Who you know might get you in the door, but what you know keeps you inside. One of my favorite lines is "good luck comes from hard work." I believe that. There is no law that says you must be in college from ages 18 to 22. If you do not know what you want to do when you graduate, that's fine. If you do not know why you are in college, then consider doing something else.

What advice would you give to aspiring fashion educators?

Teaching is hard work and does not come easily. Even if you have some aptitude, you still need to practice, be continually aware of what is happening in the classroom, and take risks. You need to have a tough skin and put all your creativity to work. Being an educator is an incredible opportunity to make a positive impact. It really is the "toughest job you'll ever love."

Source:

Courtesy of Dr. Catherine Amoroso Leslie

chapter 15

Visual Merchandising, Retail Design, and Interior Design

Envision a fashion business as a Tiffany necklace; think of its environment as the turquoise suede jewelry pouch encased in the signature blue box embossed with a beautiful logo and tied up with white ribbon (Figure 15.1). The building housing a retail store, a kiosk in a mall, a boutique in a strip center, and a Web site's landing page can function as the boxes that house various types of fashion businesses.

Think about fashion retailers focusing on the business environment for new brick-and-mortar stores. They strive to locate the right building or storefront; if the right facility cannot be found, someone (the architect) may design the building to order. Another person (the interior designer) may design and oversee the installation of the interior—from the ceiling and lights to the floor coverings and furnishings. Yet another person (the visual merchandiser or store planning director) may select the fixtures and mannequins, then set up the sales floor to entice consumers to come into the store and buy. If the retailer is in e-commerce, the Web site designer or developer helps create the "store" exterior and interior, its Web site with its imagery and content, as examined in Chapter 12 and illustrated in Figure 15.2. All of these career professionals are responsible for creating the most attractive and functional box possible for the business within the space and budget allocated by the retailer.

The fashion industry is a visual one. As a result, the way a fashion business's building and interior look can affect the business's profitability and image. Architects work to create

■ **Figure 15.1**
The exterior and interior of a brick-and-mortar store can be related to the wrappings of a Tiffany product—with the box being comparable to the store exterior.

or renovate the right exterior for a fashion business. Combining knowledge with aesthetic vision, the interior designer often collaborates with the architect and visual merchandising professional to develop interior environments that are functional and attractive to meet the physical, convenience, and aesthetic needs of the people using the space. Once the space design is complete in a mall, the mall manager works to keep the interior environment looking fresh and appealing for consumers. Careers involved in developing the environments of fashion businesses are examined in this chapter and categorized in terms of exteriors, interiors, and visual merchandising. They include the following: architect, interior designer, visual merchandising professional, store planning director, and mall manager.

Architect

Just as a Web developer builds a virtual business, the architect builds the brick-and-mortar business. The **architect** is a building designer who may work with a wide variety of structures. Those who specialize in serving retail clients have opportunities for projects ranging from small freestanding retail stores to large malls. These types of business locations are referred to as **commercial real estate**. **Architecture** is the creative blend of art and science in the design of environments for people. The plans for a building ultimately focus on the needs of the people who use them, to include aesthetics, safety, and environmental factors.

The architect and client first collaborate on the client's vision and discuss options, costs, and materials. The architect creates concept drawings, often on the computer, for the client to review. At this point, the architect spends time consulting closely with the client and builders, selling, costing, and explaining concepts. When the concepts are approved by the client, the architect draws up plans that illustrate not only how the building will look but also how to build it. The drawings show the beams that hold up the building; heating, air-conditioning, and ventilation; electrical and plumbing systems; and so on. Architects communicate the design and oversee the work of builders, contractors, plumbers, painters, carpenters, air-conditioning and heating specialists, and others. Although most commercial work has strict budgets and practical limitations, Figure 15.3 presents the opposite scenario, with an example of an elaborate architectural façade with its triptych windows, the Cynthia Rowley boutique in Boston.

■ **Figure 15.2**
Web site development and design are concerned with constructing Web sites from both aesthetic and marketing perspectives, as illustrated by the landing page of *shop/ten/25*.

■ Figure 15.3
Exterior of the Cynthia Rowley boutique in Boston, an example of customized commercial real estate for a fashion designer and retailer.

Qualifications

The profession of architect requires the following educational goals, experiences, and personal characteristics:

- *Education.* Becoming an architect is a long process. A prospective architect must complete an academic degree specifically focused on architecture. This can be earned through a five-year bachelor's of architecture program, possibly with an affiliated two-year master's of architecture program. Many students also prepare for a career in architecture with a four-year (undergraduate) liberal arts degree followed by a three- to four-year (graduate) master's of architecture degree. To be an architect, it is also necessary to be licensed in the state where one works; all states require applicants to pass a rigorous examination. In addition, candidates are expected to have completed an internship period with an architecture firm. Employers place greater preference on applicants who have mastered computer-aided design programs, which have become required knowledge for any architect as technology develops.

- *Experience.* Many college students gain work experience through an internship with an architect, which is required by some colleges and universities. Most new architects begin in an assistant position, working with an experienced architect in an area of specialization in which they plan to build a career. Once experienced, architects move into a variety of employment venues and often develop an area of specialization.

- *Personal characteristics.* Architects must be able to visualize projects and communicate these visions through drawing and computer-generated images. Presentation skills, effective writing, and public-speaking abilities are also important. Decision making, team leadership, and creativity are key attributes of the successful architect. The architect must have high attention to detail and strong time-management and budgeting skills.

Career Challenges

The first career challenge the architect faces is the amount of money, time, and effort it takes for the education and licensing needed to start this career track. It takes a great deal of perseverance and dedication to complete a degree successfully and become certified in architecture. For most, this profession requires paying one's dues for possibly years before actually gaining hands-on professional experience. Beginning architects research zoning, building codes, and legal filings; draft plans from others' designs; and build models at the side of a more experienced architect. Once in the field, the architect faces daily challenges of constant revision of plans based on client needs, contractor issues, and budget restrictions. Plans and priorities have to be reevaluated regularly and revised accordingly. Additionally, there are legal aspects of the architect's career, as the architect must stay on top of building codes, safety requirements, and legal filings.

Interior Designer

Interior designers work in a wide range of environments, including homes and businesses. They can work alone, as part of a team of professionals, or in collaboration with other professionals in related careers, as with the interior designer and the architect. Some interior designers work primarily in **residential design**, focusing on home environments. These interior designers function as fashion service providers for the home of their clients. Others function as interior providers for retail clients or businesses. They may work with architects and other designers to provide exterior and interior services for public structures. Some architectural firms include an interior design department. Referred to as **commercial designers**, these interior designers concentrate on public spaces, including projects such as retail stores; hotels, motels, and restaurants; office buildings; and so on. Some commercial designers work with the visual merchandising divisions of retail operations, whether planning a store's layout, locating furnishings and props, or designing major visual displays.

Interior designers often specialize in an area within either residential or contract interior design. The residential interior designer may develop a reputation and clientele through working in a certain type of home, such as vacation properties or high-end residences. The commercial interior designer may specialize in retail operations or, even more specifically, high-fashion boutiques, as seen in Figure 15.4, a Betsy Johnson boutique. Yet another commercial designer may earn a good living through work on hotels, stores, or museums. As designers gain work experience, they often identify a niche, an area of particular interest, which uses their skills, pays well, and in which they build industry contacts and a positive reputation.

Successful interior designers know how to plan a space and how to present that plan visually so that it can be communicated to the client. Interior designers must also know about the materials and products that will be used to create and furnish the space. These materials are constantly changing, as new products are introduced daily. The effective designer knows how texture, color, lighting, and other factors combine and interact in a space. On a more

■ **Figure 15.4**
The commercial interior designer aims to reflect the personality of the designer through the store's aesthetics, as shown in one of Betsey Johnson's boutiques.

technical level, interior designers understand the structural requirements of their plans, the health and safety issues, building codes, electrical and plumbing requirements, and many other practical aspects.

What exactly do interior designers learn to do the job effectively? They must be knowledgeable in the areas of building construction, building materials, specification writing, building codes, technical drawing, and business practices. Interior designers analyze the client's needs and problems, develop detailed design solutions to present to the client, and then organize and supervise projects to full completion while being attentive to the client's desires and resources. Interior designers collaborate with suppliers and other building specialists throughout the process. Box 15.1 provides a listing of the tasks that may be required of an interior designer.

CASE STUDIES IN CAREER EXPLORATION

Box 15.1 A Task Listing for an Interior Designer's Typical Project

---

1. Research and analysis of the client's goals and requirements and development of documents, drawings, and diagrams that reflect those needs

2. Formulation of preliminary space plans and two- and three-dimensional design concept studies and sketches that integrate the client's program needs and are based on knowledge of the principles of interior design and human behavior

3. Confirmation that preliminary space plans and design concepts are safe, functional, and aesthetically appropriate and meet all public health, safety, and welfare requirements, including code, accessibility, environmental, and sustainability issues

4. Selection of colors, materials, and finishes to appropriately portray the design concept and meet functional, maintenance, life-cycle performance, environmental, and safety requirements

5. Selection, specification, and documentation of furniture, furnishings, equipment, and trim work, including layout drawings and detailed product description; and contract documentation to facilitate pricing, shipping, and installation of new furnishings

6. Provision of project management services, including preparation of project budgets and schedules

7. Preparation of construction documents, consisting of plans, elevations, details, and specifications to illustrate nonstructural and/or nonseismic (relating to earthquakes) partition layouts, power and communications locations, reflected ceiling plans and lighting designs, materials and finishes, and furniture layouts

8. Confirmation that construction documents adhere to regional building and fire codes, municipal codes, and any other jurisdictional statutes, regulations, and guidelines that are applicable to the interior space

9. Coordination and collaboration with other allied design professionals who may be retained to provide consulting services, including but not limited to architects; structural, mechanical, and electrical engineers; and various specialty consultants

10. Confirmation that construction documents for nonstructural and/or nonseismic construction are signed and sealed by the responsible interior designer and are filed with code-enforcement officials

11. Administration of contract documents, bids, and negotiations as the client's agent

12. Review and reporting on the implementation of projects while in progress and upon completion

Source:

www.asid.org

Qualifications

A list of the education, experience, and personal characteristics of a successful interior designer follows:

- *Education.* A bachelor's degree in interior design, housing and interior design, visual arts, or a related field is a minimum requirement. After receiving an interior design degree from an accredited university or college and working in the industry for two years, an interior designer can take the National Council for Interior Design Qualification (NCIDQ) exam. Passing all sections of this exam will advance the interior designer's career by allowing opportunities for professional memberships and state licensing. In addition to college coursework, interior design is a discipline that demands research, analytical skills, a command of technology, and knowledge of products.

- *Experience.* Many college students majoring in interior design must complete an internship or two before graduation. This experience, especially for students with internships in more than one area, opens the door to contacts and knowledge within the interior design field. Retail sales or visual merchandising work with a home fashions retailer, a do-it-yourself building firm, or a textile store provides a strong background for the prospective interior designer.

- *Personal characteristics.* Interior designers are creative, imaginative, and artistic, yet they also need to be disciplined and organized businesspeople. As members of a service profession, interior designers depend on their ability to satisfy clients. The top interior designers know how to sell their ideas to clients, create informative and persuasive presentations, and maintain good client relationships. They understand the artistic and technical requirements of a project. In terms of interpersonal skills, most interior designers are comfortable meeting and dealing with many kinds of people. They communicate clearly and effectively and are attentive listeners. Because they often must work with architects, contractors, and other service providers, interior designers are constantly working as part of a team. Negotiation and problem solving are parts of their daily routines.

Career Challenges

Succeeding at interior design requires energy, technical proficiency, vision, and, often, entrepreneurial knowledge. Many interior designers own their businesses and must have the skills to run a business. Watching expenses, working with vendors, meeting deadlines, and managing projects can be huge undertakings. Working on more than one project at a time under demanding deadlines is part of the job. Within each project, there are bound to be changes along the way. Clients change their minds, and suppliers no longer have products available. The interior designer is challenged with keeping the client, vendors, contractors, and builders on the same track.

Visual Merchandising Professionals

What is visual merchandising? Often called the "silent salesperson," **visual merchandising** refers to the design, development, procurement, and installation of merchandise displays that enhance the ambiance of the environment in which the displays are shown. Effective visual merchandising aims to create an image that reflects the company and, most important, sells the company's product lines. Some visual merchandising efforts are institutional, such as Macy's large boulevard windows that feature holiday extravaganzas of mechanical dolls and a 12-foot tree made of glass lollipops. Others are product-driven, such as Tiffany's shadow-box windows that highlight new jewelry pieces.

Visual merchandisers are the people responsible for window installations, in-store displays (Figures 15.5a and b), signage, fixtures, mannequins, and decorations that give a retail operation aesthetic appeal and a distinct image. Visual merchandisers are stylists of sorts; they have the ability to look at the merchandise selected by the buyers and, through their creativity and expertise, create an image of the store that entices customers to enter the store or Web site and purchase merchandise. Think about an outfit displayed in a retail window or on a mannequin. As a result of seeing the presentation of the garment and accessories, you may have decided to buy the items on display. This purchase can be attributed, at least in part, to the successful work of a visual merchandiser.

The field of visual merchandising has grown as a career area and as a spin-off of the tremendous growth of interiors businesses and e-retailing, as well as the value consumers place on image and branding. Promoting the image of a product line, store, or service through visual merchandising is an effective way for fashion firms to market their products to prospective customers.

The visual merchandiser is responsible for several key tasks:

- Designing an aesthetically appealing environment that reflects the company's image

- Creating exciting visual displays to educate customers and to sell merchandise

- Presenting the merchandise in ways that will maximize sales, such as displaying the full range of colors of a new handbag and matching footwear

Frequently, the visual merchandiser consults with the retail operation's buyers to determine which merchandise should be featured. Because one of the main goals of visual merchandising is to increase revenue, merchandisers will ask the visual merchandiser to create displays for new, fashion-forward key items that have been purchased in depth, as in Figure 15.6, at Lord & Taylor in New York. Alternatively, the buyer may ask the visual merchandiser to feature products that are not selling well to increase sales on the items so that the merchandiser will not have to mark them down, thereby decreasing the retailer's profit. Some visual merchandisers have numerous job responsibilities in addition to designing and installing window displays. They may set up new stores for openings, locate and purchase props and fixtures for installations, create in-store displays and department floor arrangements, and produce signage for display windows and the sales floor.

Growing Visual Merchandising Career Opportunities

Many auxiliary businesses have developed from the increasing emphasis on the importance of visual merchandising; all hire visual merchandising professionals. A growing area of visual merchandising is the **prop house**, or prop company. These firms rent furniture, fixtures, mannequins, and décor accessories to visual merchandisers, saving the company money on limited-use display pieces while reducing the amount of warehouse space and labor needed to inventory and store visual merchandising props. Other areas of employment in visual merchandising are with mannequin, equipment, and fixture suppliers. These companies sell all

■ Figure 15.5a
Lord & Taylor, New York.

■ Figure 15.5b
Bergdorf Goodman, New York.

■ Figure 15.6
Lord & Taylor, New York.

that one needs to outfit a store. Fixtures, such as T-stands, rounders, and four-ways, are offered; wall slats and hanging bars provide additional merchandising space. The visual merchandising professional working for one of these interior-related firms is, in essence, responsible for in-house promotion that will be seen by the company's clients.

Some fixture and equipment companies hire visual merchandising professionals to work with their clients, retailers, and manufacturers on efficient and attractive space usage. Often using a computer-aided design system, the visual merchandising professional develops plan-o-grams. As depicted in Figure 15.7, a **plan-o-gram** is a floor plan on which the placement and types of racks, fixtures, display units, and merchandise is laid out in order to create an easy flow of traffic and to present the merchandise most effectively. The plan-o-gram is used as an effective interior design tool to show the retailer or manufacturer how many different types of fixtures will be needed and what the interior of the business will look like when it is furnished. It is also an essential tool for corporate retailers wanting to ensure that stores, particularly chains, have a uniform appearance so that customers will know where the merchandise they want can be found quickly, no matter where the location is. The store managers and staff can see exactly how their stores should look by following the plan.

Yet another employer of the visual merchandiser (commonly freelance, in this case) is the designer or manufacturer of apparel and accessories. Take, for example, a manufacturer's showroom on Broadway in the Fashion District of Manhattan. The manufacturer may hire a visual merchandising professional to design and install displays in the showroom and its windows with every market week, just as retailers around the world do with every new fashion season (shown in Figures 15.8a–c and Box 15.2).

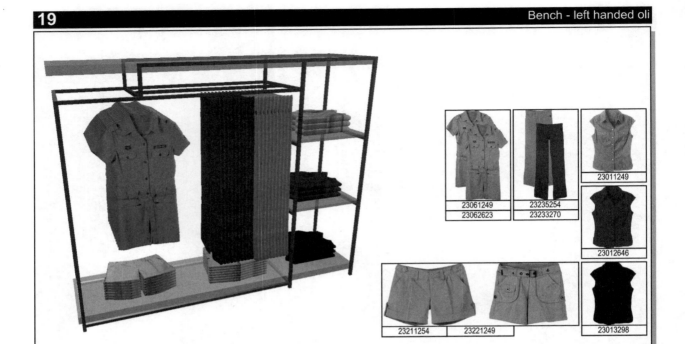

23061249
23062623

23235254
23233270

23011249

23012646

23211254　　23221249

23013298

■ Figure 15.7
MockShop, with its
visual merchandising
software, allows the
retailer to create a
virtual floor layout that
indicates the placement
of wall units, furnishings,
fixtures, and displays.

Qualifications

Are you a person who is artistic, resourceful, and loves creating visual displays? If so, this may be the career path for you. Successful visual merchandising professionals are likely to possess the following qualities:

- *Education.* A two- or four-year college degree in fashion merchandising, fashion design, interior design, retail planning and design, fine arts, visual arts, or visual merchandising is often a minimum requirement.

- *Experience.* Many visual display professionals begin as a member of the visual merchandising team for a retailer, installing window and interior displays. Others may come from the fields of interior design, fashion styling, or store planning. With all of these backgrounds, employers expect job candidates to have a variety of visual merchandising work experiences, sales training, and a solid portfolio of work. One of the best ways to prepare for the job search is to build a portfolio of work: photographs of displays created for local merchants, class projects, or internships in visual merchandising. Most visual merchandisers have experience in drafting, either computer-generated or sketched, which allows them to visualize concepts before executing them.

- *Personal characteristics.* The visual merchandising professional must understand design, marketing, and merchandising. An excellent aesthetic sensibility, computer-aided design skills, and an understanding of visual art principles are keys to securing a position in this area. The ability to create effective displays using props, mannequins, and other display components is critical. The successful visual merchandiser requires a breadth of skills and

■ **Figure 15.8a**
Larusmiani, Milan.

■ **Figure 15.8b**
Galeries Lafayette, Paris.

■ **Figure 15.8c**
Macy's, New York.

knowledge: an understanding of fashion marketing and merchandising; an eye for color, line, balance, and proportion; a theatrical vision; a strong sense of fashion; the ability to develop and follow time and budget schedules; computer-aided design skills to develop schematics of displays; and the ability to rethink and reuse props, mannequins, and other display components. The effective visual merchandiser is not only self-motivated but also able to take directions to execute work as a team member. This position requires one to be able to work well under pressure.

Career Challenges

People interested in pursuing a visual merchandising career often start at the first rung of the career ladder as a display associate, paid a fairly low hourly wage. Beginning a career in visual merchandising is not easy. The jobs are available in many sectors of the fashion industry, including retail stores, manufacturers' showrooms, and visual merchandising companies; however, not everyone is interested in making the sacrifices that are often required to get started in this field. Low pay, hard work, and long hours, including nights and weekends, describe the start of many visual merchandising careers.

In addition, the job of visual merchandiser does not consist solely of selecting beautiful merchandise and designing attractive displays. It includes vacuuming the floors of the store windows, cleaning the glass, refurbishing props to stay within budget, and working evenings to install displays when customers are not in the store. After paying their dues in this position, display associates may move into assistant visual merchandising director positions and upward to the position of director.

Future Outlook for Visual Merchandisers

Career opportunities in this field are increasing, because the retail industry understands how important visual image is to the consumer. It is significant to note that the job of visual display can be accomplished at all levels of the fashion industry—from the manufacturer/designer to the retailer to ancillary service providers, such as special event producers. Many companies outside of the retail industry hire visual merchandisers as part of their staffs. These include home furnishings and accessories manufacturers, beauty and cosmetics firms, trend-forecasting firms, fabric and notions representatives, and online visual merchandising trend Web sites, as illustrated in Box 15.3. There are also opportunities to work as either a self-employed or company-employed visual merchandiser in all levels of the fashion industry.

Store Planning Director

A store planning director develops a plan that details fixture placement, lighting, dressing rooms, restrooms, windows, aisles, and cash and wrap areas of a store. Store planning directors keep several goals in mind when laying out store floor plans. Aesthetic appeal, image consistency, visibility and security of merchandise, comfort and ease of staff and consumers, and merchandising flexibility are among these objectives. Once a floor plan is finalized, all of the supplies (e.g., hangers, bags, and tissue) are purchased, along with the equipment (e.g., four-way fixtures, T-stands, slat walls, mirrors, and computer registers) to set up the retail floor. All of this must be accomplished within a predetermined budget.

The store planning director often works with the visual merchandising director to design the store layout. Window and interior display areas and cases to exhibit small goods, fixtures, and mannequins are of interest to both. The store planner who has work experience in visual merchandising often has an edge over one who does not.

Qualifications

What else does it take to have a successful career in store planning? Education, experience, and personal qualifications are the following:

- *Education.* A bachelor's degree in fashion merchandising, interior design, retailing, or a related field is a minimum requirement.

- *Experience.* Between two and five years of experience in retail management, visual merchandising, interior design, or buying are preferred.

- *Personal characteristics.* Store planners are detail oriented, computer literate (CAD), and task oriented. They have effective communication skills—oral, written, and visual. Additionally, they have strong quantitative skills, as space allocation and budgeting are core responsibilities of someone on this career path.

Box 15.3 Online Visual Merchandiser and Stylist

As an Online Visual Merchandiser/Stylist you must have strong editorial/ curatorial taste level to hand-select products to feature across the Web site, email newsletters, and social media, as well as the pieces to push in editorial photo shoots.

We believe in the curious people, passionate people and mindful people. We're looking for a talented Online Visual Merchandiser and Stylist with a passion for fashion and technology to join our team in the heart of Soho, NYC. You'll be joining an experienced team recruited from companies such as Condé Nast, J. Crew, and Gilt Groupe.

The role will require you to work towards having strong product knowledge of brands on site, while working with the brands team and Content Director on content calendar.

Responsibilities:

- Work with the Content Director to deliver visual experiences and product-based content

- Merchandise emails

- Pitch themes

- Source images

- Test email campaigns

- Affiliate marketing

- Work with affiliate e-shops on curation

- Facilitate site merchandising

- Maintain shop categories merchandised

- Select featured products weekly and featured brands on Shop pages

- Style Web site, marketing, and other images

- Work closely with Content Director on Style shoot every six weeks, from concept development to production

Required:

Must have 2 to 3 years of experience in e-commerce, merchandising, and/or styling with knowledge of HTML.

The job outlook for this field is good. Most large retail operations rely on store planning directors for updating facilities, setting up new departments or stores, and keeping the equipment and supplies for the retail floor in stock, up to date, and safe.

Career Challenges

The store planner has a great deal to consider when designing or remodeling a retail operation. Store managers, buyers, sales associates, customers, receiving clerks, and maintenance staff have specific space needs and desires. While working under the control of a budget, the store planner must consider the comfort and safety of all constituencies, while keeping in mind the main goal of the retailer—selling merchandise. Designing a space to meet all of these objectives takes observation, patience, and perseverance.

Mall Manager

A **mall manager** is responsible for everything in the mall, from planning its budget and promotional activities to developing its mix of tenants and building community relations. On a given day, the mall manager is involved with marketing, tenant leasing, increasing capital, building improvement, construction, as well as tenant, customer, and staff security. What makes a mall successful is often the mix of stores available to the customer (Figure 15.9). The mall manager examines the mall's retail mix to determine its strengths and weaknesses. Incorporating interesting stores and concepts that are unique to the area, as well as balancing the number of apparel, home, service, and food retailers, are key to a mall's success.

Mall managers calculate customer demand into the equation, striving to meet the needs of the current demographic segment and anticipate through research what the future demographics may be. They look at home ownership, income, and customer profiles within the community to understand what the customer is looking for and who that customer is. The ultimate goals of the mall manager are to grow the value of the property while improving tenant listings and leasing capacity. To be 100 percent filled is the objective, as is finding ways to complement an already integrated mix of stores. A classified advertisement for a mall manager is featured in Box 15.4.

Assistant Mall Manager

In larger malls, the mall manager may supervise one or more assistants. An **assistant mall manager** is responsible for administering mall programs under the supervision of the property's mall manager. This person is critical in communicating operational issues to tenants, contractors, and staff.

Qualifications

A list of the educational requirements, work experiences, and personal characteristics for the successful mall manager and assistant mall manager follows:

- *Education.* A bachelor's degree in management, merchandising, marketing, retailing, business administration, real estate (leasing), property management and/or retail management, or a related field is a minimum requirement.

- *Experience.* Retail sales experience with a variety of retail operations provides an excellent background, including summer or part-time employment during college. An internship

■ Figure 15.9
The image and aesthetics of the mall reflect the type of tenants that mall management will seek out—from restaurants to retailers.

Box 15.4 Mall Manager

Position: Mall Manager

Company: Mall Property Development Group

Location: Columbus, Ohio

Description:

Managers are responsible for leasing (long-term and temporary), negotiation of contracts, staff supervision, office management, budgeting and monthly financial analysis and reporting, tenant and public relations, and operational issues, all with the goal of maximizing the asset value of the property.

Position Requirements:

- Bachelor's degree in the areas of marketing, merchandising, business administration, real estate (leasing), property management and/or retail management, or related field

- Understanding of business administration principles

- Minimum of five years professional management experience; preference given for shopping center management

- Excellent communication and organizational skills

- Temporary and/or permanent leasing experience

- Must possess superior communication and interpersonal skills with a high degree of human relations skills

- Strong management skills

- Proficient in applicable software (e.g., Word, Adobe, Excel, etc.)

with a mall management firm is an excellent way to gain experience in this career path. Many mall managers also secure store management experience, so they can understand the needs and concerns of their mall tenants. Assistant mall managers usually work a minimum of three to five years before moving up to the position of mall manager.

- *Personal characteristics.* The mall manager must be a strong leader who knows what needs to be done. Because multiple tasks arise daily, the mall manager must be a self-motivated individual who is able to work independently. Working in a mall with staff, tenants, and consumers demands being a good listener and an effective problem solver. The assistant mall manager must be able to adapt to a changing work environment and be an ambassador with staff and tenants in representing the mall manager.

Career Challenges

The mall manager and assistant mall manager have a team of bosses: all of the tenants in the mall. It is not easy to please a group of employers with different needs, expectations, and lease costs. Communicating with a group of this size is another challenge. Mall management reports to yet another audience: the mall's customers. It can be stressful to strive for a leasing level of full capacity, particularly when existing tenants and customers have specific ideas on which retailers will complement the current tenant mix. For example, the owner of an athletic footwear store that has made its home in the mall for years may be extremely dissatisfied to find that the mall manager has leased space to a similar retail operation. Keeping both tenants and customers happy and encouraging growth in the mall are two key objectives that may be tough for mall management to accomplish.

Summary

Exterior, interior, and visual merchandising environments profoundly influence image and profitability of all types of businesses in the fashion industry. Pursuit of a career in environments demands both technical and aesthetic know-how. The architect is a building designer who may work with a wide variety of structures. Those who specialize in serving retail clients have opportunities for projects ranging from small freestanding retail stores to large malls. The interior designer works with clients and other design professionals to develop inside spaces that are functional and attractive and that meet the needs of the people using the space. Visual merchandising professionals work with retailers, online and brick-and-mortar, fashion manufacturers and designers, and ancillary companies, such as mannequin manufacturers, prop houses, home furnishings manufacturers, equipment and fixture vendors. They are responsible for presenting an aesthetically appealing environment that reflects the company's image and sells merchandise. The mall manager and assistant mall manager are responsible for everything in the mall, from planning its budget and creating promotional activities to developing its mix of tenants and building community relations.

Physical and virtual spaces are continually expected to create, buy, sell, and transform. As with many careers, the key to success in these fields is satisfying the client. If you have strong technical, visual, and communication skills, consider a future in environments.

Key Terms

architect
architecture
assistant mall manager
commercial designer
commercial real estate
interior designer

mall manager
plan-o-gram
prop house
residential design
visual merchandisers
visual merchandising

Online Resources

www.1stdibs.com

www.houzz.com

www.architonic.com

www.dirtt.net

www.getdecorating.com/interiors.cfm

www.interiordesign.net/

www.mydeco.com/plan-my-room

www.sfd.co.uk/

www.vmsd.com

www.wallpaper.com/architecture

www.wallpaper.com/interiors

Discussion Questions

1. Compare and contrast the careers of architect, interior designer, and visual merchandiser. Examine the education, licensing requirements, and position responsibilities common to these three professions.

2. Consider a shopping district in the area where you live. What types of businesses stand out? How do the exteriors, interiors, and visual merchandising strategies relate to one another within each business? Evaluate how the sum of the business's environments can create a successful entity.

3. Visit a mall or other type of shopping center and record some of the major tenants (i.e., types of businesses, including retail, restaurant, and entertainment), their adjacencies, and any voids in types of tenants that would draw customers to the facility. Describe the lifestyle approach the shopping facility represents. Identify the most desirable location in the facility based on customer traffic, proximity to parking, and nearness to the best neighboring stores.

4. Take a tour of the mall and note and/or photograph the visual merchandising themes you are seeing in window and in-store displays there. Review your notes and develop a list of the top three fashion retail trends you identify as being repeated in the displays of these retailers.

Profile: Interview with Interior Designer Abbe Fenimore

Interviewed by Michele Granger

Abbe Fenimore is an interior designer located in Dallas, Texas, and the owner of the design firm, Studio Ten 25 (www.studioten25.com), and an online boutique, Shop Ten 25 (www.shopten25.com). She is a beauty who creates beautiful environments that reflect her design style while integrating the clients' needs, wants, and personal aesthetics—a balancing act, for certain. Her work has been recognized through a number of prestigious awards: D (Dallas) Home's Best Designers 2012, 2013, and 2014; ASID Legacy of Design 2013.

Can you tell us a little about yourself?

I was born and raised in Arkansas and attended Louisiana Tech University for Interior Design. After graduation, I moved to Austin, Texas, and worked for Herman Miller and a boutique design firm. After a few years, I moved to Dallas and began representing interior finish products. In 2007, I decided it was time to step out on my own and Studio Ten 25 was born. Through the founding of my firm, I was able to combine all of my experience, from furniture design to commercial and residential interiors, while showcasing my own personal style: an eclectic balance of vibrant color, mix of rich materials, and true sense of space.

When did you realize you wanted to design?

I think I was born with the light bulb on! Even as a little girl, I was always rearranging my bedroom and changing out little details in my dollhouse. My mother is a talented seamstress, so we were always making new drapes and bedding for my dollhouse out of her fabric scraps. In high school, I became obsessed with decorating my bedroom. My parents went out of town one weekend, and I was given the credit card to work on my room. I was instructed to keep it around a certain amount, which didn't happen. When my parents returned, even after much sweet-talking and begging to keep everything, I ended up grounded, relegated to ironing duty for a week, and forced to return over

Profile Figure 15a Dallas Interior Designer and e-Retailer, Abbe Fenimore.

half of my purchases. It was through this experience that I learned the importance of staying in budget! It was also during my high school days that I began dreaming up names for my future interior design business, which I recently happened upon at my parents' home in Arkansas.

What is an average day for you?

What I love about my job is that it is different every day. Flexibility is an important skill to have as an interior designer, as it's key to staying organized.

My days are typically filled with client meetings, pulling samples, placing orders, installations, and occasionally running back across town because I forgot something that I needed for the day. If I'm lucky, I grab lunch around 2 p.m. I'm determined to be better at stopping to catch my breath during the day, including making time for lunch.

What kinds of skills have you learned from your experiences, and what skills do successful interior designers need to develop?

Multitasking is a critical skill for interior designers, as we wear many hats. Over the years, I have learned to multitask on my terms and in a manner that suits me best. Time management is also very important. Navigating various deadlines can be challenging, but being able to prioritize and manage my time is key. Taking care and doing everything with intent are imperative. Rushing through projects can be a killer. Being able to think both big and small picture is crucial. I stay focused on the end result: a happy client. And the ability to learn from your experiences is vital. I strive to learn from both my mistakes and successes.

What does your company do?

We are a boutique interior design firm located in Dallas, Texas. We specialize in residential and small commercial projects.

How do you get inspired?

I frequently find myself inspired after reading one of my favorite magazines or blogs, spending time outdoors, checking out a new home furnishings

Profile Figure 15b A contemporary and colorful living room in the signature style of Abbe Fenimore.

(continued on next page)

(continued)

brand, or trying a new restaurant in Dallas. I never know when inspiration will hit, so as long as I keep my eyes open, it will continue to flow.

What do you love most about what you do?

I love the relationships with my clients and vendors. I am a people person and have found that solid relationships have been an integral component to my success.

Why are you drawn to this career?

I have always been drawn to the design industry. The creative field requires me to constantly think outside of the box and collaborate with other creative people. It's something that I have always been passionate about and have loved to do, so I have never imagined doing anything else.

What have been your toughest challenges as an interior designer?

The business side of design and business ownership has proven to be challenging for me. Tasks like bookkeeping and taxes have never been my strong suits, but I have learned to let go and ask for help when needed.

What advice would you give to aspiring designers and retailers?

Spend some time really thinking about your career and business objectives. Create goals, but understand that it's important to stay flexible, as they can change over time. Connect with others in the industry and create a network of support. It's these connections that you can rely on for advice, even if what they say is hard to hear. Stay focused on the end goal, but celebrate little successes along the way. And be open to failure, but be ready to overcome it. Success doesn't come overnight, but if you work hard and are passionate about what you're doing, you'll find it.

Profile Figure 15c An urban mix of textures, patterns, and styles in this multifunction room by Abbe Fenimore.

Which blogs and Web sites do you use as the go-tos for your work?

When searching for inspiration, I usually start with Pinterest. I have folders already organized by room or color, so I start there to see what I have already pinned. I usually set up a private board on Pinterest for each client and pin inspirational images that are specific to their project, style, or color palette.

(continued)

From there, I go to a few of my favorite design blogs, like MaterialGirls, TheDecorista, Sketch42, Made By Girl, Mix and Chic, Waiting on Martha, and I Suwannee are a few of my favorites. They are all so different with regard to their design aesthetic, but I love how they each stay true to their own style and flare for design. You can see how much they love what they do, their passion for design, it inspires me.

Do you use social media for your work? If so, which ones and how?

Social media is a major part of my business and a constantly moving part of what I do each day. I love being able to communicate with thousands in an instant, and the amount of inspiration out there is never-ending. I have been able to meet and interact with so many wonderful designers, bloggers, and editors over the years through social media. It is an easy way to show the world and potential clients what you are all about and what makes you tick.

With so many new social media outlets popping up often, it can become overwhelming. I stick with my favorites and limit it to the ones where I have the most interaction with others. If there is no interaction, it can feel like you're just throwing ideas and inspiration out into a big black hole. Instagram is my favorite by far; I love the filters and ability to show off "real" design situations, instead of just posting pretty pictures. Facebook, Twitter, Pinterest, and Pippet are the other forms of social media that I use on a daily basis.

Courtesy of Abbe Fenimore

Profile: *Careers in Interior Design* co-author, Interior Designer, and College Instructor Nancy Asay

Interior design is an industry with many facets. This is one of the reasons why my co-author, Marciann Patton, and I wrote the *Careers* book. Currently, this book is used in colleges and universities to help interior design students understand the numerous directions this career choice can take. I think the book is a great read, even for those without a college direction, but who are looking for a creative career. When looking for a career in interior design, a person needs to look around and see which areas are actively hiring. Health care is a great example. When the economy is slow, interior design professionals need to take advantage of the lack of new construction and understand that money is being spent to renovate existing spaces. Now it is all about the interior, instead of the leftover budget that we many times get to deal with as a result of the new construction cost overruns. This is true for both residential and commercial interior designers.

I have been a professional interior designer for forty years. I have a NCIDQ certificate, am a professional member of ASID, a registered interior designer in the state of Missouri, and, currently, a senior instructor at Missouri State University in the Interior Design progam. I also maintain a small business, Nancy Asay Interiors, and work with clients who I have worked with in the past. Time does not permit me to take new clients or to do large commercial jobs. Maintaining a small business also keeps me current with products and other industry professionals. These contacts are extremely helpful now, as I teach students at the university.

Profile Figure 15d Author, Interior Designer, and College Instructor, Nancy Asay.

When I went to college, I wanted a career that I could work at part time, giving me a way to support myself, and, potentially, my children. I always pictured myself married with children and wanted to be able to handle everything if something happened to my husband (which my mother went through). This was my pre-college thought.

I have a Bachelor of Fine Arts in Interior Design from the University of Kansas. When I graduated from college, I had a difficult time finding an interior design job because everyone wanted someone with experience. I chose to work in commercial interior design because I wanted an eight-to-five day job. Because I was unable to find employment

(continued)

with an existing interior design firm, I selected six businesses that marketed commercial furniture but did not have an interior design department. I applied to all six, explaining that I could start an interior design department for them and increase their business. All six agreed to the idea, so I selected from six firms. Starting a commercial interior design business gave me great experience and a very marketable future in commercial interior design.

I have always enjoyed my career in interior design and have specialized in space planning and health-care design. I earned a master's degree in education from Drury University for the purpose of teaching interior design as my latest career. It has been a great way to give back.

Courtesy of Nancy Asay

chapter 16

Beauty, Spa, and Wellness

There is a sector of the fashion industry that is dramatically affected by evolving consumer and style trends, particularly in the areas of color, environmental aesthetics, demographic shifts, technology, and science, to include medicine, psychology, and physiology. Fashion as a lifestyle includes personal beauty, health, and body image choices. As there are changing trends in the fabrics, colors, and themes of apparel and home fashions, there are shifts in "what is in fashion" in the areas of personal care, health, and fitness. Aerobics and jogging are being upstaged by Hatha yoga and Pilates. Plastic surgery is being augmented by microfacials, fillers, and Botox. Makeup shifts from a natural to a glamour look, and back. Hairstyles rely on a straightener and, later, a curling iron. If you think of fashion as lifestyle in which people strive to look good and stay current, then choices they make in spending their personal time and money on looking and feeling good fit seamlessly as part of the fashion industry (Figure 16.1).

The **beauty and wellness industries** focus on cosmetics, fragrances, hair and skin care, as well as spa, fitness, or wellness centers and their services. As a consumer, you contribute financially to this sector every day. When you wash your hair and style it, put on your makeup or skincare products, take your vitamins, apply sunscreen, go to the fitness center, and head to your pedicure and massage appointments at the spa, you are adding to the increasing revenues of the beauty and wellness industries. The beauty and wellness industries are growing fields with a wide range of career tracks that require fashion and nonfashion training. If you have an interest in fitness and health and enjoy the image changes that hair and makeup can create, then the beauty and wellness sectors of the fashion industry can offer you a variety of career options.

■ Figure 16.1
In the cosmetic, skin care, and fragrance industries, the marketing and research development areas work closely with each other on a common goal: developing products that fulfill consumers' needs.

■ Figure 16.2
A counter manager stocks and displays cosmetics at L'Oréal Paris's counter at a department store in Tokyo.

In this chapter, the following career paths are explored: beauty merchandising and marketing professional, makeup artist, aesthetician, hairstylist, and director of a spa or wellness center.

To begin, the **beauty industry** and its producers of cosmetics, fragrances, and hair and skincare products is examined. There are many well-known mass marketing companies in this field: Esteé Lauder, Lancôme, and L'Oréal, to name just a few (Figure 16.2). There are two classifications of beauty industry corporations: mass market and prestige market. **Mass market** beauty companies, such as Cover Girl and Revlon, distribute their product lines through a wide variety of retailers, including drugstores, discount merchants, and mass merchandising retailers. **Prestige market** beauty companies, such as Chanel and MAC, distribute their product lines through prominent department and specialty store retailers, primarily in leased departments. Some companies, like Sephora, distribute the products of prestige market beauty companies and under their own private labels (Box 16.1). Within these corporations, there are many subsidiaries through which product lines are developed, marketed, and sold to the retail operations that offer them to the consumer. Some companies work with the creation of products, to include goods and services, promote the product lines under various labels, and sell them to selected retailers, as with Clarins Paris (Box 16.2).

SOCIAL MEDIA STRIKES

Box 16.1 Sephora

Sephora was founded in 1970 in France by Dominique Mandonnaud, who, in 1993, fashioned the store's unique name by blending the Biblical name of Zipporah (Moses' exceptionally beautiful wife) with the ancient Greek term for "pretty," *sephos*. Today, Sephora is the leading chain of perfume and cosmetics stores in France and a powerful beauty retailer around the world. Sephora operates approximately 1,300 stores in 27 countries worldwide, with an expanding base of more than 300 stores across North America. It is owned by Louis Vuitton Moet Hennessy (LVMH), the world's leading luxury goods group. Sephora's North American headquarters is located in San Francisco, with corporate offices in New York and Montreal.

Sephora's unique, open-sell environment features an ever-increasing number of classic and emerging brands across a broad range of product categories, including skin care, cosmetics, fragrance, body, dental care, and hair care, in addition to Sephora's own private label. In addition to its own full-line stores and mini-stores in JCPenney, Sephora sells these products through its top beauty Web site, which continues to advance this arena through mobile and social media initiatives. Sephora has a notable social media presence, with more than one million Twitter followers, five million Facebook fans, almost one million Instagramians, and more than 200,000 Pinterest followers. And Sephora wants more.

In 2014, Sephora launched a new social media platform, entitled Beauty Board. The main goal for the launch was to boost sales and consumer interaction. Through the Beauty Board platform, users create their own profiles where they can upload and share photos. Sephora stores will also have their designated profiles. The concept is that pictures are everywhere (consider Sephora's success with Instagram). Beauty afficionados love to see ideas for looks and products to buy. Beauty Board makes it more practical; it is a place for consumers to browse for inspiration and discover products to buy at sephora.com.

Sources:

www.sephora.com; www.brandingmagazine.com/2014/03/18/sephora-beauty-board/

CASE STUDIES IN CAREER EXPLORATION

Box 16.2 Clarins Paris

Sometimes a simple decision can change your life. For example, when a young medical student named Jacques Courtin-Clarins decided to treat circulatory problems with massage, a strange thing started happening. After their treatments, Courtin-Clarins's patients not only felt better, but their skin looked dramatically better too. He started Clarins in 1954, naming the company after a character he played in a school play and later (in 1974) added this name to his own. Over the next 50 years, Courtin-Clarins devoted his research to improving the way his clients felt and looked, and what started off as a few simple botanical body oils ballooned (at the request of his clients) into Clarins Instituts de Beauté, a $1 billion global beauty company, including revenue from spas and salons in many countries. In 2014, *Beauty Inc.*, *WWD*'s beauty magazine, designated Clarins as one of its top ten power players in the beauty industry. What began at Clarins in the 1950s are now top trends for beauty product manufacturers around the world—plant-based formulas, medical knowledge teamed with skin care, and the mind-body connection. Next, Christian Courtin-Clarins talks about his father and the botanically enriched products of Clarins from skin care to massage to cosmetics.

Jacques Courtin-Clarins developed treatments and products using natural botanical ingredients first for the body and then for the face. He once said, "From a very young age, I was exposed to the curative effects of plants by my mother and relatives, who used herbs for medicine and treatment. Ever since, I looked to plants for answers. I cannot conceive a product without plants." In line with his father's words, today Clarins uses only the best natural botanical extracts.

The Clarins research and development team travels extensively throughout the world to exotic places, such as tropical rainforests in the Amazon, Asia, and other remote locales in Europe to find new ingredients and cutting-edge research that helps make the skin beautiful. One of Clarins's top-selling products is Total Body Lift, which uses powerful ingredients from these exotic locations to help minimize cellulite.

In addition to botanical products, Clarins offers spa treatments in massage. The company believes that poor circulation is at the root of all skin problems and understands that circulation slows down with age. Massage is an excellent way to improve circulation and the health of the skin. The Clarins massage technique is composed of no less than 80 movements. At the Clarins Institute in Neuilly, France, massage is paired with Clarins products to contour the face and body, stimulate the lymphatic system and blood circulation, preserve the skin's integrity and health, and restore balance and energy to the body and mind.

Clarins also produces a makeup collection, which is inspired by couturiers' runway shows. The company bases its cosmetic products on their abilities to adapt to the innuendos of everyday life: some days a woman wants full-out glamour, whereas other days she's rushing to apply makeup in a taxicab. Just like the skin and body care products, Clarins makeup is rich in natural botanicals. The foundations contain moringa extract to moisturize, nourish, and revitalize skin. The lipsticks contain natural oil and vegetable extracts to soothe and soften lips. The mascaras contain plant waxes to condition and coat lashes. Today, Clarins produces cleansers, moisturizers, firming products, exfoliating treatments, and sun-protection and tanning lotions, as well as perfumes under the brand names of Clarins, My Blend, Mugler, Swarovski, Azzaro, and Zadig & Voltaire.

Sources:

www.nytimes.com/2007/04/06/business/06clarins.html

www.sephora.com/browse/brand_hierarchy.jhtml?brandId=Clarins&contentId=C15102

www.time.com/time/magazine/article/0,9171,1135638,00.html

www.washingtonpost.com/wp-dyn/content/article/2007/04/01/AR2007040100958.html

Beauty Merchandising and Marketing Professionals

A **beauty merchandising and marketing professional** is involved in the promotion and sales of cosmetic, fragrance, and skin care products. Beauty merchandising and marketing professionals include the retail account coordinator, trainer, retail account executive, and counter manager. An **account coordinator** organizes special events and promotions for a cosmetic, fragrance, or skin care line, traveling to different retail locations. The account coordinator develops and implements marketing programs that perpetuate the image of the brand, introduce new products, and generate customer traffic and press for the retail accounts. A **trainer** works for the cosmetic, fragrance, or skin care line by educating sales and marketing employees on the company's product line and how to sell it. The trainer directs seminars on new products, how they are to be used, and what results the consumer can expect. An account executive can work in two main areas: retailing and public relations. The **retail account executive**, or *retail account coordinator*, sells the line to retailers and oversees the sales performance of the line in large retail accounts. The retail account executive works with retailers that carry the line by providing marketing and merchandising suggestions to maximize consumer sell-through. This account representative assists store accounts with inventory management, making recommendations to increase sales. On-site staff training, incentives to motivate sales personnel, and assistance with consumer promotional events are parts of the retail account executive's job. The **public relations account executive** works with beauty media contacts, such as fashion publications like *Marie Claire*, *Vogue*, *Allure*, *Elle*, *W*, and *InStyle*, to promote the line in magazine editorials and feature stories. Box 16.3 features a variety of beauty career positions offered by a beauty retailer.

In the retail operation, the **counter manager**, or *line manager*, coordinates special events and promotions in the retail operation, manages employees, and works closely with buyers. Selling the product line and servicing the customer are key objectives for the counter manager. Counter managers are constantly acquiring product knowledge through corporate training materials and seminars to educate sales associates and customers. They also develop merchandise displays and demonstrate products to staff and clients. They coach and develop a sales staff to achieve their personal productivity and company sales goals, often through building a **client registry file**, a computerized or print record of the names and contact information of the line's customers. The counter manager is also responsible for replenishing inventory through back stock or reorders. Finally, counter managers also develop and participate in special events that will increase business. For most mass market brands, counter managers are employed by the retailer; in prestige market brands, they usually work directly for the cosmetic, fragrance, hair, or skin care companies.

Qualifications

Account representatives, trainers, and counter managers have similar requirements in education, work experience, and personal characteristics, as follows.

- *Education.* A bachelor's degree in fashion design, fashion merchandising, communications, marketing, journalism, or a related field is a minimum requirement.

- *Experience.* Sales experience, especially in the cosmetic, fragrance, and skin care areas, is preferred. An internship in the beauty division of a department store is an excellent

CASE STUDIES IN CAREER EXPLORATION

Box 16.3 Beauty Products Career Tracks

If you are contemplating a career in the fashion industry, you may initially think about the apparel manufacturer or the accessories retailer; however, a wide range of job opportunities is available in the beauty industry, from representative positions at retail stores to field sales positions and corporate opportunities. More information about these job opportunities in the world of skin care, cosmetics, and fragrance follows.

Positions with a Retailer

In the following three roles, you may be employed by the department store or the beauty company that consigns space in the retailer's store.

Client Advisor
The client, or customer, advisor represents the product line in department stores by working with consumers. The ideal candidate enjoys providing assistance and sharing expertise in skin care, makeup, and fragrance. Providing exceptional customer service and achieving sales goals are the client advisor's primary goals. If you're in college, have prior sales and/or service experience, and can work flexible hours, this may be the start of a great career for you.

Counter Manager
The counter manager schedules, motivates, and supervises a team of client advisors to exceed standards for exceptional customer service and sales goals. The counter manager trains new client advisors, calculates their individual sales goals, and works with client advisors to execute the beauty line's promotions. Most counter managers are promoted from the rank of client advisors.

Retail Account Executive
The retail account executive is a liaison between the beauty product company and the department store management. Responsibilities include coaching counter managers to lead and develop their teams, traveling to stores in a specific territory,

and providing performance reviews for staff. This position is a step up the career ladder from counter manager.

Field Sales Positions

Several types of field sales positions are available in the beauty industry; two are described as follows.

Account Coordinator
The account coordinator is employed by the beauty company and is responsible for multiple stores within a territory. This person collaborates with personnel in the retail stores to manage sales goals and service objectives. Ultimately, the account executive ensures that the counter team best represents the beauty company to customers.

Education Executive (Trainer)
The education executive provides counter teams with information about new products, their uses, and applications. They also provide training on strategies to engage repeat customers, to achieve service standards, and to surpass sales goals. The account executive also educates line representatives on industry trends, to include seasonal fashion trends, upcoming color palettes, and the makeup products to complement all of these.

Corporate Positions

In most major beauty companies, a wide breadth of corporate positions exist—from marketing and product development to finance and human resources to digital and social media. Next is a classified advertisement for a social media manager with a company based in London.

Social Media Director
This is an amazing opportunity for a passionate social media guru to work for a high growth, entrepreneurial beauty brand with a highly engaged social audience and to take this activity to the next level.

way to gain work experience. Several years of work experience in the beauty industry is a minimum requirement. Some large companies prefer a candidate who also holds aesthetics certification or has training and experience as a makeup artist. A strong knowledge of the beauty industry is expected. The candidate who can show successful sales experience through awards, a client listing, and so on, moves ahead of the competition. Evidence of exceptional customer service skills and the abilities to multitask, lead, and coach teams are also helpful.

• *Personal characteristics.* Great people skills and a love of travel are important in this career field. Common skills of beauty merchandising and marketing professionals include the ability to be energetic and articulate in conversation and writing. People in this career field are often ambitious self-starters, competitive spirits, and have creative and optimistic attitudes. In the beauty business, an image that exudes professionalism and a sense of style that fits with the employer's image is essential.

Career Challenges

Beauty merchandising and marketing professionals have a variety of job challenges. The account coordinator works under the pressure of coming up with innovative special events and promotions for the company every season. The trainer must continually find ways to educate employees on the company's new products and how to sell them. The retail account executive must meet or surpass sales goals in selling the line to retail accounts. The counter manager has the same objective, exceeding the sales goal set by the manufacturer and the retailer. Persons in both of these positions have to balance sales and inventory so that both the retailers and the beauty product manufacturer are satisfied and making a profit. Extensive travel to different retail locations is often part of these jobs. Finally, the public relations account executive needs to persuade beauty media contacts to feature new product lines. All of these jobs have the following in common: the possibility of high stress, involvement in a fast-paced environment, and the need to sell one's self and the product line.

Makeup Artist

The person interested in working with cosmetics is not limited to working for a single beauty product firm. The **makeup artist** works hands-on with a variety of product lines and has a variety of employment opportunities. Makeup artists work with cosmetics, wigs, and other costuming materials to color and enhance a client's face and body. Working in television, film, music videos, commercials, and print ads, they use makeup to improve or alter actors' and models' appearances. Other makeup artists work at the retail level, applying products, such as lipstick and mascara, on customers at store cosmetic counters and showing them how to use these products. Some makeup artists work on photo shoots and runway shows for designers and magazines or cosmetic companies as consultants or sales representatives. Makeup artists also provide their services as independent contractors in beauty salons, retail stores, large hotels and resorts, spas, or the medical profession—from updating daytime or evening makeup looks to providing camouflage techniques to help clients following injuries or surgeries.

What is the work of makeup artists in the video, media, television, film, and theater industries? They apply makeup for presenters, performers, and others appearing on-screen. Some have completed training in both makeup and hair techniques (e.g., styling, cutting, and coloring) to prepare and work on the makeup and hair design required for each individual production. Makeup artists who are skilled in both makeup application and hairstyling have better job prospects. Makeup designers and chief makeup artists research and design the makeup required for a production. The style of makeup and hair depends on the type of production. It varies from straightforward, contemporary makeup and hairdressing (i.e., for news broadcasters and presenters in conservative, public settings) to more creative, specialized techniques (e.g., varying historical periods, different nationalities, aging, or special effects). This may entail researching the looks and learning the techniques for elaborate makeup and wigs needed for period films, such as *Marie Antoinette*. It may also require technological knowledge and skills to change the shape of a face, as in the film *Maleficent* (Box 16.4 and Figure 16.3).

The makeup artist or assistant makeup artist must ensure the availability of materials, such as the correct colors and brands of various cosmetics, period makeup, prosthetics like false noses and scars, as well as wigs and hair extensions. The makeup artist is expected to own an extensive kit of cosmetics to take to each job, although larger productions such as films and ongoing television series usually provide a makeup budget. Some makeup artists specialize in a medium, such as theater, film, runway, or photography, whereas others work in all of these areas.

Makeup artists in the entertainment industries collaborate closely with producers, directors, costume designers, hairdressers, and performers. Together, they develop and design the characters' looks, evaluating the length of time and cost required to complete each character. Most of these makeup artists are freelance and are engaged for each film production, television series, fashion season, or other project. As such, they are paid set or negotiated fees for each

Box 16.4 Film Makeup Artistry with Special-Effects Makeup Artist Rick Baker

When Angelina Jolie said she wanted to wear some prosthetics for *Maleficent*, her personal makeup artist Toni G recommended Rick Baker. Angie then went to a meeting with Disney and made a deal: "We have to get Rick Baker," she said. And that's when the threesome got to work. "I would have loved to do a copy of the Disney cartoon, because I thought it was great, but because it was Angie and she's so spectacular-looking, I thought it should be her own face. I drew up an idea on Photoshop with the horns and pointy ears, showed it Angie, and she said she wanted more," Rick said. (Jolie's response was, "I'm playing a creature, and it should be a creature.") Jolie wanted to change her bone structure to play Maleficent and pointed out Gaga's protruding forehead bones in her "Born This Way" video. Rick reflects on this: "I thought it didn't make sense for her to have bones like that, but she really liked the idea of something under her skin showing a ridge. So I moved them to her cheekbones, where I thought it would create a more elegant line. If you look closely, they actually follow the line of Maleficent's cowl in the Disney cartoon." The prosthetics used to create Maleficent's razor-sharp cheek bones, elongated nose, and pointed ears were made of silicone that had to be glued on and removed every day. It took two and half hours daily to transform Jolie into the Mistress of All Evil, tough on her patience, she says, and tough on that beautiful face. Toni devised a mix of coconut oil and argan oil, which not only took off the prosthetics but was also good for the skin.

When they moved on to the black horns that Jolie wore when she became evil Maleficent, they devised a skullcap that she could slip on with the lightweight horns attached by magnets. How did she get into that costume? "I did actually have to take it very slowly. I had two different sets of horns. I had horns I could pop off because I kept banging them into things. When they were wrapped in leather, I couldn't. I was this 7 1/2-foot-tall thing, with my staff," Jolie reported in an interview with George Stephanopoulos on abcNEWS.com. And those eyes? Her contact lenses are inspired by the eyes of goats. "That's also something Angie wanted. They have horizontal pupils. It's funny. Usually, I'm the one pushing for prosthetics and weirdness, and it was kind of the reverse on this film," Rick tells us.

Sources:

www.allure.com/beauty-trends/blogs/daily-beauty-reporter/2014/05/angelina-jolie-makeup-in-maleficent.html

abcnews.go.com/GMA/video/maleficent-scene-angelina-jolie-call-hard-work-23910441

www.eonline.com/news/543405/angelina-jolie-reveals-how-long-she-spent-each-day-in-the-maleficent-makeup-chair-watch-now

project. Some trade organizations in the media industries set minimum rates for independent productions and require membership in a trade union. Training and educational requirements for makeup artists vary. Many cosmetology schools specialize in makeup studies, but some schools specialize in film, television, and theatrical makeup.

Qualifications

If you love art, color, makeup, and drama, this may be the career path for you. Education requirements, work experience, and key personal characteristics for the career of a makeup artist are as follows:

- *Education.* The common educational requirements are a one-year vocational program or a two-year associate's degree. After completing educational programs, the makeup artist

■ Figure 16.3
The prosthetics used to create Maleficent's razor-sharp cheek bones, elongated nose, and pointed ears were made of silicone that had to be glued on and removed every day. It took two and a half hours daily to transform Jolie into the Mistress of All Evil.

often trains on the job in retail, television, or film, by assisting experienced makeup artists. Some industries, such as filmmaking, require that the makeup artist have specific certifications and union membership.

- *Experience.* An internship or apprenticeship with an established makeup artist is a great way to get through the career door. Sales experience in the cosmetics department of a retail store provides additional knowledge and on-the-job experience. Volunteering as a makeup artist with a local theatrical production company provides excellent hands-on experience. Many makeup artists keep their skills sharp and current through professional development workshops, where they learn about new products and application techniques.

- *Personal characteristics.* The successful makeup artist enjoys working with people and communicates well at all levels, including listening and empathizing. A strong visual sense and a creative imagination are a makeup artist's most important traits. The ability to look at a face and picture what it will look like with makeup and under specific lighting is a great talent. An awareness of health and safety and sanitation procedures is also necessary. A makeup artist must be organized and able to work well under pressure while paying attention to detail and as part of a team of often diverse colleagues.

The outlook for the career track of makeup artists is good, as the number of employees in this occupation is expected to increase over the next two to three years. It is becoming more common for people to have their makeup done professionally for job interviews, school dances, weddings, or other special occasions. Another trend is for makeup artists to work alongside hairstylists in salons, applying clients' makeup after they have their hair done.

Career Challenges

Starting out, the makeup artist earns low pay and works long hours, often weekends and nights. If a film director or photographer decides to shoot a scene at sunrise, then the makeup artist must be ready to go before dawn. Extensive travel with little downtime during a project can be exhausting. Setting one's ideas of the best makeup approach aside to defer to those of the producer can be challenging. The makeup artist needs the confidence and tact to suggest changes to accomplish the goal in an individual's appearance. For these reasons, flexibility is key. Building a business of regular clients can be difficult, and work may be irregular initially; however, once established, makeup artists often remain in this industry for a long time.

Some makeup artists choose to work in a spa, either as an independent contractor or as an employee. As the spa industry grows, so do the opportunities for makeup artists to work as part of a team of aesthetics professionals.

Wellness and Aesthetics

Wellness and personal care are topics of keen interest in today's beauty industry as it prepares for the future. As baby boomers become youthful seniors, there is an increasing consumer interest in slowing down or reversing the aging process (Figure 16.4) and preventing health problems. Additionally, consumers are seeking a higher quality of life through reduced stress; greater self-care; and safer, healthier diet and product choices. They are beginning to view services like massages and facials as ongoing wellness necessities, rather than occasional luxuries. The increasing customer interest in health, youth, and longevity has attracted new participants to the wellness industry. They include alternative medicine providers, pharmaceutical firms, energy drink and food supplement producers, full-service beauty salons, fitness and nutrition centers, and spas. Trends in the wellness industry include anti-aging and protection through skin care, relaxation and rejuvenation, facial treatments and body sculpting, stress management, and health concerns management.

Aesthetician

Aesthetics is a relatively new field that combines wellness, science, and beauty. The field views the client as a whole person by providing integrated aesthetic services through comprehensive makeovers and beauty-enhancement treatments that combine medical, beauty, and spa treatments for men and women in safe and comfortable environments. Many of these spas employ nail manicurists and pedicurists, masseuses, makeup artists, and facial technicians. An **aesthetician**, or *esthetician*, is a licensed professional who provides services such as facials, makeup, and hair removal to improve one's physical appearance.

Qualifications

Here are the educational and experience requirements, as well as personal characteristics, for a successful career as an aesthetician:

- *Education.* In most cities, vocational schools offer a program based on a curriculum, up to two years, covering the following subjects: anatomy, physiology, hygiene, skin disorders and diseases, skin analysis, massage, makeup application, hair removal, basic medical

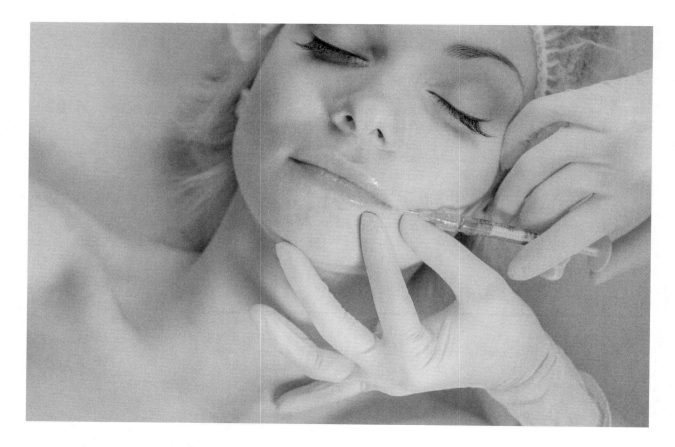

■ Figure 16.4
Spa and wellness centers are prospering because of consumer lifestyle shifts, efficacy of treatments, and education.

terminology, professional ethics, the business of aesthetics, retailing, marketing and promotion, customer service, interpersonal skills, salon administration, as well as salon layout and design.

- *Experience.* After completion of an aesthetics program and becoming licensed (requirements vary from state to state), many graduates opt to practice aesthetics in a salon or spa or open their own businesses. Others may also be employed by a makeup artist or an image consultant. Some work in medical practices such as dermatology, plastic surgery, oncology, or burn treatment centers. Additional career opportunities exist in the beauty and skin care industry.

- *Personal characteristics.* The aesthetician has good manual dexterity, a high energy level, effective communication skills, and a high level of sensitivity. The ability to work with different types of people and to build relationships with clients are important attributes of the successful aesthetician.

Four factors contribute to the level of income an aesthetician earns, as well as for most of the careers examined in this chapter. They are (1) location; (2) quality and reputation of the employer (i.e., the salon or spa); (3) whether the candidate is taking over an established clientele or starting a new clientele base; and (4) the candidate's skills and references. Some salons and spas pay a salary; others pay commission. The commission on services may start at 40 percent and increase gradually as one gains experience. Additional money can be made through tips and commission on products sold.

Career Challenges

The aesthetician must have an understanding of and interest in the three Ss: science, sanitation, and safety. Working with the human body requires a sensitive approach with strong attention to detail and methodical procedure. Because aestheticians need to stay up to date on skin care products, technology, and services, continuing education is an integral part of the job. Starting out in this career track can be tough, because it takes time to build a clientele, and aestheticians are paid for the number of services they provide.

Hairstylist

As with apparel and accessories, hairstyles change with fashion. People recognize that it is not simply apparel and accessories that express their personalities. It is also their hair, which is one reason why customers are becoming more experimental and open to change. **Hairstylists** not only work in hair salons, but also in the film and television industry for fashion companies, magazines, photo studios, and special events firms. Hairstyling is a creative art, and a good hairstylist is a valuable commodity (ask anyone who has had a bad hair day).

Qualifications

The professional hairstylist is trained in the areas of hair and scalp care, cutting, styling, and coloring, and has the following credentials, background, and personal attributes:

- *Education.* Most cities offer an array of vocational schools that specialize in hair and cosmetics training, which may take up to a year or two. Once a hairstylist has earned a license, the next step is often to apprentice under an established stylist before working solo to build a clientele. Different states have different rules governing hairstylists. Some simply require a one-time test to keep the license current, whereas others require continuing education, license renewals, and health tests associated with working with the public. Although some states do not require continuing education, most good stylists keep their skills sharp by learning new things and honing current skills through professional development workshops.

- *Experience.* Stylists can often secure positions as soon as they complete training and receive a license; however, they often begin in an assistant capacity working with an established stylist.

- *Personal characteristics.* Creativity, imagination, and continual training are necessary parts of the hairstylist's profession. Dealing effectively with people is critical. Hairstylists need effective communication skills to talk to clients and build good relationships. They should have an attractive presence, a friendly manner, and good listening skills. Because it is a physically demanding job, the stylist must have good stamina.

In terms of remuneration, hairstylists working in salons or spas may be paid on commission; the more clients they have, the more money they make. Many stylists earn additional money through tips from clients and commission on products they sell. Some firms pay stylists a salary, believing the guaranteed paycheck creates a team atmosphere. Another approach to hair salon ownership is leasing space to the stylist. The stylist pays a monthly fee for the use of a booth, often also paying a portion of the receptionist's salary so that appointments can be made at all times. Hairstylists who have training and certification in additional fields, such as makeup application and nail or facial aesthetics, have greater career and salary advancement opportunities.

Career Challenges

There is a great deal of competition in hairstyling. Think about how many hair salons exist in a midsize city. The number is often large enough that the competition is intense, and salons go out of business regularly. Finding an employer who has a solid base of repeat clientele and long-term stylists and is willing to take on a new hairstylist is a challenge. Skill and personality are critical factors in making it in this business. Continuing education is essential, as products, techniques, equipment, and looks change frequently in this industry.

Director of a Spa or Wellness Center

Resort and hotel spas originally began to make headway as a leisure time amenity and were not often thought of as profit centers for the beauty, health, and wellness industries. That has changed; now spas and medi-spas are prospering because of consumer lifestyle shifts, efficacy of treatments, and education. **Medi-spas** combine traditional spa services with those that must be offered by a physician, such as health screenings and minor outpatient surgery. **Day spas** often offer all beauty and wellness services, making the idea of a separate hair salon somewhat obsolete as spas incorporate hair and makeup services, massages, hair removal, skin rejuvenation, and other aesthetic services. In fact, the term "day spa" may eventually be replaced by "wellness and beauty center," or a similar term. The **wellness center** is becoming a place of treatment and education through well-designed nutrition and exercise programs, such as the popular fitness trends that involve combining what might seem like opposing exercises. Hot Yoga, Cy-Yo (stationary cycling followed by a yoga cool-down), and blended Yoga-Pilates are three examples of this trend. Whether referred to as a spa or a wellness center, the operation must be guided by an efficient and effective leader, its director.

The **director of a spa or wellness center** is responsible for keeping the spa running smoothly by managing customer service, budgets, marketing plans, and environment and staff appearance standards. In terms of human resources, the director ensures that employees have the training needed to perform their jobs and the knowledge they need to sell the retail product lines. Spa directors ensure the staff operates with peak efficiency through coordination, communication, and cooperation. They schedule, plan, and facilitate team meetings. Personnel duties include directing the recruitment, interviews, selection, and training of new employees. They mediate problems, organize and set work schedules, and effectively communicate and enforce company and health rules. Finally, directors are responsible for maintaining an inventory of supplies and purchasing new products. In essence, the spa director manages all of the personnel and services that make the organization a success.

Qualifications

Here are the educational, experiential, and personal characteristics needed to be a successful spa director:

- *Education.* A bachelor's degree in management, hospitality, marketing, business administration, or a related field is a minimum requirement. CPR and first-aid training are often required. It is desirable to have training, certification, and licensing in spa-related services.

- *Experience.* The director position usually requires a minimum of three to five years of experience in spa or salon management. Most spa directors have "worked in the trenches," as an aesthetician or makeup artist, for example. The position requires a working knowledge of computers, in particular, spa software skills.

- *Personal characteristics.* Spa or wellness center directors must have strong leadership skills, the ability to motivate others, excellent organizational and communication skills, and the ability to multitask. Their approach to work must be customer service oriented, diplomatic, and composed. Excellent problem-solving skills are essential.

Career Challenges

In managing all of the personnel and services that make the organization, the spa director may work long hours, including nights and weekends. This position requires many skills; chief among them are scheduling and motivating employees and creating a peaceful and immaculate environment. The successful spa director is highly attuned to image and ambiance, as well as a high level of customer service. Day after day, it can be challenging to work with personnel, customers, and vendors concurrently in a calm and controlled manner. The spa director sets the tone for the wellness center.

The Future of Spas and Wellness Centers

What does the future look like for the wellness industry? The wellness center will focus on physiological relief of fatigue and stress, while functioning as a haven for rest and relaxation. It will also be a source of education for the customer on anti-aging, brain and energy maintenance, and holistic principles of health. The products and treatments of the future will continue to concentrate on anti-aging and protection, but they will also heavily involve increasing the immune system. Although body treatments and products now take second place to the face in the spa, body skin care may be the greatest growing segment in the beauty and wellness industries of tomorrow. After all, if technology can improve the tone and texture of the face, why not use it for the entire body? As stress levels and fast-paced lifestyles continue to increase, there will be a natural need for the consumer to explore the value of detoxification for overall energy and wellness. The key to growing the beauty, health, and wellness industries lies in educating consumers on the physical and psychological benefits of self-care as a necessity, not a luxury (Figure 16.5).

■ Figure 16.5
Trends in the wellness industry include anti-aging and protection through skin care, relaxation and rejuvenation, facial treatments and body sculpting, stress management, and health concerns management.

Summary

After the cosmetics, fragrance, and skin care products are developed and produced, beauty product merchandising and marketing professionals are called on to promote and sell them. The account coordinator organizes special events and promotions for product lines, traveling to different retail locations. A trainer works to educate employees and directs seminars on new products—how they are to be used and how to sell them. The retail account executive works to sell the line to retailers carrying the product line, and the public relations account executive works with beauty media contacts to solicit promotion in consumer publications. The counter manager's key objectives are to sell the product line at the retail store and service the customer through product knowledge and special promotions in the retail operation.

The creative talents in the beauty industry are makeup artists, who work with cosmetics, wigs, and other costuming materials, to color and enhance the client's face and body, and hairstylists, who are trained in the areas of hair and scalp care, cutting, styling, and coloring. Makeup artists and hairstylists may provide their services as independent contractors in beauty salons, retail stores, large hotels and resorts, or spas. They may also work for runway productions, as well as the video, music, television, film, and theater industries.

The beauty industry is no longer just concerned with hair and makeup, however. The popularity of alternative physical treatments has broadened concepts of personal care and the career options within the beauty and wellness industries. Spas, or wellness centers, offer a variety of treatments and services, including anti-aging and protection through skin care, relaxation and rejuvenation, facial treatments and body sculpting, stress management, and health concerns management, and services provided by aestheticians. A spin on the traditional spa, the medi-spa combines long-offered spa services with those that must be provided by a physician. The director of a spa or wellness center is responsible for keeping the spa running smoothly by managing customer service, budgets, marketing plans, and environment and staff appearance standards.

Beauty, health, and wellness businesses are rapidly growing sectors of the fashion lifestyle industry. Career opportunities are flourishing, with new ones developing as innovative products and techniques are introduced. Increasing consumer interest and awareness in the well-being, longevity, and beauty that results from self-care indicates that this area will be one to watch in the future.

Key Terms

account coordinator
aesthetician
aesthetics
beauty and wellness industries
beauty industry
beauty merchandising and marketing professional
client registry file
counter manager
day spa

director of a spa or wellness center
hairstylist
makeup artist
mass market
medi-spa
prestige market
public relations account executive
retail account executive
trainer
wellness center

Online Resources

www.eonline.com/news/556160/getting-to-know-the-glam-squad-hairstylist-marcus-francis

online.wsj.com/news/articles/SB10001424052702303376904579137573642671870

smallbusiness.chron.com/become-successful-makeup-artist-13404.html

www.wwd.com/beauty-industry-news/beauty-features/the-2013-beauty-inc-top-100-7824155

www.huffingtonpost.com/news/organic-beauty-products/

www.prweb.com/releases/2013/1/prweb10363396.htm

www.startupbizhub.com/how-to-start-a-health-and-wellness-business.htm

Discussion Questions

1. Which skin and cosmetic products and treatments do you incorporate into your lifestyle? Describe what the future of these and new products and treatments may be in response to the growth of the wellness industry.

2. Are department-store-branded beauty products superior to generics and drugstore lines? Compare and contrast the differences in product development, merchandising, and promotion.

3. Many of the job descriptions in the beauty and wellness industry compare to those of positions discussed earlier in the chapters on marketing, merchandising, and management. Compare and contrast three positions in this chapter with those requiring similar backgrounds and skills in three other chapters. What would it take for a professional to move from the apparel or accessories sectors of the industry into beauty and wellness?

4. Search the Internet to find out who the major manufacturers of cosmetics and beauty products are. Construct a four-column chart of 10 beauty product corporations, listing the name of the corporation in the first column and the brand names in the second column. In column three, indicate whether the brands are mass or prestige market; in the fourth, list examples of retailers that sell each brand.

Profile: Interview with Spa Director Jeremy McCarthy

Jeremy McCarthy has had a lifelong career of pampering guests at luxury resorts in the spa and hospitality industry, including over a decade with Four Seasons Hotels and Resorts and several years opening and operating the spa at the famed La Costa Resort. As the Director of Global Spa Development and Operations for Starwood Hotels and Resorts, he is responsible for the development of spas across Starwood's many hotel brands around the world.

As the Starwood Spa guru, what is an average working day like?

Unfortunately, I spend a lot of time in my office staring at a computer screen or on a telephone. I think of it as managing by "remote control." I miss the days of working on a resort campus where I could get up and walk around a beautiful property, talk to guests, meet with employees. That being said, I am able to rub elbows with a lot of really smart people in Starwood's headquarters and can liaise with those who work on our hotel brand teams, marketing teams, technology channels, design, architecture, etc. A large part of my job is making sure that all of Starwood's resources are used to drive our spa business just as well as they do the rest of the hotel. There is no way that I could manage our massive portfolio of over 300 spas plus another 100-plus in development without leaning on all of the other resources that Starwood has driving our performance.

So, your team has decided that it's time to build a new spa or revamp an existing one. What comes after this?

First, the decision isn't made by us alone. Usually it comes out of discussion between our ownership groups, our property teams, our regional teams, with feedback from our customers and our associates. Once we know a project will have a spa, we have to determine what the spa will be:

managed by us or by a third party? One of our brands or an external brand? These decisions vary property by property depending on the vision of the owner, the economics of the project, and the demographics of the location. Assuming it will be one of our branded spas, we approach it with an intense design focus. We believe that ensuring the spa is set up right in the beginning is a critical part of its future success.

What, in your opinion, is the up-and-coming place for new hospitality developments?

China, India, Russia, Brazil, and Abu Dhabi are all somewhat hot right now in terms of an infusion of new spa and hospitality projects. A lot of our new development has been and continues to be in Asia (with a lot of that in China), but I am excited to see the wheels turning in North America again. A lot of spa projects that were on hold for the past few years are starting to move again, and Starwood is seeing both new hotel developments in the U.S. as well as owners desiring to convert their existing hotels to one of Starwood's brands. Our reputation for strong brands and our ability to drive business through channels like our SPG loyalty program create opportunities for us even in a down economy.

What would you like to see more of in the health and wellness industry?

I see the health and wellness industry, taken broadly, as highly segmented into three divergent categories: (1) There is the health care component, which is evidence based (interventions and services are substantiated by research on large populations) but mechanical and bureaucratic in its delivery and failing to take into account the holistic nature of human health; (2) then there is the spa side of the coin, which is highly holistic, considers lifestyle and transformation that extends beyond a mere physical intervention, and delivers healing experiences that are enjoyable and that people want to have more

(continued on next page)

(continued)

of. To me, the spa world, however, is all philosophy and no science; and (3) finally, there is the medi-spa side of the industry that is more scientific but less holistic. The medi-spa arena focuses on superficial treatments to enhance beauty and appearance. I classify anti-aging into this section since most anti-aging treatments only impact the appearance of aging, rather than truly extending human flourishing into more years of the lifespan. I would like to see more convergence in the health and wellness industry with more places for healing that are scientific in their approach, holistic in their scope, and nurturing in their delivery. There are very few entities that live in this sweet spot.

There are many emerging design trends for spas; are there any that really stick out for you?

Given that most of the world has just come out of an economic pummeling and are cautiously trying to determine how to move forward, I'm seeing a trend towards smaller spas. I'm embracing the challenge to explore ways to take smaller spaces and create rich, meaningful experiences for our guests. The guest doesn't know how many square feet or how many treatment rooms a spa has, so the key is to make the spa experience just as good in a 200-square-meter spa as it is in a 2,000-square-meter spa.

Jeremy, we know you have a keen interest in psychology. How would you say the health and wellness sectors combine with the field of mental health?

My real interest is in holistic wellness. The reason I study and write about psychology is because I feel like that is the part that is undervalued in most health models. Even in the spa industry, where we talk a lot about "body, mind, spirit," we could do better at really understanding the science behind people's mental and emotional states or their sense of meaning and spirituality. Researching these areas connects me with a great community of like-minded people who are also passionate about human wellness. In our society we tend to compartmentalize both health and science into different departments, so mental health and physical health are viewed separately. Unfortunately, this glosses over the complex interactions that we all experience between body, mind, and emotion. The scientists like to simplify down to categories that are easier to measure, while the holistic approach is to embrace the complexity, but don't bother with trying to understand it or measure it using the scientific method. I think there is room to do both: accept the complexity of human nature and keep pushing the science to evolve so our understanding of it continues to grow.

Courtesy of Jeremy McCarthy

appendix a

Career Tracks and Salaries Chart

Below is a list of online resources for those interested in exploring employment opportunities in the fashion industry. Following the online resources, there is a chart of the fashion career positions that were discussed in the book. They are sorted by median salaries and major cities representing different regions of the U.S.

- *www.wwd.com/wwdcareers* Browse jobs by category; read about featured employers and jobs; check out the student center and internships; and much more.

- *www.payscale.com* Here, you can enter a job title and location to find an annual salary, as well as an average salary.

- *www.fashionista.com/2013/08/fashionistas-first-ever-salary-survey-the-results-are-in-and-theyre-fascinating* Five thousand fashion professionals responded to this survey. Browse through the Web pages to get an idea of average salaries in more than 40 different fashion-related job tracks, including retail and sales, marketing, publicity, design, social media, and creative tracks, such as art departments.

- *www.careerbuilder.com* Lots of good information on job descriptions and salaries at this site. There is an interesting section entitled "8 Jobs for Fashionistas."

- *www.indeed.com* A place to find actual fashion jobs by location. This is a good resource for checking out salaries by company and geography. It also provides prerequisites for hiring.

- *www.stylecareers.com* This site provides a detailed listing of positions available by employer, location, and type of job. It is updated regularly and used by a great number of key employers in fashion manufacturing, wholesaling, and retailing.

For the following chart, www.bls.gov is used as the primary source, www.glassdoor.com (indicated with one asterisk) is used as a secondary source, www.fashionista.com as a third source for New York City (indicated with two asterisks), and www.indeed.com as a fourth source (indicated with three asterisks). For all positions, a bachelor's degree is a prerequisite for employment.

Job Title	Location	Annual Mean Wage
Account Coordinator, Beauty (Ch 16)	New York	$37,720*
	Dallas	$32,480*
	Los Angeles	$35,000*
	Chicago	$36,784*
Account Executive, Beauty (Ch 16)	New York	$54,280*
	Dallas	$59,354*
	Los Angeles	$59,943*
	Chicago	$53,161*

Accountant (Ch 5)	New York Dallas Los Angeles Chicago	$93,480 $77,100 $78,090 $74,460
Advertising/Promotions Director (Ch 8)	New York Dallas Los Angeles Chicago	$150,000*** $105,000*** $110,000*** $123,000***
Aesthetician (Ch 16)	New York Dallas Los Angeles Chicago	$36,930 $30,630 $32,180 $31,810
Architect (Ch 15)	New York Dallas Los Angeles Chicago	$80,100 $80,570 $90,300 $73,060
Archivist/Technician, Museum (Ch 14)	New York Dallas Los Angeles Chicago	$58,590 $47,580 $49,300 $42,990
Art Director (Ch 9)	New York Dallas Los Angeles Chicago	$132,980 $84,720 $116,800 $82,510
Assistant Buyer, Retail (Ch 10)	New York Dallas Los Angeles Chicago	$45,000** $44,332* $43,645* $51,366*
Assistant/Associate Fashion Designer (Ch 6)	New York Dallas Los Angeles Chicago	$35,000*** $29,000*** $31,000*** $35,000***
Assistant Importer/Agent (Ch 3)	New York Dallas Los Angeles Chicago	$47,000*** $39,000*** $41,000*** $47,000***
Assistant Museum Curator (Ch 14)	New York Dallas Los Angeles Chicago	$45,124 $32,090 $37,878 $27,540
Assistant Store Manager (Ch 11)	New York Dallas Los Angeles Chicago	$45,865* $42,343* $44,360* $42,322

Blogger (Ch 12)	New York	$74,000***
	Dallas	$63,000***
	Los Angeles	$66,000***
	Chicago	$61,000***
Buyer/Fashion Merchandiser (Ch 3, 10)	New York	$71,280
	Dallas	$69,000
	Los Angeles	$55,960
	Chicago	$53,570
Chief Marketing Officer, Retail (Ch 9)	New York	$186,000***
	Dallas	$157,000***
	Los Angeles	$165,000***
	Chicago	$185,000***
Chief Financial Officer, Retail (Ch 5)	New York	$182,960
	Dallas	$135,490
	Los Angeles	$146,650
	Chicago	$132,710
Colorist, Textiles (Ch 2)	New York	$37,000***
	Dallas	$35,000***
	Los Angeles	$37,000***
	Chicago	$42,000***
Company Salesperson/ Representative (Ch 5)	New York	$80,780
	Dallas	$64,180
	Los Angeles	$61,790
	Chicago	$65,080
Copywriter, Corporate (Ch 9)	New York	$74,000***
	Dallas	$63,000***
	Los Angeles	$66,000***
	Chicago	$74,000***
Costume Designer (Ch 13)	New York	$66,000***
	Dallas	$56,000***
	Los Angeles	$59,000***
	Chicago	$66,000***
Counter Manager, Beauty (Ch 16)	*See Account Executive, Beauty*	
Creative Fashion Director (Ch 1)	New York	$191,000**
	Dallas	$105,000***
	Los Angeles	$110,000***
	Chicago	$123,000***
Customer Service Manager (Ch 11)	New York	$40,280
	Dallas	$31,230
	Los Angeles	$38,020
	Chicago	$37,570
Department Manager (Ch 11)	New York	$36,613
	Dallas	$31,449
	Los Angeles	$33,722
	Chicago	$41,240

Digital Media Director, Corporate (Ch 12)	New York	$141,000***
	Dallas	$119,000***
	Los Angeles	$125,000***
	Chicago	$140,000***
Digital Media Artist (Ch 12)	New York	$75,400
	Dallas	$70,000
	Los Angeles	$70,190
	Chicago	$64,520
Distribution Manager/Allocator (Ch 10)	New York	$54,623
	Dallas	$54,844
	Los Angeles	$56,300
	Chicago	$53,060
Divisional Merchandising Manager (Ch 10)	New York	$124,000***
	Dallas	$105,000***
	Los Angeles	$110,000***
	Chicago	$123,000***
Fashion Designer (Ch 6)	New York	$80,620
	Dallas	$62,120
	Los Angeles	$71,910
	Chicago	$66,200
Fashion Photostylist, Entry Level (Ch 8)	New York	$23,000***
	Dallas	$19,000***
	Los Angeles	$20,000***
	Chicago	$23,000***
Fashion Show/Special Events Planner (Ch 8)	New York	$61,520
	Dallas	$54,550
	Los Angeles	$58,350
	Chicago	$49,190
Fashion Stylist for Television/Film/Video (Ch 13)	New York	$155,000***
	Dallas	$131,000***
	Los Angeles	$138,000***
	Chicago	$154,000***
Fashion/Trend Forecaster (Ch 1)	New York	$130,400
	Dallas	$118,710
	Los Angeles	$115,530
	Chicago	$102,820
Fashion Photographer, Retail (Ch 13)	New York	$55,780
	Dallas	$35,650
	Los Angeles	$62,780
	Chicago	$33,020
Fashion Stylist/Personal Shopper, Retail (Ch 9)	New York	$44,914
	Dallas	$39,044
	Los Angeles	$39,224
	Chicago	$43,000***

General Merchandising Manager	New York	$141,840
(Ch 10)	Dallas	$119,530
	Los Angeles	$125,980
	Chicago	$93,190
Graphic Designer	New York	$65,000
(Ch 12)	Dallas	$44,750
	Los Angeles	$57,100
	Chicago	$52,650
Hairstylist, Salon	New York	$31,960
(Ch 16)	Dallas	$30,880
	Los Angeles	$27,960
	Chicago	$28,920
Hiring Manager	New York	$55,415*
(Ch 5)	Dallas	$48,797*
	Los Angeles	$53,123*
	Chicago	$47,103*
Human Resources Manager/Director, Corporate	New York	$136,480
(Ch 5)	Dallas	$123,260
	Los Angeles	$115,840
	Chicago	$103,050
Import Production Coordinator	New York	$49,000***
(Ch 3)	Dallas	$42,000***
	Los Angeles	$44,000***
	Chicago	$49,000***
Import Manager	New York	$74,000***
(Ch 3)	Dallas	$63,000***
	Los Angeles	$66,000***
	Chicago	$74,000***
Interior Designer	New York	$66,600
(Ch 15)	Dallas	$59,320
	Los Angeles	$60,420
	Chicago	$54,040
Licensing Director, Corporate	New York	$140,000***
(Ch 3)	Dallas	$119,000***
	Los Angeles	$125,000***
	Chicago	$140,000***
Makeup Artist	New York	$44,000***
(Ch 16)	Dallas	$37,000***
	Los Angeles	$39,000***
	Chicago	$44,000***
Mall Manager	New York	$49,000***
(Ch 15)	Dallas	$42,000***
	Los Angeles	$44,000***
	Chicago	$49,000***

Manufacturer's Representative (Ch 5)	New York	$96,450
	Dallas	$75,380
	Los Angeles	$80,780
	Chicago	$73,497
Media Planner (Ch 8)	New York	$51,035*
	Dallas	$41,876
	Los Angeles	$48,563*
	Chicago	$47,923*
Merchandise Coordinator (Ch 5)	New York	$48,092*
	Dallas	$43,336*
	Los Angeles	$33,428
	Chicago	$41,234
Merchandise Planner (Ch 10)	New York	$86,275*
	Dallas	$65,460*
	Los Angeles	$48,182
	Chicago	$46,734
Merchandising/Management Trainee (Ch 10)	New York	$55,000***
	Dallas	$46,000***
	Los Angeles	$49,000***
	Chicago	$54,000***
Marketing Manager/Director (Ch 9)	New York	$177,400
	Dallas	$134,410
	Los Angeles	$136,350
	Chicago	$115,530
Model (Ch 13)	New York	$42,940
	Dallas	$36,789
	Los Angeles	$41,220
	Chicago	$27,280
Model /Talent Agency Director (Ch 13)	New York	$100,240
	Dallas	$78,620
	Los Angeles	$131,540
	Chicago	$72,310
Museum Conservator (Ch 14)	New York	$58,590
	Dallas	$48,620
	Los Angeles	$49,300
	Chicago	$42,990
Museum Director (Ch 14)	New York	$73,790
	Dallas	$42,960
	Los Angeles	$70,130
	Chicago	$51,750
Museum Curator (Ch 14)	New York	$83,000***
	Dallas	$70,000***
	Los Angeles	$73,000***
	Chicago	$82,000***

Operations Manager (Ch 11)	New York	$98,000***
	Dallas	$83,000***
	Los Angeles	$87,000***
	Chicago	$98,000***
Patternmaker (Ch 4)	New York	$63,410
	Dallas	$45,947
	Los Angeles	$55,160
	Chicago	$31,260
Stylist, Retail (Ch 9)	New York	$31,000***
	Dallas	$26,000***
	Los Angeles	$27,000***
	Chicago	$31,000***
Product Development Manager/Director, Beauty Industry (Ch 16)	New York	$89,610
	Dallas	$89,639
	Los Angeles	$86,198
	Chicago	$81,279
Product Development Manager/Director, Wholesale/Manufacturing (Ch 7)	New York	$127,000***
	Dallas	$107,000***
	Los Angeles	$113,000***
	Chicago	$126,000***
Product Development Manager/Director, Retail (Ch 7)	New York	$106,322*
	Dallas	$87,375
	Los Angeles	$80,184
	Chicago	$87,742*
Production Assistant (Ch 4)	New York	$38,820*
	Dallas	$32,374
	Los Angeles	$32,516*
	Chicago	$30,000***
Production Manager (Ch 4)	New York	$72,281*
	Dallas	$58,900*
	Los Angeles	$72,706*
	Chicago	$66,565*
Production Planner (Ch 4)	New York	$52,520
	Dallas	$46,810
	Los Angeles	$48,880
	Chicago	$45,730
Promotion Director/Manager, (Ch 8 and 10)	New York	$166,140
	Dallas	$90,140
	Los Angeles	$143,990
	Chicago	$132,730
Public Relations Manager (Ch 8)	New York	$70,320
	Dallas	$57,000
	Los Angeles	$73,190
	Chicago	$67,190

Quality Control Manager (Ch 4)	New York	$55,441
	Dallas	$54,366
	Los Angeles	$56,980
	Chicago	$52,848
Regional (District) Store Manager (Ch 11)	New York	$71,000***
	Dallas	$60,000***
	Los Angeles	$63,000***
	Chicago	$71,000***
Resource Room Director/Reference Librarian (Ch 2)	New York	$48,240
	Dallas	$45,410
	Los Angeles	$41,349
	Chicago	$41,000
Retail Account Executive, Beauty (Ch 16)	New York	$105,000***
	Dallas	$89,000***
	Los Angeles	$93,000***
	Chicago	$105,000***
Retail Store Owner/Entrepreneur (Ch 11)	New York	$111,000***
	Dallas	$104,000***
	Los Angeles	$98,000***
	Chicago	$110,000***
Security Manager, Retail Store (Ch 3)	New York	$27,000***
	Dallas	$22,000***
	Los Angeles	$24,000***
	Chicago	$26,000***
Showroom Manager/Sales (Ch 5)	New York	$96,000***
	Dallas	$81,000***
	Los Angeles	$85,000***
	Chicago	$95,000***
Social Media Manager, Midlevel (Ch 8)	New York	$76,000***
	Dallas	$63,000***
	Los Angeles	$67,000***
	Chicago	$75,000***
Sourcing Manager (Ch 3)	New York	$116,244*
	Dallas	$105,553
	Los Angeles	$110,720*
	Chicago	$119,081*
Specification Technician (Ch 6)	New York	$85,158*
	Dallas	$83,378*
	Los Angeles	$71,813*
	Chicago	$64,515*
Store Manager (Ch 11)	New York	$65,400**
	Dallas	$49,000***
	Los Angeles	$52,000***
	Chicago	$58,000***

Technical Designer (Ch 6)	New York	$79,000***
	Dallas	$67,000***
	Los Angeles	$70,000***
	Chicago	$79,000***
Store Planning Director (Ch 10)	New York	$110,000***
	Dallas	$93,000***
	Los Angeles	$97,000***
	Chicago	$109,000***
Technical Designer (Ch 7)	New York	$79,000***
	Dallas	$67,000***
	Los Angeles	$70,000***
	Chicago	$79,000***
Textile/Apparel Cutter (Ch 4)	New York	$26,130
	Dallas	$25,190
	Los Angeles	$23,810
	Chicago	$26,370
Textile Designer (Ch 2)	New York	$80,000***
	Dallas	$68,000***
	Los Angeles	$71,000***
	Chicago	$80,000***
Textile Engineer (Ch 2)	New York	$96,000***
	Dallas	$81,000***
	Los Angeles	$85,000***
	Chicago	$95,000***
Traffic Manager (Ch 4)	New York	$74,000***
	Dallas	$63,000***
	Los Angeles	$66,000***
	Chicago	$74,000***
Visual Merchandising Assistant, Entry Level (Ch 15)	New York	$38,220
	Dallas	$28,980
	Los Angeles	$34,610
	Chicago	$28,320
Visual Merchandising Director/Manager (Ch 15)	New York	$86,000***
	Dallas	$73,000***
	Los Angeles	$77,000***
	Chicago	$86,000***
Web Site Designer/Developer (Ch 12)	New York	$80,750
	Dallas	$71,080
	Los Angeles	$68,030
	Chicago	$66,330
Writer/Journalist (Ch 12)	New York	$57,000***
	Dallas	$49,000***
	Los Angeles	$51,000***
	Chicago	$57,000***

appendix b

Résumé Tips, Interview Guidelines, Employer Research, and Résumé Samples

The Résumé

Your Résumé Should:

- *Be more an outline than a narrative.* Think of it as a calling card or an offering to a prospective buyer. Keep it simple and to the point. Tried-and-true résumé tips and a sample résumés follow to assist you in making your calling card a memorable one that spurs the employer to contact you immediately.

- *Be specific, particularly in the Objective section.* Most interviewers do not want to conduct career counseling. Know what types of career positions you are prepared for and want to pursue before you send your résumé, and indicate this under the *Objective* heading. If you are interested in more than one type of position, develop different objectives and design separate résumés for each type of position, focusing on the needs of the employer and the specific career track.

- *Be factual.* Tell the truth and nothing but the truth. Do not get caught having to explain a point that is not clear and does not have support.

- *Read like the trailer for a great movie.* The résumé should help you get through the door without telling the whole story. You need to be ready to jump in and to fill in the gaps during phone or online screenings and personal interviews.

Support Your Résumé With:

- *A good letter of application* (often referred to as a cover letter). It should be short and to the point. It should show that you have done your homework and know a thing or two about the company you are pursuing. Make sure the recipient knows what you want (e.g., a full-time job, an internship, an informational interview, a contact, etc.) and how you have prepared to succeed.

- *A good listing of references.* Ask references for permission before including them on your reference listing. Include the job title and complete contact information (e.g., postal mailing address, e-mail address, and telephone number) of each reference. Some job seekers add a brief description of their relationship and work experiences with the reference (e.g., intern, part-time sales associate, etc.).

- *Excellent target employers provided by your contacts.* Ask alumni (graduates of your institution); they want to help if they can. Ask family, friends, faculty, guest speakers, internship contacts, former employers, and hometown contacts. This is how you develop your network, one that you build throughout your career.

- *The informational interview.* Identify key professionals within your target career path and schedule meetings to learn more about the business or the career path. Contact people in both human resources and other areas. The more people in support of you, the better your opportunity for success.

Tried-and-True Résumé Tips

No matter if your résumé is scanned and e-mailed, sent through the postal system, or hand-delivered, its content is most important. Follow these tried-and-true résumé tips as you work toward résumé perfection.

- Always use spellcheck.
- Begin with a goal or an objective. It should include key words that are pulled from the position description and/or job advertisement.
- For *Education*, include your major, minor, and month and year of graduation. You may include your grade point average. Some employment professionals suggest listing the grade point average only if it is 3.0 or above on a 4.0 scale. Most professionals also recommend that you do not include high school information if you are a college student or graduate.
- *Work Experience* should include internships and part-time jobs (within reason).
- If you are lacking relevant employment experience, include information about college projects that would relate to the position for which you are applying.
- Include extracurricular activities, keeping in mind these tips:
  - Identify the skills and experiences you will need in your target field and look for organizations on campus where you will get these.
  - If you hold an officer position within the organization, or head up various committees within the organization, mention these.
  - Have a variety of extracurricular experiences to demonstrate your ability to work with a range of people.
  - Be involved throughout your college career, not just during your final year in school.
  - Many companies place a high value on service activities, such as volunteer work on campus, in your community, or in the world community.
- List specific skills related to your career goals, such as computer skills, language fluency, international experiences, etc.
- List outcomes whenever possible. For example, if you led a fundraising project for a philanthropic organization, state the amount of money raised and the name and a brief description of the charity.
- You may choose to list highlights of your coursework (courses that relate to the position) under the *Education* section, if you do not have adequate experience to fill a one-page résumé. If you do have enough experiences to effectively fill a one-page résumé, courses can be listed on a separate sheet of paper, along with a brief description if the course titles do not adequately explain them. You may want to have this list in case the interviewer asks for this information.
- Keep the résumé to one page. Although you may have many great experiences in college, you likely have not had enough yet to warrant more than a one-page résumé.
- For hard copies, use light-colored, standard size (8 1/2" x 11") paper. Use high-quality paper and a good printer. Choose white, eggshell, beige, or light gray paper. Avoid grainy paper.
- Place your name and contact information at the top (in the header) of each page after the first one, such as a reference listing.
- If you are sending your résumé via postal mail, do not fold the résumé; send it in a flat envelope. Do not use staples.

Interview Guidelines

Planning for the Interview

- Be prepared. Research the company *and* the industry *before* the interview. Know exactly when and where to go for the interview well ahead of time.
- Come prepared with good questions to ask and know the good questions the interviewer will likely ask (it's even better if you know the answers).
- Be polite and courteous. You are building your professional reputation.
- Think of the interview in the following segments:

The Time Breakdown of an Interview by Minutes

0–5	Size it up. Be impressive. You are both evaluating each other and first impressions count.
5–20	Sell yourself. This is the part when you explain your résumé. Know which parts of your background to stress. Do not be shy about your accomplishments—specifically, outcomes. Describe yourself and your experiences, but remember the time. You will be judged on how well you organize your thoughts. If the interviewer asks you a yes or no question, answer it that way. Watch and listen to know if he or she wants you to elaborate.
20–25	Let the interviewer sell you. Ask questions about the organization. Why is it such a great place to work? Remember, this is an important decision for you.
25–30	Wrap it up. Determine what will happen next. Will the interviewer call you, or should you contact him or her? When?

- A well-written thank-you letter is essential after the interview.

Points to Keep in Mind for the Interview

1. Be strategic and focused.
2. Even if you do not know exactly what you want, sound like you at least have an idea.
3. Really understand the reality of the workplace and the reality of really working.
4. Service businesses in the fashion industry are good places to look. Be creative.
5. New industries and businesses are often the ones seeking new employees with fresh ideas.
6. Think about the environments in which you would like to work (e.g., a large company, a big-city location, a formal structure, etc.).
7. Find a good training program. Down the road you will benefit greatly from a good foundation. Sales and retail management often have the best programs. Internships can also provide excellent training.
8. Consider the merits of graduate school. Then, consider working first. Evaluate the pros and cons of each. More and more young professionals have advanced degrees. They are likely the people you will compete with on the career ladder. In contrast, you may want to

gain some experience in the workplace in order to add personal and professional value to further education. You may even find an employer who will pay for graduate coursework.

9. Whether you are completing or have completed a bachelor's or master's degree, consider yourself fortunate to have a solid education. Your college or university has provided you with a strong foundation for lifelong learning and diverse exposure. Recruiters appreciate that.

10. Enjoy yourself. Have fun! Sell yourself; you are your most important and valued resource. Many doors can be opened for you, but it is up to you to sell yourself in order to walk through them.

11. Be realistic. Send out many more letters of application and résumés than you believe you will need. There is much competition in the job market. The more opportunities you have, the higher your chances of having several positions offered, giving you the chance to choose from among them.

Researching Employers

Why Research Employers?

Researching prospective employers is—surprisingly—a frequently overlooked step when applying for a job. It is easy to get excited when you believe you have found the perfect opportunity; however, not digging deep into an employer's current and past situations and its reputation can prove to be a costly mistake. You can be certain that employers are checking your references, online profiles, and college credentials before extending an offer. You would be remiss not to do the same with any prospective hiring organization. The more you know about a company, the better you will be able to communicate your value to this employer during your interview. The hard work that you put into your research will pay off by reflecting your interest, confidence, and enthusiasm to employers, and providing you with the confidence that this is a secure employment opportunity. Taking the time to learn about a company and then sharing what you learned about it is a form of flattery to company representatives. Before you complete your letter of application and send out your résumé, we will take a closer look at why you should research employers, what to look for, and how to investigate like a detective.

The majority of college graduates have held some type of employment; some have had wonderful experiences on these jobs, whereas others may have been wondering what the employer was thinking, how bad it could get, and when it would be over. In the latter case, they learned the hard way to spend dedicated time learning about an employer before applying for a job. Why should you do some investigative work on prospective employers?

- *To determine if the company is a fit for you.* You may find you do not particularly like a specific career path in the industry. You may dig up unfortunate corporate digital dirt, or uncover information on poor employee relations.

- *To decide if you are right for the company.* Some companies or industries may not be the right fit for your skill sets, values, or corporate culture preferences. It is also possible to find that you are not really interested in the company's products or services. Be sure to consider your goals, desires, and ethics to see how they fit given the information you have revealed.

- *To help tailor your résumé and letter of application to the position.* Knowing specifically what makes the company successful can turn your application into the winning ticket.

- *To give you the information required to effectively address the organization's needs.* Knowing why the company needs to hire is key to addressing how you can help the company.

- *To help you prepare effective interview questions.* Knowing specific industry information or advanced product knowledge can get you closer to an offer as you impress the interviewer with insightful questions and answers.

- *To demonstrate sincere interest in the company.* A common interview question is "Why do you want to work for us?" Having an educated answer puts you ahead of the competition. One of the most important ways to distinguish yourself in an interview is to speak knowledgeably about the organization.

- *To educate yourself about a particular career path in the industry.* Perhaps this job is in a new sector of the industry for you. Get in the know before writing your résumé and shopping for an interview.

When to Research Employers

The best time to research employers is before you prepare your résumé and letter of application to request an interview with a company. By doing some due diligence early, you can quickly rule out firms and positions that do not match your personal needs, academic requirements, or desired career path.

Where to Conduct Employer Research

Conducting employer research is much like preparing a college assignment or project. The idea is to develop two lists: one of companies for which you are interested in working and another of resources for researching businesses. Next are examples of a few good places to start your list of resources to help your investigation of prospective employers:

- *Corporate Web site.* Look for industry information, product or service details, and management information. Most corporate sites indicate company age, size, ownership, locations, and leadership or management details, often in the "About the Company" or "About us" link at the top or bottom of the Web site's landing page. Check the Web site to see if the company is public or private. A review of annual reports may reveal interesting corporate details, such as the firm's financial situation, health of the industry, mission statement, and number of employees.

- *Google.* Search forums, Web sites, blogs, and online articles that will enable you to see what others have to say about the company's products, services, and employee relations. You may be surprised. Take these as they are—opinions and comments. Make a decision that is based on facts, yet allows room for majority opinion.

- *Better Business Bureau.* This organization can alert you to complaints against companies in specific geographic areas or cities. You may want to contact them to see if your prospective employer is on the list.

- *Consumer and trade publications.* Research the employer's industry activity through print, in addition to Internet sources. Read magazines, newspapers, trade publications, and journals related to the field and organization.

- *Trade associations.* Is the company affiliated with an association? Consult association Web sites to see if the prospective employing organization is in good standing and how it contributes to the profession.

- *Chambers of Commerce.* You may want to begin by contacting the Chambers of Commerce in the communities where the companies you are interested in are located. You will often find a searchable comprehensive directory online.

- *Public relations and promotions.* Check out any product or service advertisements the company runs in the media. Locate press releases about the company. Many companies have these at their Web sites; however, keep in mind that these are usually positive reflections of the firm. Employer recruitment brochures are a great marketing tool for the company and provide a good overview for the prospective employee. Brochures and sales flyers also offer a good look at the company.

- *Former or current employee references.* Do you know any current or former employees? Ask them why they left, who supervised them, and if they would ever work there again.

Types of Information to Uncover Through Employer Research

Begin by locating general information about each company in which you are interested. Keep an accurate record of what you learn. If you are ready to go onto the Internet to begin your research, keep the following in mind:

1. Know what you are looking for before you go online. Keep a list beside you so that you can check off items as you locate them. An electronic spreadsheet is ideal to post information as you find it. It is easy to get frustrated or disinterested in the research phase when you don't keep organized records.
2. Bookmark major Web sites as you come across them. Create folders to organize the sites.
3. Although the Internet is an invaluable research tool, the library is still one of the best places to locate information. The reference librarian at your college, university, or local library should be able to point you in the direction of many useful directories and indexes. Examples of resources that you will find in the library are *Dunn and Bradstreet* reports, *Standard & Poor's* corporation records and rating services, *World Business Directory*, *Hoovers*, and *Ward's Business Directory*. Now that you know where to look for general information, you may want to format a spreadsheet of which details to uncover.
4. Consider these variables when researching an employer:
   - Mission, philosophy, and objectives of the company
   - Source(s) of funding, including assets, earnings, and losses
   - Company ownership (e.g., private or public, sole proprietorship or partnership, foreign or domestic ownership, etc.)
   - Company divisions or subsidiaries and their locations
   - Board of directors or advisory board
   - Reputation of the company
   - History or background and age of company
   - Products (to include services) that the company sells or provides

- Target market or clientele list
- Strategies and goals
- Market positioning or repositioning efforts
- Areas of specialization
- New projects and major achievements
- Size of the company and number of employees
- Patterns of growth or decline
- Forecast of future growth
- Recent issues or events (e.g., layoffs or hiring, closings or expansion, etc.)
- Number of employees
- Location of the company headquarters and length of time it has been established there
- Office/facility environment
- Personnel policies
- Types of people employed and from where employees are recruited
- Corporate culture
- Health of the industry
- Compensation and benefits for entry-level employees
- Career path or promotion opportunities within the company

Be sure to consider other details specific to the types of positions in which you are most interested. It is important not to be slow, vague, or inaccurate about this process, as any employer worth your time and effort on the job is well worth your time and effort now.

The Final Word on Researching Before Sending Out Your Résumés

Finding the right job is work. Researching a prospective employer is work, but the results can be very rewarding, especially if you find the ideal positions based on your findings. It just makes sense to do some homework on a company before sending out résumés and letters of application to just any firm you hear about or stumble across. You are not simply applying for any job. This is the start of your career, and you are determining who will be the provider of your paycheck in the future. You are your most important investment of time and energy. Next, samples of résumés for a range of fashion careers are presented.

Sample Résumés

The résumé of a product developer needs to illustrate abilities in trend forecasting, knowledge of various target markets, and strong analytical, negotiation, and leadership skills. In addition, the product developer must show a detail orientation, which is important when communicating with factories, tracking sample status, calculating costs, and communicating details to the merchandising/design team and/or factories. Creative and business skills are required, with problem-solving abilities in both areas. The ability to work under pressure is essential. To follow is a résumé example for a product developer position.

JARED
BAJKOWSKI
(beɪ-kaʊ-ski)

Objective
To secure an internship in product development and trend forecasting in which I can test and apply skills in a way that allows continued development and benefits the firm.

Employment
Intern
Cotton, Inc., May 17 - Aug. 2, 2014; New York, NY
- Created a 20-page spring/summer 2016 menswear forecast for the Product Trend Analysis (PTA) team that consisted of macro trend, color, silhouette, fabric, and print/pattern analysis
- Researched, analyzed, and synthesized over 50 text sources and over 400 runway and street style images from spring 2014 shows in Milan, Paris, and London.
- Explored the New York City streets, taking street style and art exhibit photos to inspire the PTA team.

Intern
BridgeBlue Sourcing Partners, Jan. – May 2014, Springfield, MO
- Developed social media and video marketing strategies for home products line
- Created trend forecasting and analysis materials through visual media
- Collaborated with teammates through entire creative theming and product development process by editing/revising blog post copy and writing copy of my own

Intern
Baldwin Denim, Standard Style, LLC., Jun. 2013 - Aug. 2013; Kansas City, MO
- Cultivated relationships with clients to create a community dynamic around brand and product
- Conveyed unique selling points of brand to clients through superior product knowledge
- Developed styling expertise through exercise and practical application for clientele

Education
University of Kansas, GPA 3.38; 4.0 scale
Fall 2011-Present
Anticipated Graduation: May 2015
Bachelor of Science – Entrepreneurship

Awards, Honors, Community Experience
Inter-Fraternity Council
President, Fall 2013 – Present
- Administrate and govern student community of over 1,000 members
- Coordinate executive council of 10 vice-presidents and $30,000 budget
- Increased annual IFC membership by 12%, exceeding a goal of 10% (422 to 472)

Pi Kappa Phi
President, Fall 2012- Fall 2013
- Applied for and won the Fraternity and Sorority Life Chapter of the Year Award for 2013
- Oversaw 27 officers and committee chairs and a budget of $20,000
- Increased chapter membership from 40 to 70 over one year

Fraternity and Sorority Life Outstanding Male Sophomore of the Year, 2012

Skills
Software Proficiency: Microsoft Word, Excel 2013; Adobe Photoshop, Illustrator, InDesign CS6

A résumé for a digital media artist or graphic designer should be eye catching and creative. A résumé in this field is viewed as an extension of a candidate's work. Social media should be highlighted, and the résumé writer's own social media should be representative of the image/brand she or he is intending to convey. Social media fluency and incorporating a three-dimensional presence through the résumé will help the prepared candidate secure an interview. The résumé will open the interviewer's door, but the portfolio (online, more frequently) often lands a job in this field. It is okay to be different, but be certain to show familiarity with a wide array of techniques and software skills within your portfolio, as well as branding your own unique design style. Next, a résumé example for a digital media artist or graphic designer in fashion is presented.

Coty Beasley
Graphic Designer
& Web Developer

 Email
design@beasleycreative.com

 Telephone
816.200.2889

 Address
1234 E Madison Ave
Kansas City, Mo 64138

 LinkedIn
linkedin.com/in/cbeasleyb

 Facebook
facebook.com/beasleycreative

 Twitter
twitter.com/beasley

I am currently looking for freelance and consultant work.

My Work

For more info and examples of my work, please visit

beasleycreative.com

Personal Statement

 Well-rounded designer with extensive experience in multimedia. Enthusiastic, intuitive, insightful, and hardworking.

Views technology as an incredible tool for improving communication between people and understands that above all, the user experience is key.

Great in a pinch and knowledgeable in current industry shifts and trends.

References

Brent Mariott - CEO
reference@domain.com
Brent managed me directly at MIS Technologies.

 Joan Varner - Accountant
reference@domain.com
Joan managed me indirectly at The Bobblehead.

 Roberto Cruz - Account Manager
reference@domain.com
Roberto is a colleague that works for Ikros.

 Steven Ashley - System Admin
reference@domain.com
Steven is a friend who works for the USDA.

Education and Work

○ Education ● Work Experience

Fort Osage High - High School Diploma
2003 - 2007
Took advanced coursework in desktop publishing, photography, and biosciences.

MIS Technologies - Webmaster, Creative Manager & Consultant
September 2007 - Present
As webmaster and creative manager, I maintained the company's server, designed marketing graphics, maintained websites, and created an internet presence. I also created flash animations, optimized web graphics, and programmed UIs for control units.

M.C.C. - Associate of Arts
2007 - 2009
Additional coursework in graphic design, marketing, and web design.

The Bobblehead LLC - Webmaster & Creative Manager
September 2008 - Present
I maintained company servers, created promotional artwork, designed web content, managed the company's website, and oversaw all internet marketing including SEO and SMO. We rose from page ten on Google to page one in a year.

Beasley Creative - CEO/Owner
July 2009 - Present
Specialization in UI design for web, mobile, and applications, always keeping UX in mind. Best-practice knowledge leads to groundbreaking presentations. Understanding the implications of the web and its medium and its ability to reach very targeted audiences.

U.M.K.C. - B.A. Communications (Emph. Film & Media Arts)
2009 - 2012
Additional coursework in graphic design, marketing, and web development.

Ikros / Crossover Graphics - Technical Account Manager
July 2010 - October 2010
I was responsible for maintaining client relationships, overseeing web projects, developing detailed project mock-ups and wireframes, reinforcing and furthering industry-standard UX practices, and building department processes for an online presence and an intranet.

Technical Expertise

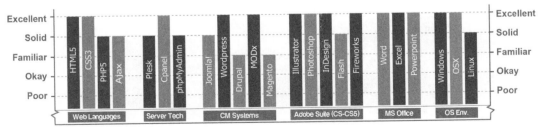

A résumé for the public relations director of a fashion company should be both creative and informational. The fashion public relations specialist interacts with media and other outlets to ensure that the company's products and corporate image are consistently presented in a positive manner in the public eye. The public relations specialist strategizes new and creative ways to gain the attention of the media, often generating buzz by holding press conferences and events, working with publication editors and bloggers, and sending press releases. The résumé needs to show that the writer can develop and cultivate relationships with media counterparts. It must also illustrate excellent communication and interpersonal skills, high energy, fashion knowledge, and the ability to multitask.

ELLEN DIANNE WORTHINGTON

COMMUNICATIONS & PUBLIC RELATIONS EXPERT HIGHLY SKILLED IN WRITING, SPEAKING, COACHING AND FOSTERING AWARD-WINNING EMPLOYEE WORK ENVIRONMENTS. TWENTY YEARS TOTAL EXPERIENCE IN VARIOUS CHANNELS OF PROMOTIONS, DESIGN AND PUBLIC RELATIONS. DEDICATED, LOYAL EMPLOYEE; AWARDED MULTIPLE PROMOTIONS WITH AN INNOVATIVE, FAST-GROWING COMPANY. PROFICIENT WITH NUMEROUS DESKTOP-PUBLISHING, SPREADSHEET, AND COMMUNICATIONS SOFTWARE APPLICATIONS ON BOTH MAC OS AND PC PLATFORMS.

CAREER HISTORY

VERMILLION CORPORATION

2005-PRESENT • COMMUNICATIONS DIRECTOR
- Oversee all communication vehicles to 3,000 employees including CEO & VP messages, newsletters, videos, brochures
- Direct the FORTUNE 100 Best Companies to Work For application program
- Facilitate celebrity promotional events
- Advise clients and colleagues at all levels on how to best communicate key messages to employees; strategize proactive and reactive plans
- 2006, 2012 ADDY Award Winner

1999-2005 • HR SPECIALIST
- Published two-way communication vehicle on intranet for VP of Operations
- Implemented company-wide employee focus groups

May 1999 • COMMUNICATIONS COORDINATOR
- Facilitated cross-functional teams
- Executed efficient communication plans
- Designed, developed, and maintained company intranet

1997-1999 • GRAPHIC DESIGNER
- Designed all corporate publications
- Coordinated various web and print projects
- Led press runs for internal publications

<1997
Previous work experience includes serving as the MARKETING DIRECTOR for the Williamson County Illinois Tourism Bureau

EDUCATION
B.S. Psychology • University of Tennessee

An effective résumé for a buyer or merchandiser should highlight the following qualities: an eye for fashion and an understanding of the target market, the ability to keep up with the latest trends, skills in organization and interpersonal relationships, the ability to work under pressure, and strong mathematical abilities. Following is an example of a merchandiser's résumé.

NATHAN GREGORY CATES

Objective
Obtain a position in a growth-oriented firm where I can contribute to the bottom line.

Related Industry Experience

Bombfell, Inc., New York, NY   **June 2013 - Present**

E-Commerce Merchandise Assistant – Assist Head Buyer (HB) with all necessary tasks, manage calendar, schedule appointments for Market week both locally and nationally; partner with HB to procure buying selections and assortments for improved sales performance; coordinate assortment to enable best merchandising for multiple brands and classification parings with HB; execute and manage purchase order process from entry to maintenance and receiving logistics; mediate logistics between vendor and 3rd party warehouse, resolving all discrepancies; continually update vendor guidelines and ensure follow through.

E-Commerce Coordinator and Stylist – Created and maintained digital and physical filing system/library for financials, line sheets, and all essential buying materials enhancing workplace efficiency; excelled in vendor relations and new brand procurement; delivered repeat and referral business while increasing projected revenue by over 2x in less than 6 months; directed commercial and editorial photo shoots focusing on web strategy and execution; assisted developers to increase programming effectiveness by sourcing glitches and creating web enhancements; strategized with marketing team to implement ideas for user acquisition, increased over 3x.

E-Commerce Intern – Met daily styling goals for extensively growing clientele base; handled daily customer service requests promptly and accurately; maintained stock room organization; increased social media presence by over 2.2x in 3 months, achieved through planned content distribution, search optimization, and strategic user interaction.

Aldo Group, Springfield, MO   **March 2012 – May 2013**

Senior Sales Lead/Key Holder – Excelled in training both new managers and brand associates; aided in the merchandise planning and set EOD/EOW/EOM/EOY financial objectives; ensured brand associates met sales quotas and followed corporate regulations; coordinated frequent communications with regional and district management; conducted store opening and closing procedures directly under management.

Brand Representative – During the six months before promotion to Sales Lead, accomplished personal and corporate initiatives resulting in consistently performing with some of the highest numbers within our district and nationally, maintaining excellent customer relations as noted by consumer feedback; addressed customer concerns/queries regarding purchases, returns and repairs; stimulated sales via visual merchandising and extensive brand/product quality knowledge.

Freelance Stylist/Personal Shopper   **August 2009 - Present**

Style experience led to TV spot on KOLR 10 News as a style consultant; produced multiple fashion shows, raised over $10,000 to effectively execute senior fashion show; assisted the Dean of the College of Business to educate business students about appropriate industry attire. Success led to evaluating the Dean's personal image/wardrobe issues, worked as her Personal Shopper/Stylist; developed costumes for theatrical stage and film productions.

Education

Bachelor of Science, Fashion Merchandising/Design and Minor Advertising and Promotion
College of Business, Missouri State University, Springfield, MO   **Graduation August 2013**
    Dean's List Honors 2010-2013; graduated as Merchandiser of the Year.

Related Volunteer Experience

Couture Fashion Week, New York, NY   **September 2013**
    Worked as assistant to the director, completing all tasks in a timely and efficient manner.
The Plaid Door Resale Boutique – The Junior League of Springfield   **April 2011**
    Visual Merchandising Volunteer - Supports abused women and children. Incorporated knowledge of visual merchandising and retail planning by redesigning/merchandising entire floor layout and window displays to increase sales/engage traffic; provided comprehensive plan for continued implementation.

Skills and Proficiencies

Computer – Extensive knowledge of Microsoft Excel, Word and Power Point; equivalent Macintosh programs; Adobe Photoshop and Illustrator; Lectra Knit, Print, Weave and Style.

Talents – Working proficiency in French language; Can toe touch, landing in a split for comedic value or a needed distraction.

The résumé for a fashion writer is almost as important as an interview because it reflects the essence of the position—communicating through writing. The writer who actively bridges the gap between print and digital media has what it takes to be a 21st-century journalist. In fact, many employers will investigate the number of followers a journalism candidate has on Facebook, Instagram, Twitter, and the like. Of course, you need to show that you can write well, but personal qualities to illustrate in the writer's résumé include a curious and positive attitude, a proactive approach, the ability to multitask effectively, and a generalist's knowledge of the fashion industry. An excellent article for fashion writer candidates to review is located at www.huffingtonpost .com/2014/05/27/fashion-editor-career-advice-eva-chen-_n_5372007 .html. Next, a sample résumé for a fashion journalist is presented.

CELINE DURAN

A Frustrated Breed of Slasher

Fashionista/ Writer/ Make-up Artist

Professional Experience

- **Beauty and Fashion Intern**
  (April-May 2013)
  MEGA Magazine
  Beauty Editor Kim Reyes-Palanca
  -Kakuyasu Uchiide, International Artistic Director
  Shu Uemura
  -NARS international Make-Up Stylist Sada Ito
  MEG Magazine
  Fashion Editor Rain Degala

- **Content Curator**
  (April-June 2012)
  Progressive Pinoy Perspectives
  Mark Bantigue
  -Coverage of Spoken Herb Festival
  -Interview with the 2006 Make-Up Head
  for Shu uemura, Ms. Xeng Zulueta

- **Food & Establishment Blogger**
  (May-June 2012)
  Zodio (Mobile application)
  Nina Comsti

Core Competence and Skills

- Fashion and Communications
  Fashion Forecasting: Familiarity in the styles and
  latest trends in Women's Fashion, Vertical
  Integration Trends, Knowledgeable in Brand
  Imaging.
  Styling: Personal and Theatrical Make-Up,
  Store Display Styling
  Capable Production Assistant: Knowledgeable in
  Wardrobe Styling, Make-up and Design,
  is organized, willing, driven and attentive.
  Maintains a personal blog on fashion, make-up and
  campus life:
  www.missCELINEous.blogspot.com

- Public Relations and Performing Arts
  Skilled in Social Communications and Public
  Relations, sociable, visible in major SNS
  Theater Arts, Television and Productions,
  Radio Disk Jockeying

- Technical Skills
  Digital Art and Layout: Adobe Photoshop CS5,
  Typography, Color Theory
  Web design: Adobe Dreamweaver, Basic
  HTML and CSS
  Photography: Basic DSLR Photography
  Word Processing: Microsoft Office 2010

Recognition and Positions Held

- **Creative Director/ Presenter**
  IMCQuest 2013: CocoQuench
  #Agency of the Year, #Best in Marketing Strategy
  #Best Creatives, #Best in PR, #Best Female Presenter

- **Creative Director/ Presenter**
  AdQuest 2013: Pure n' Fresh Account
  #Agency of the Year, #Best Creatives, #Best TVC,
  #Print Advertising, #Best in Social Media
  #Best Female Presenter

- **Best Female DJ**
  Kapisanan ng mga Broadcaster ng Pilipinas
  & Communication Arts Student Association
  PODCAST 2013: National Student's Forum on
  Responsible Radio Broadcasting

- **Make-Up Head**
  Mediartrix
  Rent (2013), Miss Saigon (2012)

- **Graphic Artist**
  Faculty of Arts and Letters Student Council 2013

- **Artist of the Year**
  St. Matthews College (March 2010)

- **Literary Head**
  St. Matthews College official School Paper
  Mathean Gazette, 2009-2010

AFFILIATIONS

- Metro Manila Alliance of Communication Students
  (MACS) 2010-Present
- UST-Mediartrix 2011-present
- Thomasian Cable TV 2010-2012
- Romwe Clothing 2012-present
- LuckyMag.com Contributor 2012-present

Educational Background

UNIVERSITY OF SANTO TOMAS — AB Communication Arts
2010-present

St. Matthews College — Secondary Education
2006-2010

References

Prof. Irene M. Lising PhD — Chairperson, Department of Humanities
Vice-Rector for Academic Affairs
University of Santo Tomas

Ms. Ethel T. Vendiola — Officer for Academic Affairs
St. Matthews College

Know more about Me

Scan

scan.me/5cdj6c

download free app at get.scan.me

glossary

academic curator training Instruction for the prospective museum curator on how to direct the accession, deaccession, storage, and exhibition of collections; the study of managing museum collections. (Chapter 14)

accession The addition of an artifact to a museum collection. (Chapter 14)

account coordinator For the beauty industry, this person organizes special events and promotions; travels to different retail locations; develops and implements marketing programs; introduces new products; and helps generate customer traffic and press for retail accounts. (Chapter 16)

account executive Sells to a manufacturer and manages accounts. May also be called *manufacturer's representative* or *sales representative*. (Chapter 2 and Chapter 16)

accounts payable Monies owed to creditors for goods and services; the amount owed by a business to its suppliers or vendors. (Chapter 5)

accounts payable manager Directs the accounts payable division of a company under the organization's established policies and monitors monies owed to creditors. (Chapter 5)

accounts receivable Amounts of money owed to a business that it expects to receive for goods furnished and services rendered, including sales made on credit, reimbursements earned, and refunds due. (Chapter 5)

accounts receivable manager Supervises the accounts receivable function, oversees monies owed to the business within an organization's established policies. (Chapter 5)

advertising A type of promotion that is paid, nonpersonal communication delivered through mass media. (Chapter 8)

advertising director Develops and implements a company's paid promotional strategy for the purpose of increasing visibility, image, and, ultimately, sales. (Chapter 8)

advertising photography Expresses a product's personality or illustrates a magazine story and is usually classified as still life, food, transportation, portraiture, or landscape. Also known as *editorial photography*. (Chapter 13)

advertising promotion staff Develops presentations to help the sales representatives of print and electronic media firms sell advertising to new and existing accounts. (Chapter 8)

advertising research assistant Helps sales representatives sell advertising space, in a publication for example, by supplying facts that an advertiser will want to know, such as the number of issues sold and top locations in terms of sales volume, or the profile and buying power of the publication's readers. (Chapter 8)

advertising sales representative Sells advertising for consumer and trade publications. (Chapter 8)

aesthetician A licensed professional who provides services such as facials, makeup application, and hair removal to aid in improving an individual's physical appearance. (Chapter 16)

aesthetics A field that combines wellness, science, and beauty—providing the client with comprehensive makeovers and beauty-enhancement treatments that combine medical, beauty, and spa treatments. (Chapter 16)

architect Building designer who works with a wide range of structures that may range from small, freestanding retail stores to large malls. (Chapter 15)

architecture The creative blend of art and science in the design of environments for people. The plans for a building ultimately focus on the needs of the people who use them, to include aesthetics, safety, and environmental factors. (Chapter 15)

archive technician In a museum, this person helps archivists organize, maintain, and provide access to historical documentary materials. (Chapter 14)

archivist Analyzes, describes, catalogues, and exhibits records and documents that are retained by museums because of their importance and potential value, benefiting researchers and the public. (Chapter 14)

art director Develops and implements the creative concepts for advertising, catalogues, mailers, and signage; this person provides an overall and consistent visual view of the manufacturing or retailing company, including signage, photography, direct mail, and packaging. (Chapter 9)

assistant buyer Supports the buyer, often working with the six-month plan, open-to-buy, inventory, and vendor follow-up; takes direction from the buyer. (Chapter 10)

assistant curator Supports the museum curator, often serving as the registrar of museum collections by coordinating the collections' accessions. (Chapter 14)

assistant fashion designer Supports designers by helping them create, modify, and locate new materials, styles, colors, and patterns for fashion brands and labels. (Chapter 6)

assistant importer Works for the import production coordinator and follows up on orders with overseas suppliers. He or she also communicates with freight companies and customs agents, processes documents, and checks pricing agreements. (Chapter 3)

assistant mall manager Responsible for administering mall programs under the supervision of the property's general manager (mall manager). This position is critical in communication among tenants, contractors, consumers, and mall staff. (Chapter 15)

assistant photographer Supports the photographer and works with clients and suppliers; organizes estimates, invoices, and payments; arranges props and assists with lighting; communicates with photographic labs and stylists; helps the photographer on shoots; and maintains the photographer's Web site and portfolio. (Chapter 13)

assistant piece goods buyer Often works with the piece goods buyer to calculate quantities of fabrics needed, to follow up on deliveries, and to locate fabric sources, while training for a buying position in the future. (Chapter 3)

assistant store manager Assists the store manager in scheduling employees, overseeing sales performance in the store, planning promotions, etc.—all of the daily responsibilities of operating a store successfully. (Chapter 11)

assistant stylist Supports the stylist; responsible for contacting public relations companies, manufacturers, and retailers to locate the best assortment of merchandise to be used in a shoot. (Chapter 13)

assistant textile designer Works under the direction of the textile designer in developing new fabric prints and colorways, sourcing new patterns for fabrics, and modifying successful fabric prints and patterns. (Chapter 2)

associate store manager This position lies between the assistant store manager and the store manager; assists with employee hires, personnel scheduling, promotional activities, employee training, and other responsibilities assigned by the store manager. (Chapter 11)

beauty and wellness industries Focus on cosmetics, fragrances, hair and skin, as well as spa, fitness, or wellness centers and their services. (Chapter 16)

beauty industry The producers of cosmetics, fragrances, and hair and skin care products. (Chapter 16)

beauty merchandising and marketing professional Involved in the promotion and sales of cosmetics, fragrances, and skin care products. (Chapter 16)

block A basic flat pattern that is used as a starting place for pattern modifications. Also called a *sloper*. (Chapter 6)

body scanning Use of light beams to accurately measure the human body. (Chapter 4)

branding The sum of all the associations, feelings, beliefs, attitudes, and perceptions customers have with a company and/or its products. (Chapter 9)

brand marketing manager Strategically develops and executes multichannel brand marketing and promotional programs in order to drive brand awareness, support and reinforce the brand's character, and ultimately generate increased revenue. (Chapter 9)

brick-and-click store A retail business that offers its products to consumers through a store facility and through the Internet. (Chapter 7)

brick-and-mortar-store A retail business that has a physical appearance, as opposed to an Internet-based company. This includes department stores, mass merchants, specialty stores, boutiques, discount stores, and outlet stores located in buildings. (Chapter 7)

bridal show Event also called a *bridal fair*, where bridal wear manufacturers and retailers team up with auxiliary businesses, such as wedding planners, caterers, florists, and travel agents, to offer a fashion presentation of the season's offerings for brides-to-be, their friends, and their families. (Chapter 8)

broad-spectrum firm A company that provides forecasting services for a wide range of target markets and product categories or industries. (Chapter 1)

business plan A document used to solicit business funding that details strategies for the business concept and target market, location and space needs (i.e., building lease, facility purchase, or Web site requirements), growth and exit strategies, sales and inventory levels, and financing needs. (Chapter 11)

buyer Typically responsible for all of the product purchases and inventories for a company or particular department of a company, within a certain budget; this position is also referred to as *fashion merchandiser*. (Chapter 10)

buying plan A financial plan that takes into account past and projected sales, inventory, markups, and markdowns by department; it is also referred to as a *six-month plan*. (Chapter 10)

carryover A best-selling item from one season that is featured again with minor modifications in the next season. (Chapter 7)

channel of distribution The method(s) selected for moving goods from producer to consumer. (Chapter 9)

chargebacks Credits to a vendor for damaged merchandise and returns on defective goods. (Chapter 3)

chief financial officer (CFO) Top director of the overall financial plans and accounting practices of an organization. (Chapter 5)

chief marketing officer (CMO) A higher executive position to the marketing director; develops, implements, and facilitates the marketing plan in fashion retailing. (Chapter 9)

client/customer relationship management (CRM) Marketing that encompasses the analysis of significant amounts of data to understand consumer demographics, key market segments, and best practices for recruiting or retaining those customers. (Chapter 9)

client registry file A computerized or print record of the names and contact information of the retailer's or the line's customers. (Chapter 16)

collection Grouping of related styles. (Chapter 3)

collections manager Supervises museum personnel working in a specific area within a museum classification, such as historical textiles, 18th-century millinery, or Egyptian jewelry. (Chapter 14)

colorist Chooses the color palette or color combinations that will be used in creating product lines. (Chapter 7)

color palette The specific color selections for a particular pattern, print, or a collection or season of apparel or accessories. (Chapter 7)

colorway Color selections for a particular pattern or print. (Chapter 2, Chapter 7)

commercial designer Interior designer who concentrates on public spaces, including projects for retail stores, hotels, motels, schools, etc. Also referred to as *contract designer*. (Chapter 15)

commercial real estate Public properties that include malls, business districts, and shopping centers. (Chapter 15)

company salesperson Sales representative employed directly by a particular firm. (Chapter 6)

computer-aided design (CAD) The process of developing garments, prints, and patterns on a computer screen; this is an important trend in textile design. (Chapter 2, Chapter 6)

computer-aided pattern making Manipulation of the components of pattern pieces on a computer screen. (Chapter 6)

computer-integrated manufacturing (CIM) Computers are tied together to communicate throughout the entire product development and manufacturing processes, from design to distribution. (Chapter 4)

consumer publication Magazine or newsletter that is written for and made readily available to the general consumer. (Chapter 8)

consumer tracking information Findings gathered from sales data and credit card applications that are interpreted as customer demographics and psychographics. (Chapter 1)

contractor Can either be a factory that makes and finishes goods or a firm that is hired to manufacture

a product line domestically or abroad. (Chapter 2, Chapter 3)

controller Responsible for a company's financial plans and policies, its accounting practices, its relationships with lending institutions and the financial community, the maintenance of its fiscal records, and the preparation of its financial reports. (Chapter 5)

copywriter The person responsible for writing the words (e.g., slogans, promotions, and scripts) that accompany promotional visuals—online and in print. (Chapter 9, Chapter 12)

corporation Company that is owned by stockholders, and may be run by an individual or a group. (Chapter 11)

cost price (*cost*) Wholesale price. (Chapter 5)

costume designer This person collaborates with film and video directors to design, consign, or construct apparel and accessories that fit with the mood, time frame, and image of the visual; also referred to as *fashion costumer*. (Chapter 13)

costume plot A list or chart that shows characters as they appear in each scene, what they are wearing, and what their overall movements are throughout a play. (Chapter 13)

country of origin The nation in which goods are primarily manufactured. (Chapter 3)

counter manager Coordinates special events and promotions in the retail operation, manages employees, and works closely with buyers. Key responsibilities include selling the product line and servicing the customer. Sometimes referred to as a *line manager*. (Chapter 16)

creative director Determines the primary fashion trend for upcoming seasons (Chapter 1); oversees art directors and other in-house art staff. (Chapter 9)

croquis A rendering or miniature visual of a textile pattern or print. (Chapter 2)

cross-shopping A customer's inclination to purchase a wide variety of products in an array of brands and prices from any number of providers—directly from the manufacturer, in a resale store, at a flea market, or through a couturier. (Chapter 7)

curatorial traineeship Internship or apprenticeship for the prospective museum curator. (Chapter 14)

customer service manager Assists customers with issues or complaints and implements the retail operation's policies and procedures for returns, exchanges, out-of-stock merchandise, product warranties, and the like. (Chapter 11)

cutter Uses electronic machines, knives, or scissors to precisely cut around the pattern pieces through layers of fabric, often several inches in thickness. (Chapter 4)

cut-to-order Considered the safest method of projecting manufacturing needs, this refers to producing the quantity of products specified on orders received. (Chapter 4)

cut-to-stock Involves purchasing fabrics and other product components before orders are secured. (Chapter 4)

day spa An environment that offers a variety of beauty and wellness services, such as massages, hair removal, skin rejuvenation, and other aesthetic services. (Chapter 16)

deaccession The removal of items from a museum collection because of repetition of artifacts, the receipt of better examples, loss, or decay. (Chapter 14)

decentralized buying The process used by individual stores or groups of stores within a retail chain that have a buyer who selects from the company's primary buyer's purchases. (Chapter 7)

demographic data Consumer data that can be interpreted as numbers (e.g., age, income, education attained, and number of family members). (Chapter 1)

department manager Oversees a specific area or department within a store and maintains the sales floor by supervising sales associates, placing new merchandise on the sales floor, adding signage for promotions, recording markdowns, and executing floor sets. (Chapter 11)

design-driven brand A brand that is led by a designer expressing a personal artistic vision and sense of taste. (Chapter 7)

design process The conception of a style, to include its inspiration or theme, the color palette, fabric selection, form, and fit. (Chapter 7)

diffusion labels Secondary clothing lines, often priced much lower than the designer's original line, such as Vera Wang's Simply Vera line for Kohl's. (Chapter 9)

digital marketing manager Works to further develop and manage a company's digital marketing presence and oversees the digital marketing strategy for the brand. This person is responsible for managing online brand and product campaigns to raise brand awareness. (Chapter 9)

digital media artists Also known as *multimedia artists*, they create animation and digital effects for various media outlets, such as television, movies, and video games. (Chapter 12)

digital twin Refers to a solution to fit preference in which a scanner takes a customer's measurements digitally; *body scanning.* (Chapter 4)

digitizer An electronic tool that is used to manipulate the size and shape of pattern pieces. (Chapter 6)

direct competition A manufacturer producing or a retailer selling a similar product at roughly the same price point as another, targeted toward the same customer or market niche. (Chapter 7)

direct market brand Describes a brand that is the name of the retailer. Often, this brand is carried by a specialty store chain, such as Ann Taylor, IKEA, and Banana Republic. (Chapter 7)

director of a spa or wellness center Responsible for keeping the spa running smoothly by managing customer service, budgets, marketing plans, and environment, and dealing with staff-related issues. (Chapter 16)

director of product development Ultimately responsible for strategic planning of the division, this person specifies exactly what the company will make and market, as well as when it will do this. (Chapter 7)

distribution Concerned with making sure that the product is available where and when it is wanted; includes determining how much inventory to hold, how to transport goods, and where to locate warehouses. (Chapter 9)

distribution manager Also referred to as an *allocator* or a *replenishment analyst*, this position is responsible for planning and managing the flow of goods received from the vendors, as ordered by the buyers, to the retail locations. (Chapter 10)

divisional merchandising manager (DMM) Works under the general merchandising manager and provides leadership for the buying staff of a division or a related group of departments, such as menswear, women's wear, or home furnishings. (Chapter 10)

draping method Process in which a pattern maker shapes and cuts muslin or the garment fabric on a dress form or a live model to create a pattern. (Chapter 6)

educational event A presentation during which a fashion event planner, a manufacturer's representative, or an employee hired by the planner educates an audience about a product. (Chapter 8)

electronic data interchange (EDI) Refers to the transfer of computer-generated information between one company's computer system and another's. (Chapter 4)

end product The final product to be purchased by the customer. (Chapter 4)

entrepreneur The business owner who is financially responsible for the company and oversees all aspects of the retail business. (Chapter 11)

entry-level accountant Maintains records of routine accounting transactions and assists in the preparation of financial and operating reports. (Chapter 5)

evergreen Refers to writing online content (e.g., blog, Web site, social media) so that it is relevant for a long period of time, not just the present. (Chapter 12)

exclusive An item limited to a retailer in a trade area. In some cases, a retailer may negotiate to be the only one in a geographic region to carry a particular item or the only one in the country to carry a particular color. For example, the label may read: "Burberry Exclusively for Neiman Marcus." (Chapter 7)

exports Products that are bought by an overseas company from a vendor in the United States and sent out of the country. (Chapter 3)

Family and Consumer Science Education (FCSEd) Certification for an instructor who teaches high school, vocational, or college courses in textiles, fashion, interior design, consumer education, personal financial literacy, clothing construction, careers in the fashion industry, and similar topics. (Chapter 14)

fashion blog Online coverage of fashion topics through which a narrator discusses and shares opinions and information about products, retailers, designers, and anything else related to clothing and accessories. (Chapter 12)

fashion bloggers Are much like *fashion writers*, but with a definitive online presence, a distinct personality, and an informal writing style. (Chapter 12)

fashion curators Work within historical and socioeconomic frameworks to educate others about fashion through accessing and archiving fashion artifacts, then sharing many of these with the public. (Chapter 14)

fashion design The development and execution of wearable forms, structures, and patterns. (Chapter 6)

fashion designer A creative who supervises a team of design assistants at a company, works under the label of a big-name designer or manufacturer, freelances for others while creating a personal line, or produces a line under his or her own name. (Chapter 6)

fashion director Responsible for determining the trends, colors, themes, and textures for piece goods or fabrics that a firm will feature for a specific season. In retailing, this position is responsible for designating the trends, themes, colors, and fabrics that the buyers will purchase for the retail operation. (Chapter 2)

fashion event producer Someone who increases the visibility of a design house, organization, brand, product, or fabric by coordinating special events, such as fashion shows and seminars, which provide exposure for these products; works with budgets, media, and customers in producing cost-effective and high-profile events. Also known as *fashion show producer*. (Chapter 8, Chapter 13)

fashion exclusivity Refers to having merchandise that is unique to a particular company. (Chapter 7)

fashion journalists Develop stories and materials such as articles, advertisements, and product descriptions, for books, magazines, newspapers, and online Web sites and blogs. Also known as *fashion writers*. (Chapter 12)

fashion photographer Takes photographs of models wearing the latest apparel, accessories, hairstyles, and makeup, or highlighting the newest home furnishings and other fashion products, primarily for commercial use. (Chapter 13)

fashion photostylist Responsible for bringing to life a photographer's or director's vision for a fashion photography shoot, magazine layout, music video, television or film commercial, or print advertisement. (Chapter 8)

fashion production planner Projects timelines for manufacturing the products in a line. (Chapter 3)

fashion scholar A person who studies, researches, writes, and teaches students in a classroom or online about the industry (past, present, and future), its careers, and the skills needed to succeed in it. (Chapter 14)

fashion shoot Photography session of models and/or fashion items. (Chapter 8)

fashion stylist Consults with clients on hair, makeup, footwear, jewelry, and apparel to create total looks, often for specific events. (Chapter 8)

fashion visual Refers to the images used in the fashion industry, such as photographs, trend boards, and magazine clippings. (Chapter 13)

fashion writer See *fashion journalist*. (Chapter 12)

fast fashion Apparel and accessories trends that are designed and manufactured quickly, and in an affordable way, to allow the mainstream consumer to take advantage of current fashions at a lower price. (Chapter 7)

fiber house A company, also called a *fabric house*, that represents a fiber source or a fabric. (Chapter 1)

findings Functional product components that may not be visible when viewing the final product; they include zippers, thread, linings, and interfacings. (Chapter 3)

findings buyer Responsible for purchasing zippers, threads, linings, and such for a manufacturer. (Chapter 3)

finishing Enhances the appearance of fabric and also adds to its suitability for everyday use or durability. Finishes can be solely mechanical, solely chemical, or a combination of the two. (Chapter 2)

first cost Wholesale price, in the country of origin. (Chapter 3)

first pattern Used to cut and sew the prototype. (Chapter 6)

fit model This is the model on whom a designer may drape, cut, and pin fabric and on whom the designer will check the sizing and proportion of garments. Also referred to as the *fashion house model*. (Chapter 13)

flat pattern method Uses angles, rulers, and curves to create patterns. (Chapter 6)

floor set The arrangement of fixtures and merchandise on the sales floor to create a fresh look and highlight brand-new or undersold merchandise. (Chapter 11)

foundations Similar to museums, they are institutions formally set up with endowment funds. (Chapter 14)

freelance costumer Hired for specific productions by a theater company or production studio and may or may not actually be local to the theater for which he or she is designing. (Chapter 13)

functional finish A finish that imparts special characteristics to the cloth (e.g., durable press treatments). (Chapter 2)

funder Financing source, such as a bank or the Small Business Administration, used by a prospective business owner with a well-written business plan that justifies financing due to a good potential for profit, minimized risk, and a strong long-range plan. (Chapter 11)

general finish A finish, such as scouring or bleaching, that simply prepares the fabric for further use. (Chapter 2)

general merchandising manager (GMM) Leads and manages the buyers of all divisions in a retail operation. (Chapter 10)

general web developers Deal with the construction and maintenance of a site, whereas other career paths, including programmers, designers, and Web masters, are more specialized. (Chapter 12)

globalization The process of interlinking nations of the world with one another; this is a growing trend in the fashion industry. (Chapter 3)

global sourcing Refers to the process of locating, purchasing, and importing or exporting goods and services from around the world. (Chapter 3)

graphic designers Use skill and software to create unique ideas, images, and concepts in order to attract customers and convey a specific message. (Chapter 12)

gross margin Actual profit after cost of goods, markdowns, and other expenses are deducted. (Chapter 10)

hairstylist Person specializing in hair design, color, and care. (Chapter 16)

hiring manager Responsible for locating and employing personnel for the various positions within a company. (Chapter 5)

human resources (HR) Refers to the department in charge of an organization's employees, which has responsibilities including finding and hiring employees, helping them grow and learn in the organization, and managing the process when an employee leaves. (Chapter 5)

human resources development (HRD) The field of business concerned with recruiting, training, maintaining, motivating, and managing personnel. (Chapter 5)

human resources manager Also known as a *human resources director*, this person plays a leadership role in the business- and people-related issues of the company. After identifying issues in the workplace, he or she meets with supervisors and managers to determine effective solutions. (Chapter 5)

import production coordinator Works as a liaison between the domestic apparel or home furnishings company and the overseas manufacturer or contractor. (Chapter 3)

imports In North America, products that are purchased from an overseas vendor and shipped to the United States or Canada. (Chapter 3)

informal fashion show is a show without extravagant staging and technical assistance, often taking place in a conference center, hotel, or restaurant in which models circulate among the tables as refreshments are served. (Chapter 8)

interactive display Exhibit ancillary in which viewers can press a button to run a video or actively participate in the exhibition's subject matter. (Chapter 14)

interior designer Often working with either homes (i.e., residential) or businesses (i.e., commercial or contract), this person is responsible for creating the facility's inner environment, with attention to aesthetics, safety, and the well-being of those using the space. (Chapter 15)

intermediate accountant Prepares and maintains accounting records that may include general accounting, costing, or budget data. Also called a *midlevel accountant*. (Chapter 5)

internal theft Refers to merchandise or money stolen by employees within the company. (Chapter 11)

international store manager Supervises store sales and staff performance in a different country, or group of countries, not in the company's country of residence. (Chapter 11)

inventory The selection of products available for sale in a fashion operation; this is also referred to as *merchandise assortment*. (Chapter 10)

inventory replenishment Reorders and stock placement on the sales floor to replace or fill in merchandise sold. (Chapter 5)

key account For a manufacturer, this term refers to a large retailer, in terms of sales volume, which carries the manufacturer's line consistently and in depth. (Chapter 5)

key vendor Manufacturers' lines featured as the greatest proportion of inventory in a retail operation. (Chapter 10)

knockoff A copy of another style, often of lesser quality and with minor modifications. (Chapter 7)

labdip A swatch of dyed fabric sent by mills to the product development team for color approval prior to dyeing large yardages of fabric. (Chapter 7)

landed costs The actual price of goods after taxes, tariffs, handling, and shipping fees are added to the cost of imported goods. (Chapter 3)

lead time Number of days, weeks, months, or years needed for the intricate planning and production steps that are implemented before fashion products actually arrive at the retail store; it is also the amount of time needed between placing a production order and receiving the shipment of products. (Chapter 1, Chapter 4)

letter of credit A document issued by a bank authorizing the bearer to draw a specific amount of money from the bank, its branches, or associated banks and agencies. (Chapter 3)

license An agreement in which a manufacturer is given exclusive rights to produce and market goods that carry the registered name and brandmark of a designer, celebrity, character, or product line. (Chapter 3)

licensee The manufacturer of a licensed product. (Chapter 3)

licensing director Responsible for overseeing the look, quality, labeling, delivery, and distribution of the company's licensed product lines. (Chapter 3)

licensor The owner of the name or brandmark who receives a percentage of wholesale sales or some form of compensation based on a licensing agreement. (Chapter 3)

lifestyle trends A population segment's values, interests, attitudes, dreams, and goals. (Chapter 1)

line plan Shows the number of styles in the line, the number and general types of fabrics and yarns to be used, colors per style, anticipated stock-keeping units (SKUs), and approximate preferred costs. (Chapter 7)

makeup artist Works with cosmetics, wigs, and other costuming materials to color and enhance the client's face and body. (Chapter 16)

mall manager Responsible for everything in the mall from formulating its budget and planning promotional activities to developing its mix of tenants and building community relations. (Chapter 15)

management The process of organizing and controlling the affairs of a business or a particular sector of a business. (Chapter 11)

manager-in-training (MIT) An employee who is being trained to move into a management position. (Chapter 11)

manufacturer's representative Also referred to as a manufacturer's rep, this person is a wholesale salesperson who is often independent. (Chapter 5)

marker The layout of pattern pieces on the fabric from which the pieces will be cut. (Chapter 4)

marker maker Traces pattern pieces by hand or by computer into the tightest possible layout, while keeping the integrity of the design in mind. (Chapter 4)

marketing director Develops, implements, and facilitates the marketing plan in fashion retailing. (Chapter 9)

marketing manager A position that is just below that of marketing director in the executive hierarchy and has qualifications similar to those of marketing director. (Chapter 9)

marketing mix The Four Ps of marketing include: price, product, placement, and promotion. A fifth P of marketing can be added—the people or consumers who are targeted as potential customers or product users, referred to as the target market. (Chapter 9)

marketing plan Helps to define and quantify user benefits; establishes the market size as well as potential customer interest; and addresses the competition. (Chapter 9)

market representative A specialized buyer of individual merchandise classifications who works closely with his or her client stores, keeping them up to date on new product offerings in the marketplace, recommending new vendors, and assisting them in locating needed goods. (Chapter 3)

market week Scheduled at the apparel and trade marts throughout the year in conjunction with the introduction of the new, seasonal lines presented by manufacturers. Also called a *trade show*. (Chapter 5)

mass customization Strategy that allows a manufacturer or retailer to provide individualized products to a consumer. (Chapter 4)

mass market Consumer group targeted for low to mid-priced product lines sold through a wide variety of retailers, including drugstores, discount merchants, and mass merchandising retailers. (Chapter 16)

master pattern Final pattern; often evolved from adjusting and perfecting a sample pattern. (Chapter 4)

media planner Determines prices, including quantity discounts, for a media buy that may include several venues, such as radio, television, and newspaper. The media planner determines how the advertising budget is best spent to generate the most exposure and sales. (Chapter 8)

medi-spa Combines traditional spa services with those that must be offered by a physician, such as health screenings and minor surgery. (Chapter 16)

merchandise coordinator Employed by a manufacturer and works in retail stores carrying the manufacturer's line within a certain geographic area, restocking products, installing displays, reordering top-selling styles, and educating sales staff and customers on the product line. (Chapter 5)

merchandiser Collaborates with the director of product development to decide what to produce and organizes and manages the entire product development process; this person is responsible for the development of a balanced, marketable, profitable, and timely line. (Chapter 3, Chapter 9)

merchandising Refers to all of the activities involved in the buying and selling of a product line. (Chapter 10)

merchandising calendar The product development team's schedule, created to deliver the right product (i.e., style, quality, and price) at the right time. (Chapter 7)

merchandising-driven brand Void-filling brand; a market-based brand designed to fill a niche in a market (i.e., an underserved customer) and create products to appeal to a distinct customer. (Chapter 7)

merchandising executive training program Designed for new hires, former interns, college recruits, or current employees who have shown skills in merchandising, to prepare them for their first assignment as assistant buyers; also referred to as *merchant executive training program*. (Chapter 10)

micro blogs Provide shorter stories that are easy to read and are accompanied by video clips and links that are smaller in size and easy for readers to share with one another; often focused on a specific niche in the industry. (Chapter 12)

modeling and talent agency director Ultimately responsible for locating and contracting new models, training them, and securing modeling jobs for them. (Chapter 13)

multiline rep An independent salesperson who carries a number of lines, often working with noncompetitive product lines and manufacturers. (Chapter 5)

museological training Instruction that covers how to preserve, maintain, and interpret museum collections. (Chapter 14)

museum conservator Manages, cares for, preserves, treats, and documents works of art, artifacts, and specimens; with regard to fashions or costumes, conservators acquire and preserve important visuals (e.g., photographs, illustrations, or sketches), costumes, accessories, furnishings, and other valuable items for permanent storage or display; this position may be referred to as a *restoration and preservation specialist*. (Chapter 14)

museum curator Works under the supervision of the museum director. A curator directs the accession, deaccession, storage, and exhibition of collections. This position may also be referred to as a *museum keeper*. (Chapter 14)

museum director Runs the business of the museum, manages the general operations and staffing of the organization, and coordinates the public affairs mission of the museum. (Chapter 14)

museum managerial training Educational program for a museum curator on how to run a museum, from personnel to finances to operations. (Chapter 14)

open-to-buy The amount of money allocated for the buyer to make new merchandise purchases each month, based on sales and inventory amounts. (Chapter 10)

operations manager Develops and maintains effective sales and operational programs with a focus on superior customer service for all of the retail units in the company or for units in a region. (Chapter 11)

outsourcing Having an aspect of a company's work performed by nonemployees in another company and, perhaps, in another country. (Chapter 2)

partnership A business owned by two or more people. (Chapter 11)

partnership event An event in which a fashion firm collaborates with another company outside of the fashion industry with the intent of drawing in customers. (Chapter 8)

party planning Can involve manufacturer, a designer, a PR director, or an organization hiring a fashion event producer to put together a celebratory event. (Chapter 8)

pattern grader Develops a pattern in the full range of sizes offered by the manufacturer. (Chapter 4)

pattern maker Translates the design concept into a flat pattern to create an actual garment. (Chapter 6)

personnel The employees or staff of an organization. (Chapter 5)

philanthropic fashion show A fashion show with ticket sales and/or donations that benefit a nonprofit or charitable organization. (Chapter 8)

photographic model Hired to be photographed in the studio or on location. Although a select few top models work in high-fashion magazines, most opportunities exist through mail-order catalogues, newspaper advertisements, and television. Also known as a *print model*. (Chapter 13)

photography stylist Works with teams of people such as photographers, designers, lighting technicians, and set builders. Sets up the shoot for the photographer, scouts locations, and selects appropriate props, fashions, accessories, and, perhaps, the models to enhance the shoot. (Chapter 13)

physical inventory The merchandise actually in the retail or manufacturing operation. (Chapter 11)

piece goods Fabrics or materials, such as leather, used to create products. (Chapter 2)

piece goods buyer Purchases the textiles used in the production of final products. (Chapter 3)

planner Works in collaboration with the buyer to develop sales forecasts, inventory plans, and spending budgets for merchandise to achieve the retailer's sales and profit objectives. (Chapter 10)

planning manager Provides leadership, direction, and support at the merchandise division level to plan appropriately; this person also distributes and monitors inventory within a company's various retail locations to maximize sales. (Chapter 10)

planning module A chart constructed by a planner that details inventory ratios, such as top-to-bottom ratios of junior sportswear. (Chapter 10)

plan-o-gram Floor plan showing the placement and types of racks, fixtures, display units, and/or merchandise in order to create an easy flow of traffic and present the merchandise most effectively. (Chapter 15)

pop-up shop A project that is like a hide-and-seek boutique that pops up within other retail locations or at vacant retail spaces with few preliminary announcements. They quickly draw crowds, are open for a limited period of time, and then disappear or morph into something else. (Chapter 8)

portfolio A collection of work that illustrates a job candidate's range of skills and outcomes. This is also referred to in some sectors of fashion as a *book*. (Chapter 13)

press photography Also known as *photojournalism*, this focuses on images directly related to news stories, both events and personalities. (Chapter 13)

prestige market Product lines that are distributed through high-end department and specialty store retailers. (Chapter 16)

primary level The sector of the fashion industry that includes fiber, fabrics, and manufacturing. (Chapter 2)

print service Company that sells print designs to mills, wholesalers, product developers, and retailers. (Chapter 2)

private brand A name owned exclusively by a particular store that is extensively marketed with a definite image, such as Target's Mossimo and Isaac Mizrahi brands. (Chapter 7)

private label A line name or brand that the retailer develops and assigns to a collection of products and that is owned exclusively by a particular retailer, such as Antonio Melani at Dillard's. (Chapter 7)

product development Creating and making a product, such as a dress, belt, or chair, from start to finish. (Chapter 7)

product development designer The creator of a product or product line; he or she is a trend forecaster in his or her own right by determining what the customer will be ready for next. Going through the design process with each new season, this person in a retail firm is also referred to as a *private label designer*. (Chapter 7)

product development pattern maker Takes accurate measurements and develops a pattern, either by using draping, CAD, or flat pattern methods, to create a pattern that, if correctly developed, ensures that the designer's vision will be implemented. (Chapter 7)

product manager Responsible for all products within a company's product lines or for a specific product category within the line. (Chapter 4)

product marketing manager Anticipates when to get into a fashion style, color, or theme and when to get out. (Chapter 9)

product void Merchandise category in which there are few, if any, items to fill consumer needs and desires. (Chapter 4)

production assistant Supports the production manager with detail work and record keeping. This person may track deliveries, assist development of production schedules, and communicate the workflow of the factory to the production manager. (Chapter 4)

production authorization The process of selecting and quantifying styles that will be manufactured. (Chapter 7)

production efficiency manager Responsible for monitoring the speed and output of a manufacturing facility and for managing waste. (Chapter 4)

production manager Also referred to as a *plant manager*, this person is responsible for all operations at the manufacturing plant, whether it is a domestic or overseas location and contracted or company owned. Job responsibilities of a production manager include supervising or completing the estimation of production costs, scheduling workflow in the factory, and hiring and training production employees. (Chapter 3, Chapter 4)

production planner Estimates the amount and types of products a company will manufacture, either based on previous seasonal sales or on orders being received from the sales representatives on the road and in the showroom. (Chapter 4)

professional development Includes continuing education, perhaps toward a higher degree; internships within a field; conference participation; and memberships in trade and educational organizations. (Chapter 14)

promotion The endorsement of a person, a product, a cause, an idea, or an organization (Chapter 5); these activities communicate a company's or product's attributes to the target consumers using two primary tools: publicity and advertising. (Chapter 8)

promotion director Guides the marketing activities of a fashion operation and finds hooks, or topics of interest, for a network of media sources. (Chapter 8)

promotion product Can refer to an item, such as a press release or an advertisement, or an event, such as a fashion show or music video, used as an endorsement tool. (Chapter 8)

prop house Firm that rents furniture, fixtures, mannequins, and décor accessories to visual merchandisers, saving the company money on limited-use display pieces while reducing the amount of warehouse space and labor needed to inventory and store visual merchandising props. (Chapter 15)

prototype First sample garment, accessory, or home product. (Chapter 6)

psychographics Refers to lifestyle choices, values, and emotions of a population. (Chapter 1)

public affairs As a mission in museums, this refers to collaborating with the community, the government, industry, and social and academic organizations to develop exhibitions and collections that appeal to and educate the community and its visitors. (Chapter 14)

public relations account executive Works with media contacts such as fashion publications like *Vogue*, *Elle*, *W*, and *InStyle* to promote the line in magazine editorials and feature stories. (Chapter 16)

public relations director Responsible for finding cost-effective ways to promote the company he or she represents. (Chapter 8)

puck A mouselike device used for computer-aided design. (Chapter 6)

purchase order (PO) A contract for merchandise between the buyer, as a representative of his or her firm, and the vendor. (Chapter 3)

quality control manager Also known as the *quality control engineer*, this person develops specifications for the products that will be manufactured and is responsible for the final inspection of garments from the manufacturer, checking fabric, fit, and construction for quality and adherence to product specification guidelines. (Chapter 4, Chapter 7)

radio-frequency identification technology (RFID) Increases supply-chain management through the tagging of containers, pallets, and individual items so that they can be accurately tracked as they move through the supply chain. (Chapter 4)

reference librarian Responsible for managing the inventory of books, samples, and resources of a fashion company, such as a fiber house or manufacturer, and for procuring new ones. (Chapter 2)

regional store manager Responsible for the retail stores of a particular company that are located in a segregated area of the United States and/or overseas; this position is also referred to as a *district manager*. (Chapter 11)

reorder A fill-in on merchandise that is selling well. (Chapter 5)

residential costumer Hired by a specific theater to design and develop costumes for an extended series of productions. (Chapter 13)

residential design Interior design focusing on home environments. (Chapter 15)

resource room Reference library of product samples and sources, such as books, photographs, and other images. (Chapter 2)

resource room director Responsible for managing the inventory of books, fabrics, garments, and resources and for procuring new ones for a fashion library or resource room. (Chapter 2)

retail account executive Also referred to as a *retail sales account executive*, this person sells a product line to retail accounts and oversees the sales performance of the line in large retail accounts. (Chapter 16)

retailer A business that sells products to the ultimate consumer and can include the vast range of brick-and-mortar stores (e.g., department stores, mass merchants, specialty stores, boutiques, discount stores, and outlet stores), as well as catalogue, brick-and-click, and online stores. (Chapter 7)

retail label A brand with the retailer's name on it, such as Neiman Marcus, Custom Interiors, or Saks Fifth Avenue. A retailer may negotiate with a manufacturer to put its label on a group of items instead of or in addition to the manufacturer's label, although the retailer may not have anything to do with the design or development of the items. (Chapter 7)

retail store manager Oversees all aspects of a retail store's operation, from promotions and inventory

to the customers and employees, often consisting of assistant managers, department managers, sales associates, and staff. (Chapter 11)

sales forecast Includes projections of sales by category, style, color, and size based on historical data and statistical analysis. This information may be used to place preliminary fabric and trim orders and block out production time in factories. (Chapter 7)

sample line Includes a prototype of every style available in the final product line and is used by sales representatives to show and sell the line to buyers. (Chapter 5)

sample size Used for testing fit and appearance, in addition to selling purposes. (Chapter 6)

search engine optimization (SEO) Used to ensure that search engine "spiders" are "liking" a blog and are moving it up in search engines. The decision of whether they "like" it or not can be based on traffic, content, competition, etc. (Chapter 12)

secondary vendor Manufacturers' line featured in a retailer's inventory in small quantities. (Chapter 10)

security Refers to the safekeeping of the merchandise in the store. (Chapter 11)

security manager Works to prevent merchandise theft; collaborates with receiving, accounting, and management to be certain that accurate accounting procedures are in place and true losses are identified when the physical inventory is taken. (Chapter 11)

senior accountant Responsible for establishing, interpreting, and analyzing complex accounting records or financial statements for management. (Chapter 5)

show model Employed by a modeling agency that takes bookings from clients who need to display clothes at fashion shows, exhibitions, or trade markets; also referred to as a *runway model*. (Chapter 13)

showroom A place where product lines are displayed; usually caters only to the trade. (Chapter 5)

showroom salesperson Also referred to as a *showroom representative*, this person works at a manufacturer's and/or designer's place of business, where he or she meets with visiting retail buyers and presents the latest product line to them. (Chapter 5)

shrinkage Merchandise losses due to theft. (Chapter 11)

single-line rep Manufacturer's representative who prefers to sell solely one manufacturer's line as an independent salesperson, rather than as a company employee. (Chapter 5)

social media The tools and social Web sites of the Internet that are used to communicate online with others. (Chapter 8)

social media director Develops, manages, and oversees the implementation of public relations programs in the social media venue. This includes creating content and generating coverage for social media efforts in all forms. (Chapter 8)

social networking The online communication of individuals, often with relationships or similar interests. (Chapter 8)

social Web site A Web site that functions like an online community of Internet users (e.g., Facebook and LinkedIn). (Chapter 8)

sole proprietorship A business owned by an individual. (Chapter 11)

sourcing The activities of determining which vendor can provide the amount of product needed, negotiating the best possible price and discounts, scheduling deliveries, and following up on actual shipments to make certain due dates are met and that quality control is maintained. (Chapter 3)

sourcing manager Director of the activities related to locating goods and producers of goods. (Chapter 3)

specification technician Also known as *spec tech*, attends the fittings of the sample garments, takes measurements, and compiles these measurements into packets to hand off to production. (Chapter 6)

spec pack Contains detailed information taken from the designer's sketch, translated into measurements in order to ensure desired fit and styling details, such as the placement of pockets, the length of zippers, the size of buttons, etc. Also called a *tech pack*. (Chapter 6)

spec sheet Specification list; typically provides detailed measurements and construction guidelines. (Chapter 7)

spreader Lays out the selected fabric for cutting. (Chapter 4)

stabilizing Saving and maintaining museum artifacts. A museum curator stabilizes artifacts when preparing them for storage or an exhibition. (Chapter 14)

stock-keeping unit (SKU) Identification data for a single product. (Chapter 3)

store-owned foreign buying office Large retailers and exclusive boutiques often use and pay for this ancillary operation located in major fashion capitals overseas, whose buyers support and advise other buyers of their respective stores. (Chapter 3)

street style blogs Encompass fashion trend, environments, and styles seen on the streets. Whether an object, a group, or an individual, they can be action shots or posed, usually taken in the middle of a city. (Chapter 12)

strike-off A few yards of fabric printed by a mill and sent to the product developer (i.e., colorist, designer, and sample maker) to be made into a sample. (Chapter 2, Chapter 7)

stylus A computerized pen. (Chapter 6)

surface designer Knitters, weavers, or embroiderers for industries ranging from apparel to upholstery. (Chapter 2)

supply-chain management (SCM) All of the activities required to coordinate and manage every step needed to bring a product to the consumer, including procuring raw materials, producing goods, transporting and distributing those goods, and managing the selling process. (Chapter 4)

target market The people or consumers who are targeted as potential customers or product users. (Chapter 9)

tearsheet A page that has been pulled from a newspaper, model book, or magazine. They are excellent to include in the portfolio for the photographer who has been published. (Chapter 13)

technical design Use of drawings, measurements, patterns, and models to develop the "blueprints," or technical plans, needed for the manufacturing of products. (Chapter 6)

technical designer Liaison between the designer and factory, responsible for working closely with the designers to communicate their specific product requests to the factory overseas. (Chapter 6)

technical photographer Produces photographs for reports or research papers, such as textile durability analyses. (Chapter 13)

technical writers Translate highly technical information into easy-to-understand text. (Chapter 12)

terminal degree Highest educational degree available in a particular field. (Chapter 14)

textile colorist Chooses the colors or color combinations that will be used in creating each textile design. (Chapter 2)

textile design The process of creating the print, pattern, texture, and finish of fabrics. (Chapter 2)

textile designer Creates original patterns, prints, and textures for the fabrics used in many types of industry, from fashion to interiors. (Chapter 2)

textile engineer Works with designers to determine how a design can be applied to a fabric in terms of more practical variables, such as durability, washability, and colorfastness. (Chapter 2)

textile stylist Modifies existing textile goods, altering patterns or prints that have been successful on the retail floor to turn them into fresh, new products. (Chapter 2)

textile technical designer Creates new textile designs or modifies existing fabric goods, altering patterns or prints that have been successful on the retail floor to turn them into fresh, new products. (Chapter 7)

textile technician Works with the issues that are directly related to the production of textiles, such as care factors, finishing techniques, and durability. (Chapter 2)

trade mart Houses temporary sales booths and permanent showrooms leased either by sales representatives or manufacturers. Also called an *apparel mart*. (Chapter 5)

trade publication Periodical designed for readers interested in or employed in specific professions, vocations, or merchandise classifications. (Chapter 8)

trade school An institution that may offer fashion programs and provide certificates, rather than degrees, upon the student's completion of the program, including programs in such areas as fashion design, illustration, retailing, photography, and merchandising. (Chapter 14)

traffic manager Supervises workflow on the factory floor, monitoring the product from start to finish. (Chapter 4)

trainer An educator who works with employees to provide them with certain knowledge or skills to improve performance in their current jobs. (Chapter 7) Someone who works for a cosmetic, fragrance, or skin care line by educating sales and marketing employees on the company's product line and how to sell it. (Chapter 16)

trend board The tool forecasters use to communicate seasonal fashion moods and trends to designers, buyers, product developers, and manufacturers. Key terms and images of the trend's fabrications, colors, and styling details are composed on a "board." In the past, these boards were created by hand; today, they are more likely created and disseminated to design and merchandising personnel digitally. (Chapter 1)

trend book Design resource publication intended to assist creative teams and manufacturers in developing future product lines. Trend books may include photos, fabric swatches, materials, color ranges, drawings of prints, product sketches, silhouettes, commentaries, and related materials. (Chapter 1)

trend forecaster Continually monitors the consumer and the industry through traveling, reading, networking, and, most important, observing; this person creates formal reports that summarize important fashion trends with seasonal themes. The trend forecaster in the product development division of a retailer identifies the fashion trends and then interprets them for the retailer's particular customer or market. (Chapter 1)

trendspotter A person located at a university or other location worldwide who provides information to a forecasting company, such as WGSN, on the latest trends in the locale. (Chapter 1)

trimmings Decorative components designed to be seen as part of the final product (e.g., buttons, appliqués, and beltings). (Chapter 3)

trimmings buyer Person who is responsible for locating and ordering decorative components for products. (Chapter 3)

trunk show Consists of a fashion event planner and/or a manufacturer's representative bringing a manufacturer's full seasonal line to a retail store that carries that particular manufacturer. (Chapter 8)

vendor The person selling a product or service, or a manufacturer or distributor from whom a company purchases products or production processes. (Chapter 3)

visual merchandisers Responsible for the window installations, displays, signage, fixtures, mannequins, and decorations that give a retail operation aesthetic appeal and a distinct image. This position is also known as *visual merchandising director*. (Chapter 15)

visual merchandising Design, development, procurement, and installation of merchandise displays and the ambiance of the environment in which the displays are shown. (Chapter 4, Chapter 10)

vocational school Provides training for students who elect not to participate in a four-year college degree program upon high school graduation. Courses taught include commercial clothing construction, apparel alteration, patternmaking, and retailing. (Chapter 14)

volume driver Top-selling merchandise for a manufacturer or retailer. (Chapter 3)

Web masters Maintain the Web sites and ensure that they are constantly up-to-date and in working order; sometimes referred to as a *Web designer* or *developer*. (Chapter 9)

Web programmers Deal with the coding and technical aspects of a Web site. (Chapter 12)

Web site designers People who not only create Web sites but also focus on the ongoing visual and user aspects of the site. This position may also be referred to as *Web site developer*. (Chapter 12)

Web site developer Constructs, maintains, and builds a company's Web site; this person must possess general design skills and knowledge of Web-specific design factors (e.g., screen resolution and accessibility). He or she designs a Web site's look and feel, incorporating features such as e-commerce, online community, animations, and interactive applications into the site. This position may also be referred to as *Web site designer*. (Chapter 12)

wellness center A type of spa that often incorporates health programs, such as exercise (e.g., yoga and Pilates) and nutrition. (Chapter 16)

wholesale A company that sells the goods to the retailer for subsequent resale to the consumer. (Chapter 9)

writers See *journalist* (Chapter 12).

yardage A given amount of fabric, based on its length in yards. (Chapter 3)

credits

Chapter 1

1.0 Chinsee/WWD/© Condé Nast; 1.1 Achard/WWD/© Condé Nast; 1.2 Giannoni/WWD/© Condé Nast; 1.3 © Première Vision; 1.4 Sardella/WWD/© Condé Nast; 1.5 Ollyy/Shutterstock; 1.6 Goran Bogicevic/Shutterstock; 1.7 Sardella/WWD/© Condé Nast; 1.8 © Marleen Daniëls; 1.9 Sipa via AP Images; 1.10 © Everett Kennedy Brown/epa/Corbis; 1.11 Kyle/WWD/© Condé Nast; Box 1.1 Courtesy of Henry Doneger Associates, Inc.; Box 1.2 © Philippe Munda; Box 1.3 Courtesy of Henry Doneger Associates, Inc.; Box 1.4 Eichner/WWD/© Condé Nast; Box 1.5 Courtesy of Henry Doneger Associates, Inc.; Profile 1.1 Courtesy of Henry Doneger Associates, Inc.

Chapter 2

2.0 Jaguar PS/Shutterstock; 2.1 © 2015 Lectra S.A. All rights reserved. www.lectra.com; 2.2 Manfredo Pinzauti/Grazianeri/WWD/© Condé Nast; 2.3 Giannoni/WWD/© Condé Nast; 2.4 © 2015 Lectra S.A. All rights reserved. www.lectra.com; 2.5 © 2015 Lectra S.A. All rights reserved. www.lectra.com; 2.6 Courtesy of Ellis Developments Ltd.; design by Peter Butcher; 2.7 Photo by Patrick Cline for Lonny LLC; 2.8 Fairchild created and owned; 2.9 Image courtesy of Cotton Incorporated; 2.10 Courtesy of the Woolmark Company; 2.11 Logo courtesy of Fur Council of Canada; 2.12 Mohair Council of America; Box 2.1 Courtesy of ITP, Inkjet Textile Printing, LLC; Profile 2.1a © 2015 Lectra S.A. All rights reserved. www.lectra.com; Profile 2.1b © 2015 Lectra S.A. All rights reserved. www.lectra.com; Profile 2.1c © 2015 Lectra S.A. All rights reserved. www.lectra.com

Chapter 3

3.0 © Serge Kozak/Corbis; 3.1 Baird/WWD/© Condé Nast; 3.2 Photo by Erin Fitzsimmons; 3.3 Shutterstock/Adisa; 3.4 Shutterstock/Arvind Balaraman; 3.5 Shutterstock/Gertan; 3.6 Iannaccone/WWD/© Condé Nast; 3.7a Thornton/Footwear News/© Condé Nast; 3.7b Guzel Studio/Shutterstock

Chapter 4

4.0 Delbo/WWD/© Condé Nast; 4.1a Sullivan/WWD/© Condé Nast; 4.1b Aquino/WWD/© Condé Nast; 4.1c Chinsee/WWD/© Condé Nast; 4.1d Sullivan/WWD/© Condé Nast; 4.2 Reuters/Lucy Nicholson/Landov; 4.3 Jitendra Prakash/Reuters/Landov; 4.4 © Diana Hirsch/iStockphoto; 4.5 © 2015 Lectra S.A. All rights reserved. www.lectra.com; 4.6 © 2015 Lectra S.A. All rights reserved. www.lectra.com; 4.7 © 2015 Lectra S.A. All rights reserved. www.lectra.com; 4.8 © S.G./Alamy; 4.9 Delbo/WWD/© Condé Nast; 4.10 Courtesy Nike Inc.; 4.11a © Mark Peterson/Corbis; 4.11b © Mark Peterson/Corbis; 4.11c © Mark Peterson/Corbis; 4.12 Scott Olson/Getty Images; Box 4.3a © Keith Bedford/Reuters/Corbis; Box 4.3b Aquino/WWD/© Condé Nast; Box 4.3c Courtesy of Laser Cutting Shapes (Dress by Marchesa; Laser-cut fabric by Laser Cutting Shapes of Columbus, Ohio, USA); Box 4.3d Courtesy of Laser Cutting Shapes (Dress by Marchesa; Laser-cut fabric by Laser Cutting Shapes of Columbus, Ohio, USA); Profile 4.1 Eichner/WWD/© Condé Nast

Chapter 5

5.0 Andrey_Popov/Shutterstock; 5.1 Churchill/WWD/© Condé Nast; 5.2a Churchill/WWD/© Condé Nast; 5.2b Churchill/WWD/© Condé Nast; 5.3 Courtesy of WWD/© Condé Nast; 5.4 Shari Smith Dunaif, High Noon Productions, LLC, New York; 5.5 © Blend Images/Alamy; 5.6 © Randy Faris/Corbis; 5.7 Maitre/WWD/© Condé Nast; 5.8 Twin Design/Shutterstock; 5.9 Andrey Popov/Shutterstock

Chapter 6

6.0 Mitra/WWD/© Condé Nast; 6.1 Seckler/WWD/© Condé Nast; 6.2 Giannoni/WWD/© Condé Nast; 6.3 Anton Oparin/Shutterstock; 6.4 Eichner/WWD/© Condé Nast; 6.5 Whalen/WWD/© Condé Nast; 6.6 Aquino/WWD/© Condé Nast; 6.7 Keenan/WWD/© Condé Nast; 6.8 Courtesy of Fairchild Publications; 6.9 © Ariel Skelley/Blend Images/Corbis; Profile 6.1 Melissa McGraw/The Fashion Potential; Karol Duclos; Profile 6.2a Iannoccone/WWD/© Condé Nast; Profile 6.2b Photograph by Chelsea Euliss Photography

Chapter 7

7.0a Ericksen/WWD/© Condé Nast; 7.0b Ericksen/WWD/© Condé Nast; 7.1 © Kim Kulish/Corbis; 7.2 Alhovik/Shutterstock; 7.3 Iannaccone/WWD/© Condé Nast; 7.4 Courtesy of WWD/© Condé Nast; 7.5 winhorse/Istock; 7.6a Mitra/WWD/© Condé Nast; 7.6b Mitra/WWD/© Condé Nast; 7.6c Mitra/WWD/© Condé Nast; 7.7 Aquino/WWD/© Condé Nast; 7.8 © Gareth Brown/Corbis; 7.9 Dodds/WWD/© Condé Nast; 7.10a © 2015 Lectra S.A. All rights reserved. www.lectra.com; 7.10b © 2015 Lectra S.A. All rights reserved. www.lectra.com; 7.11 Courtesy of Fairchild Publications

Chapter 8

8.0 Sardella/WWD/© Condé Nast; 8.1 © Pascal Perich/Corbis Outline; 8.2 Courtesy of WWD/© Condé Nast; 8.3a © Moviestore collection Ltd/Alamy; 8.3b Carin Baer/© AMC/Courtesy Everett Collection; 8.4 www.andreakamal.com/Getty Images; 8.5 Courtesy of WWD/© Condé Nast; 8.6 Photo by Marquita Sayres; 8.7 omgimages/istockphoto; 8.8 Iannaccone/WWD/© Condé Nast; 8.9 Keenan/WWD/© Condé Nast; 8.10 Eichner/WWD/© Condé Nast; 8.11 Matarazzo/WWD/© Condé Nast; Profile 8.1 Courtesy of John Marino

Chapter 9

9.0 © Peter Horree/Alamy; 9.1 Courtesy of Fairchild Publications; 9.2 Aquino/WWD/© Condé Nast; 9.3 J2R/Shutterstock; Profile 9.1a © I Love Fashion Retail, All Rights Reserved.; Profile 9.1b © I Love Fashion Retail, All Rights Reserved.

Chapter 10

10.0 Action Sports Photography/Shutterstock; 10.1a Lakruwan Wanniarachchi/AFP/Getty Images; 10.1b Aquino/WWD/© Condé Nast; 10.1c Eichner/WWD/© Condé Nast; 10.2 Getty Images for Tommy Hilfiger; 10.3 Mitra/WWD/© Condé Nast; 10.4 Keenan/WWD/© Condé Nast; 10.5 acorn/Shutterstock; 10.6 © Justin Guariglia/Corbis; Profile 10.1 Lauren Wzorek Earl

Chapter 11

11.0 Andresr/Shutterstock; 11.1 © John Scott/iStockphoto; 11.2 © Matej Michelizza/iStockphoto; 11.3 Photo by Jay Freis/Getty Images; 11.4 DmitriMaruta/Shutterstock; 11.5 bikeriderlondon/Shutterstock; 11.6 Bikeriderlondon/Shutterstock; Profile 11.1 Erin Burke/Louver Studio

Chapter 12

12.0 www.styledefinedNYC.com; 12.1 Kundra/Shutterstock; 12.2 BONNINSTUDIO/Shutterstock; 12.3 Slaven/Shutterstock; 12.4 antart/Shutterstock; 12.5 BONNINSTUDIO/Shutterstock; 12.6 Yuka/Shutterstock; 12.7 marcogarrincha/Shutterstock; 12.8 Courtesy of www.manrepeller.com; Profile 12.1 Monica Schipper/Getty Images

Chapter 13

13.0 Photo taken by Hugh Stewart, 2014; 13.1 Paul Warner/WireImage/Getty Image; 13.2 © Stephen Power/Alamy; 13.3 © Micro Discovery/Corbis; 13.4a © Disney; 13.4b © Disney; 13.5 Ericksen/WWD/© Condé Nast; Box 13.5 Photo taken by Hugh Stewart, 2014; Profile 13.1 Courtesy of Susan Jackson

Chapter 14

14.0 Ericksen/WWD/© Condé Nast; 14.1 © Jim Holde/Alamy; 14.2 © Jeff Greenberg/Alamy; Box 14.1 Chomel/WWD/© Condé Nast; Box 14.2 Ericksen/WWD/© Condé Nast; Box 14.3 Maitre/WWD/© Condé Nast; Box 14.4 Maestri/WWD/© Condé Nast; Profile 14.1 Melissa McGraw/The Fashion Potential; Joshua Spafford, Starboard Photos, http://starboardphotos.com; Profile 14.2 Courtesy of Kent State University

Chapter 15

15.0 Courtesy of Abbe Fenimore; 15.1 © Simon Lord/Alamy; 15.2 shopten25.com; 15.3 Colangelo/WWD/© Condé Nast; 15.4 Maestri/WWD/© Condé Nast; 15.5a WindowsWear PRO, http://pro.windowswear.com; 15.5b WindowsWear PRO, http://pro.windowswear.com; 15.6 WindowsWear PRO, http://pro.windowswear.com; 15.7 vr Software 2011; 15.8a WindowsWear PRO, http://pro.windowswear.com; 15.8b WindowsWear PRO, http://pro.windowswear.com; 15.8c WindowsWear PRO, http://pro.windowswear.com; 15.9 Maitre/WWD/© Condé Nast; Profile 15.1a Kelly Rucker Photography; Profile 15.1b Melanie Johnson Photography; Profile 15.1c Melanie Johnson Photography; Profile 15.2 Courtesy of Missouri State University

Chapter 16

16.0 Poznyakov/Shutterstock; 16.1 vnlit/Shutterstock; 16.2 © Yuriko Nakao/Reuters/Corbis; 16.3 Walt Disney Pictures/Photofest; 16.4 Wallenrock/Shutterstock; 16.5 Pressmaster/Shutterstock

Color Insert

Color Insert 1 Falk/WWD/© Condé Nast
Color Insert 2 Mitra/WWD/© Condé Nast
Color Insert 3 Giannoni/WWD/© Condé Nast
Color Insert 4 Falk/WWD/© Condé Nast
Color Insert 5 Eichner/WWD/© Condé Nast
Color Insert 6 Giannoni/WWD/© Condé Nast
Color Insert 7 Antonov/WWD/© Condé Nast
Color Insert 8 Celeste/WWD/© Condé Nast
Color insert 9 Giannoni/WWD/© Condé Nast
Color Insert 10 Giannoni/WWD/© Condé Nast
Color Insert 11 Chinsee/WWD/© Condé Nast
Color Insert 12 Eichner/WWD/© Condé Nast
Color Insert 13 Eichner/WWD/© Condé Nast
Color Insert 14 Chinsee/WWD/© Condé Nast
Color Insert 15 Iannaccone/WWD/© Condé Nast
Color Insert 16 Pressmaster/Shutterstock

index